Tax Policy and Labor Market Performance

CESifo Seminar Series
Edited by Hans-Werner Sinn

See http://mitpress.mit.edu for a complete list of titles in this series.

Tax Policy and Labor Market Performance

Jonas Agell and Peter Birch Sørensen, editors

CESifo Seminar Series

The MIT Press
Cambridge, Massachusetts
London, England

MIT Press books may be purchased at special quantity discounts for business or sales
promotional use. For information, please email special_sales@mitpress.mit.edu or write
to Special Sales Department, The MIT Press, 55 Hayward Street, Cambridge, MA 02142.

This book was set in Palatino on 3B2 by Asco Typesetters, Hong Kong. Printed and
bound in the United States of America.

Library of Congress Cataloging-in-Publication Data

Tax policy and labor market performance / Jonas Agell and Peter Birch Sørensen, editors.
   p.   cm. — (CESifo seminar series)
Includes bibliographical references and index.
ISBN-13: 978-0-262-01229-4
ISBN-10: 0-262-01229-4
1. Taxation—Europe. 2. Welfare state—Europe. 3. Labor market—Europe. I. Agell,
Jonas. II. Sørensen, Peter Birch. III. Series.

HJ2599.5.T26   2006
331.1094—dc22   2006044442

10 9 8 7 6 5 4 3 2 1

Contents

Series Foreword

This book is part of the CESifo Seminar Series. The series aims to cover topical policy issues in economics from a largely European perspective. The books in this series are the products of the papers and intensive debates that took place during the seminars hosted by CESifo, an international research network of renowned economists organized jointly by the Center for Economic Studies at Ludwig-Maximilians-Universität, Munich, and the Ifo Institute for Economic Research. All publications in this series have been carefully selected and refereed by members of the CESifo research network.

Acknowledgments

The initial versions of the papers in this volume were presented and discussed at the 2003 CESifo Summer institute in Venice, held on July 21–23. We are highly indebted to the staff at CESifo for organizing an excellent meeting, and for creating a highly stimulating environment. We are also grateful to our knowledgeable referees who assisted us in selecting the papers to be included in this volume. Finally, we thank all authors for patiently revising papers and for speedily responding to all our deadlines.

Introduction and Summary

Jonas Agell and Peter Birch
Sørensen

In many European OECD countries unemployment remains high, and many commentators worry that wages are too rigid. Widespread concern exists that mobility between jobs and between regions is too low, and that a compressed distribution of net-of-tax pay discourages education and skill formation. At the low end of the labor market, it is feared that the interaction of high taxes and generous social benefits discourages labor supply and labor force participation. In many countries, there is also a concern that an increasing share of the workforce responds to high tax wedges by working in the underground economy, or by engaging in do-it-yourself work in the household sector.

The studies in this book are devoted to the analysis of how tax policy, and welfare state incentives more broadly, affects the performance of the labor market. The eight chapters cover both theoretical and empirical approaches, include broad overviews as well as in-depth analysis of specific policies, address normative as well as positive issues, and offer examples of both aggregate and microeconomic analysis. It is our hope that both the policy analyst and the academic theorist will find it worthwhile to read the book.

In the following, we offer a brief overview of the contributions included in this volume.

I Taxation and Labor Markets—The Broader Perspective

In chapter 1, A. Lans Bovenberg provides a survey of the effects of taxation on labor supply, employment, and unemployment in the conventional model of a competitive labor market as well as in more realistic models with imperfect labor markets. In particular, he focuses on distortions stemming from trade union wage setting and externalities arising from the search behavior of workers and firms. Bovenberg's analysis includes the effects of taxes on hours of work, on labor force participation and job search, and on structural unemployment. One key finding is that the effects of taxation on unemployment depend crucially on the rules for indexation of unemployment benefits. To a first approximation, a change in tax policy can reduce unemployment only if it succeeds in reducing the net (after-tax) replacement ratio offered by the benefit system. Another finding is that while an increase in tax progressivity harms economic efficiency in a competitive labor market, it may play an efficiency-enhancing role in labor markets with job search. By increasing the job loss associated with any given increase in the after-tax wage rate, a higher marginal tax rate may induce wage moderation. This makes it profitable for employers to post more vacancies, thereby helping to reduce unemployment. At the same time, higher tax progressivity may involve costs by reducing hours of work, work effort, human capital investment, and labor mobility, while stimulating tax avoidance and evasion.

To illustrate the points made in the theoretical analysis, Bovenberg performs simulation experiments with an elaborate applied general equilibrium model for the Netherlands. The model incorporates a disaggregated household sector, human capital accumulation, efficiency wage setting, job search behavior and costly job matching, and an underground economy. The simulations highlight a number of difficult trade-offs for tax policy. According to the model, the most effective way to reduce unemployment (in particular, low-skilled unemployment) and to stimulate labor force participation via changes in tax policy is to introduce a targeted Earned Income Tax Credit (EITC) that is phased out as income goes up. However, since such a policy increases the progressivity of the tax system, it also reduces hours of work and discourages investment in human capital by many of those who are already employed. To boost human capital formation and work hours, cuts in the marginal tax rates of higher-income workers are most effective, but such a policy also increases income inequality. Bovenberg's chapter ends with a discussion of some ways for the government to alleviate the inevitable equity-efficiency trade-off—for example, by compulsory savings schemes and workfare programs.

The starting point for chapter 2 by Stephen Nickell is the observation that people in some countries appear to work harder than people in other countries. For example, the average person of working age works almost 50 percent more in the United States than in Belgium. As noted by Nickell, such differences in labor supply go a long way toward explaining the variation in GDP per capita among the advanced countries of the OECD. Nickell's chapter discusses to what extent differences in taxes can explain why Americans devote so much more time to market work than do Europeans. He presents calculations on how the overall tax wedge on labor income has evolved over time in OECD countries, reviews aggregate econometric evidence on how tax wedges affect the real labor cost per employee, and discusses studies that have tried to directly estimate the effect of taxes on aggregate employment. Based on "average" results reported in the literature, Nickell concludes that the 16-percentage-point difference in the tax wedge between the three big countries of continental Europe (France, Germany, and Italy) and the United States may explain around one quarter of the overall difference in the employment rate. Thus, the conclusion seems to be that though taxes are an important determinant of employment, most of the observed market work differentials between Europe and the United States must be explained by other factors. Nickell conjectures that more generous European social insurance programs might account for the major part of the work differential.

In chapter 3, Frederick van der Ploeg discusses a similar theme by raising the question "Do social policies harm employment and growth?" The chapter reviews a large literature dealing with the potential for progressive taxes and redistributive categorical benefits to counteract some of the nontax distortions found in imperfect labor markets. Van der Ploeg shows that tax progressivity may boost employment by moderating wage claims not only in unionized labor markets, but also in labor markets where employers pay efficiency wages and in markets with search frictions. He proceeds to study the effects of conditional and unconditional unemployment benefits in an extended version of the shirking model of efficiency wages originally introduced by Shapiro and Stiglitz. The model is used to demonstrate that whereas a higher unconditional benefit drives up equilibrium unemployment, a conditional benefit that is granted only to workers who have lost their jobs through no fault of their own (workers who have not been fired because of misconduct or shirking) will actually reduce unemployment. Intuitively, if the conditional unemployment benefit is high relative to the unconditional welfare benefit, workers are more eager to avoid being fired for shirking, and hence employers need to pay less to induce workers not to shirk. The resulting drop in wage pressure lowers equilibrium unemployment. Van der Ploeg also uses a well-known political economy model of redistributive taxation attributed to Meltzer and Richard to show that a more equal skill distribution—and hence a more equal distribution of pretax incomes—results in a voting equilibrium with less distortionary taxation. This may be an argument for public investment in education to improve the distribution of skills. Van der Ploeg also discusses the consequences of assuming that people care about their relative levels of consumption and income. He finds that in this case the majority of the electorate will prefer a more progressive tax system that deliberately discourages work and material consumption because of the negative external effect of an individual's consumption on the utility of others.

II Taxation, Labor Supply, and Wage Formation

Most studies of how tax incentives and tax reform affect labor supply and welfare have concentrated on the behavioral response along the intensive (hours-of-work decision) margin. At the same time, recent empirical work on labor supply behavior indicates that the response along the extensive margin (participation decision) is a stronger one. In chapter 4, Nada Eissa, Henrik Jacobsen Kleven, and Claus Thustrup Kreiner shed theoretical and empirical light on the issues. They develop a model incorporating both the intensive and the extensive labor supply decisions, and they show how nonlinearities in the tax system make it necessary to distinguish explicitly between the intensive and extensive margins in welfare analysis of tax reform. While the intensive margin will depend on the marginal tax rate, the extensive margin will depend on the average tax wedge on labor income.

As an illustration of the quantitative importance of the theoretical results, Eissa, Kleven, and Kreiner compute the welfare effects for female household heads of the United States Tax Reform Act of 1986 (TRA86). Their simulations show that TRA86 created substantial welfare gains, which were primarily associated with adjustments along the extensive labor supply margin; that is, labor force participation increased. More generally, the simulation experiments of Eissa, Kleven, and Kreiner strongly suggest that tax policy simulations that do not account for labor force participation decisions may underestimate the welfare effect by a significant amount.

An important element in the various tax reforms carried out in the United States since the mid-1980s was the expansion of the EITC granted to individuals and families with low labor incomes. In recent years several other OECD countries, in particular the United Kingdom, have also experimented with various forms of EITCs. In line with the analysis of Eissa, Kleven, and Kreiner, proponents of the EITC have emphasized its likely positive effects on the extensive margin of labor supply. However, since the EITC increases the effective marginal tax rate in the income range where the credit is phased out, and since it has a positive income effect on the demand for leisure, skeptics have pointed out that the EITC is likely to reduce the hours worked by many of those who are already employed, leaving an ambiguous net effect on total labor supply. In the light of this ambiguity, it is obviously important to study the effects of the EITC on the intensive as well as the extensive labor supply margin.

While several empirical studies of the EITC have considered its effects on the labor supply of single women, very few have examined its impact on hours worked by married couples in the United States. In chapter 5, Nada Eissa and Hilary Hoynes set out to fill this important gap in the literature on the EITC. As a starting point, they note that most secondary earners among married couples may be expected to reduce their work hours in response to the EITC, since most eligible couples with two earners are likely to be in the income range where phasing out the credit raises the effective marginal tax rate. Using Current Population Survey data from 1984 to 1996, Eissa and Hoynes proceed to estimate hours of work equations for married couples. To account for the fact that the after-tax wage rate depends endogenously on labor supply, they use an instrumental variable technique that allows them to trace the budget sets of individual households, taking advantage of time variation as well as cross-sectional variation in tax schedules. The estimates confirm the existing evidence that the labor supply of married men is not responsive to taxes. By contrast, Eissa and Hoynes estimate the net wage elasticity of hours worked by married women to be between 0.1 and 0.4. On this basis, they perform simulations to show that EITC expansions between 1984 and 1996 induced married women to decrease their work hours by 1–4 percent.

What are the effects of progressive income taxes on wages? The traditional view maintains that progressive income taxes can be expected to push up wages, the reason being that progressive taxes reduce labor supply, which in a competitive labor market can be expected to increase the equilibrium wage. The alternative view—exemplified by Frederick van der Ploeg's contribution to this volume (chapter 4)—maintains that in imperfectly competitive labor markets, where there is bargaining over wages, progressive taxes can actually be expected to lead to wage moderation, with positive employment effects as a consequence. The reason is that tax progression changes the trade-off between workers' real take-home pay and employment—when the tax system is steeply progressive, a given increase in the real wage after tax will be more costly in terms of employment. In recent years, empirical studies have presented results for some European countries that are compatible with the alternative view.

In chapter 6, Torben Tranæs, Søren Arnberg, and Anders Holm take a fresh look at the issues. Using unique microdata from the highly unionized labor market in Copenhagen, and using a first-difference estimator that factors out unobserved individual effects, they report evidence suggesting that tax progression actually increases wages at all levels of the occupational hierarchy. Thus, the results are in line with the traditional view, and in contradiction to the alternative view. For unionized workers, Tranaes, Arnberg, and Holm find that an increase in tax progression tends to generate a noncompetitive wage moderating effect, as predicted by the alternative view. However, even among unionized workers the net effect of increased tax progression is a wage-increasing one.

III   Taxation and the Underground Economy

Rather than inducing people to work less and take more leisure, high taxes on labor income may motivate workers to go "underground" to work in the informal economy where taxes are evaded. Measuring the size of the underground economy is obviously difficult, but existing empirical studies suggest that it accounts for a significant share of total economic activity even in the most developed OECD countries. Most of the literature seeks to explain the size of the underground economy by focusing on the incentives to avoid high taxes, or to avoid government "red tape" and corruption. However, in chapter 7, Dan Anderberg uses data for fifteen OECD countries to document a high correlation between the standard OECD index of employment protection and the estimated size of the underground economy. Indeed, this correlation seems to be much higher than the partial correlation between the level of taxation and the magnitude of the underground economy.

Anderberg develops a theoretical labor market model that offers an explanation for the correlation between labor market rigidity and underground activity. In his model, unemployed workers divide their time between job search in the formal labor market and work in the underground economy to supplement their income from unemployment benefits. In this setting, stricter employment protection slows down the flows of firing and hiring in the formal labor market. This has two offsetting effects on the incentives to engage in underground activities. On the one hand, when formal jobs are expected to last longer they become more attractive, and this increases the incentives for job search. On the other hand, employment protection also makes it less attractive for employers to create jobs, thereby increasing the length of the average unemployment spell and strengthening the incentive for the unemployed to go underground rather than searching for a regular job. In Anderberg's model the latter effect dominates, so institutions that prolong job tenure also tend to increase the incentives for unemployed "outsiders" to seek alternative sources of income on the fringe of the economy.

Anderberg's analysis suggests that labor market reforms that increase the flexibility of the formal labor market would also help reduce the size of the underground economy. In practice, governments often rely on policy instruments such as penalties and auditing in their efforts to discourage underground economic activity. In the literature, the effects of such policies have typically been studied in partial equilibrium models where wages are exogenous or in general equilibrium models with competitive labor markets.

In chapter 8, Ann-Sofie Kolm and Birthe Larsen analyze the labor market effects of tighter controls of the underground economy in a more realistic general equilibrium model of an imperfect labor market with matching frictions and wage bargaining between workers and firms. Empirical studies indicate that underground activities are often highly concentrated in particular sectors of the economy such as construction and certain personal services. Kolm and Larsen therefore set up a two-sector model where one sector represents the formal economy and the other sector—producing a different good—represents the underground economy. The government influences the size of the underground economy by imposing a penalty for tax evasion discovered through auditing. Kolm and Larsen show that a higher penalty rate causes the formal sector to expand at the expense of the informal sector, while at the same time reducing unemployment. The reason is that higher penalties reduce the value of the "outside option" (the option of working in the underground economy) for workers bargaining over the wages for formal jobs. Hence it reduces wage pressure in the formal sector, thereby inducing more employers to enter that sector. While this result is hardly surprising, a more surprising feature of the model developed by Kolm and Larsen is that a higher audit rate has an ambiguous impact on unemployment and the size of the underground economy. Indeed, it may even cause the underground economy to expand. Other things being equal, more intensive auditing reduces the profitability of entering the informal sector, but in general equilibrium it may also drive up the relative price of goods supplied by the underground economy to such an extent that it actually becomes more attractive to enter the sector.

I

**Taxation and Labor
Markets: The Broader
Perspective**

1   Tax Policy and Labor Market Performance

A. Lans Bovenberg

1.1   Introduction

This chapter explores the link between tax policy and labor market performance. As far as labor performance is concerned, we focus on labor supply, employment, and the difference between these two variables: unemployment. As regards tax policy, we consider a number of elements: first, the level of taxation as measured by average tax burdens for major groups of workers; second, the composition of the tax burden over payroll taxes, personal labor income taxes, capital income taxes, and consumption taxes; third, the progressiveness of the tax system (as measured by the speed with which average tax rates rise with income levels) and—related to this—the magnitude of marginal tax rates for workers with middle and high incomes; and fourth, marginal tax rates faced by low-income earners and nonparticipating or unemployed individuals as a result of means-tested safety net provisions and retirement benefits. The analysis is mainly theoretical. Nevertheless, at several stages we survey evidence on the empirical importance of various theoretical mechanisms.

The chapter is structured as follows. After section 1.2 provides information about the tax and benefit systems in various OECD countries, the chapter turns to the labor market effects of taxation in representative agent models. Section 1.3 explores how tax reform affects employment through the channels of labor supply and equilibrium unemployment. It shows that whether a tax reform succeeds in cutting unemployment depends crucially on its influence on the effective replacement rate. In addition to the replacement rate, the progressiveness of the tax system is an important determinant of the unemployment rate. In particular, progressive taxes moderate wages by taxing wage increases, thereby reducing unemployment.

Section 1.4 employs an applied general equilibrium model with heterogeneous agents to investigate the consequences of tax reform for not only aggregate employment but also income distribution. The simulations reveal several trade-offs between various objectives. These objectives include cutting unemployment in general and low-skilled unemployment in particular, stimulating the participation of women in the labor force, raising the quality and quantity of labor supply (both in hours and in persons), and establishing an equitable income distribution, including a reasonable income level for those dependent on social benefits. Indeed, these objectives imply different priorities for how tax cuts should be structured. In particular, cutting unemployment primarily requires widening the gap between labor incomes and transfer incomes in unemployment. Stimulating labor force participation of women calls for widening the gap between, on the one hand, after-tax incomes of households with two partners who are active on the formal labor market and, on the other hand, after-tax incomes of households with a nonparticipating partner. Such a larger income gap encourages partners to start participating in the labor force so that the latter households turn into the former households. Raising the quantity and quality of labor supply in the formal economy calls for widening the income differentials between low formal labor incomes and high formal labor incomes.

Sections 1.5 and 1.6 investigate the optimal progressiveness of labor income taxes. Section 1.5 explores the efficiency case for progressive taxes in a representative agent model without an intensive margin of labor supply. In that setting, a progressive labor tax eliminates nontax distortions on wage setting by allowing workers to commit to not expropriating specific investments of firms. Section 1.6 explores the optimal progression of the labor income tax in the presence of search unemployment, heterogeneous households, and distributional concerns. With an intensive labor supply margin, the government does not completely eliminate nontax distortions on wage setting because it faces a trade-off between creating more jobs and encouraging a smaller group of agents to work harder on the intensive margin. Section 1.7, finally, summarizes the main policy conclusions.

1.2 Taxes and Labor Market Performance

Labor market performance can be assessed in several ways. This chapter focuses on unemployment and labor supply, which can be measured as the participation rate (i.e., the labor force as percentage of the working-age population (15–65)) and average number of hours worked by employees (see table 1.1). Together, unemployment and labor supply yield employment. The fifth column of table 1.1 gives the average hours worked per member of the working-age population as a percentage of a full-time workweek (of 40 hours). This can be considered as the best available aggregate measure of labor-market performance. It in fact measures the share of the potential labor-market endowment that is actually used. Table 1.1 ranks countries in decreasing order of this utilization rate of labor resources. On this measure, the United States, Canada, and Japan perform better than Europe, and continental Europe in particular. Within Europe, the largest continental European countries (Germany, France, and Italy) do worse than most other European countries.

Also tax policy can be assessed in different ways. Table 1.2, which ranks countries according to their aggregate labor market performance, contains average tax rates and marginal tax rates at different income levels for a single-person household.[1] The tax wedges used here include personal income taxes, employers' and employees' social security contributions,[2] payroll taxes, and indirect consumption taxes (such as VAT and excises). The marginal tax wedge drives a wedge between marginal labor costs (which a competitive, profit-maximizing employer equates to the marginal productivity of labor (i.e., the social benefit of labor)) and after-tax disposable income from work (which a utility-maximizing household sets equal to the monetary value of the marginal disutility of labor (i.e., the reservation wage or the social costs of labor)).

Tax rates are quite high. Marginal tax rates for the average production worker exceed 60 percent in most countries on the European continent. Although marginal rates of personal income tax generally rise with income, overall marginal tax rates do not rise substantially with income. This is because social security contributions are typically due only on incomes below a ceiling. The United Kingdom and the United States combine high employment rates with relatively low marginal and average tax burdens. Within continental Europe, however, labor market performance and tax rates do not show a clear correlation.

Other taxes may also harm the reward to labor, even though they are not assessed on labor income. To illustrate, reducing labor productivity can result in source-based taxes on capital being shifted onto labor in a small open economy with internationally mobile capital.

Table 1.1
Indicators of labor market performance, 2001

	Labor force participation rate (%)[c]	Unemployment rate (%)[c]	Employment/population ratio (%)[c]	Average hours worked per person in employment	Employment indicator[d]	Employment/population ratio for older workers (55–64)	Long-term unemployment share[e]
United Kingdom	74.9	4.8	71.3	1711	58.7	52.2	27.7
Sweden	79.3	5.1	75.3	1603	58.0	67.0	22.3
Finland	74.6	9.2	67.7	1694	55.1	45.9	26.2
Denmark	79.2	4.2	75.9	1482	54.1	56.6	22.2
Ireland	67.5	3.7	65.0	1674	52.3	46.6	55.3[b]
Spain	65.8	10.5	58.8	1816	51.3	39.2	44.0
Greece	62.1	10.4	55.6	1921	51.3	38.0	52.8
Netherlands	75.7	2.1	74.1	1346	48.0	39.3	43.5[b]
Germany	71.6	8.0	65.9	1467	46.5	36.8	51.5[a]
France	68.0	8.8	62.0	1532	45.7	36.5	37.6
Belgium	63.6	6.2	59.7	1528	43.9	25.2	51.7
Italy	60.7	9.6	54.9	1606	42.4	18.6	63.4
Portugal	71.8	4.3	68.7	n.a.	n.a.	50.3	38.1
Austria	70.7	4.0	67.8	n.a.	n.a.	27.4	23.5
Luxembourg	64.2	1.9	63.0	n.a.	n.a.	24.8	27.6
United States	76.8	4.8	73.1	1821	64.0	58.4	6.1
Canada	76.5	7.3	70.9	1801[a]	61.4	48.3	9.5
Japan	72.6	5.2	68.8	1821[a]	60.2	62.0	26.6
OECD Europe	66.8	8.6	61.1	n.a.		37.9	40.4
Total OECD	69.8	6.4	65.3	n.a.		48.4	27.5

Source: OECD 2002a.

[a] Data refer to 2000.

[b] Data refer to 1999.

[c] Persons aged 15–64 years.

[d] (column 3 × column 4)/2080.

[e] The share of long-term (12 months and over) in employment in total unemployment.

n.a. Not available.

Table 1.2
Effective tax[a] rates on labor income, 1999

	Total average tax rate (ta) % of gross labor costs[b]			Total marginal tax rate (tm) for a single-person household % of gross labor costs[c]		
	0,67*APW[d]	APW[d]	1,67*APW[d]	0,67*APW[d]	APW[d]	1,67*APW[d]
United Kingdom	37.2	41.4	43.7	49.4	49.4	41.9
Sweden	59.9	61.3	64.9	64.6	62.8	71
Finland	53.9	57.7	63.3	63.6	67.2	70.7
Denmark	54.9	57.4	63	62.4	62.4	71.9
Ireland	37.1	45.8	53.8	47.2	66	63.4
Spain	42.7	46.9	50.1	52.3	53.8	56.4
Greece	45.2	46.4	50	48	53.4	61.7
Netherlands	50	53.4	53.3	60.6	65	58.1
Germany	55	59.2	62.5	66.1	68.9	68.9
France	52.1	58.4	59.8	78.7	62.5	60.9
Belgium	59.3	64.2	68.4	71.9	72.8	75.7
Italy	54.5	57	59.8	59.8	63.6	63.6
Portugal	43.1	45.7	50.1	50.6	51.3	57.9
Austria	52.7	56.2	60.1	60.9	64.5	68.6
Luxembourg	43.9	48	54.6	53.3	60	67.1
United States	35.2	37	42.2	40.4	40.4	51.5

Source: Cnossen 2001.
[a] Taxes include direct taxes, namely; personal income taxes, employers' and employees' social security contributions, and payroll taxes (if levied), plus indirect taxes, namely, VAT and excises.
[b] $ta = (a + c)/(1 + c)$, where a is the total direct average tax rate and c is the average effective indirect tax rate.
[c] $tm = (m + c)/(1 + c)$, where m is the total direct marginal tax rate.
[d] APW stands for the income level of an average productive worker. For a definition, see OECD 2002b.

These implicit taxes on labor are not included in table 1.2. The same holds true for labor market regulations that give rise to implicit taxes on employment. Minimum wage policies, for example, in effect levy implicit taxes on employers hiring low-skilled workers, with the revenues being transferred to these workers.[3] Other implicit taxes on employers include employment regulations that constrain the ability of employers to reduce the labor force in response to weak business conditions. By reducing labor demand, the implicit taxes associated with these regulations harm employment.

For low-income levels, the average and marginal tax burdens as contained in table 1.2 become a less reliable indicator of the incentives to supply labor because social insurance benefits and means-tested welfare benefits (including other safety-net benefits, such as housing allowances) imply significant implicit tax burdens on work. Indeed, many of these benefits are withdrawn when a worker finds work or works more hours. To provide some information about the magnitude of these implicit tax rates, table 1.3 contains the replacement rates (in after-tax terms) for both the short-term and the long-run unemployed. The desire to protect households with young children from poverty implies that lone-parent families and two-parent families feature the highest replacement rates. These replacement rates are closely related to the effective marginal tax rate on finding a full-time job. In particular, to arrive at the overall implicit rate on work $\bar{t}$ (in terms of before-tax wages), one should perform the following calculation: $\bar{t} = t + (1 - t)r$, where t is the (average) tax wedge (as given in the first three columns of table 1.2, but then for the relevant household types) and r is the net replacement rate (as provided in table 1.3).

Table 1.4 contains the implicit tax rates for several transitions.[4] In particular, the first two columns consider the transition of an unemployed average production worker, with a nonemployed spouse and two children, to part-time employment (40%) and full-time employment, respectively. The third and fourth columns present the effective tax rates for a secondary earner previously out of the labor force who starts working part-time or full-time, while the principal earner within the same household continues to work full-time. These data reveal that effective tax rates on principal earners typically substantially exceed those on secondary earners. The main reason is the benefit system. In particular, means-tested benefits and unemployment benefits are withdrawn if the principal earner finds work. Secondary earners do not have access to welfare benefits if the primary worker (i.e., the breadwinner) is employed. Moreover, if they do not have an employment history, these workers are also ineligible for benefits from unemployment insurance. Table 1.4 reveals that effective tax rates differ substantially across various households, even within the same country.

The first two columns of table 1.4 suggest that marginal effective tax rates are relatively high for primary workers at the bottom of the labor market, especially since many OECD countries have cut top marginal tax rates over the last two decennia. Another important reason why marginal tax rates are highest at the bottom of the labor market is that unemployment insurance benefits for high-income earners are typically only limited in duration. For high-income earners, therefore, the short-run replacement rates on which the data in table 1.4 are based

Table 1.3

Net replacement rates for three family types at two earnings levels, 1999 (after tax and including unemployment benefits, family, and housing benefits)

	APW[a]			66.7% of APW[a]		
	Single	Couple, two children	Lone parent, two children	Single	Couple, two children	Lone parent, two children
In the first month of benefit receipt						
United Kingdom	46	49	49	66	54	55
Sweden	71	78	85	82	90	93
Finland	65	83	87	79	88	92
Denmark	63	73	78	89	95	96
Ireland	31	57	52	42	67	59
Spain	74	73	76	76	76	77
Greece	47	44	47	48	46	50
Netherlands	82	89	81	88	85	80
Germany	60	70	71	67	75	76
France	71	72	72	78	82	83
Belgium	64	64	65	85	79	81
Italy	42	53	50	39	49	47
Portugal	79	79	80	88	87	87
Luxembourg	82	87	87	82	88	88
Austria	60	76	73	61	82	78
United States	58	57	58	59	49	49
Canada	62	91	91	62	97	97
Japan	67	64	70	82	77	82
In the sixtieth month of benefit receipt						
United Kingdom	46	80	71	66	88	81
Sweden	54	85	59	79	110	70
Finland	53	89	62	73	100	69
Denmark	60	80	79	85	102	97
Ireland	31	56	56	41	66	64
Spain	23	39	37	32	57	51
Greece	8	10	11	8	11	12
Netherlands	60	71	61	74	85	76
Germany	54	65	63	63	71	71
France	30	42	43	43	59	60
Belgium	45	68	69	60	84	86
Italy	0	18	14	0	21	17
Portugal	49	63	64	70	87	87
Luxembourg	50	75	59	70	93	82
Austria	55	72	69	58	78	74
United States	7	46	38	10	59	48
Canada	24	62	60	35	81	80
Japan	33	68	61	49	87	84

Source: OECD 2002b.

[a] APW stands for the income level of an average productive worker. For a definition, see OECD 2002b.

Table 1.4
Average effective tax rates on transitions for two-earner couples, 1999[a]

	From unemployed breadwinner and nonemployed partner to		From full-time employed breadwinner and non-employed partner to	
	Part-time (40%) employed breadwinner/ nonemployed partner	Full-time employed breadwinner/ nonemployed partner	Full-time employed breadwinner/ part-time (40%) employed partner	Full-time employed breadwinner/ full-time employed partner
United Kingdom	18	56	15	26
Sweden	87	84	29	34
Finland	86	87	21	34
Denmark	86	81	51	51
Ireland	101	61	21	34
Spain	166	76	18	19
Greece	103	43	16	18
Netherlands	84	92	50	46
Germany	52	75	51	53
France	80	72	32	37
Belgium	107	74	46	51
Italy	80	60	33	41
Portugal	174	81	15	20
Austria	142	79	21	30
Luxembourg	17	87	13	26
United States	99	63	19	25
Canada	73	92	30	34
Japan	151	68	14	14

Source: OECD 2002b.
[a] If employed, the earnings are as a percentage of the full-time employed salary of an average production worker.

may overstate disincentives to seek work. For low-income earners, in contrast, safety-net provisions, which are typically unlimited in duration, imply high replacement rates for longer periods of time. A comparison between the short-run and long-run replacement rates in table 1.3 does indeed reveal that benefits tend to drop less over time for low-income earners, thus producing higher long-run replacement rates than for those earning higher incomes. This implies substantial disincentives for low-income earners. Indeed, the duration rather than the magnitude of unemployment benefits may be the main determinant of disincentives to work and maintain human capital.

Older workers often face very high marginal tax rates on continuing to work because early retirement benefits are withdrawn if workers continue to work instead of retire. In any case, pension benefits are typically not increased in an actuarially fair manner if older workers delay retirement. Gruber and Wise (1999) show that marginal tax rates for older workers may sometimes exceed 100 percent. Their analysis reveals that high marginal tax rates on older workers are strongly correlated with labor force participation of older workers, which is in fact quite low in most European countries (see the next-to-last column in table 1.1). In addition to workers facing these high explicit tax rates, employers of older workers may be subject to implicit tax rates as a result of downward rigid wages. The government could offset these implicit taxes by explicit job subsidies for employers who employ older workers. These job subsidies, however, need to be financed through distortionary taxation. A more direct way to protect employment of older workers is to make wages of older workers more flexible. In this way, wages can be more in line with individual productivity. To achieve this, age-related pay schemes have to be reconsidered. For example, occupational pension systems that link pension benefits to final pay discourage gradual retirement through occupational downgrading with lower rates of pay. Ljungqvist and Sargent (1998) show how generous unemployment and disability benefits based on previous earnings prevent the labor market from easily adjusting to adverse shocks. In particular, in the face of generous insurance benefits that exceed their labor productivity, older skilled workers who suffer a substantial capital loss on their human capital (e.g., as a result of being laid off) are discouraged from searching for new jobs and from reducing their reservation wage in line with their reduced productivity. In this way, social insurance sets in motion a vicious circle of high unemployment and skill loss. This contributes to the high incidence of long-term unemployment and disability among European workers (see the last column of table 1.1).[5] As the workforce ages, these moral hazard problems associated with social insurance benefits based on previous earnings become more serious. Indeed, social insurance benefits based on final pay discourage workers from maintaining their human capital, since workers can rely on generous social benefits when their human capital becomes obsolete. Private insurance policies supplementing public disability and unemployment insurances worsen these moral hazard problems (Pauly 1974).[6]

Welfare, unemployment, and early retirement benefits are typically *conditional* benefits. In particular, unemployment benefits are paid only if one has left one's job involuntarily and if one is actively looking for work. Furthermore, many countries are enforcing obligations on welfare recipients, sometimes in the form of welfare-to-work programs or workfare programs. Early retirement benefits may be similar to disability benefits in that they are conditional on failing health. Countries may differ substantially in the eligibility criteria for categorical benefits like unemployment and disability benefits and in how strictly they enforce these criteria.[7] In interpreting the replacement rates and implicit tax rates in tables 1.3 and 1.4, one needs to be aware of these considerations. Indeed, the duration of the benefits and the obligations associated with social benefits (workfare, training, work tests) are key aspects of the design of unemployment insurance.[8]

1.3   Tax Reform and Employment

This section uses representative agent models to explore the impacts of tax reform on employment. It first considers the channel of labor supply before it turns to the channel of equilibrium unemployment. The analysis in this section is positive rather than normative. Normative aspects of labor taxation in representative agent models are explored in section 1.5.

1.3.1   Labor Supply

A representative household derives utility from consumption of goods (C) and leisure (V). The utility function $U(C, V)$ is concave and homothetic. Total time available to each household is normalized to one, which can be used to enjoy leisure V or to work $L^s = 1 - V$. The only source of income is labor income. The household budget constraint is thus given by $P^c C = (1 - T^a)WL^s$, where P^c stands for the consumer price and W denotes the market wage. $T^a \equiv T(WL^s)/WL^s$ represents the average personal income tax rate on labor, where the income tax paid by the household $T(WL^s)$ is a function of the market value of labor supply. Households determine labor supply from the condition that the marginal rate of substitution between leisure and consumption should equal the marginal consumer wage, namely, $U_v/U_c = (1 - T^m)W/P^c$, where subscripts stand for partial derivatives. $T^m \equiv$

$dT(WL^s)/d(WL^s)$ denotes the marginal tax rate on labor income. Both the marginal and the average tax rates depend on the market value of wage income WL^s.[9]

A measure of the progressivity of the income tax is the elasticity of after-tax labor income with respect to pretax labor income, namely, $S \equiv d \log(WL^s - T(WL^s))/d \log(WL^s) = (1 - T^m)/(1 - T^a)$. This coefficient is also known as the coefficient of residual income progression (Musgrave and Musgrave 1976). In a proportional tax system, the average and the marginal tax rates coincide so that $S = 1$. In a progressive tax system, in contrast, the average tax rate $T^a \equiv T(WL^s)/WL^s$ rises with pretax labor income WL^s, so that the marginal tax rate exceeds the average tax rate (i.e., $T^m > T^a$) and thus $S < 1$.

We employ lowercase variables to denote loglinear deviations from an initial equilibrium (e.g., $c \equiv dC/C$), except for the tax rates where we define $t^i \equiv dT^i/(1 - T^i)$, $i = a, m$. The logarithmic change in the degree of progressivity is thus given by $s = t^a - t^m$. The household budget constraint in relative changes is given by $p^c + c = S(w + l^s) - t^a$. Using the loglinearized optimality condition (i.e., $c - v = \sigma(w - t^m - p^c)$ where $\sigma \equiv -d \log(C/V)d \log(U_c/U_v)$ represents the elasticity of substitution between leisure and consumption goods in utility), we obtain the relative change in labor supply:[10]

$$l^s = \epsilon^u(w - p^c) - \epsilon^c t^m - \epsilon^i t^a = \epsilon^u(w - t^a - p^c) + \epsilon^c s. \tag{1}$$

Here, $\epsilon^i \equiv -V < 0$, $\epsilon^c \equiv V\sigma > 0$, and $\epsilon^u \equiv V(\sigma - 1) = \epsilon^c + \epsilon^i$ stand for the income, compensated wage, and uncompensated wage elasticities of labor supply, respectively.

Other things being equal, the average tax rate T^a and the market wage W, a higher marginal tax rate $t^m > 0$ reduces the opportunity cost of leisure at the margin. Hence, households substitute leisure for consumption and thus reduce labor supply. The compensated elasticity of labor supply ϵ^c reflects the strength of this substitution effect on account of a more progressive tax system (i.e., $s < 0$ with $t^a = 0$).

For a given marginal tax rate T^m, a higher average tax $t^a > 0$ makes workers poorer and thus increases the incentive to work. The magnitude of this income effect is reflected in the income elasticity of labor supply ϵ^i. The average and marginal tax rates thus exert opposite effects on labor supply: whereas higher marginal tax rates harm labor supply through the substitution effect, higher average tax rates raise it through the income effect.

If both the marginal and average tax rates are increased in tandem such that the progression of the tax system is unaffected (i.e., $t^m = t^a$ so that $s = 0$), the uncompensated wage elasticity of labor supply (i.e., $\epsilon^u = \epsilon^c + \epsilon^i$) captures the combined labor supply impact of the substitution effect of a higher marginal tax rate and the income effect of a higher average tax rate. The negative substitution effect dominates the positive income effect on labor supply if the elasticity of substitution between leisure and consumption goods exceeds unity (i.e., $\sigma > 1$) so that the uncompensated wage elasticity of labor supply is positive.

The previous analysis has assumed that the market wage W is constant. To explore the impact on the market wage, we model the demand side of the labor market. A representative firm maximizes profits, taking wages as given. It may have some market power on the commodity market in that the (absolute value of) price elasticity of demand for its output ε remains finite. Profits are given by $\Pi \equiv P_y(AF(L^d))AF(L^d) - (1 + T^l)WL^d$, where T^l denotes the payroll tax rate and L^d represents labor demand. $AF(L^d)$, $F' > 0$, $F'' < 0$ stands for a production function with diminishing returns to labor. These diminishing returns are due to a second production factor (e.g., capital), which is taken as fixed in the short run. Hence, profits originate not only in market power on commodity markets but also in this second production factor. Exogenous technology shocks are captured by changes in the productivity parameter A. Firms hire labor until the marginal revenue from the last worker equals the producer wage, namely, $P_y\left(1 - \frac{1}{\varepsilon}\right)AF'(L^d) = (1 + T^l)W$. Using $t^l \equiv dT^l/(1 + T^l)$, loglinearizing the marginal productivity condition for firms, and taking the producer price P_y as numeraire, we obtain the relative change in the demand for labor:[11]

$$l^d = -\epsilon^d(w + t^l - a), \tag{2}$$

where ϵ^d stands for the wage elasticity of labor demand.[12] Expression (2) reveals that an adverse productivity shock (i.e., $a < 0$) acts like a payroll tax. Indeed, we investigate not only changes in explicit taxes on labor income but also exogenous changes in labor productivity. This enables us to explore the impact of implicit labor taxes that reduce the productivity of labor. To illustrate, in a small open economy, source-based taxes on capital act as implicit taxes on labor do by reducing the productivity of labor if capital is perfectly mobile internationally. In the same fashion, if world prices of energy are fixed, a tax on the intermediate use of energy into production exerts similar adverse effects on labor productivity.[13]

In a competitive labor market, the market wage ensures that aggregate labor supply equals labor demand. Ignoring open economy considerations, we define the consumer price as $P^c \equiv 1 + T^c$, where T^c denotes the consumer tax rate. Using $t^c \equiv dT^c/(1 + T^c) = p^c$ and imposing equilibrium on the labor market (i.e., $NL^s = L^d$ where N denotes the fixed number of households), we can solve for employment, wage costs per unit of output, and the consumer wage:

$$l = -[\epsilon^d/(\epsilon^u + \epsilon^d)][\epsilon^c t^m + \epsilon^i t^a + \epsilon^u(t^l - a + t^c)] \tag{3}$$

$$= [\epsilon^d/(\epsilon^u + \epsilon^d)][\epsilon^c s + \epsilon^u(a - t)],$$

$$w + t^l - a = [\epsilon^u(t - a) - \epsilon^c s)/(\epsilon^u + \epsilon^d)], \tag{4}$$

$$w - t^a - p^c = [\epsilon^d(a - t) - \epsilon^c s]/(\epsilon^u + \epsilon^d), \tag{5}$$

where $s = t^a - t^m$, $t \equiv t^a + t^l + t^c$, and the labor demand elasticity ϵ^d applies to the macroeconomic level.

1.3.1.1 Tax Progression and Overall Tax Burden

We consider the impact of three exogenous policy shocks, namely (1) a higher marginal tax rate ceteris paribus the average tax wedge (i.e., $t^m = -s > 0$; $t = 0$); (2) a higher average tax wedge ceteris paribus the marginal tax rate (i.e., $t = t^a = s > 0$; $t^m = 0$); and (3) a higher average tax wedge ceteris paribus the coefficient of residual income progression (i.e., $t = t^m > 0$; $s = 0$). The average tax wedge between the producer wage and the consumer wage consists of the sum of the employees' tax rate, employers' tax rate, and consumer tax rate.[14]

The equilibrium effects are driven by labor supply effects (compare the impact of t^m and t^a in equations (1) and (3)). As described earlier, the marginal average and average tax rates shift the labor supply curve down and up, respectively. A higher average tax wedge between the producer and consumer wage while leaving the tax structure in terms of the degree of progressivity unaffected (i.e., $t > 0$ and $s = 0$) lowers employment and raises the producer wage if the substitution effect dominates the income effect in labor supply (i.e., $\sigma > 1$ so that $\epsilon^c > -\epsilon^i$), that is, if the uncompensated wage elasticity of labor supply is positive (i.e., $\epsilon^u > 0$).

Unemployment benefits do not have a natural place in this equilibrium model of the labor market. However, if one is willing to interpret unemployment as leisure, one can model unemployment benefits as a subsidy to leisure (Pissarides 1998; van der Ploeg 2003). Unemployment benefits hurt labor supply through both substitution and income effects. Indeed, unemployment benefits raise the effective marginal tax on work while reducing the overall average tax rate.[15]

1.3.1.2 Composition of Tax Burden

All components of the average tax wedge exert the same impact on employment. The reason is that flexible wages ensure that firms can partially shift a higher payroll tax (i.e., $t^l > 0$) onto workers through lower wages, while higher wages allow workers to shift higher income taxes and consumption taxes (i.e., $t^a, t^c > 0$) onto employers. This equivalence of various taxes depends on flexible wages. If market wages W were rigid, in contrast to income and consumption taxes, payroll taxes would hurt employment. In the presence of a fixed binding statutory minimum wage, therefore, replacing payroll taxes by income taxes boosts employment. Such a tax reform in effect undoes some of the implicit labor tax that workers impose on employers as a result of the minimum wage. Why the same employment effect cannot be achieved by simply lowering the implicit tax through a direct reduction in the minimum wage is unclear. Indeed, if the statutory minimum wage is raised to protect the purchasing power of workers after the income tax is raised, the tax reform does not succeed in raising employment.

An adverse productivity shock ($a < 0$) yields exactly the same effects as does a rise in the payroll tax rate—namely, a drop in after-tax wages and a fall in (boost to) employment if the substitution effect dominates (is outweighed by) the income effect in labor supply.[16] Hence, an adverse supply shock amounts to an implicit labor tax. To keep employment constant in the face of a steady increase in productivity, one needs to impose a unitary elasticity of substitution between leisure and consumption of goods (King, Plosser, and Rebelo 1998). In that case, not only productivity shocks but also changes in the average tax rate leave employment unaffected.

1.3.1.3 Human Capital

Labor taxes impact not only the quantity of labor (i.e., hours worked) but also the quality of labor (i.e., effort and human capital).[17] With exogenous labor supply, proportional labor taxes do not affect human capital accumulation if all costs of training are deductible against the proportional tax rate. Intuitively, just as cash-flow taxes leave capital investment unaffected,[18] proportional labor taxes affect the costs and benefits of investments in human capital in the same way. The neutrality of proportional labor taxes no longer holds if the number of hours worked is endogenous. At fewer hours worked, human capital accumulation becomes less attractive because human capital is utilized less intensively. This so-called utilization effect makes schooling and labor supply complementary activities.[19]

This indirect complementarity is further strengthened in learning-by-doing models (Heckman, Lochner, and Cossa 2002). In these models, learning and working are directly complementary, whereas in the traditional learning-or-doing model work and schooling compete for a worker's time. Nevertheless, if the labor market appropriately prices the benefits from learning-by-doing in wages,[20] the implications of learning-by-doing turn out to be equivalent to those of learning-or-doing. In any case, with endogenous leisure, both models predict that permanent tax policies that stimulate labor supply also boost human capital accumulation. At the same time, policies that encourage schooling increase long-run labor supply. Labor supply and human capital thus exert positive feedback effects on each other.

Apart from inducing the utilization and learning-by-doing effects, labor taxes may harm human capital if not all costs of schooling are tax deductible (see, e.g., Trostel 1993). Similarly, if marginal taxes rise with income, benefits of schooling may be taxed at higher rates than the rates against which costs are tax deductible, thereby discouraging human capital accumulation (Bovenberg and van Ewijk 1997). Residence-based taxes on capital income, in contrast, stimulate schooling because they encourage agents to substitute human capital for financial capital. These taxes can therefore help offset the human-capital distortions due to nondeductible training costs or rising marginal tax rates (Nielsen and Sørensen 1998). Alternatively, training subsidies or compulsory schooling may be employed to alleviate the adverse effect of progressive labor taxes on human capital accumulation (Bovenberg and Jacobs 2002).

1.3.2 Equilibrium Unemployment

Turning to the analysis of labor taxes in imperfect labor markets, we enter the realm of second-best economics. Distortionary labor taxes may either alleviate or exacerbate nontax distortions in the labor market that give rise to involuntary unemployment. Whereas section 1.3.1 considered only a representative agent and did not address distributional issues at all, this section investigates the separate impacts of taxes on employed and unemployed agents. Workers, however, are still homogeneous.[21]

1.3.2.1 Right-to-manage Model

To illustrate the impact of taxes in imperfect labor markets, we formulate a right-to-manage model of the labor market.[22] Many symmetric decentralized unions exert market power in a labor-market segment but are too small to internalize the effects of higher wages on prices, profits, and the government budget constraint. Unions and employers bargain about wages, after which firms set employment.

Union preferences are characterized by the following objective function:[23]

$$Lv(W^a) + (N - L)WU^r; \quad v'(W^a) > 0, \, v''(W^a) \leq 0, \tag{6}$$

where N denotes the number of trade union members, of which L are employed. $W^a \equiv W - T(W)$ represents after-tax wages earned in the industry, where W and $T(W)$ represent the market wage and the personal income tax function, respectively. A concave felicity function $v(W^a)$ implies risk-averse workers. In several cases, we will assume that felicity is isoelastic; that is, $v(W^a) = (W^a)^{1-\rho}/(1-\rho)$, where ρ stands for the (constant) coefficient of relative risk aversion.

In wage bargaining, the union takes the outside option (i.e., expected utility outside the industry U^r) as given and accounts for labor demand behavior by firms, which is modeled along the lines of section 1.3.1. The perceived wage elasticity of labor demand ϵ^d depends on the price elasticity of demand for the bargaining unit as a whole (i.e., the industry). This price elasticity is likely to be smaller than the price elasticity facing an individual firm. Nash bargaining maximizes $[L(v(W^a) - U^r)]^\beta \Pi^{1-\beta}$ with respect to W, where profits Π are given by $P_y(AF(L))AF(L) - (1 + T^l)WL$. This yields

$$\frac{v(W^a) - U^r}{v(W^a)} = Sm, \tag{7}$$

where $m \equiv \left(\frac{v'(W^a)W^a}{v(W^a)}\right)/\left[\epsilon^d + \frac{1-\beta}{\beta}\frac{(1+T^l)WL}{\Pi}\right]$. The union sets utility in work as a markup on outside utility U^r.[24] A more progressive tax system, which implies a lower coefficient of residual income progression

S, moderates wages. Intuitively, a high marginal tax rate implies that higher wages accrue mainly to the government rather than to union members. Hence, from the union's point of view, the payoff from higher wage costs (and the associated loss in employment) in terms of higher net incomes for working members is only low, so that the union moderates wages. By affecting wage-setting behavior, a more progressive tax system for workers thus combats inequality between employed union members enjoying utility $v(W^a)$ and union members who only obtain outside utility U^r.

Apart from S, however, tax policy cannot affect this inequity as measured by the ratio $v(W^a)/U^r$. In particular, unions undo the effect on $v(W^a)/U^r$ of a higher tax on union members employed in the sector by raising the before-tax reward to work, W, so that $v(W^a)/U^r$ does not decline. In this way, union behavior limits the scope for redistribution between workers and the unemployed.[25]

Various nontax factors affect the markup m. To explore these factors, we assume that other production factors besides labor are fixed. In that case, the markup can be written as follows:

$$\frac{v'(W^a)W^a}{v(W^a)} \left/ \left[\frac{1}{\left(\frac{1-\alpha}{\sigma^f}+\frac{\alpha}{\varepsilon}\right)} + \frac{1-\beta}{\beta}\frac{\alpha\left(1-\frac{1}{\varepsilon}\right)}{\left[1-\alpha\left(1-\frac{1}{\varepsilon}\right)\right]} \right] \right. .$$

Wages are thus moderated if bargaining firms as a unit do not yield much market power on the commodity market (i.e., $1/\varepsilon$ is small), labor is a good substitute for the fixed factor (i.e., σ^f is large), profits account only for a small share of value added (i.e., α is large), and unions do not exert much bargaining power (i.e., β is small).[26] The first two conditions ensure that the (quasi) rents parties bargain over are only small.

In order to solve for wages in general equilibrium in which outside utility U^r is endogenous, we use the following expression for outside utility:

$$U^r = g(u)[v(B)+\delta] + (1-g(u))v(\overline{W}^a), \tag{8}$$

where B and $\overline{W}^a$ denote the unemployment benefit and after-tax wages of workers employed in other sectors, respectively, and $\delta \geq 0$ is the utility of leisure if unemployed.[27] $(1-g(u))$, measures the probability of finding a job outside the current sector. This probability is decreasing with the aggregate unemployment rate (i.e., $dg/du > 0$). In a symmetric equilibrium, all unions set the same wages, so that $\overline{W}^a = W^a$.

Using this equilibrium condition in (8) to eliminate $\overline{W}^a$ and using the result in (7) to eliminate U^r, we arrive at the following expression for equilibrium unemployment u:

$$g(u) = \frac{Sm}{[1 - (v(B) + \delta)/v(W^a)]}. \tag{9}$$

This expression can be interpreted as the wage-setting curve. Together with the labor demand function (2), the curve determines labor-market equilibrium. Thus, compared to the competitive equilibrium analyzed in section 1.3.1, the wage-setting curve rather than the labor-supply curve affects actual wages. The labor supply curve implicit in the reservation wage is given by $v(B) + \delta$. It is thus horizontal in (L, w) space, reflecting an infinite elasticity of labor supply associated with constant utility of leisure δ.

1.3.2.2   Net Replacement Rate Fixed
We first look at the special case in which the effective net (i.e., after-tax) replacement rate $R \equiv B/W^a$ is fixed, utility is isoelastic, utility of leisure is absent (i.e., $\delta = 0$), and S and the markup m are fixed. In these circumstances, the wage curve determines equilibrium unemployment:

$$g(u) = \frac{Sm}{[1 - R^{1-\rho}]}.$$

The wage curve is vertical in (L, W) space. Intuitively, an increase in the wage rate does not make work more attractive because the fixed replacement implies that such a wage increase is accompanied by an equivalent increase in the unemployment benefit B.

Tax Progression   The tax system affects employment through the coefficient of residual income progression S. The employment impacts of a higher marginal tax rate (ceteris paribus the average tax wedge, namely, $t^m = -s > 0$) and a higher average tax wedge (ceteris paribus the marginal tax rate, namely, $t = t^a = s > 0$) have the opposite sign as the employment impacts established in section 1.3.1. In particular, whereas section 3.3.1 showed that a higher marginal tax rate hurts employment by harming labor supply, we now find that it actually boosts employment by moderating wages.[28] Indeed, in our second-best setting, a high marginal tax rate alleviates the distortions implied by the market power of unions.

Overall Tax Burden   Given a fixed effective replacement rate $R = B/W^a$, a higher average tax wedge (ceteris paribus the coefficient of residual income progression, namely, $t = t^m > 0; s = 0$) leaves equilibrium unemployment unaffected. Raising the tax burden while maintaining the structure of taxation (as measured by the coefficient of residual income progression) thus does not have an impact on labor market transactions. Workers completely accommodate the higher tax burden in terms of lower after-tax wages so that wage costs (and hence labor demand) remain constant. This is known in the literature as the complete absence of real wage resistance.

The intuition behind this lack of real wage resistance is that the unemployed are in effect subject to the higher tax burden. With the outside option thus effectively being taxed, the bargaining position of the union weakens so that wages are moderated. Indeed, the key effective tax rate in this model is the effective (after-tax) replacement rate. As long as the tax system does not affect this key variable, unemployment remains unaffected. With a vertical wage-setting curve, payroll taxes or capital taxes harming labor productivity (thereby shifting the labor-demand curve) also do not affect employment but are transmitted fully as changes in market wages.

This result of lack of real wage resistance has been quite popular for both theoretical and empirical reasons. Regarding the theoretical reasons, one would like to separate clearly the unemployment impact of the tax burden and that of the social insurance system (and the replacement rate). A higher tax burden affects equilibrium unemployment only through the channel of the effective (after-tax) replacement rate. Another reason for the popularity of this result is that most labor-market models impose conditions that ensure that productivity growth does not impact unemployment. Fixing the replacement rate ensures that the models replicate this stylized fact. As regards empirical reasons, several cross-country studies could not establish significant empirical correlation between average tax rates and unemployment (see, e.g., Layard, Nickell, and Jackman 1991). Indeed, as long as one correctly measures the after-tax replacement rate $R = B/W^a$ and the coefficient of residual income progression S, one would not expect to find an additional separate effect of the tax burden.

Composition of the Tax Burden   Changes in the tax structure (i.e., replacing payroll taxes by consumption taxes) do not affect equilibrium unemployment. A upward shift in the labor demand curve as a consequence of lower payroll taxes results in higher wages. This protects the purchasing power of workers and benefit recipients after the increase in consumption taxes.

1.3.2.3 Gross Replacement Rate Fixed

Daveri and Tabellini (2000) have challenged the result that a higher tax burden does not affect unemployment, which has been supported by empirical studies that could not find any significant correlation between cross-section variations in unemployment and tax rates. They argue that labor market institutions differ significantly across countries and that fixed effects thus dominate cross-sectional variations in unemployment rates. Accordingly, they rely on time-series instead of cross-sectional evidence to establish the link between the labor tax burden and unemployment. They find that time variation in labor taxes tends to be strongly correlated with unemployment changes in highly unionized countries of continental Europe. The correlation is substantially weaker, however, in the Scandinavian countries with centralized trade unions. Hence, the unemployment impact of labor taxes depends importantly on the nontax institutions of a country.

To establish real wage resistance theoretically, Daveri and Tabellini (2000) assume that the replacement rate is fixed in before-tax terms and that unemployment benefits are not subject to income tax.[29] With isoelastic utility but without leisure (i.e., $\delta = 0$), equilibrium employment amounts to

$$g(u) = \frac{Sm}{[1 - (R^g/(1 - T^a))^{1-\rho}]},\tag{10}$$

where $R^g = B/W$ is the fixed gross (i.e., before-personal tax) replacement rate.

Overall Tax Burden At fixed S, a higher average tax burden T^a raises unemployment by in effect increasing the net replacement rate $R^g/(1 - T^a)$, thereby making unemployment relatively more attractive. Union members pay for the higher tax burden less in terms of lower after-tax wages, and more in terms of a higher probability of becoming unemployed. The intuition behind the higher unemployment rate can be understood as follows. Equation (7) implies that the utility of non-employed union members is proportional to employed union members. Hence, a higher tax burden raising the net replacement rate does not make nonemployed union members better off compared to employed members. The effect of a higher net replacement rate is offset by a higher unemployment rate increasing the expected duration of unemployment. Indeed, a change in the net replacement rate is powerless to affect the relative position of the unemployed compared to the employed.

Whether the higher tax burden makes the employed and the unemployed worse off depends on the elasticity of labor demand.[30] With inelastic labor demand, a higher tax burden may even raise after-tax wages so that workers can shift more than 100 percent of the tax burden onto employers. The intuition for the overshifting is that higher wages increase unemployment benefits, thereby improving the outside option and thus increasing wage pressure. If at the same time labor demand is inelastic, the higher wages do not result in much additional unemployment, so that wage pressures remain.[31] Indeed, with inelastic labor demand, workers are able to shift the tax burden onto profits, consumers, and other taxpayers. With overshifting, despite the higher unemployment rate increasing the expected duration of unemployment, the unemployed also gain because higher wages raise income not only in employment but also in unemployment (since unemployment benefits are linked to wages).

One way to justify the separate unemployment effect of T^a in empirical wage equations (even if they directly measure S and the after-tax replacement rates from social insurance benefits) is that, in addition to taxed unemployment benefits, the unemployed may derive untaxed incomes from the informal sector (Bovenberg and van der Ploeg 1998; Holmlund 2000) or enjoy utility of untaxed leisure (Sørensen 1997). The official replacement rates, which include only public unemployment benefits, thus do not correctly measure the *effective* replacement rates. Indeed, with a fixed net replacement rate from unemployment insurance R, isoelastic utility, and positive nontaxed other income in unemployment (measured in terms of utils) δ, the wage-setting curve (from (9)) is given by

$$g(u) = \frac{Sm}{[1 - R^{1-\rho} - \delta/(W(1 - T^a)^{1-\rho}]}.$$

With nontaxed sources of unemployment income, productivity growth is consistent with stationary unemployment if nontaxed incomes rise with productivity in the formal economy so that $\delta^* \equiv \delta/W$ is fixed. In that case, the wage-setting curve is vertical again. With a fixed net official replacement rate R, in contrast to the situation without nontax sources of unemployment income, an increase in the average tax burden T^a moves this vertical curve to the right.[32] Hence, conditions that ensure that changes in labor productivity do not impact unemployment do not necessarily imply that a higher tax burden leaves unemployment unaffected.

The result that the tax burden raises the equilibrium unemployment rate is an important and controversial policy conclusion. In the Netherlands, for example, the empirical result that—even if one controls for the official replacement rate—the tax wedge significantly affects equilibrium unemployment has been quite robust (see, e.g., Graafland and Huizinga 1999). It has played an important role in supporting policies to contain the tax burden. Indeed, the numerical impacts of a lower tax wedge can be substantial. To illustrate, Daveri and Tabellini (2000) find that the rise of 10 percentage points in the rate of effective labor tax in continental Europe in the 1970s and 1980s can explain about 3 percentage points of the increase in European unemployment during this period. Nickell and Layard (1999) estimate an unemployment effect of about 2 percentage points for such a tax increase.[33]

Tax Progression   Tax progression raises the net replacement rate if unemployment benefits are subject to the same tax schedule as wage income, while the replacement rate is fixed in before-tax terms. This is in fact the case in many OECD countries (see OECD 2002b). In that case, more progression exerts two offsetting effects in equilibrium unemployment. In addition to moderating wages, it boosts wages by raising the net replacement rate. To illustrate these two effects, we assume a tax schedule featuring a constant coefficient of residual income progression S. In particular, the tax schedule is given by $T(Y) = Y - \zeta Y^S$, where ζ and S are positive constants and Y is gross (labor or unemployment) income. This tax schedule implies that the coefficient of residual income progression is fixed at S. With this tax schedule and $\delta = 0$, equilibrium unemployment amounts to

$$g(u) = \frac{Sm}{1 - (R^g)^S}, \tag{11}$$

where R^g denotes the fixed replacement rate (in before-tax terms).[34] In that case, the wage moderation effect of more progression still dominates the replacement rate effect. Accordingly, more progression alleviates unemployment, even if high gross replacement rates imply that more progression raises effective net replacement substantially.[35] Replacing a proportional consumption tax by a progressive income tax thus boosts employment.

This result is modified if we allow for positive utility from leisure δ. In that case, a more progressive tax schedule may actually raise equilibrium unemployment. Intuitively, with high leisure, the replacement rate effect becomes relatively more important compared to the wage moderation effect. At high replacement rates, a progressive tax system thus becomes less powerful in boosting employment. Indeed, a more progressive tax schedule raises unemployment if nontaxable income $\delta^* = \delta/W(1 - T^a)$ and the gross replacement rate R^g are large, while the tax system is quite progressive to start (i.e., S is small). Together, these three factors contribute to a high net replacement rate.

Starting from a proportional income tax system, the introduction of some progression may help to fight unemployment. At higher levels of progression, however, further increasing progression may be counterproductive in terms of the objective of reducing unemployment. There is thus a level of progression that minimizes unemployment, defined by the following implicit equation for S:[36]

$$1 - \delta^* = (R^g)^S(1 - S \log R^g).$$

The optimal tax system is progressive (i.e., $S < 1$) as long as the gross replacement rate and utility from leisure δ^* are not very large, so that $(R^g)(1 - \log R^g) < 1 - \delta^*$.

This example suggests that the unemployment impacts of taxes and unemployment benefits are related. If tax systems are progressive, a given gross replacement rate implies a higher after-tax replacement rate, so that this replacement rate worsens unemployment more. At the same time, at higher replacement rates, changes in progression are less likely to reduce unemployment, as the replacement rate effect of more progression becomes stronger compared to the wage-moderating effect.

Composition of the Tax Burden   The differential impacts of productivity and explicit labor taxes in case the gross compensation ratio is fixed generate scope for tax policies to boost employment. In particular, replacing explicit labor taxes with implicit labor taxes boosts employment. Intuitively, such a tax switch reduces the net replacement rate and shifts the tax burden onto nonlabor income. With their nontaxed incomes being tied to before-tax wages, the unemployed bear the burden of the implicit labor taxes (since these taxes reduce before-tax wages), yet escape the burden of explicit labor taxes. Hence, this tax reform succeeds in shifting the tax burden toward the unemployed so that the outside option becomes less attractive. This stimulates wage moderation and thus employment.

Implicit labor taxes can take various forms. Source-based capital income taxes in small open economies are one example. With mobile capital, these taxes are shifted onto labor (and with unemployment benefits and other nonlabor income δ being linked to wages also onto the unemployed) in the form of lower labor productivity. Environmental taxes on tradable intermediate inputs such as energy are another example. Bovenberg and van der Ploeg (1998), Koskela and Schob (1999), and Koskela and Schob (2002) show that green tax reforms and substituting source-based capital taxes for labor taxes may boost employment if these reforms succeed in shifting the tax burden to nonlabor income (and income of the unemployed, in particular). If they succeed in increasing employment, these reforms are thus an indirect way to cut the effective net replacement rate. These conclusions are consistent with Bovenberg (1995), who argues that a green tax reform boosts employment only if the tax burden is shifted away from workers to people outside the active labor force (e.g., pensioners, owners of natural resources, transfer recipients). A change in the tax structure thus succeeds in alleviating unemployment if it replaces a tax that is borne solely by workers with a tax that is also paid by the unemployed.[37]

The Role of the Bargaining Level   The employment effect of labor taxes depends crucially on wage-setting institutions (see also Daveri and Tabellini 2000). Up to now, we have assumed decentralized wage setting. Some countries, however, feature more centralized wage setting. Centralized unions may internalize the adverse impacts of high unemployment on the government budget constraint, thereby moderating wages (Calmfors and Driffill 1988; Summers, Gruber, and Vergara 1993).[38] In fact, taxes may no longer affect unemployment at all. Intuitively, unions see through the veil of the government budget constraint and offset changes in the tax rate through transfers that offset exactly the real effects of taxes. This is a mixed blessing. The good news is that a higher average tax burden is less harmful for employment if (part of) income in unemployment is untaxed.[39] The bad news, however, is that a high marginal tax rate becomes less effective in reducing the monopoly distortion. This latter distortion is absent, however, if unions also internalize the impact of wages on profits (e.g., because union members derive their pensions from shareholdings in the firms) and consumer prices (because union members consume commodities produced at home). Indeed, unions may internalize the effect of high wages not only on the government budget constraint but also on profits and prices.[40]

In addition to centralization, another important aspect of wage-setting institutions is the time horizon used by unions in setting wages. In particular, if they have a short-term horizon, unions can take the capital stock as given. The labor demand elasticity in wage bargaining is thus rather low, implying a relatively high wage markup m and thus a high equilibrium unemployment rate. If reputational considerations allow unions to commit, in contrast, unions use a longer time horizon in considering the effects of high wages. Hence, they employ larger labor demand elasticity in setting wages. With a smaller union markup, changes in labor taxes exert a smaller impact on unemployment.[41]

Unemployment Benefits Linked to Consumer Prices Unemployment benefits may be linked to prices rather than wages, especially in the short run.[42] Indeed, these benefits may be associated with an exogenous minimum income a country wants in order to keep liquidity-constrained households above the poverty line. In this case, the wage-setting curve is no longer vertical, but slopes upward. Intuitively, higher wages are no longer transmitted into higher income during unemployment. This makes a higher wage more effective in equilibrating the labor market. In particular, a higher wage makes work more attractive compared to unemployment, thereby boosting employment.

If unemployment benefits are linked to consumer prices and are thus fixed in real terms, the wage-setting curve describing the target real wage (in terms of producer prices) is given by (from (9))

$$v(W(1 - T^a)/(1 + T^c)) = [v(B) + \delta]\left[1 - \frac{Sm}{g(u)}\right]^{-1}.$$

In this case, taxes are paid only by workers, while the unemployed are protected. Since higher taxes make work less attractive compared to unemployment, a higher overall tax burden raises unemployment, just as in the case in which the gross replacement rate is fixed. Moreover, there is real wage resistance in that after-tax wages do not fully absorb a higher tax burden.

How much wage costs increase and after-tax wages decline in response to a higher tax burden depends on the slopes of the labor demand and wage-setting curves. Workers shift most of the tax burden onto firms if labor demand is inelastic (i.e., vertical in (L, W) space) and unemployment hardly affects the target real wage, so that the wage-setting curve is horizontal in (L, W) space. In that case, employed union members and nonemployed union members do not experience much of a loss in utility. Utility of nonemployed union members, U^r, does not decline much, as unemployment does not increase substantially. The initial decrease in inequity between workers and the unemployed is thus restored mainly through an increase in W^a. The other extreme case involves elastic labor demand and elastic wage setting (with respect to unemployment). In this case, the initial gap between utilities of workers and unemployed agents is reestablished through higher unemployment reducing U^r rather than through higher market wages increasing W^a.

1.4   Employment and Distribution: Applied General Equilibrium Analysis

This section explores the impact of labor tax reform with the help of an applied general equilibrium model for the Netherlands, the so-called MIMIC model developed at CPB Netherlands Bureau for Economic Policy Analysis. The model combines a rich theoretical framework based on modern economic theories, a firm empirical foundation, and an elaborate description of the actual tax and social insurance systems in the Netherlands. The model considers the two main transmission channels through which tax policy impacts the labor market—namely, labor supply and wage determination. In addition, it considers various other ways through which taxes and benefits affect the labor market— namely, the black economy, human capital accumulation, efficiency wages, costly job matching, and search behavior of the unemployed. Hence, in addition to wages, unemployment, and the quantity of labor supply, taxes affect the quality of labor supply. Through the replacement rate, the benefit system affects not only wage setting but also search intensity and the reservation wages of the unemployed.

1.4.1   MIMIC Model

This section provides a bird's-eye view of MIMIC (Graafland et al. 2001 provides a more detailed overview of the model). MIMIC allows for considerable heterogeneity among households. In particular, the model accounts for heterogeneity in household composition (including the number of children), educational level, age, ability, preferences for leisure, and labor market status. Incorporating this heterogeneity allows one to explore the income distribution and hence various trade-offs between equity and efficiency. Moreover, tables 1.3 and 1.4 document the fact that replacement rates and marginal tax rates vary considerably across various individuals, depending on household composition and income level. The same holds true for labor supply elasticities.[43] Whereas particular policies may have little impact on a representative individual, they may significantly affect the behavior of particular types of individuals, such as secondary part-time workers, low-skilled agents, and older employees close to retirement (Disney 2000). A careful analysis of the labor supply effects of tax policy therefore requires substantial disaggregation. Indeed, representative agent models conceal this variation in effective tax rates and labor supply behavior.

MIMIC embeds a standard microsimulation model in a general equilibrium setting. As an applied general equilibrium model, MIMIC draws on microeconomic theory to derive supply and demand from optimizing behavior by decentralized agents. This allows one to interpret the model results in terms of microeconomic behavior of households and firms. In modeling equilibrium on the labor market, the model departs from the traditional assumption of market clearing in most general equilibrium models. In modeling labor market imperfections that give rise to involuntary unemployment, MIMIC employs modern labor market theories. In particular, in addition to legal minimum wages, it includes elements of wage bargaining, efficiency wages, and costly job matching. In this way the model describes equilibrium unemployment in terms of the structure of the tax system, minimum wages, and the features of social insurance and assistance.

MIMIC has a firm empirical basis. Various crucial relationships in the model, including contractual wage formation and the production function, have been estimated from time-series data. Furthermore, microeconometric estimates on Dutch labor supply helped calibrate the labor supply model. Moreover, income distributions are based on micro data.

MIMIC describes the institutional features of taxation and social insurance in much detail. This institutional detail makes the model especially relevant for policymaking because actual policy proposals typically involve particular details of the tax and social insurance systems. Moreover, as section 1.3.2 documents, the impact of tax policies depends crucially on how unemployment and welfare benefits respond to changes in wages and taxes.

Incorporating the main transmission channels of tax policy in an empirically based model with substantial household heterogeneity is not without costs. In particular, the various submodels are not fully consistent with each other. To illustrate, the wage-setting model does not take into account endogenous labor supply. Moreover, the labor supply model assumes that households are not rationed on the labor market. At the same time, the models describing search behavior of the unemployed and training and schooling are not part of the household model describing labor supply.

1.4.1.1 Households and Labor Supply

MIMIC distinguishes forty types of households in order to adequately describe labor supply and explore the income distribution. In particular, it distinguishes couples, single persons, single parents, pensioners, and students. To model the specific labor supply behavior of those close to retirement, people aged between 55 and 65 years are represented by a separate household type. Couples consist of a so-called breadwinner (i.e., the individual with the highest personal income) and a partner (i.e., the adult with the lowest personal income). Couples are subdivided into families with children and those without. Individuals within each household may differ with respect to their skill level (high-skilled, low-skilled, or unskilled) and their job status (i.e., holding a job in the formal sector, unemployed and collecting a social benefit, or not participating in the labor force).

For each household type, MIMIC employs class frequency income distributions based on microdata to describe the distribution of gross incomes. These income distributions are important determinants of the efficiency costs of high marginal tax rates: the more people are concentrated in a particular income range, the higher the efficiency costs of high marginal rates in this income range. By applying the corresponding statutory tax and premium rates to gross incomes, MIMIC determines net incomes and the average and marginal tax rates that affect labor supply decisions.

The labor supply model has been calibrated so that the model reproduces labor supply elasticities estimated in the empirical literature for the Netherlands. In particular, the uncompensated wage elasticity of labor supply by partners is set at 1.0; single persons and most breadwinners feature corresponding elasticities of 0.25 and 0.1, respectively. Older breadwinners, who may change their retirement decisions in response to changes in wages, feature a somewhat higher elasticity of 0.15. The income elasticities of labor supply are smaller than the corresponding wage elasticities—namely, 0.2 for partners, 0.05 for single persons, and almost zero for breadwinners. In addition to supplying labor to the formal labor market, households can supply labor to the black labor market. The model has been calibrated to reproduce the size of the black economy in the Netherlands, which is estimated at about 3 percent of GDP, and an uncompensated wage elasticity of black labor supply of 0.75.

A separate training model endogenizes the distribution of the labor force over unskilled, low-skilled, and high-skilled workers. By engaging in training activities, workers can increase the transition rates to higher skill levels with higher wages. In setting their training level, workers trade off (nontaxable) effort costs and the benefits of training (in terms of a higher probability of moving toward a higher skill level earning a higher wage). Based on Groot and Oosterbeek 1995, the model is calibrated such that a 10 percent increase in after-tax wage differentials raises the share of workers participating in training by 8 percent.

1.4.1.2 Wage Formation and Job Matching

The black labor market is modeled as the competitive labor market in section 1.3.1; for each of the three skill categories, the wage clears this market. Firms in the sheltered sector and the construction sector[44] demand labor from the black market. The elasticity of substitution between black and formal labor in the production function is set at 2.0, which is based on empirical evidence in Baartmans, Meyer, and van Schaik 1986. Furthermore, firms may pay formal labor in part informally, namely, without reporting the wages to the tax authorities. Firms determine this informal labor by trading off lower taxes against a potential penalty for fraud.

The formal labor markets for the three skill categories do not clear. The imperfections of this market originate in market power of unions, efficiency wages, and costly job matching. To describe wage formation in these markets, MIMIC distinguishes between contractual wages (which are determined in collective bargaining between employers and unions) and incidental wages (which are set by individual employers based on the tightness of the skill-specific labor markets). Social benefits are linked to contractual, rather than incidental, wages.

Contractual wages are determined by a right-to-manage model in which employers and unions bargain over wages at the industry level. The rents that unions and employers bargain over originate in the market power of firms on product markets. In particular, each industry produces a good that is an imperfect substitute for goods produced by other domestic industries or by foreign firms. The unions are small compared to the labor market as a whole, and therefore they do not internalize the impact of their bargain on the government budget constraint, profits, and prices.

The resulting wage equation is calibrated on the basis of estimates by Graafland and Huizinga (1999). Using macrodata, they found that the positive elasticity of the average tax rate is six times as large in absolute value as the negative elasticity of the marginal tax rate (-0.1). The elasticity of the consumer price equals the sum of the elasticities of the marginal and average tax rates, which is 0.5. Accordingly, at constant unemployment and replacement rates, the incidence of a higher tax wedge (by simultaneously increasing average and marginal tax rates) is split equally between employers and employees through higher gross wages and lower after-tax wages. On average, the wage elasticity of the replacement rate is about 0.2.[45]

The wage structure among skills is further modified by a skill-specific, so-called incidental wage component. This incidental wage component is used by employers to minimize search costs and can thus be interpreted as an efficiency wage associated with hiring costs. It is set as a markup on the contractual wage. This markup rises with the tightness of the labor market.

To model labor market tightness and mismatch, MIMIC incorporates costly job matching. Heterogeneity in the matching process also allows MIMIC to model the adverse impact of high minimum wages and high reservation wages on the efficiency of the matching process. In particular, low-productivity matches may fail because they do not meet the minimum productivity standard of the employer (determined by the minimum wage) or the reservation wage of the unemployed.

1.4.1.3 Public Institutions

MIMIC contains several public institutions, including the Dutch personal income tax system in 1998. The personal income tax features a tax-free allowance and three tax brackets. A partner whose labor income remains below the tax-free allowance can transfer the tax-free allowance to the breadwinner. The rate in the first tax bracket is about 36 percent in 1998. The tax rate in the second bracket is 50 percent and has to be paid on incomes above about 25,000 euros. The marginal rate in the third tax bracket, which amounts to 60 percent, is paid on incomes above about 50,000 euros. Workers benefit from a special earned income tax deduction, which amounts to 12 percent of labor income with a maximum of around 1,500 euros. Unemployment benefits are subject to the progressive personal income tax. VAT in the Netherlands imposes a low rate on necessary goods (6%) and a high rate on other goods (17%). Other public institutions in MIMIC include employee and national social insurance schemes,[46] the employers' and employees' contributions to employee social insurances, premiums for health insurance, the statutory minimum wage (which is linked to the average contractual wage rate), social assistance (which is linked to the statutory minimum wage), and a number of policy instruments targeted at specific groups, such as the long-term unemployed and the unskilled. Households with incomes just above the minimum wage face overall effective marginal tax rates close to 80 percent on account of employee insurance premiums, income-dependent public health care premiums, and means-tested housing allowances. Indeed, overall marginal taxes in this income range exceed the marginal tax rate (of 60%) facing high-income earners.

1.4.2 Cutting Taxes in MIMIC

This section employs the MIMIC model to investigate the long-run effects of a number of tax cuts. In all experiments, the ex ante (i.e., before behavioral responses have been taken into account) reduction in tax revenues amounts to 0.25 percent of GDP. A cut in public consumption balances the government budget ex post (i.e., after the effects of the behavioral responses on the public budget have been taken into account). Hence, the required cut in public consumption reflects the impact of behavioral responses on the public budget. In particular, if the reduction in public consumption is less than the ex ante cut in revenues of 0.25 percent of GDP, behavioral responses help mitigate budgetary costs.

This section first explores cuts in personal income taxes before it investigates various forms of an EITC aimed at increasing the reward of work, in general, and of low-skilled work, in particular.

1.4.2.1   Personal Income Taxation

Cutting Marginal Tax Rates   The detailed modeling of the personal income tax system allows MIMIC to explore the labor market effects of various parameters of the Dutch tax system. The first three columns of table 1.5 contain the long-run effects of cuts in each of the three tax brackets of the Dutch personal income tax (of 1.2, 6.9, and 24.5 percent points, respectively). These tax cuts reduce both marginal and average tax rates. However, the tax cut in the first bracket is inframarginal for many workers whose incomes reach into the second and third tax brackets. This particular tax cut thus reduces the average marginal tax rate (i.e., the marginal tax rate averaged over the various workers) substantially less than tax cuts in the higher brackets do (see the next-to-last row of table 1.5). Indeed, in contrast to a reduction in the tax rates in the upper brackets, a tax cut in the lowest bracket makes the tax system somewhat more progressive (as measured by the coefficient of residual income progression).

Labor Supply   All three tax cuts boost aggregate labor supply (in hours) because the substitution effect associated with a lower marginal tax rate dominates the income effect on account of a lower average tax rate. The composition of additional labor supply, however, differs. In particular, a lower tax rate in the first bracket raises especially the labor supply of partners (i.e., secondary earners). This is because partners tend to work in part-time jobs with relatively low (annual) labor incomes. Hence, their marginal labor income is typically subject to the tax rate in the first bracket. A cut in this tax rate therefore encourages partners to work longer hours, especially in view of the relatively large uncompensated wage elasticity of partners' labor supply.

Breadwinners and older workers generally earn higher labor incomes than partners do. Indeed, the incomes of many of these workers reach

Table 1.5
Macroeconomic effects of cuts in income and payroll taxes

	First income tax bracket	Second income tax bracket	Third income tax bracket	Basic income tax allowance
Percentage deviations				
Private consumption	0.51	0.64	0.62	0.39
Exports	0.36	0.53	0.53	0.12
Imports	0.21	0.30	0.30	0.09
Formal production	0.37	0.57	0.57	0.09
Black production	−0.02	−0.20	−0.63	0.06
Employment	0.39	0.47	0.44	0.07
unskilled	0.46	0.20	0.20	0.18
low-skilled	0.50	0.17	0.07	0.10
high-skilled	0.35	0.60	0.60	0.04
Labor supply (pers.)	0.39	0.05	−0.02	−0.07
Labor supply (hours)	0.18	0.26	0.30	−0.04
breadwinners	0.03	0.28	0.54	−0.02
partners	0.39	0.02	−0.20	−0.16
single persons	0.26	0.31	0.08	−0.06
55+	0.09	0.42	0.77	0.03
Black labor (hours)	−0.03	−0.14	−0.33	0.07
Training				
unskilled and low-skilled	0.04	0.10	0.03	−0.05
high-skilled	−0.09	0.65	0.89	−0.06
Absolute deviations				
Unemployment rate	−0.13	−0.12	−0.08	−0.08
unskilled	−0.21	−0.37	−0.27	−0.07
low-skilled	−0.18	−0.12	−0.08	−0.13
high-skilled	−0.10	−0.08	−0.04	−0.07
Share long-term unemployment	−1.29	−0.74	−0.47	−0.48
Replacement rate[a]	−0.03	−0.29	−0.18	0.15
Average tax burden[a]	−0.35	−0.36	−0.33	−0.25
Marginal tax burden[a]	−0.32	−0.91	−1.07	−0.07
Government consumption[b]	−0.17	−0.15	−0.14	−0.21

Source: Graafland et al. 2001.
[a] Average over all households.
[b] In percentage of GDP.

into the second or third tax brackets. For these workers, a lower tax rate in the first bracket reduces the average tax rate without affecting the marginal tax rate. The inframarginal character of the tax cut in the first bracket for many breadwinners explains why such a cut barely affects the aggregate labor supply of breadwinners and older workers; the income effect is relevant for all breadwinners and older workers, while the substitution effect applies only to those workers whose marginal labor income falls in the first bracket.

In contrast to tax cuts in the first bracket, tax cuts in the second and third brackets are effective in stimulating labor supply of breadwinners and older workers. Although these groups feature relatively low labor supply elasticities, the relatively large cuts in marginal tax rates produce significant labor supply responses. The impact on aggregate labor supply (in hours) is substantial because breadwinners, single persons, and the elderly account for a large share of aggregate labor supply (in hours). Tax cuts in the highest bracket discourage partners from supplying labor, because the income effect rather than the substitution effect mainly impacts the labor supply of partners. In particular, by raising the incomes of breadwinners, a tax cut in the highest bracket reduces partners' labor supply through means of higher household incomes. At the same time, the substitution effect is not important because only few partners earn incomes that are sufficiently high to be marginally taxed in the third bracket.

These simulations illustrate the added value of the extensive labor supply model of MIMIC, which accounts for heterogeneity in preferences and wages, incorporates the actual Dutch tax system, and explicitly models the labor supply of partners. The incorporation of the actual income distribution and the institutional detail of the Dutch tax system allows MIMIC to determine to what extent cuts in particular tax brackets are (infra)marginal. Furthermore, the explicit modeling of labor supply behavior of partners and breadwinners modifies the predictions from aggregate models. To illustrate, tax cuts in the first brackets are more inframarginal and thus reduce marginal tax rates, on average, only a third as much as tax cuts in the higher brackets do (see the next-to-last row of table 1.5). Despite the relatively small decline in average marginal tax rates, tax cuts in the first bracket are still quite effective in stimulating aggregate labor supply. The reason is that these tax cuts reduce marginal tax rates of partners—the group featuring the most elastic labor supply. Indeed, these tax cuts are most effective in raising labor supply in persons, as more partners are encouraged to enter the labor force.

Black Labor Supply and Training   All three tax cuts reduce the size of the black economy. Supply of black market labor declines because lower marginal income taxes make formal labor supply more attractive. Firm demand for black labor decreases because formal wage costs decline on account of a lower average tax burden. This encourages firms to hire formal rather than informal labor. Tax cuts in the higher brackets are most effective in combatting the black economy because these tax cuts reduce marginal tax rates most.

The lower marginal tax rates in the upper tax brackets raise the marginal return on training activities. Accordingly, human capital and labor productivity increase, and the expansion of production exceeds the rise in employment.

Unemployment   The income tax cuts reduce equilibrium unemployment for two main reasons.[47] The first is the drop in the average tax burden, which moderates contractual wages. The lower marginal tax wedge produces upward wage pressure, but the positive elasticity of the average tax burden in the contractual wage equation (of 0.6) substantially exceeds the absolute value of the negative elasticity of the marginal tax burden (of 0.1). Hence, the overall effect of the tax cut is to moderate wages, thereby reducing equilibrium unemployment. Cutting taxes in the first bracket is most effective in reducing unemployment this way because it combines the decline in the average tax burden (the magnitude of which is similar for tax cuts in each of the three brackets) with the smallest decline in the marginal tax rate.

The second factor explaining the decline in unemployment is the lower replacement rate; workers tend to benefit more from lower marginal rates of personal income tax than transfer recipients do because the incomes of workers tend to exceed those of transfer recipients. This is especially so for tax reductions in the second bracket of the income tax.[48]

Subtracting the results of the second column from those of the first, one finds the impact of increasing tax progression by using revenues from a higher tax rate in the second tax bracket to cut the first tax bracket. Increasing progression in this way leaves the unemployment rate more or less unaffected. The replacement rate effect thus offsets the direct wage moderation effect associated with a higher marginal tax rate.[49]

Employment   The three tax cuts raise aggregate employment through both lower unemployment and higher labor supply. In fact, all tax cuts generate a similar increase in aggregate employment, although the composition of the employment gains differs. A tax cut in the first bracket is most effective in raising employment for the unskilled, low-skilled, and partners. The other tax cuts are somewhat more effective in boosting aggregate labor supply (in hours) and high-skilled employment and in combating the black economy.

Raising the Tax Allowance   We now turn to the effects of raising the general tax allowance (see the fourth column in table 1.5). Partners who do not earn sufficient labor income to fully use the tax allowance can transfer the allowance to the breadwinner. The tax credit is thus actually refundable for households with nonparticipating partners. This tax credit thus reduces the average tax burden but leaves the marginal tax burden unaffected—even for partners with small part-time jobs.[50] The tax allowance applies to both transfer recipients and workers. This is in contrast to the earned income tax credit explored later. This latter credit applies only to workers.

Formal labor supply falls because the tax credit exerts only income effects on labor supply. Unemployment declines, despite an increase in the average replacement rate. The unemployed benefit relatively more from a tax credit than those in work because the unemployed typically collect lower incomes than the employed. The main reason for lower equilibrium unemployment is that the lower average tax burden, together with the constant marginal tax burden, moderates contractual wages.

To summarize, a lower average tax rate at a constant marginal tax rate reduces both labor supply and unemployment. On balance, aggregate employment expands somewhat. The main difference with the cuts in tax brackets is thus that labor supply falls.

1.4.2.2   Earned Income Tax Credit

Table 1.6 contains the long-term effects of introducing various forms of a tax credit that applies only to workers—the so-called EITC—In several EU countries, this instrument is increasingly perceived as an attractive instrument to combat unemployment by raising the return to

Table 1.6
Macroeconomic effects of an earned income tax credit

	Fixed	Annual	Hourly 80	Hourly 50	Hourly 30
Percentage deviations					
Private consumption	0.56	0.30	0.51	0.51	0.51
Investment	0.47	0.12	0.46	0.48	0.45
Export	0.52	0.17	0.50	0.51	0.48
Imports	0.29	0.09	0.28	0.29	0.28
Formal production	0.55	0.13	0.53	0.55	0.52
Black production	0.09	−0.17	0.55	0.64	0.67
Employment	0.61	0.17	0.67	0.74	0.71
unskilled	1.00	1.50	2.89	3.81	4.07
low-skilled	0.72	0.14	0.47	0.28	0.08
high-skilled	0.51	−0.03	0.39	0.42	0.39
Labor supply (pers.)	0.11	0.58	0.11	0.13	0.16
Labor supply (hours)	0.19	−0.22	0.12	0.14	0.13
breadwinners	0.01	−0.33	−0.13	−0.12	−0.17
partners	0.44	0.54	0.42	0.50	0.59
single persons	0.28	−0.55	0.26	0.30	0.31
55+	0.10	−0.29	0.06	0.05	0.03
Black labor (hours)	0.09	−0.19	0.55	0.69	0.78
Training	−0.08	−0.49	−0.94	−1.29	−1.42
unskilled and low-skilled	−0.14	−0.14	−0.26	−0.37	−0.28
high-skilled	−0.03	−0.07	0.17	−0.24	−0.20
Absolute deviations					
Unemployment rate	−0.26	−0.28	−0.36	−0.39	−0.37
unskilled	−0.40	−0.16	−0.23	−0.22	−0.32
low-skilled	−0.37	−0.47	−0.62	−0.70	−0.66
high-skilled	−0.21	−0.25	−0.32	−0.35	−0.33
Share long-term unemployment	−1.64	−1.75	−2.30	−2.54	−2.45
Replacement rate[a]	−0.42	−0.28	−0.60	−0.78	−0.74
Average burden[a]	−0.50	−0.43	−0.51	−0.52	−0.51
Marginal burden[a]	−0.14	0.63	0.80	0.67	0.38
Government consumption[b]	−0.12	−0.16	−0.09	−0.08	−0.08

Source: Graafland et al. 2001.
[a] Average over all households.
[b] In percentage of GDP.

low-skilled work. This policy in effect directly reduces the net replacement rate, as the unemployed do not benefit from the EITC. Hence, an EITC corresponds to the case in which unemployment benefits are not subject to tax (see section 1.3.2.3).

Flat EITC   The first column of table 1.6 contains the impact of a flat EITC of 140 euros per year (corresponding to about 0.5% of the median gross wage). This nonrefundable EITC reduces the marginal tax rate on small part-time jobs so that partners find it more attractive to enter the labor force. Accordingly, the participation rate (i.e., labor supply in persons) increases.

Unemployment declines substantially. The reason is that the EITC accrues only to those in work and hence reduces the replacement rate. The lower replacement rate enhances job matching by reducing the reservation wage and by encouraging the unemployed to search more intensively for a job. Moreover, it moderates contractual wages. This wage moderation reduces the current incomes of transfer recipients because social benefits are linked to gross wages.

Targeted EITC Based on Annual Labor Incomes   The second column of table 1.6 explores the impact of an EITC that focuses on raising the reward to low-skilled work. The EITC analyzed here depends on the annual labor income of an individual.[51] It amounts to 3 percent of annual labor income of the individual in a phase-in range up to the statutory minimum wage (13,500 euros), and it stays at 340 euros in a flat range up to 115 percent of the minimum wage. Subsequently, the EITC is phased out linearly up to 180 percent of the minimum wage.

The EITC reduces the marginal tax burden on small part-time jobs, thereby encouraging partners to join the labor force. Accordingly, the participation rate increases, although aggregate labor supply measured in hours drops. Only partners raise their average labor supply (in hours) because many partners fall in the phase-in range of the EITC. Breadwinners and single persons, in contrast, reduce their labor supply because of a positive income effect and, to the extent that they fall in the phase-out range, a negative substitution effect associated with a higher marginal tax rate. On balance, for labor supply in hours, the reduction in labor supply on account of the substitution effect in the phase-out range and the income effect dominates the positive effect on the participation rate.

The high marginal tax rate in the phase-out range harms the incentives for training. This reduces the rates of transition into higher skill levels. Hence, unskilled labor supply rises at the expense of low-skilled labor supply. The changing composition of labor supply affects the distribution of employment and unemployment over skill levels. Whereas the training effect mitigates the decline in unskilled unemployment, it raises unskilled employment. Since unskilled workers face a higher replacement ratio than low-skilled workers do, this tends to contain the decline in the average replacement ratio, thereby moderating the employment gains.

Targeted EITC Based on Hourly Wages   If the objective is to reduce the number of unskilled who collect unemployment and welfare benefits, the targeted EITC explored earlier suffers from the disadvantage that it accrues also to part-time workers with high hourly wages but low annual incomes. This is relevant especially in the Netherlands, which features the highest share of part-time work of all OECD countries. Hence, in the Dutch policy discussion, a targeted EITC has been proposed that depends on hourly wages rather than annual incomes. Workers who earn the hourly minimum wage and hold a full-time job are eligible for the full EITC. The credit is reduced proportionally for workers who work less than a full-time job. It also gradually drops with the level of the hourly wage rate. By reducing the credit for part-time workers with high wages, the EITC for full-time workers who earn an hourly wage up to 115 percent of the statutory minimum wage can almost be doubled to 625 euros. The phase-out range runs up to an hourly wage of 180 percent of the minimum wage.

This EITC reduces the marginal tax burden only on part-time jobs with low hourly wages. Hence, the effect on the participation rate is smaller than in the previous experiment. The higher marginal tax rate in the phase-out range applies only to higher hourly wages and not to higher labor incomes on account of more hours worked. In fact, additional hours worked raise the credit for unskilled workers. This explains why, in contrast to the case with an EITC based on annual labor income, labor supply (in hours) increases slightly.

The marginal tax rate on higher hourly wages in the phase-out range is higher than in the previous experiment because the maximum credit is about twice as large. This harms the incentives to accumulate human capital. Hence, compared to an EITC that depends on annual incomes, an EITC that depends on hourly wages does less harm to the quantity of labor supply but more harm to the quality of labor supply. Another drawback to this variant of the EITC is that it relies on additional information (i.e., the number of hours worked in the formal sector) that is vulnerable to fraud. Indeed, the black economy expands substantially.

Unemployment This EITC reduces the replacement rate for low-skilled workers more substantially than the other EITCs explored earlier. Through skill-specific wage formation, this decline in the replacement rate reduces low-skilled wages, thereby boosting demand for low-skilled labor. Moreover, the lower replacement rate stimulates search and lowers the reservation wage, thereby facilitating the matching process for low-skilled labor. Accordingly, the unemployment rate for the low-skilled drops more substantially than under the EITCs analyzed previously.

Trade-offs The comparison between an EITC that depends on annual incomes and an EITC that depends on hourly wages reveals a trade-off between two objectives: increasing the participation rate of partners and reducing the unemployment rate for the low skilled. An EITC that depends on annual incomes advances the first objective, while an EITC that depends on hourly wages is more effective in cutting low-skilled unemployment. This trade-off is similar to that uncovered in studies for the United States and the United Kingdom (see, e.g., Blundell et al. 2000). In these countries, the EITC depends on household rather than individual incomes. The advantage is that the tax incentives can be better targeted at low-income households who often face high replacement rates, thereby stimulating employment of primary wage earners and single mothers. The disadvantage, however, is that income effects and higher marginal tax rates in the phase-out range harm labor supply incentives facing secondary earners with working partners. This illustrates how reducing one obstacle to employment may increase another.

Another trade-off involves the quality versus the quantity of labor supply. Compared to an EITC that depends on annual incomes, an EITC that depends on hourly wages enhances the quantity of labor supply (in hours) but harms its quality (in terms of human capital).

Targeting the EITC The last two columns of table 1.6 show the effects of two EITCs (based on hourly wages) that are phased out more rapidly than in the previous experiment, namely, at 150 percent (the fourth column) and 130 percent (the fifth column) of the minimum wage. Fewer people fall in the phase-out range, but those who remain in that range face even higher marginal tax rates. The advantage of more targeting is that the maximum credit for people who earn the minimum wage rate can be larger, thereby cutting the replacement rate of the unskilled more substantially. The disadvantage is that the marginal tax rate in the phase-out range increases more sharply and the (larger) decline in the replacement rate applies to fewer persons.

A moderately targeted version of the EITC (in the fourth column of table 1.6) is slightly more effective in reducing the aggregate unemployment rate than is the most-targeted EITC (in the fifth column of table 1.6). Also, compared to the less-targeted EITC (in the third column of table 1.6), the moderately targeted EITC is more effective in reducing the aggregate unemployment rate. This suggests that an inverse U-shaped curve describes how the effectiveness of the EITC in cutting unemployment varies with the degree of targeting. Hence, moderately targeting the EITC seems the most effective way to reduce the overall unemployment rate. At the same time, these simulations illustrate the drawbacks of targeting: more targeting implies that more workers remain unskilled. Indeed, the adverse shift in the skill composition boosts unskilled employment at the expense of low-skilled employment and limits the decline in unskilled unemployment.

1.5 Optimal Taxes: Efficiency

1.5.1 Progressive Taxation and Efficiency

In a second-best world, progressive taxes may help alleviate various imperfections. Section 1.3 considered one specific labor market imperfection—namely, the monopoly power of unions. In the particular model we explored, a 100 percent marginal tax rate (i.e., $S = 0$) would be optimal to eliminate the markup of unions on the reservation wage. High marginal tax rates may also help combat the leapfrogging of employers when they set efficiency wages. To illustrate, if effort depends on relative wages (i.e., the wage paid in a firm compared to the average wage level in the economy), employers impose adverse externalities on other firms if they raise wages in order to stimulate effort of their own workers. High marginal taxes on wage increases may help internalize these externalities.

Marginal labor taxes may internalize adverse externalities also if utility from consumption depends in part on one's relative position in society (Layard 1980). In that case, an individual raising his consumption by working harder reduces the utility of others. Marginal taxes help combat these negative external effects of additional consumption.

In addition to addressing labor market imperfections, progressive tax systems may also help alleviate distortions on capital markets. In particular, poor agents and young agents may suffer from liquidity constraints when they want to borrow in order to invest in human capital or to smooth consumption over their lifecycle. Progressive taxes redistribute income toward the poor and the young (since young workers tend to earn less than older workers) and thus help alleviate these capital market imperfections (Hubbard and Judd 1986).

Another relevant nontax market failure concerns insurance markets. Parents can not sign contracts insuring their children against career risks. Moreover, insurance against various human capital risks suffers from adverse selection. Hence, private insurance contracts are not available or are excessively expensive. Agents may thus demand a high-risk premium on their investments, which inhibits risk taking and entrepreneurship (Sinn 1995). By helping pool human capital risks, a progressive labor tax helps create the missing market for insurance of human capital (Eaton and Rosen 1980). Indeed, from an ex ante point of view (i.e., behind the veil of ignorance), a redistributive labor tax can be viewed as insurance of human capital; what is insurance ex ante (before the uncertainty has been realized) becomes redistribution ex post (after one knows the outcome).

Two considerations are important when deciding whether or not to employ high marginal tax rates on labor income as an instrument to address these imperfections. As a first consideration, benefits must be weighed against costs. Indeed, high marginal tax rates impose various costs. Section 1.3.1 focused on labor-leisure distortions. However, other potential costs are diminished work effort and human capital accumulation, thereby harming not only the quantity but also the quality of labor supply. Moreover, high marginal taxes may hamper labor mobility, stimulate tax avoidance and tax evasion, and redistribute activities from the formal sector into the informal sector or the black economy. Finally, they may encourage jobs with substantial nontaxable nonpecuniary benefits.

The second, related, consideration is whether alternative instruments are available to combat market imperfections. Often more direct instruments are available to address market imperfections.

1.5.2   Optimal Progressivity from an Efficiency Point of View

This section explores the optimal progressivity of the labor income tax in a standard search model of the labor market. With homogeneous households, a progressive income tax does not generate any distributional benefits. Hence, optimal progressivity is explored from a pure efficiency point of view. In emphasizing the pure efficiency case for tax progressivity in imperfect labor markets, the approach is similar to that of Sørensen (1999), who investigates the optimal progressivity of the labor income tax in various labor market models. Whereas Sørensen relies on numerical simulations, we derive an explicit analytical solution for the optimal labor income tax. This allows us to gain more insight into the determinants of optimal progression.

To investigate optimal progression in imperfect labor markets, we simplify the workhorse of modern labor economics—the search model developed by Mortensen and Pissarides (see, e.g., Pissarides 1990; Mortensen and Pissarides 1999)—by formulating a one-shot, static version of the model. While facilitating the interpretation of the results considerably, the simplified model still contains the main determinants of the optimal system. Most important, it retains the major market failure of the standard search model: search activities, which amount to specific investments in a labor market relationship, are noncontractible and may thus be held up.[52] We explore how the tax system, by acting as a commitment device, can prevent a holdup of search activities. By efficiently allocating property rights, the tax system in effect acts as a substitute for complete contracts in protecting the appropriate incentives for search activities. In this way, the tax system internalizes both positive and negative search externalities.

The crucial element here is that wages are negotiated *after* search efforts on both sides of the labor market have been sunk. The quasi rents from the search activities are thus distributed on the basis of ex post bargaining power rather than the marginal effectiveness of search in generating matches. Accordingly, if the marginal productivity of search activities exceeds the ex post bargaining power, specific investments in the match are held up. This holdup problem arises because the party with excessive bargaining power cannot credibly commit to rewarding his partner according to her contribution to concluding the match. Indeed, parties can bargain only after they have met. Since contracts can thus be signed only after the contracting parties have sunk their search activities, the market for search is missing. The missing market for specific investments in the match is the key nontax distortion in the model.

1.5.2.1 Model

The sequencing of decisions is as follows. Tax policy is set in the first stage of the one-shot game. In the second stage, firms enter. In the third stage, workers and firms (or entrepreneurs or employers), which are unmatched, search for a partner on the labor market. At the supply side of the labor market, workers $i \in [0, 1]$ select their search intensities $0 \le X_i \le 1$ at a cost $\gamma(X_i) \ge 0$, with $\gamma''(.) > 0$ and $\lim_{X_i \uparrow 1} \gamma'(X_i) \to +\infty$. At the demand side, entrepreneurs simultaneously decide how many vacancies to create. Vacancy costs are linear, so that economywide vacancy costs amount to cD, where D denotes the economywide number of vacancies and c is the per-unit vacancy cost.

In the fourth stage of the game, workers and entrepreneurs are matched; the number of matches equals $m(X, D)$, where $X = \int_0^1 X_i \, di$. The matching function $m(.,.)$ is increasing in its two arguments. Moreover, it exhibits constant returns in both arguments together, but decreasing returns in each of the arguments separately. Since a Cobb-Douglas matching function fits the data rather well,[53] we assume that the matching function is of the Cobb-Douglas form, where the exponent of the vacancies is given by η.

After they have been matched, workers and entrepreneurs bargain about the (after-tax) wage rate W in the fifth stage of the game. Entrepreneurs and workers who do not find a match receive a payoff of, respectively, zero and the (after-tax) unemployment (or welfare) benefit B. The unemployment benefit B can be interpreted as the minimum standard of living guaranteed by the government.[54] Finally, output is produced, taxes are collected, and tax revenue G is spent on a public good.

The model is solved backward. Accordingly, before determining search intensity X and labor market tightness $\theta \equiv \frac{D}{X}$, we solve for (after-tax) wages.

Production   Each matched firm-worker combination produces Y units of output. Output is the numeraire. Output net of search costs, Ω, is given by

$$\Omega = m(X, D)Y - \gamma(X) - cD, \tag{12}$$

where $m(X, D)Y$ represents total output and $\gamma(X) + cD$ stands for total search costs. The exogenous public good G and the exogenous unemployment benefit B are financed by a linear tax on wages:

$$G + B = m(X, D)(\tau(W - B) + \tau_a + B). \tag{13}$$

Here, τ represents the proportional (or ad valorem) tax on wages (net of the unemployment benefit B). The other component of the linear wage tax, τ_a, is a fixed (or specific) tax on the match. This tax depends on only the existence of a match and is not conditioned on how the quasi rents from the match are shared between firms and workers. Wage taxation is progressive (i.e., the average tax burden rises with the wage) if the specific tax τ_a is negative.

Wage Setting   Wages are determined by Nash bargaining after a match has been found. The bargaining is about the (after-tax) quasi rent (or surplus) from the match, $Y - \tau(W - B) - \tau_a - B$. The after-tax wage W that maximizes the Nash bargaining function $(W - B)^\beta (Y - W - \tau(W - B) - \tau_a)^{1-\beta}$ is given by

$$W = \frac{\beta(Y - \tau_a + \tau B) + (1 - \beta)(1 + \tau)B}{1 + \tau}. \tag{14}$$

This is the value of the match for the worker, where for analytical convenience we abstract from risk aversion. The value of a match for the entrepreneur, Π, amounts to

$$\Pi \equiv Y - W(1 + \tau) + \tau B - \tau_a = (1 - \beta)(Y - \tau_a - B). \tag{15}$$

The burden of the fixed tax component τ_a is shared between the worker (i.e., the supply side of the labor market) and the firm (i.e., the demand side of the labor market) in proportion to their respective bargaining powers β and $(1 - \beta)$; after-tax wages W decline and before-tax wages (i.e., wage costs) $W(1 + \tau) + \tau_a$ rise with τ_a. The proportional tax rate τ, in contrast, reduces only the worker's value of a match (14); before-tax wages $W + \tau(W - B) + \tau_a$ and the firm's value of the match (15) are not affected by τ. The proportional tax rate thus bears on the supply side rather than the demand side of the labor market. Intuitively, by taxing the quasi rents that accrue to workers (i.e., the after-tax wage W), the proportional tax not only reduces the (after-tax) surplus from the match but also raises the effective bargaining strength of employers. In the presence of a higher proportional tax, employers bargain more aggressively because a given increase in the after-tax wage W results in a larger increase in wage costs $W(1 + \tau) + \tau_a$.

Search Intensity and Vacancies   The wage agreed upon in ex post bargaining (i.e., after the match has been concluded) affects the incentives facing workers and firms to search for a partner in the preceding stage of the game. In selecting their search intensity, workers trade off additional search costs against the higher probability of finding a job. With a constant-returns-to-scale matching function, the probability that a worker with search intensity X_i is matched with a firm can be written as a function of labor market tightness only: $\frac{X_i}{X} m(X, D) = X_i m(\theta)$, where $m(\theta) \equiv m(1, \theta)$. The risk-neutral worker selects search intensity X_i so as to maximize the expected surplus from search

$$\max_{X_i \geq 0}\{X_i m(\theta)(W - B) - \gamma(X_i)\}.$$

With homogeneous individuals, all households feature the same search intensity

$$\gamma'(X) = m(\theta)(W - B),\tag{16}$$

where the left-hand side represents the marginal costs from higher search intensity and the right-hand side the corresponding expected marginal benefit in terms of raising the probability of finding a job. The net expected surplus for the worker, $Xm(\theta)(W - B) - \gamma(X) = X\gamma'(X) - \gamma(X)$, is assumed to be positive.

The expression for optimal search intensity (16) can be interpreted as the implicit labor supply equation. With the aid of (14), labor supply can alternatively be written as

$$\gamma'(X) = m(\theta)\frac{\beta(Y - \tau_a - B)}{1 + \tau}.\tag{17}$$

Demand for labor is determined by firms. The probability that a firm is matched with a worker equals $\frac{m(X,D)}{D} = \frac{m(\theta)}{\theta}$. With free entry of firms, expected profits from posting an additional vacancy are zero:

$$c = \frac{m(\theta)}{\theta}\Pi = \frac{m(\theta)}{\theta}(1 - \beta)(Y - \tau_a - B).\tag{18}$$

Here the left-hand side represents the costs for a firm entering the labor market, while the right-hand side stands for the firm's expected benefits from doing so. By reducing the probability of filling a vacancy $\frac{m(\theta)}{\theta}$, a tighter labor market decreases the expected benefits from posting a vacancy. Since labor market tightness θ is the only endogenous variable in (18), the free-entry condition determines tightness as a function of τ_a. As in most noncompetitive models of the labor market, a more progressive tax system (i.e., a smaller value for τ_a) raises the employment rate (i.e., the number of matches per unit of labor supply) $m(X, D)/X = m(\theta)$.

Welfare Substituting the government budget constraint, $Xm(\theta)Y = Xm(\theta)[W + \Pi] + G + (1 - Xm(\theta))B$ into the expression for Ω in (12), we find

$$\Omega = Xm(\theta)[W - B + \Pi] + G + B - \gamma(X) - c\theta X$$

$$= X\gamma'(X) - \gamma(X) + G + B.$$

With the free-entry condition ensuring a zero expected return for entrepreneurs, welfare consists of the ex ante return to workers $Xm(\theta)(W - B) - \gamma(X) + B$ and the resources allocated to the government G. The second equality follows from (16) (to eliminate W) and (18) (to eliminate Π). Since G and B are exogenously given and $X\gamma'(X) - \gamma(X)$ is rising in X, maximizing welfare is equivalent to maximizing search X.

Optimal Progressiveness If the government employs τ and τ_a to maximize welfare and search, it sets τ_a according to

$$\tau_a \equiv \frac{1 - \beta - \eta}{1 - \beta} Y - B \tag{19}$$

(see the proof in the appendix).

The optimal degree of progressiveness of the income tax ensures that the matching process is efficient by establishing an efficient distribution of property rights over the fruits from noncontractible specific investments in search. In particular, the party that carries out the most important noncontractible investments should be able to reap most of the quasi rents from the relationship. In this way, property rights act as a substitute for complete contracts in protecting the incentives for specific investments. By moderating wages, a progressive tax system in effect allows firms to increase their share in the quasi rents from search. A progressive tax system is thus optimal if firms can not reap the full social benefits of their search effort in a laissez-faire equilibrium. This is the case if vacancies are important in generating matches (as reflected in a high value for η) and if workers can appropriate a large share of the surplus from the match because of substantial bargaining power β and a good outside option B.[55] In that case, workers in effect levy an implicit tax on the specific investments of employers (i.e., the posting of vacancies) by expropriating part of the marginal social benefits of these investments.[56] With employers being held up by workers, labor demand (i.e., the posting of vacancies) is too low from a social point of view. A progressive tax undoes the implicit "holdup" tax levied by workers on employers so that employers face adequate incentives to enter the labor market. By in effect subsidizing labor demand and taxing labor supply, tax policy restores the socially optimal mix of labor demand and supply.

Tax policy, which is set before search activities are determined, allows workers to commit to not expropriating firms. In this way, tax policy effectively creates the market for search that is missing in the laissez-faire equilibrium. Before workers and firms meet each other after they match, tax policy in effect allows them to conclude a contract stipulating that their search activities will be rewarded according to the marginal contribution to the match. Indeed, if workers were to vote on the tax rate in the first stage of the game (i.e., when they are still unmatched and in effect face infinitely elastic labor demand), they would vote for the optimal social contract (i.e., the optimal allocation of property rights) implicit in the optimal tax structure.

The results can be interpreted also in terms of the distortions due to imperfect competition. If workers exercise too much power ex post (i.e., $\frac{1-\beta-\eta}{1-\beta}Y - B < 0$ so that θ is too low), the market can be characterized as being monopolized. Tax policy corrects the associated monopoly distortions by levying a tax on the excessive wages, thereby offsetting the price distortion imposed by the party with excessive market power.

An efficient matching process maximizes the incentives of workers to participate in this matching process through labor supply. If the bargaining power of workers is too strong (i.e., $\tau_a - \frac{1-\beta-\eta}{1-\beta}Y + B > 0$), workers are discouraged from looking for a job by a low probability of finding a job on account of a lax labor market (as reflected in a low value for tightness θ).[57] The unemployment rate is too high in that case. If workers' bargaining power is too weak (i.e., $\tau_a - \frac{1-\beta-\eta}{1-\beta}Y + B < 0$), workers' search is depressed by excessively low wages. Accordingly, beyond the point at which $\tau_a \equiv \frac{1-\beta-\eta}{1-\beta}Y - B$, a more progressive tax system harms the efficiency of the matching process by reducing labor supply and in effect giving the supply side of the labor market in-sufficient bargaining power compared to labor demand.[58] As a direct consequence, labor supply is too low compared to labor demand. The resulting excessively tight labor market implies that the unemployment rate $1 - m(X, D)/X$ is too low from a pure efficiency point of view.

The optimal τ_a does not depend on revenue requirements. The intuition behind this result is as follows. The linear vacancy costs imply that demand for labor is infinitely elastic. Hence, firms are able to shift the entire tax burden required to finance government spending to workers. Thus, whereas a tax on labor supply, τ, taxes the supply side directly through a lower after-tax wage W, a tax on labor demand τ_a is also borne by labor supply—albeit indirectly (i.e., through the general equilibrium effect of fewer firms entering the labor market, which reduces the probability of finding a job by producing a less tight labor market). It is more efficient to tax workers directly through τ than indirectly through the general equilibrium effect on θ; both ways distort search intensity, but the second way also distorts labor market tightness.[59]

This result is closely related to the celebrated Diamond and Mirrlees (1971) result on the optimality of production efficiency. With constant-returns-to-scale production (or tax instruments to tax away rents due to decreasing returns) and sufficient tax instruments to tax consumers directly, the government should ensure production efficiency. The government finds it optimal to tax consumers directly through consumer taxes rather than indirectly through taxes that violate production efficiency. Similarly, in the current context, the government should not distort labor market tightness, θ, by raising revenues through τ_a. Indeed, keeping labor market tightness at its first-best level can be viewed as maintaining efficiency in the production of matches.

A higher unemployment benefit is translated into an equivalent increase in in-work benefits τ_a (i.e., $-d\tau_a = dB$). A higher unemployment benefit thus results in a more progressive tax system, as a higher in-work benefit in effect offsets the adverse impact of the unemployment benefit on job creation. The benefit system thus determines the optimal progressiveness of the labor tax. The combination of an unemployment benefit and a job subsidy can be interpreted as a basic income. Indeed, if the Hosios condition is met, the overall tax on job creation is zero (i.e., $\tau_a + B = 0$). The higher marginal tax rates depress labor supply, but it is more efficient to depress labor supply through lower after-tax wages than to depress labor supply indirectly through violating production efficiency.[60] A progressive tax (i.e., $\tau_a < 0$) thus offsets the distortions of the welfare system.

1.6 Optimal Redistribution

We turn now to a model of risk-averse agents with heterogeneous abilities. Accordingly, progressive taxes not only affect the efficiency of the labor market but also insure agents against the risk of being born with heterogenous abilities. Moreover, in addition to an extensive labor supply margin, we allow taxes to impact labor supply on the intensive margin. Hence, whereas progressive taxes may stimulate job search, they may harm the incentives of workers to exert effort and work long hours after workers have found a job. Compared to the analysis in section 1.5, we thus include both an additional benefit of progressive taxation (i.e., income redistribution) and an additional cost (i.e., lower labor supply on the intensive margin). As another extension, welfare benefits may be set optimally. Moreover, the income tax does not have to be linear but may be nonlinear, since the government can observe individual labor incomes. Furthermore, the government can imperfectly monitor the search effort of agents. This allows us to investigate how the monitoring technology affects the optimal welfare benefit and the optimal tax system.

In order to incorporate the additional complications of heterogenous, risk-averse agents with endogenous work effort, we simplify the model of section 1.5 in two ways. First, we abstract from wage bargaining and search (and the associated externalities) at the demand side of the labor market: workers are paid their marginal product.[61] Second, we simplify the formulation of search at the supply side so that the search margin is relevant for low-skilled workers only. Our formulation of labor market matching allows for two types of unemployment: first, involuntary unemployment of high-skilled agents and, second, voluntary unemployment of low-skilled agents who do not face sufficient incentives to search. As regards this last type of unemployment, optimal unemployment benefits in effect set a wage floor below which agents no longer search for work. Hence, the desire to protect the involuntarily unemployed produces an optimal rate of voluntary unemployment.

1.6.1 The Model

The economy is populated by agents featuring homogeneous preferences but heterogeneous skills. A worker of ability (or skill or efficiency level) n working E hours (or providing E units of work effort) supplies nE efficiency units of homogeneous labor. With constant unitary labor productivity, these efficiency units are transformed in the same number of units of output. With output as the numeraire, the before-tax wage per hour is thus given by exogenous skill n. Hence, overall gross output produced by a worker of skill n, $Z(n)$, amounts to $Z(n) = nE(n)$. Since workers collect only labor income, this gross output $Z(n)$ corresponds to total gross (i.e., before-tax) income collected by a worker of that skill n. The density of agents of ability n is denoted by $f(n)$, and $F(n)$ represents the corresponding cumulative distribution function. The support of the distribution of abilities is given by $[n_0, n_1]$, while $f(.)$ is differentiable.

Workers share the following quasi-linear utility function over consumption C and hours worked (or work effort) E:

$$u(C, E) = v(C) - E,$$

where $v(C)$ is increasing and strictly concave: $v'(C) > 0$, $v''(C) < 0$ for all $C \geq 0$. The specific cardinalization of the utility function affects the distributional preferences of a utilitarian government. In particular, the concavity of $v(.)$ implies that a utilitarian government aims to fight poverty. In other words, such a government seeks to insure agents against the risk of a low consumption level.

As in Lollivier and Rochet 1983, Weymark 1987, Ebert 1992, and Boadway, Cuff, and Marchand 2000, utility is linear in work effort E and separable in work effort and consumption C. This has three important consequences. First, consumption C is not affected by income effects. A higher average tax rate thus induces households to raise work effort E rather than to cut consumption C. Second, the specific quasi-linear utility function allows for a closed-form solution of the standard optimal income tax problem. Third, a utilitarian government cares only about aggregate work effort in the economy. Such a government thus aims at an equal distribution of consumption (i.e., the alleviation of poverty) rather than an equal distribution of work effort over the various agents.

In line with the optimal income tax literature, the government is assumed not to be able to observe skills n, but to know the distribution function $f(n)$ and before-tax income of each individual $Z(n)$. We depart from the standard optimal tax literature by incorporating job search: agents have to search for a job and the government can only imperfectly monitor agents' search effort (see this section). In particular, we allow agents to adjust their labor supply not only on the intensive margin (i.e., by varying hours of work) but also on the extensive margin (i.e., by deciding whether or not to look for a job). In particular, by searching with intensity $X \in [0, 1]$, agents find a job with probability X. Agents' search costs $\gamma(X)$ are given by

$$\gamma(X) = \begin{cases} \gamma X & \text{if } X \in [0, \bar{X}] \\ +\infty & \text{otherwise,} \end{cases}$$

where $\gamma \geq 0$ is a parameter representing the magnitude of the search costs. $\bar{X} < 1$ captures the idea that agents may fail to find a job, even if they search at full capacity. By modeling the costs and effectiveness of search, the parameters γ and $(1 - \bar{X})$ represent labor market imperfections that give rise to unemployment. Agents thus differ in both ability n and employment status and face two types of risks: being born with low ability n and being involuntarily unemployed.

If an agent does not succeed in finding a job, (s)he receives a welfare (or social assistance) benefit $B \geq 0$.[62] An agent who does not search for a job, while (s)he is expected to look for a job by the government, has a probability $p_c \in \langle 0, 1 \rangle$ of receiving a penalty $\pi \geq 0$. This penalty is in the form of lost leisure time.

An agent of ability n who is expected to search by the government searches at full capacity if and only if

$$-\gamma\bar{X} + \bar{X}U(n) + (1 - \bar{X})v(B) \geq v(B) - p_c\pi. \tag{20}$$

The linear specification of the search cost function implies that a worker either does not search at all (and is voluntarily unemployed) or searches at the level $\bar{X}$ (and faces a probability of $(1 - \bar{X})$ of involuntary unemployment).

After a worker has found a job, (s)he has to determine her work effort. Ex post utility of a type n agent who finds a job is determined by type n's choice of gross income Z:

$$U(n) = \max_Z \left\{ v(Z - \tilde{T}(Z)) - \frac{Z}{n} \right\}, \tag{21}$$

where $\tilde{T}(Z)$ denotes the tax schedule as a function of gross income Z. We can write $\tilde{T}(n) = T(Z(n))$, since type n chooses gross income $Z(n)$

in equilibrium. The envelope theorem yields the first-order incentive compatibility constraint[63]

$$U'(n) = \frac{Z(n)}{n^2}. \tag{22}$$

The utilitarian government maximizes ex ante expected utility (i.e., expected utility before ability and labor market status have been revealed)

$$\Omega \equiv \int_{n_0}^{n_1} -\gamma X(n) + X(n)[U(n) + \xi] + (1 - X(n))[v(B) - \kappa^e(n)]f(n)\,dn,$$

where $\kappa^e(n)$ represents the expected penalty for type n with $d\kappa^e(n)/dn \geq 0$. We allow for positive employment externalities $\xi > 0$. If these externalities are positive, the government attaches more value to work than individual agents do.

The government faces the following budget constraint:

$$\int_{n_0}^{n_1} f(n)X(n)[B + T(n)]\,dn = G + B, \tag{23}$$

where G represents exogenously given exhaustive government expenditure and $T(n) \equiv Z(n) - C(n)$ denotes the tax paid by type n. The government employs the nonlinear income tax and welfare benefits to optimize social welfare and takes public spending G and the search monitoring and penalty system as given.

1.6.2   The Optimal Tax Problem

In optimizing social welfare, the government faces three constraints: the incentive compatibility constraint (22), the participation constraint (20), and the government budget constraint (23). Since $Z(n) \geq 0$, incentive compatibility (22) implies that utilities do not decline with skill (i.e., $U'(n) \geq 0$). Accordingly, if the participation constraint $U(n) \geq \gamma + v(B) - \kappa^e(n)$ is met for skill $\bar{n}$, it is met also for higher skills $n > \bar{n}$. Defining n_w as the lowest skill that looks for work, we thus have $X(n) = 0$ for $n < n_w$ and $X(n) = \bar{X}$ for $n \geq n_w$. The agents with skill $n < n_w$ can be viewed as being voluntarily unemployed. The higher skills $n > n_w$ look for work but may be involuntarily unemployed (if $\bar{X} < 1$). The productivity level n_w is called the minimum productivity level. It is in fact the minimum gross wage implied by the welfare and tax systems.

These observations allow us to formulate the social planner's problem as[64]

$$\max_{n_w, U(.), Z(.), B} F(n_w)v(B) + [1 - F(n_w)] - \gamma\bar{X} + (1 - \bar{X})v(B)$$

$$+ \int_{n_w}^{n_1} \left\{ \bar{X}[U(n) + \xi]f(n) - \lambda_U(n)\left[U'(n) - \frac{Z(n)}{n^2}\right] + \lambda_E[f(n)\bar{X}T(n)] \right\} dn$$

$$- \lambda_E\{B[F(n_w) + (1 - F(n_w))(1 - \bar{X})] + G\}$$

$$- \eta_w\left(\gamma - U(n_w) + v(B) - \frac{p_c}{\bar{X}}\pi\right), \tag{24}$$

where $T(n) \equiv Z(n) - C(n) = Z(n) - v^{-1}\left(U(n) + \frac{Z(n)}{n}\right)$. $\lambda_U(n)$ represents the Lagrange multiplier of the incentive compatibility constraint, and λ_E stands for the multiplier of the government budget constraint. η_w denotes the Lagrange multiplier on the participation constraint for type n_w. It measures the social value of increasing employment by forcing more people to search, and it can therefore be interpreted as the value of a work test (and the required information on search intensity) inducing more skills to look for work.

Boone and Bovenberg (2003b) derive the first-order conditions for the optimal tax problem and establish the following proposition:

PROPOSITION 1 If $\gamma\bar{X} > p_c\pi$, employed agents of type $n > n_0$ face positive marginal tax rates. If, in addition, $\bar{X} < 1 - n_0 f(n_0)$, there is voluntary unemployment (i.e., $n_w > n_0$), marginal taxes are positive at the bottom (i.e., $\tau(n_w) > 0$), and the following relationship holds at the minimum productivity level:[65]

$$\tau(n_w)Z(n_w) = (B + T(n_w)) + \frac{\xi - \pi\frac{p_c}{\bar{X}}}{\lambda_E}. \tag{25}$$

The inequality $\gamma\bar{X} > p_c\pi$ implies that search costs are so high that agents can be induced to search only if they can expect higher consumption levels in work than in unemployment. Since the unemployed enjoy less consumption than workers, the government wants to redistribute resources away from the employed skills $n > n_w$ to the unemployed skills $n < n_w$. This desire to redistribute toward the unemployed results in positive marginal tax rates for all workers, including the marginal workers with skill n_w.

The left-hand side of inequality $1 - \bar{X} > n_0 f(n_0)$ stands for involuntary unemployment among the skills that are actively searching for a

job. Hence, if these labor market imperfections as measured by this involuntary unemployment $1 - \bar{X}$ are substantial, voluntary unemployment (i.e., $n_w > n_0$ so that the least skilled do not look for a job)
becomes optimal. Intuitively, to avoid poverty among the substantial
numbers of involuntarily unemployed, the welfare level B is set at
such high levels that the participation constraint becomes binding and
the least skilled workers no longer search for work, especially if these
workers feature only low labor productivity (i.e., n_0 is small). The desire to combat poverty among the low-skilled and the involuntarily unemployed agents without imposing excessive distortions on the work
effort of high-skilled agents thus optimally creates additional, voluntary unemployment.

To interpret expression (25), we first consider the case without employment externalities and penalties (i.e., $\xi = \pi = 0$). In that case, the
right-hand side of (25) represents the direct budgetary implications of
raising employment by reducing n_w: by bringing a marginal worker
into work, the government saves a welfare benefit B and collects
additional tax revenue $T(n_w)$. The indirect implications—namely, the
effects on other workers—are captured by the left-hand side of (25).
Bringing a marginal type n_w into work encourages workers who are
marginally more skilled to work less hard—since they can now mimic
type n_w. An optimal tax system balances the welfare implications of
this latter behavioral response on the intensive margin of the more productive workers (represented by the left-hand side of (25)) with the
budgetary implications of the behavioral response on the extensive
margin of the marginal workers. The government thus faces a trade-off
between obtaining revenues from either inducing more agents to search
or encouraging a smaller group of agents to work harder. As a result,
the distortion on the extensive margin (i.e., the right-hand side of (25))
should equal the distortion on the intensive margin (i.e., the left-hand
side of (25)).

In this particular case (i.e., $\xi = \pi = 0$), the progressiveness of the income tax is directly related to the level of welfare benefits. To see this,
we rewrite (25) as $\tau(n_w) - \frac{T(n_w)}{Z(n_w)} = \frac{B}{Z(n_w)} = \frac{B}{C(n_w)}\left[1 - \frac{T(n_w)}{Z(n_w)}\right]$. For the least-
skilled worker, the marginal tax rate $\tau(n_w)$ minus the average tax rate
$\frac{T(n_w)}{Z(n_w)}$ is directly related to the replacement rate $\frac{B}{C(n_w)}$. In particular, the
tax system is progressive at the minimum productivity level n_w if and
only if the welfare benefit is positive. This result resembles the corresponding result on optimal progression in section 1.5. In particular, if
the Hosios condition holds, this latter section also establishes that the

income tax is progressive if and only if the welfare benefit is positive. An important difference is, however, that in section 1.5 the search margin is not distorted in the optimum (i.e., $\tau_a + B = 0$ so that at a wage level of B, workers collect a tax subsidy of $-\tau_a = B$). In the presence of an extensive labor supply margin, in contrast, the distortions on the search margin have to be traded off against the distortions in work effort. Hence, the search margin remains distorted in equilibrium, since the tax on search $B + T(n_w)$ is positive.

We consider now the case with positive employment externalities $\xi > 0$. In that case, ceteris paribus the gross replacement rate $\frac{B}{Z(n_w)}$,[66] the gap between the marginal tax and average tax rates widens at the minimum productivity level. Intuitively, with positive employment externalities, the government wants to subsidize the search of unskilled workers in order to have these workers internalize the positive externalities from their search. These subsidies are financed by higher-skilled agents so that marginal tax rates increase and the tax system becomes more progressive. An alternative way of understanding why employment externalities tend to make the tax system more progressive and therefore to reduce the work effort of high-skilled workers is that positive employment externalities can be viewed as implicit taxes on the search. In particular, the search is inadequate from a social point of view because of not only explicit taxation but also job externalities. With a larger overall tax distortion on the search (consisting of both the explicit tax wedge and the implicit tax wedge on account of job externalities), the optimal trade-off between distortions on the intensive and extensive margins demands that the explicit tax on the search (i.e., the extensive margin) is reduced and that the tax on effort (i.e., the intensive margin) is raised. If the employment externalities are large enough and the revenue requirements are only small (so that the marginal tax rate $\tau(n_w)$ can be small), the search may even be subsidized in equilibrium (i.e., $B + T(n_w) < 0$).

With penalties for an inadequate search (i.e., $\pi p_c > 0$), the government reduces the search distortions originating in the welfare system and can rely less on explicit search subsidies for low-skilled labor. With less need to subsidize the low-skilled, the income tax system has to be less progressive. Hence, compared to positive employment externalities, the penalty system exerts exactly the opposite effect on marginal tax rates facing workers. Indeed, whereas positive employment externalities can be viewed as an implicit tax on search, the penalty system works as an implicit subsidy on it. If the penalties are strong enough to internalize the employment externalities (i.e., $\pi \frac{p_c}{\bar{X}} > \xi$), the penalty effect dominates. Hence, (25) together with $\tau(n_w) > 0$ (see Proposition 1) implies that search is necessarily taxed (i.e., $B + T(n_w) > 0$). Intuitively, the net tax on search helps to redistribute resources away from workers to the unemployed, who are poorer than the workers.

The monitoring system allows the government to alleviate the distortions imposed by the welfare system on the search margin.[67] It thus alleviates the distortions from redistributing resources away from workers to the poorer unemployed. In particular, the agents who are required to search collect $B - \pi \frac{p_c}{\bar{X}} / \lambda_E$ rather than B in unemployment. As long as $B - \left[\pi \frac{p_c}{\bar{X}} / \lambda_E\right] > 0$, the welfare system distorts the search and the tax system is progressive at the minimum productivity level.

1.7 Conclusions

The link between taxes and labor market performance depends crucially on nontax institutions. In particular, the impact of taxes on wages and unemployment depends on how wages are set and on welfare and unemployment benefits. Indeed, a key channel through which taxes affect unemployment is the effective replacement rate. The highest effective tax rates on work typically originate in welfare and unemployment benefits that are withdrawn if work is found.

Changes in the tax structure can cut unemployment if they succeed in shifting the tax burden onto the unemployed, thereby reducing the effective replacement rate. Moreover, whether a higher tax burden raises unemployment depends crucially on whether or not the unemployed share in the higher tax burden. These two insights explain how revenue-neutral environmental tax reforms can create a double dividend by producing not only a cleaner environment but also a lower level of unemployment. How unemployment benefits are indexed is crucial in determining whether a change in the tax structure can affect the effective after-tax replacement rate and whether a higher tax burden is shared by the unemployed.[68] In particular, an environmental tax reform can shift the tax burden onto the unemployed through taxes on dirty consumption replacing labor income taxes if unemployment benefits are linked to producer prices and not subject to personal income tax. Alternatively, this can be accomplished by taxes on dirty inputs into production replacing consumption taxes if unemployment benefits are linked to wages. In all these cases, environmental tax reform succeeds in cutting the effective after-tax replacement rate.[69] With revenue-neutral reforms, the employment impact also depends on the additional implicit tax burden associated with a better quality of the public good of the environment. A double dividend is feasible only if the benefit recipients pay a more than proportional share of the larger supply of the environmental public good (Bovenberg and van der Ploeg 1998).

The tax system may also impact unemployment through rigid market wages. If statutory minimum wages prevent market wages from falling, tax policy can offset the implicit tax on employers imposed by workers by reducing payroll taxes paid by employers. The question also applies here: why must these nontax institutions be changed indirectly through tax policy rather than reformed directly?

Another channel through which the tax system impacts unemployment is the progressiveness of the tax system. In particular, by taxing wage rises, progressive taxes moderate wages, thereby reducing unemployment. However, progression may also increase the effective net replacement rate if unemployment benefits are subject to tax. This latter effect may in fact be stronger than the former if gross replacement rates and nontaxable incomes in unemployment are substantial. Moreover, even though progressive taxes combat unemployment, they typically imply other costs by reducing labor supply, work effort, human capital accumulation, and labor mobility while stimulating tax avoidance, tax evasion, jobs with substantial nontaxable nonpecuniary benefits, and the informal and black economies.

Tax policy impacts the labor market not only through wage setting but also through labor supply. The labor supply effects of tax policy require microeconomic analysis of specific, disaggregated groups (such as secondary part-time workers, low-skilled agents, and older employees close to retirement) in order to do justice to substantial variation in effective marginal tax rates and labor supply elasticities. The general equilibrium model MIMIC incorporates a disaggregated household model in a general equilibrium setting. In addition to labor supply and wage determination, various other ways through which taxes and benefits affect the labor market are incorporated—namely, the black economy, human capital accumulation, efficiency wages, costly job matching, and search behavior of the unemployed.

The simulations with MIMIC reveal several trade-offs between various objectives. These objectives include cutting unemployment in general and low-skilled unemployment in particular, stimulating the participation of women in the labor force, raising the quality and quantity of labor supply (both in hours and in persons), and establishing an equitable income distribution (including a reasonable income level for those dependent on social benefits). Targeting in-work benefits at the low-skilled is most effective in cutting economy-wide unemployment. However, by decreasing the gap between low and high labor incomes through a more progressive tax system for workers, a targeted EITC reduces the hours of labor supplied. The cost of higher marginal tax rates in the phase-out range is particularly high in European countries, where marginal tax rates are already quite high. The trade-off between cutting unemployment and raising labor supply (in hours) can be mitigated by linking the EITC to hourly wages rather than annual incomes, and by reducing the EITC proportionally for small part-time jobs. Doing so, however, raises the marginal tax burden on hourly wage increases, thereby discouraging the accumulation of human capital and stimulating the black economy. Tax cuts in the higher tax brackets are most effective in raising the quantity and quality of formal labor supply (in hours). However, cuts in higher tax brackets are less effective in reducing unemployment (by widening the income gap between being in work and collecting unemployment benefits), raising low-skilled employment, and stimulating female labor supply. Indeed, the contrast between cuts in the highest tax brackets and a targeted EITC reveals a trade-off between raising the quality and quantity of labor supply and combatting unemployment.

We formalized the trade-off between high levels of labor supply and low unemployment rates in a model of optimal taxation with involuntary unemployment. In a model with homogeneous households without an intensive margin of labor supply, a progressive labor tax eliminates nontax distortions on wage setting. In particular, a progressive tax allows workers to commit to not expropriating specific investments of firms. This is especially relevant if unions feature a short time horizon and thus set wages on the basis of low short-run labor demand elasticities rather than higher long-run labor supply elasticities. In other words, progressive taxes restore the efficient balance of power between workers and employers. A progressive tax also corrects for the impact of the welfare system on wage setting, thereby alleviating the adverse impact of the welfare benefit on job creation and the unemployment rate. The benefit system thus determines the optimal progressiveness of the labor tax: a higher welfare benefit is accompanied by a higher in-work benefit so that the improved outside option of workers as a result of the higher welfare benefit does not raise unemployment. The more progressive labor tax depresses labor supply, but it is more efficient to reduce labor supply through lower after-tax wages than through the discouraged worker effect.

In the presence of an intensive labor supply margin, the government faces a trade-off between obtaining revenues from either inducing more agents to search or encouraging a smaller group of agents to work harder. In that case, therefore, the government does not completely eliminate the impact of the welfare benefit on the unemployment rate, but rather balances the distortions on job creation and the unemployment rate against those on hours worked and work effort.

The government can improve this trade-off in various ways. First of all, agents may insure themselves against the risk of involuntary unemployment through precautionary saving and compulsory saving schemes so that the unemployment insurance benefits paid to the involuntarily unemployed can be cut.[70] Self-insurance seems a particularly attractive instrument for high-skilled agents who face relatively short unemployment spells during their careers. In this connection, the government may want to relieve liquidity constraints by offering loans to the unemployed. This combats the capital market distortions that may give rise to labor market distortions. Compulsory saving schemes with liquidity insurance in effect provide a stronger link between contributions and insurance benefits on a microlevel (Sørensen 2003). This protects incentives to search for work, to work hard, and to moderate wages.

For agents with low lifetime incomes, self-insurance does not work well. To protect these agents against poverty, the government needs to transfer resources to these agents. For these agents, other ways need to be found to improve the trade-off between the extensive and the intensive margins. In particular, the government may collect more information by monitoring job search and imposing penalties on less active job search.[71] In this connection, workfare may also play a role, even though it may to some extent crowd out private employment. In particular, the mere threat of being put on workfare is likely to boost the job search of able individuals and prevent nonworkers who highly value leisure[72] from claiming unemployment benefits (Fredriksson and Holmlund 2003). Workfare can thus be seen as a way to redistribute resources to low-skilled agents who are involuntarily unemployed.

Appendix

To establish (19), we linearize the following equations characterizing the decentralized equilibrium

$$\gamma'(X) = m(\theta)\left(Y - \Pi - \frac{G+B}{m(\theta)}\right), \tag{26}$$

$$\frac{c\theta}{m(\theta)} = \Pi. \tag{27}$$

To derive the first equation, we substituted the government budget constraint $Xm(\theta)Y = Xm(\theta)[W + \Pi] + (1 - Xm(\theta))B + G$ to eliminate the after-tax wage W from (16). The second equation follows from (15) and (18).

Loglinearization yields

$$\begin{pmatrix} \tilde{X} \\ \tilde{\theta} \end{pmatrix} = \frac{1}{\frac{c\theta(1-\eta)}{m(\theta)}\left(X\gamma''(X) - \frac{G+B}{X}\right)}$$

$$\times \begin{pmatrix} \frac{c\theta(1-\eta)}{m(\theta)} & m(\theta)\eta(Y-\Pi) \\ 0 & X\gamma''(X) - \frac{G+B}{X} \end{pmatrix} \begin{pmatrix} -m(\theta)\Pi\tilde{\Pi} - \frac{G}{X}\tilde{G} - \frac{B}{X}\tilde{B} \\ \Pi\Pi \end{pmatrix}. \tag{28}$$

We thus have (the second equality follows from (27))

$$\frac{\tilde{X}}{\tilde{\Pi}} = \frac{\Pi m(\theta)}{\frac{c\theta(1-\eta)}{m(\theta)}\left(X\gamma''(X) - \frac{G+B}{X}\right)}\left[-\frac{c\theta}{m(\theta)}(1-\eta) + \eta(Y - \Pi)\right]$$

$$= \frac{\Pi m(\theta)}{\frac{c\theta(1-\eta)}{m(\theta)}\left(X\gamma''(X) - \frac{G+B}{X}\right)}[-\Pi + \eta Y]$$

$$= \begin{cases} \geq 0 & \text{if } \Pi \leq \eta Y \\ < 0 & \text{if } \Pi > \eta Y \end{cases}. \tag{29}$$

Hence, X and thus welfare is maximized if $\Pi = \eta Y$. Using (15) to eliminate Π, we arrive at the expression for the optimal tax τ_a in (19).

Q.E.D.

Notes

This chapter was prepared for the CESifo Workshop on Tax Policy and Labor Market Performance, Venice Summer Institute, San Servolo, July 21–23, 2003. The author thanks Jan Boone, Peter Sørensen, two anonymous referees, and participants of the CESifo

Workshop on Tax Policy and Labor Market Performance in Venice for helpful comments on an earlier draft.

1. The data are for an average production worker who is 40 years of age. For more details, see OECD 2002b. Table 1.2 does not include implicit tax rates in contributions to occupational pension schemes.

2. The marginal tax rates assume that social security contributions are not linked to insurance benefits on an individual level.

3. Neary and Roberts (1980) show how rigid wages and prices can be modeled as implicit tax rates.

4. In contrast to the figures in table 1.2, these figures abstract from indirect taxes on consumption.

5. For other explanations of long-term unemployment in Europe, see Machin and Manning 1999.

6. The data in tables 1.3 and 1.4 account for only publicly provided unemployment benefits. Supplementary, private benefits, which may be provided by the previous employer, sometimes raise replacement rates further.

7. To illustrate, many countries do not strictly enforce on older unemployed persons the obligation to look for work in order to be eligible for unemployment or welfare benefits.

8. For a recent overview of the literature on the optimal design of these important elements for unemployment insurance, see Frederiksson and Holmlund 2003.

9. These tax rates may also depend on the personal characteristics of the individual. Moreover, since the tax authorities observe individual labor incomes, the tax schedule may be nonlinear in individual labor income WL^s.

10. Here we have assumed that the initial coefficient of residual income progression is unity. If this assumption is not met, labor supply is given by $[(S-1)V + 1]l^s = \epsilon^c(w - t^m - p^c) + \epsilon^i(Sw - t^a - p^c)$.

11. We assume here that firms face a constant price elasticity of demand for their output ε. An increase in market power, reflected in a decrease in ε, amounts to an implicit tax on labor. Indeed, a relative change in ε would enter (2) in the same way as t^l (but with the opposite sign). If other production factors besides labor are fixed, the labor demand elasticity is given by $\epsilon^d \equiv 1 \left/ \left[\frac{1-\alpha}{\sigma^f} + \frac{\alpha}{\varepsilon}\right]\right.$, where σ^f is the substitution elasticity between labor and the other production factor(s) and $\alpha \equiv F'(L)L/F(L)$. With a Cobb-Douglas production function (i.e., $\sigma^f = 1$) and a constant price elasticity ε, the labor demand elasticity is constant, namely, $\epsilon^d \equiv 1/\left[1 - \alpha\left(1 - \frac{1}{\varepsilon}\right)\right]$. In that case, a smaller share of fixed factors (i.e., a higher value for α) raises ϵ^d.

12. Two important aspects of the labor demand elasticity are the time horizon and the aggregation level to which the elasticity applies. As regards the time horizon, other production factors may respond to changes in wage costs, especially in the longer run. The long-run wage elasticity of labor demand is therefore likely to exceed the corresponding short-run elasticity. As regards the aggregation level, the labor demand elasticity on a macroeconomic level is likely to be smaller than on a sectoral or microeconomic level.

13. Another reason for investigating the impact of changes in productivity is that modern economies experience steady growth in labor productivity while the rate of

unemployment remains more or less stationary. In the face of this empirical observation, most models impose conditions that ensure that changes in labor productivity do not impact unemployment. Section 1.3.2 develops models in which, in contrast to productivity, the tax burden does affect the structural rate of unemployment.

14. In analyzing these policy changes, we do not explicitly consider the government budget constraint. The analysis implicitly assumes that changes in government revenues are transmitted into corresponding changes in government spending that are separable from other arguments in the utility function in households. Hence, the changes in government spending produced by public revenue effects do not affect private decisions.

15. The latter effect on the average tax rate drops out if one imposes government budget balance with exogenous public spending on other purposes besides unemployment benefits. In that case, higher tax rates required to finance the additional benefits may further raise effective marginal tax rates.

16. If other production factors besides labor enter the production function, labor productivity may decline as a result of higher taxes on either these factors or (depending on the degree of complementarity between labor and these factors) labor itself.

17. Human capital is another channel through which tax policy may affect long-run productivity growth. In fact, in endogenous growth models in which human capital drives growth (see, e.g., Lucas 1988), labor taxes may exert permanent effects on growth.

18. In the presence of uncertain returns, proportional taxes may boost investments in human capital by risk-averse agents. Indeed, in the presence of such a tax, the government in effect shares in the risk of the investment. For the role of taxes as an insurance device, see Eaton and Rosen 1980.

19. Jacobs (2002) demonstrates that positive feedback effects between human capital and labor supply raise the long-run wage elasticity of effective labor supply above the corresponding standard elasticities that assume exogenous levels of human capital. If the government optimally employs schooling subsidies to undo the effect of taxation on schooling, effective elasticities again correspond to the standard elasticities. The utililization effects depends on human capital being more productive in work time than in leisure time. Heckman (1976), in contrast, assumes that human capital is equally productive in leisure and in work.

20. Heckman, Lochner, and Cossa (2002), however, seriously doubt whether firms can differentiate wages on the basis of expected future human capital benefits of current work. Indeed, they cite empirical evidence for the learning-by-doing model (*without* sufficient wage discrimination).

21. For a more complete distributional analysis, see section 1.4, which introduces heterogeneous workers.

22. The effects of labor taxes on wages and unemployment are very similar in efficiency wage models and search models, although the normative implications for welfare may be different. See Bovenberg and van der Ploeg 1994, Sørensen 1997, and Pissarides 1998.

23. The objective function can be interpreted as an expected utility function of union members. Equation (6) assumes that hours worked in a full-time job are exogenously fixed. For a model in which unions also set hours worked in a full-time job, see Sørensen 1997. Alternatively, employed individual workers can determine working time after wages have been set (see, e.g., Holmlund 2000).

24. An efficiency wage model in which effort by workers, e, is given by $e = (W^a - W^r)^\zeta$ and firms set wages to maximize profits yields a similar expression for the wage markup, except that the markup m is replaced by the exponent ζ in the effort function.

25. The same holds true in an efficiency wage model; see Stiglitz 1999.

26. In case of a Cobb-Douglas production function, a fixed price elasticity ε, an isoelastic utility function $v(C) = C^{1-\rho}$, and a fixed S, this markup is constant and given by $\frac{S(1-\rho)\left[1-\alpha\left(1-\frac{1}{\varepsilon}\right)\right]}{1+\frac{1-\beta}{\beta}\alpha\left(1-\frac{1}{\varepsilon}\right)}$. Hence, more risk aversion (i.e., a higher value for ρ) moderates wages.

27. With an isoelastic utility function $v(C) = C^{1-\rho}$, one can interpret the coefficient of risk aversion ρ also as the reciprocal of the substitution elasticity between consumption and leisure. A lower substitution elasticity makes unemployment less attractive and thus moderates wages. In principle, δ can be negative if the unemployed are stigmatized.

28. See also Koskela and Vilmunen 1996. The wage-moderating effects of high marginal tax rates have been established empirically by Lockwood and Manning (1993), Tyrvainen (1995), and Graafland and Huizinga (1999).

29. Similar results would be found if the unemployment benefits were taxed but at a lower average rate $\bar{T}^a$ than wages and if the coefficient $(1 - \bar{T}^a)/(1 - T^a)$ were to increase with the tax burden. If the tax schedule features a constant coefficient of residual income progression S, and unemployment benefits would be subject to the same income tax schedule, the coefficient $(1 - \bar{T}^a)/(1 - T^a)$ would not vary with the overall tax burden, but would depend only on S. Indeed, as shown later in (11), equilibrium unemployment is given by $g(u) = \frac{Sm}{1-(R^g)^S}$, where $R^g = B/W$ stands for the fixed replacement rate in before-tax terms.

30. Similar conditions determine the distributional effects of a higher replacement rate R^g. Note that the (absolute value of the) elasticity of labor demand is likely to increase with the time horizon considered. In particular, the long-term labor elasticity is likely to exceed the labor demand elasticity that the union employs to estimate the employment impact of higher wage costs.

31. With higher wages raising unemployment benefits and reducing profits, the negative external effects on the government budget and profits become more substantial.

32. In addition, an increase in the consumption tax moves this curve to the right if the price of output in the formal sector is proportional to consumer prices.

33. The macroeconomic model of CPB Netherlands Bureau for Economic Policy Analysis implies that a rise in the tax wedge of 1 percentage point raises the equilibrium unemployment rate by about $\frac{1}{4}$ percentage point.

34. Note that a higher average tax burden raising the parameter ζ does not impact unemployment. Hence, a higher tax burden does not affect unemployment even if, as documented by Daveri and Tabellini (2000), the unemployed pay fewer taxes than the employed do. Hence, just as in the case with a fixed after-tax replacement rate (see section 1.3.2.2), the average tax rate does not affect equilibrium unemployment.

35. The unemployment effect of more progression (with a fixed gross effective replacement rate) is very similar to that of more risk aversion (with a fixed net effective replacement rate). To determine these effects, one takes the derivative of the function $f(a) = a/(1 - b^a)$ with respect to a. The sign of this derivative is determined by $1 - b^a(1 - a \log b)$. This expression is non-negative because $g(a,b) \equiv b^a(1 - a \log b) \leq 1$. This inequality can be established by showing that $\partial g/\partial a$ and $\partial g/\partial b$ are both positive for

$a > 0$ and $0 < b < 1$ so that $g(a,b)$ reaches a maximum of 1 at $a = 1$ and $b = 1$ (we impose the restriction $a \leq 1$, $b \leq 1$).

36. Here we assume that δ is proportional to gross wages W, while T^a is constant. We thus vary progression at a constant average tax burden on workers. The expression is found by taking the first derivative of $g(u) = S/(1 - \delta^* - (R^g)^S)$ with respect to S. The sign of this derivative depends on $h(R^g, S) \equiv 1 - \delta^* - (R^g)^S(1 - S \log R^g)$. This function is decreasing in R^g and increasing in S. Since we have $h(R^g, 0) = -\delta$, $h(R^g, 1) > 0$ (i.e., $(R^g)(1 - \log R^g) < 1 - \delta$) is a sufficient condition for the existence of a unique optimal value for $0 < S < 1$ if $\delta^* > 0$. At this unique value of S, we have $1 - \delta^* - (R^g)^S = -S(R^g)^S \log R^g > 0$ if $R^g < 1$. Hence, at the optimal value of S, $g(u) = S/(1 - \delta^* - (R^g)^S)$ is well-defined (as the denominator is positive). Note that the optimal marginal tax rate is 100 percent (i.e., $S = 0$) if $\delta^* = 0$ or $R^g = 0$.

37. If unemployment benefits are indexed to producer prices, for example, replacing the payroll tax, the income tax, or implicit labor taxes with an indirect tax on consumption raises employment by shifting the tax burden toward the unemployed (i.e., imposing a larger burden on the outside option of unions). Whereas replacing consumption taxes by implicit taxes thus boosts employment if unemployment benefits are linked to gross wages, such a tax reform hurts employment if these unemployment benefits are linked to producer prices. Accordingly, whether replacing implicit taxes by consumption taxes raises or reduces employment depends crucially on how unemployment benefits respond to prices and wages and how unemployment benefits are taxed.

38. This may be one of the explanations for why smaller European countries feature lower unemployment rates than larger ones. An alternative explanation, however, is that small countries wield less market power on commodity markets (i.e., ε^d and ε are larger) so that the union markup m in (9) is smaller.

39. Indeed, Nickell and Layard (1999, 3059) find empirical evidence that coordination in wage bargaining reduces the impact of taxes on equilibrium unemployment. If unions also set working hours (e.g., as in Sørensen 1999), taxes also leave labor supply unaffected if unions internalize the government budget constraint. Hence, in contrast to the competitive model with endogenous labor supply (see section 1.3.1), taxes are nondistortionary.

40. Indeed, if all budget constraints are linked through one representative agent, policy becomes completely neutral (Bernheim and Bagwell 1988).

41. For commitment problems facing unions, see van der Ploeg 1987. In a small open economy with mobile capital, the long-run wage elasticity of labor demand may become very large. This explains why smaller European countries feature lower unemployment rates than do larger European countries.

42. If this link were to be maintained in the long run, productivity growth would reduce the replacement rate so that unemployment would decline over time.

43. This is shown by microeconometric evidence. Econometric work on labor supply behavior increasingly exploits this microeconomic variation and, hence, is moving away from macroeconomic estimation.

44. In addition to these two sectors, MIMIC includes a mining sector, a residential sector, and an exposed sector, which consists of not only capital-intensive manufacturing industries subject to intense foreign competition but also agriculture and transport. The sheltered sector includes trade, banking and insurances, and other private services.

45. Since both skill-specific and macroeconomic factors play a role in determining skill-specific wages, skill-specific wages are determined by both a macroeconomic wage equation (which adopts macro aggregates for the average tax rate, the marginal tax rate, the replacement rate, and unemployment) and a corresponding skill-specific wage equation (which employs skill-specific explanatory variables). Based on Graafland and Lever 1996, the macro and skill-specific wage equations carry equal weights in determining the contractual wage for a specific skill.

46. Employee insurances apply only to working people and cover employment risks: unemployment, disability, and sickness. Benefits depend on previously earned wages. All residents are entitled to national social insurance, which involves family allowances, disability benefits for the handicapped, special health costs, and a basic pension. In contrast to benefits from employee insurances, benefits from national social insurance are not related to previously earned wages.

47. According to these simulations, a cut of 1 percentage point in the average tax burden reduces the unemployment rate by about 0.3 percentage point. This is somewhat higher than the estimates of Nickell and Layard (1999) and similar to the estimates of Daveri and Tabellini (2000).

48. The tax rate in the third bracket exerts a smaller effect on the replacement rate because this income range is less relevant for unemployed persons.

49. Section 1.3.2.3 identifies these two effects in an analytical right-to-manage model in which unemployment benefits are subject to the progressive labor income tax.

50. For students with low annual incomes, however, the tax allowance reduces the marginal tax rate. This explains the minor decline in the average marginal tax rate in the next-to-last row of the fourth column of table 1.5.

51. Hence, this EITC differs from the EITC implemented in the United States, which depends on family income and the number of children in a family.

52. Hosios (1990) and Acemoglu and Shimer (1998) also formulate static versions of the search model. See also Boone and Bovenberg 2002.

53. See, for example, Broersma and van Ours 1999.

54. This is in fact optimal if the utility function of individuals is given by

$$u(Y) = \begin{cases} -\infty & \text{if } Y < B \\ Y & \text{if } Y \geq B. \end{cases}$$

Note that the unemployment benefit is not subject to the labor income tax. Boone and Bovenberg (2002) explore the model developed here with $B = 0$.

55. A proportional tax is optimal if unemployment benefits are absent (i.e., $B = 0$) and the so-called Hosios condition holds. The latter condition (see Hosios 1990), which reads $1 - \beta = \eta$, states that the bargaining power of firms $1 - \beta$ should correspond to the effectiveness of firms in producing matches as measured by η.

56. Unions can affect holdup problems. On the one hand, they may worsen these problems if, by monopolizing labor supply in an industry, they are able to hold up firms' investments that are specific to this industry. On the other hand, unions tend to feature a longer time horizon than individual workers do. The reputational mechanism may thus induce them to keep their commitments to moderate wages, thereby alleviating the holdup problem. These opposite effects of unions resemble the opposite effects of industry

unions worsening monopoly distortions and national unions internalizing externalities (as discussed in section 1.3.2.3).

57. Progressive taxation and wage moderation may thus raise labor supply if workers have excessive bargaining power in the laissez-faire equilibrium. This contrasts with models (explored in section 1.3.1) that focus on the intensive rather than the extensive margin of labor supply and in which labor supply is set after workers have found a job. The discouraged worker effect is absent in these models, and the unemployment rate thus does not depress labor supply.

58. This contrasts with the union model explored in section 1.3.2. In that model, which abstracts from endogenous labor supply, the optimal marginal tax rate is 100 percent, resulting in the elimination of involuntary unemployment.

59. This strong result no longer holds if labor demand is not infinitely elastic with respect to wage costs because firms cannot freely enter the labor market and a lump-sum profit tax is not feasible (see Boone and Bovenberg 2002). In that case, not only τ but also τ_a rises with the government revenue requirement.

60. With less than infinitely elastic labor demand, higher unemployment benefits would in part be financed through lower job subsidies τ_a, so that $\tau_a + B > 0$. A similar result holds in a model in which labor supply is endogenous on not only the extensive margin but also the intensive margin (see section 1.6).

61. In terms of the model of section 1.5, $\beta = 1$ and $\eta = 0$, so that the Hosios condition is met.

62. An alternative interpretation of B is a categorial unemployment insurance benefit. Indeed, the benefit is paid only to those who have not found a job. In most countries, however, unemployment benefits depend on the previously earned wage and are thus likely to increase with ability n. This is the main reason why we interpret B as a social assistance benefit (i.e., the minimum income level provided by the government). Another interpretation of B is an early retirement or disability benefit that is paid if an agent does not work.

63. The second-order condition for the agents' optimal choice of consumption and gross income implies that consumption and gross income are nondecreasing in type n. Boone and Bovenberg (2003a) analyze these constraints (and the associated bunching implications) in depth and argue that they are not relevant for understanding optimal taxation and welfare benefits at the bottom of the labor market. We therefore ignore these constraints here and refer the interested reader to Boone and Bovenberg 2003a.

64. Instead of $C(n)$, we employ $U(n)$ as a control variable in order to facilitate the inclusion of first-order incentive compatibility (22) into the optimization problem.

65. This expression also holds if the welfare benefit is fixed exogenously.

66. Equation (25) also holds with an exogenous benefit level. If B is not optimally set, however, $\tau(n_w)$ may be negative (Boone and Bovenberg 2003a). With positive search externalities, the optimal welfare benefit B will typically be lower than without positive search externalities. Indeed, the search externalities will be internalized by reducing both B and $T(n_w)$. Indeed, redistribution away from workers toward the poorer unemployed becomes more problematic.

67. Whereas we thus model the benefits of monitoring, we do not specify the costs of monitoring. We therefore can not compute optimal monitoring levels.

68. We demonstrated that higher income or payroll tax rates can raise unemployment even though productivity growth does not affect the unemployment rate. This may happen if the "outside wage" is indexed to labor productivity in the formal sector. This case seems particularly relevant if the outside option is employment in the untaxed, informal economy.

69. This raises the question of why the government cannot cut the replacement rate directly, but has to rely on an environmental tax reform to do so. One reason may be that benefit recipients reap the largest gains from the improvement in environmental quality. With environmental benefits offsetting the decline in after-tax unemployment benefits, benefit recipients may favor an environmental tax reform that cuts their after-tax incomes whereas they would not support a direct cut in the replacement rate (Bovenberg 1999).

70. Indeed, the desire to provide income to involuntarily unemployed agents creates distortions on the extensive margin in the model laid out in section 1.6. If the government does not need to provide income to the involuntarily unemployed, even the least skilled workers can be offered sufficient incentives to look for jobs.

71. The government can also collect more information on why workers lost their jobs. If they were laid off because of misconduct or if they quit voluntarily, the government may refuse unemployment benefits. This may reduce the wage pressure from higher unemployment benefits (van der Ploeg 2003). Higher categorical benefits for verifiable disabilities (so-called tagging) may also provide valuable insurance without inducing moral hazard. Indeed, the trade-off between efficiency and equity originates in asymmetric information about the skills and behavior of agents. The agencies paying welfare and unemployment benefits typically collect much more information about the skills and health of benefit recipients than the tax office does about taxpayers.

72. In terms of the model developed in section 1.3.2, workfare in effect reduces δ (i.e., the value of leisure in unemployment).

References

Acemoglu, D., and R. Shimer. 1998. "Efficient Unemployment Insurance." *Journal of Political Economy* 107: 893–928.

Baartmans, K., F. Meyer, and A. van Schaik. 1986. "House Repair and the Informal Sector." Mimeo., University of Delft, the Netherlands.

Bernheim, B. D., and K. Bagwell. 1988. "Is Everything Neutral?" *Journal of Political Economy* 96: 308–338.

Blundell, R., A. Duncan, J. McCrae, and C. Mehir. 2000. "The Labor Market Impact of the Working Families' Tax Credit." *Fiscal Studies* 21: 75–104.

Boadway, R., K. Cuff, and M. Marchand. 2000. "Optimal Income Taxation with Quasi-Linear Preferences Revisited." *Journal of Public Economic Theory* 2: 435–460.

Boone, J., and A. L. Bovenberg. 2002. "Optimal Taxation and Search." *Journal of Public Economics* 85, no. 1: 53–98.

Boone, J., and A. L. Bovenberg. 2003a. "The Optimal Taxation of Unskilled Labor with Job Search and Social Assistance." NBER Discussion Paper No. 9785, Cambridge, Mass.

Boone, J., and A. L. Bovenberg. 2003b. "Optimal Welfare Benefits and Non-linear Income Taxation with Unemployment." Mimeo., CentER, Tilburg University, the Netherlands.

Bovenberg, A. L. 1995. "Environmental Taxation and Employment." *De Economist* 143, no. 2: 111–140.

Bovenberg, A. L. 1999. "Green Tax Reforms and the Double Dividend: An Updated Reader's Guide." *International Tax and Public Finance* 6: 421–443.

Bovenberg, A. L., and B. Jacobs. 2002. "Redistribution and Education Subsidies Are Siamese Twins." CEPR Discussion Paper No. 3099, London.

Bovenberg, A. L., and F. van der Ploeg. 1994. "Effects of the Tax and Benefit System on Wage Formation and Unemployment." Mimeo., CentER, Tilburg University, the Netherlands.

Bovenberg, A. L., and F. van der Ploeg. 1998. "Tax Reform, Structural Unemployment and the Environment." *Scandinavian Journal of Economics* 100: 593–610.

Bovenberg, A. L., and C. van Ewijk. 1997. "Progressive Taxes, Equity, and Human Capital Accumulation in an Endogenous Growth Model with Overlapping Generations." *Journal of Public Economics* 64: 154–179.

Broersma, L., and J. C. van Ours. 1999. "Job Searchers, Job Matches and the Elasticity of Matching." *Labour Economics* 6, no. 1: 77–93.

Calmfors, L., and E. J. Driffill. 1988. "Bargaining Structure, Corporatism and Macroeconomic Performance." *Economic Policy* 6: 13–62.

Cnossen, S. 2001. "Tax Policy in the European Union. A Review of Issues and Options." Studies in Economic Policy No. 5, Ocfeb, Erasmus Universiteit Rotterdam, the Netherlands.

Daveri, F., and G. Tabellini. 2000. "Unemployment and Taxes: Do Taxes Affect the Rate of Unemployment?" *Economic Policy* 30: 49–104.

Diamond, P. A., and J. A. Mirrlees. 1971. "Optimal Taxation and Public Production 1: Production Efficiency and 2: Tax Rules." *American Economic Review* 61: 8–27, 261–278.

Disney, R. 2000. "The Impact of Tax and Welfare Policies on Employment and Unemployment in OECD Countries." IMF Working Paper No. 2000/64, Washington, D.C.

Eaton, J., and H. S. Rosen. 1980. "Taxation, Human Capital and Uncertainty." *American Economic Review* 70: 705–715.

Ebert, U. 1992. "A Reexamination of the Optimal Nonlinear Income Tax." *Journal of Public Economics* 49: 47–73.

Frederiksson, P., and B. Holmlund. 2003. "Improving Incentives in Unemployment Insurance: A Review of Recent Research." Working Paper No. 5, Institute for Labor Market Policy Evaluation, Uppsala.

Graafland, J. J., and M. H. C. Lever. 1996. "Internal and External Forces in Sectoral Wage Formation: Evidence from the Netherlands." *Oxford Bulletin of Economics and Statistics* 58: 241–252.

Graafland, J. J., and F. H. Huizinga. 1999. "Taxes and Benefits in a Non-linear Wage Equation." *De Economist* 147: 39–54.

Graafland, J. J., R. A. de Mooij, A. G. H. Nibbelink, and A. Nieuwenhuis. 2001. *Mimicing Tax Policies and the Labor Market*. Amsterdam: North-Holland.

Groot, W., and H. Oosterbeek. 1995. "Determinants and Wage Effects of Participation in On- and Off-the-job Training." Tinbergen Institute Research Memorandum TI 95-122, Amsterdam.

Gruber, J., and D. Wise. 1999. *Social Security and Retirement Around the World*. Chicago: University of Chicago Press.

Heckman, J. J. 1976. "A Life-cycle Model of Earnings, Learning, and Consumption." *Journal of Political Economy* 4: S11–S44.

Heckman, J. J., L. Lochner, and R. Cossa. 2002. "Learning by Doing versus On-the-job Training: Using Variantion Induced by the EITC to Distinguish between Models of Skill Formation." NBER Working Paper No. 9083, Cambridge, Mass.

Holmlund, B. 2000. "Labor Taxation in Search Equilibrium with Home Production." Mimeo., Department of Economics, Uppsala, Sweden.

Hosios, A. J. 1990. "On the Efficiency of Matching and Related Models of Search and Unemployment." *Review of Economic Studies* 57: 279–298.

Hubbard, R. G., and K. L. Judd. 1986. "Liquidity Constraints, Fiscal Policy, and Consumption." *Brookings Papers on Economic Activity*, no. 1: 1–50.

Jacobs, B. 2002. "Public Finance and Human Capital." Thela thesis, Tinbergen Institute Amsterdam.

King, R., C. Plosser, and S. Rebelo. 1988. "Production, Growth and Business Cycles, I: The Basis Neoclassical Model." *Journal of Monetary Economics* 21: 195–232.

Koskela, E., and J. Vilmunen. 1996. "Tax Progression Is Good for Employment in Popular Models of Trade Union Behavior." *Labour Economics* 3, no. 1: 65–80.

Koskela, E., and R. Schob. 1999. "Alleviating Unemployment: The Role of Unemployment Benefits and Tax Structure." *European Economic Review* 43: 1723–1746.

Koskela, E., and R. Schob. 2002. "Optimal Factor Income Taxation in the Presence of Unemployment." *Journal of Public Economic Theory* 4: 387–404.

Layard, R. 1980. "Human Satisfaction and Public Policy." *Economic Journal* 90: 737–750.

Lockwood, B., and A. Manning. 1993. "Wage Setting and the Tax System: Theory and Evidence for the United Kingdom." *Journal of Public Economics* 52: 1–29.

Lollivier, S., and J. Rochet. 1983. Bunching and Second-order Conditions: A Note on Optimal Tax Theory. *Journal of Economic Theory* 31: 392–400.

Lucas, R. E. 1988. "On the Mechanisms of Economic Development." *Journal of Monetary Economics* 22: 3–42.

Lungqvist, L., and T. J. Sargent. 1998. "The European Unemployment Dilemma." *Journal of Political Economy* 106: 514–550.

Machin, S., and A. Manning. 1999. "The Causes and Consequences of Long Term Unemployment in Europe." In *Handbook of Labor Economics*, vol. 3, ed. O. Ashenfelter and D. Card. Amsterdam: North-Holland.

Mortensen, D. T., and C. A. Pissarides. 1999. "New Developments in Models of Search in the Labor Market." In *Handbook of Labor Economics*, vol. 3, ed. O. Ashenfelter and D. Card. Amsterdam: North-Holland.

Musgrave, R., and P. B. Musgrave. 1976. *Public Finance in Theory and Practice*, 2nd ed. New York: McGraw-Hill.

Neary, J. P., and K. W. S. Roberts. 1980. "The Theory of Household Behaviour and Rationing." *European Economic Review* 13: 25–42.

Nickell, S., and R. Layard. 1999. "Labor Market Institutions and Economic Performance." In *Handbook of Labor Economics*, vol. 3, ed. O. Ashenfelter and D. Card. Amsterdam: North-Holland.

Nielsen, S. B., and P. B. Sørensen. 1998. "On the Optimality of the Nordic System of Dual Income Taxation." *Journal of Public Economics* 63: 311–329.

OECD. 2002a. *Employment Outlook*. Paris: OECD.

OECD. 2002b. *Benefits and Wages*. OECD Indicators. Paris: OECD.

Pauly, M. V. 1974. "Over Insurance and Public Provision of Insurance: The Roles of Moral Hazard and Adverse Selection." *Quarterly Journal of Economics* 88: 44–62.

Pissarides, C. A. 1990. *Equilibrium Unemployment Theory*. Oxford: Blackwell.

Pissarides, C. A. 1998. "The Impact of Employment Tax Cuts on Unemployment and Wages: The Role of Unemployment Benefits and the Tax Structure." *European Economic Review* 42: 155–183.

Sinn. Hans Werner. 1995. "A Theory of the Welfare State." *Scandinavian Journal of Economics* 97: 495–526.

Sørensen, P. B. 1997. "Public Finance Solutions to the European Unemployment Problem?" *Economic Policy* 25: 223–264.

Sørensen, P. B. 2003. "Social Insurance Based on Individual Savings Accounts." In *Public Finances and Public Policy in the New Century*, ed. S. Cnossen and H-W. Sinn, 303–331. Cambridge, Mass.: MIT Press.

Stiglitz, J. E. 1999. "Taxation, Public Policy and the Dynamics of Unemployment." *International Tax and Public Finance* 6: 239–262.

Summers, L., J. Gruber, and K. Vergara. 1993. "Taxation and the Structure of Labor Markets: The Case of Corporatism." *Quarterly Journal of Economics* 108: 385–411.

Trostel, P. A. 1993. "The Effect of Taxation on Human Capital." *Journal of Political Economy* 101: 327–350.

Tyrvainen, T. 1995. "Wage Setting, Taxes and Demand for Labour: Multivariate Analysis of Cointegrating Relations." *Empirical Economics* 20: 271–297.

van der Ploeg, F. 1987. "Trade Unions, Employment and Investment: A Non-cooperative Approach." *European Economic Review* 31: 1465–1492.

van der Ploeg, F. 2003. "Do Social Policies Harm Employment and Growth? Effects of Taxes and Benefits on Non-competitive Labour Markets." Mimeo., European University Institute, Florence, Italy.

Weymark, J. A. 1987. "Comparative Static Properties of Optimal Nonlinear Taxes." *Econometrica* 55: 1165–1185.

2

Work and Taxes

Stephen Nickell

2.1 Introduction

One of the most interesting features of the developed world is the fact that people in some countries work much harder than in others. By work, I mean work in the market, not work overall, which is an important distinction. For example, U.S. and German households spend about the same proportion of their income on "food and beverages." However, in the United States, around a half of this goes to restaurants, compared with only one quarter in Germany. Far more time in the latter country is spent on food preparation at home (see Freeman and Schettkat 2001).[1] Despite this, in what follows I focus on market work, where the differences across countries are startling. For example, the average person of working age (16–64) works around 46 percent more in the United States than in Belgium (see table 2.1). A little over half of this difference is because more people in the United States are in employment with the remaining difference arising from the fact that those in employment in the United States tend to work more hours per year. These substantial differences explain the majority of the variation in GDP per capita among the advanced countries of the OECD, with differences in productivity making a significantly smaller contribution. These differences in labor input may be large, and indeed interesting, but are they important? Many certainly think so. At the Lisbon summit of the European Union in March 2000, the heads of government set a target that by 2010, the EU employment rate should rise by at least 6 percentage points (nearly 10%), and for older workers by 12 percentage points (over 30%). These are substantial numbers. Here, however, I do not pursue in a serious way whether more work is good or bad but merely investigate the factors generating the data.

Table 2.1
A picture of employment and unemployment in the OECD in 2001

	Unem-ployment rate (%)	Inactivity rate (%)	Employ-ment rate (%)	Hours per year	Average hours per week
Europe					
Austria	3.6	29.3	67.8	—	—
Belgium	6.6	36.4	59.7	1528	17.5
Denmark	4.3	21.8	75.9	1482	21.6
Finland	9.1	25.4	67.7	1694	22.0
France	8.6	32.0	62.0	1532	18.3
Germany	7.9	28.4	65.9	1467	18.6
Ireland	3.8	32.5	65.0	1674	20.9
Italy	9.5	39.3	54.9	1606	17.0
Netherlands	2.4	24.3	74.1	1346	19.2
Norway	3.6	19.7	77.5	1364	20.3
Portugal	4.1	28.2	68.7	2009**	26.5
Spain	10.7	34.2	58.8	1816	20.5
Sweden	5.1	20.7	75.3	1603	23.2
Switzerland	2.6	18.8	79.1	1568*	23.8
United Kingdom	5.0	25.1	71.3	1711	23.5
European Union	7.6	30.8	64.1	—	—
Non-Europe					
Australia	6.7	26.2	68.9	1837	24.4
Canada	7.2	23.5	70.9	1801*	24.6
Japan	5.0	27.4	68.8	1821*	24.1
New Zealand	5.3	24.1	71.8	1817	25.1
United States	4.8	23.2	73.1	1821	25.6

Source: OECD Employment Outlook 2002, Tables A, B, F.
Notes: *refers to 2000; **refers to 1994. Unemployment is based on OECD standardized rates. These approximate the ILO definition. Hours per year is an average over all workers, part-time and full-time. Average hours per week refers to the entire population of working age and is equal to the proportional employment rate × hours per year ÷ 52.

When confronted with these work differences, it is natural to look at the incentives to engage in market work relative to other activities in the different countries. The particular feature of these incentives on which I focus are those embedded in the tax system. To be more precise, I concentrate on taxes on employment paid by firms (payroll taxes), taxes on income paid by individuals, and taxes on consumption paid by individuals. Important features of the overall incentive structure that I do not discuss in detail include the unemployment benefit system, the sickness and disability benefit system, and the early retirement benefit system. These are obviously an important part of the overall picture given that those in the working-age population who do not work fall into five major categories—namely, full-time students, the unemployed, the sick and disabled, the early retired, and those looking after their family.

In what follows, I look briefly at the theoretical background in the next section. Then in section 2.3 I present an array of results on taxes, wages, and employment, and in section 2.4 I consider non-employment among different subgroups of the working-age population. I finish with a summary and some general conclusions.

2.2 Theoretical Background

A great deal has been written on taxation and work, and useful summaries are provided by Pissarides (1998) or Koskela (2002). My intention here is to discuss two simple, illustrative models in order to see how tax rates may influence the extent of market work. Both are far from being serious behavioral models because they make no distinction between hours worked per week, weeks worked per year, employment, unemployment, and inactivity.[2] Any worthwhile microeconomic behavioral analysis of individual labor supply has to make these distinctions. Here, I restrict myself to a broadbrush analysis because I am concerned with only broad, cross-country comparisons.[3]

A basic competitive model, based on Prescott 2002, looks something like the following. Using a representative agent model, with the working-age population normalized to unity, we may define h as (market) work and then $(1 - h)$ is non-work. Let output y be generated by the production function:

$$y = Bh^{\alpha}. \tag{1}$$

Representative utility is given by

$$u = \ln c + \theta \ln(1 - h), \tag{2}$$

where c is consumption. Suppose W is nominal labor cost per employee and P is the price of the firm's output. So $w = W/P$ is the real labor cost per employee facing the firm. Suppose we have proportional tax rates as follows. The payroll tax rate is t_1, the income tax rate is t_2, and the consumption tax rate is t_3. Then the real post-tax consumption wage is given by

$$\frac{W(1 - t_1)(1 - t_2)}{P(1 + t_3)} = w(1 - \tau), \quad \text{say.} \tag{3}$$

So τ is the "tax wedge" between the real labor cost per employee facing the firm and the real post-tax consumption wage. Note that τ is given by

$$\tau = 1 - \frac{(1 - t_1)(1 - t_2)}{1 + t_3} \simeq (t_1 + t_2 + t_3). \tag{4}$$

In equilibrium, the marginal product of labor is equal to real labor cost per employee, and the marginal rate of substitution between consumption and leisure is equal to the real post-tax consumption wage. Thus we have

$$\alpha y / h = w, \tag{5}$$

$$\frac{\theta}{(1 - h)} \Big/ \frac{1}{c} = w(1 - \tau). \tag{6}$$

If we suppose that tax revenues are returned to consumers in a lump-sum fashion in the form of consumption, then $c/y = 1$. If we eliminate w from (5) and (6) and use $c/y = 1$, employment is given by

$$h = \frac{(1 - \tau)}{(\theta/\alpha) + (1 - \tau)}, \tag{7}$$

which is diminishing in τ. The size of the impact of τ depends crucially on θ. Prescott (2002) calibrates an equation of this type, uses it to generate predicted labor supply for seven OECD countries, and finds that it matches actual labor supply quite closely. How his results square with others in this area is discussed in the next section.

It might, however, be argued that in Europe, some sort of bargaining model of wage determination would be more realistic.[4] To construct such a model, we suppose that there are N identical firms in the economy, labeled i, each with a production function

$$y_i = \frac{B}{N} h_i^\alpha, \tag{8}$$

where y_i is output. If we divide the population of working age (still normalized to unity) into N equal groups, then h_i is the proportion of group i that is working. This production framework is consistent with that in the previous model.

In our standard bargaining model, it is assumed that in each firm, wages are determined by a bargain between workers and the firm. Then the firm determines employment, h_i, to maximize profits given the wage. When the wage bargain is struck, workers may take some account of the impact of wages on their employment prospects (see Layard, Nickell, and Jackman 1991, chap. 2, for an extensive discussion of these models). If the bargained wages (labor costs per employee) are w_i, then, from (8), we see that, under profit maximization, employment $h_i(w_i)$ satisfies

$$\frac{\alpha B}{N} h_i^{(\alpha-1)} = w_i. \tag{9}$$

Using a Nash bargaining framework, we suppose wages are determined by maximizing

$$[h_i(w_i)^\gamma (w_i(1-\tau) + y_n - A)]^\beta \Pi_i \tag{10}$$

where y_n is real, post-tax, per capita nonlabor income, A is expected alternative income for a worker not employed in firm i and Π_i is the firm's profit. The parameter γ captures the extent to which workers take account of the employment effects of the wage bargain, and β reflects the relative strength of workers in the bargain.

Expected alternative income A consists of two elements, that generated by employment in another firm with income $w(1-\tau) + y_n$, with probability h, and that generated by non-employment with income $bw(1-\tau) + y_n + z$ with probability $(1-h)$. While b represents non-employment benefit relative to post-tax employment income, z captures the real value of the leisure when not employed. So A is given by

$$A = h(w(1-\tau) + y_n) + (1-h)(bw(1-\tau) + y_n + z). \tag{11}$$

Note that the probability of being employed, h, is the same as our aggregate measure of employment, namely, the proportion of the working-age population that is at work. If (10) is maximized with respect to w_i and noting that the production function (8) and the labor demand function (9) ensure that $\partial \ln h_i / \partial \ln w_i = -(1-\alpha)^{-1}$, $w_i h_i / \Pi_i = \alpha/(1-\alpha)$, the first-order condition implies that

$$\frac{w_i(1-\tau)}{(w_i(1-\tau) + y_n - A)} = \frac{\beta\gamma + \alpha}{\beta(1-\alpha)}. \tag{12}$$

Noting that the identical firms assumption implies that $w_i = w$, $h_i = h$ and using (11), (12) becomes

$$(1 - h)(1 - b - \bar{z}(w)) = \beta(1 - \alpha)/(\beta\gamma + \alpha), \tag{13}$$

where $\bar{z}(w) = z/w(1 - \tau)$. So, in this context, the only reason taxes impact employment is because the value of leisure enters "income" while not working and is unaffected by a change in the tax wedge. Nonlabor income and the way in which it is taxed play no role, essentially because in this model, only the *difference* between income when employed and when not employed is relevant and nonlabor income is eliminated. Equation (13) can be thought of as the wage equation, which in this framework is equivalent to the labor supply equation in a competitive model. The labor demand equation is given by the aggregate version of (8), namely,

$$\frac{\alpha B}{N} h^{(\alpha-1)} = w. \tag{14}$$

So in order to generate the impact of taxes on labor supply, we simply eliminate w from (13) and (14) to obtain

$$(1 - h)\left(1 - b - \frac{zNh^{1-\alpha}}{\alpha B(1 - \tau)}\right) = \frac{\beta(1 - \alpha)}{\beta\gamma + \alpha}, \tag{15}$$

which implies $\partial h/\partial \tau < 0$ so long as benefits plus the value of leisure are less than the post-tax wage. Of course, if this were not the case, no one would work.

In these models, market work depends only on the total tax wedge, τ. There are a number of reasons why the impact of the different tax elements of τ on market work may differ. First, in the previous model, suppose the utility of income is not linear. Then nonlabor income is not eliminated. Since nonlabor income is typically not subject to payroll taxes, then the impact of the payroll tax rate on work may differ from that of the income tax or consumption tax rate (see, e.g., Hoon and Phelps 1995). Second, suppose there is a wage floor, because of minimum wage laws, for example. Then, for those at or near the wage floor, a switch from income taxes to payroll taxes will reduce employment. Third, the fact that, in practice, the taxes are not applied uniformly ensures that switches between them will not be neutral. For example, it is very unusual for consumption taxes to apply to all consumption goods or for payroll taxes to apply to all of a firm's workers (e.g., the self-employed are often exempt).

Another feature of these models is that the taxes are all proportional. Income taxes are often progressive and the degree of progressivity may itself have an independent impact. For example, in a bargaining model, increased progressivity leads to lower wage demands because wage increases are less valuable and this generates more work. The standard labor supply effect, however, typically goes in the other direction. Once we allow for different skills, progressive taxes may reduce the labor supply of skilled workers relative to the unskilled, which may damage the labor market position of the unskilled by reducing their marginal productivity. However, I do not pursue these skill effects here.

To summarize, there are good theoretical reasons why the total tax wedge may have a negative impact on work and why the individual tax rates that make up the total wedge may have differing effects. The size of these potential effects is obviously an empirical matter, so this is the topic of the next section.

2.3   Tax Effects on Work and Pay

I start by looking at the general size of the tax wedge in the OECD countries over the years (see table 2.2). All countries exhibit a substantial increase over the period from the 1960s to the 1990s, although there are wide variations across countries. These mainly reflect the extent to which health, higher education, and pensions are publicly provided along with the all-around generosity of the social security system. Some countries have made significant attempts to reduce labor taxes in recent years, notably, the Netherlands and the United Kingdom. Underlying these numbers are some significant variations in the individual tax rates: for instance, Denmark and Australia have tiny payroll tax rates whereas as those in Italy and France are very substantial at around 40 percent.

Turning to the evidence, this comes typically in two forms. The first is the impact of taxes on labor costs per employee facing firms, while the second focuses directly on the effect of taxes on aspects of labor input. The former is relevant because in order for taxes to reduce work, they must raise labor costs per employee so that firms reduce their demand for labor. If tax increases leave labor costs per employee unchanged, then they are all shifted onto labor (i.e., employees *effectively* pay all the tax) and employment is unaffected. In the remainder of this section, I first consider whether different taxes have different

Table 2.2
Total taxes on labor payroll tax rate plus income tax rate plus consumption tax rate (total tax rate, %)

	1960–1964	1965–1972	1973–1979	1980–1987	1988–1995	1996–2000
Australia	28	31	36	39	—	—
Austria	47	52	55	58	59	66
Belgium	38	43	44	46	49	51
Canada	31	39	41	42	50	53
Denmark	32	46	53	59	60	61
Finland	38	46	55	58	64	62
France	55	57	60	65	67	68
Germany (W.)	43	44	48	50	52	50
Ireland	23	30	30	37	41	33
Italy	57	56	54	56	67	64
Japan	25	25	26	33	33	37
Netherlands	45	54	57	55	47	43
Norway	—	52	61	65	61	60
New Zealand	—	—	29	30	—	—
Portugal	20	25	26	33	41	39
Spain	19	23	29	40	46	45
Sweden	41	54	68	77	78	77
Switzerland	30	31	35	36	36	36
United Kingdom	34	43	45	51	47	44
United States	34	37	42	44	45	45

Notes:
These data are based on the London School of Economics, Centre for Economic Performance OECD dataset (see the data attached to DP502 at ⟨http://cep.lse.ac.uk/papers/⟩). They are mainly based on OECD National Accounts as follows:
i. Payroll tax rate $= EC/(IE - EC)$, $EC = EPP + ESS$. $EPP =$ employers' private pensions and welfare plans contributions, $ESS =$ employers' social security contributions, $IE =$ compensations of employees.
ii. Income tax rate $= (WC + IT)/HCR$. $WC =$ employees' social security contributions, $IT =$ income taxes, $HCR =$ households' current receipts.
iii. Consumption tax rate $= (TX - SB)/CC$. $TX =$ indirect taxes, $SB =$ subsidies, $CC =$ private final consumption expenditure. The inclusion of EPP in the payroll tax rate may be subject to debate. Excluding this term has little impact on the broad overall pattern of the numbers.

effects. Then I look at the impact of the tax wedge on real labor costs per employee and finally the impact of the tax wedge on aggregate labour input.

2.3.1 Different Tax Effects

The key issue here is whether different taxes exhibit differential rates of shifting onto labor. There are a large number of time series wage equations for various countries that show different degrees of shifting onto labor for different taxes. There is no pattern to these numbers, many of which are summarized in Layard, Nickell, and Jackman 1991, OECD 1994 (247), Disney 2000, and Koskela 2002. Some intensive cross-country investigations may be found in the work of Tyrväinen (1994) reported in OECD 1994 (Table 9.5) and in that of Robertson and Symons in OECD 1990 (Annex 6A). In both these wide-ranging studies, there is no significant evidence that payroll, income, or consumption taxes have a differential impact on labor costs and hence on unemployment. As reported in the former study, "Changes in the mix of taxes by which governments raise revenues can be expected, at most, to have a limited effect on unemployment" (OECD 1994, 275).

2.3.2 Tax Wedge Effects on Real Labor Cost per Employee

In OECD 1990 (Annex 6A) a simple test of the impact of tax rates on labor costs is carried out as follows. This work specifies labor demand and labor supply equations of the form

$$N^D = f^1(w)K, \quad N^S = f^2(w(1 - \tau), \omega)L,$$

where N = employment, w = ln(real labor cost), K = capital stock, $\tau = (t_1 + t_2 + t_3)$, the total tax rate, L = the labor force, and ω = exogenous factors. Then the reduced form wage equation is

$$w = g(\tau, K/L, \omega).$$

While this OECD model specifies labor demand and labor supply equations, it is perfectly possible to relabel the labor supply equation as a wage equation, as in our bargaining model in section 2.2 (see equation (13)). The model is, therefore, completely consistent with either a competitive or a bargaining framework.

If w is independent of τ in the long run, the labor market behaves as if labor supply is inelastic and taxes are all borne by labor. So if real labor costs are unaffected by taxes (τ), employment and hence unemployment is then unaffected by τ in the long run (the labor demand equation ensures that employment depends only on w). The following equation, reported in OECD 1990 (Annex 6A), represents the average coefficients and average t statistics (in parentheses) for individual time-series regressions on sixteen OECD countries (1955–1986).

$$w = 0.79w_{-1} + 0.18ln(K/L) - 0.08\tau + 0.52\Delta\tau.$$
$$\quad (8.7) \qquad (2.0) \qquad\qquad (0.6) \qquad (2.6)$$

Thus total taxes, τ, have no long-run effects on labor costs although they have a substantial and long-lasting short-run effect via $\Delta\tau$ (and the high level of persistence in wages).[5] Consistent with this result is the work discussed in Gruber 1997 on the incidence of payroll taxation. Gruber studies the impact on wages and employment at the micro level of the sharp exogenous reduction in payroll tax rates (of around 25 percentage points!) that took place in Chile over the period 1979–1986. His analysis of a large number of individual firms indicates that wages adjust completely to this payroll tax shift and there is no employment effect whatsoever.

In contrast to this result, two multicountry studies find significant tax wedge effects on labor costs. Daveri and Tabellini (2000) find that a 10-percentage-point increase in the tax wedge raises real labor costs by 5 percent in the long run for a select group of countries,[6] although there are few controls for other labor market institutions (see Table 11, col. 1). Nickell et al. (2003) report an equivalent figure of 3.7 percent controlling for a complete set of labor market institutions (see Table 12, col. 1). Many others have found significant tax wedge effects on labor costs, and some have argued that the size of these tax wedge effects depends significantly on those labor market institutions connected with flexibility (see Liebfritz, Thornton, and Bibbee 1997; Daveri and Tabellini 2000). The argument here is that tax wedge effects are bigger, the greater the degree of inflexibility of the labor market. In order to pursue this, I set out some results on the impact of the tax wedge on labour costs in table 2.3. The first point to note is how wildly the numbers and the rankings fluctuate across the columns. This is basically due to variations in the other variables included in the labor cost equations and emphasises the fragility of most of the results in this area. Second, in order to see if there is any relationship between tax wedge effects and labor market flexibility, I regressed the average

Table 2.3
Percentage increase in real labor cost in response to a 1-percentage-point rise in the tax wedge

	1 BLN	2 T	3 AP	4 P-SK	5 Kvd W	6 Average
Austria	0			0		0
Belgium	3.4		.37	.95		1.57
Denmark	0		.28	0		0.09
Finland	0.2	0.5	0.28			0.33
France	0.5	0.4	0.37	0	0.56	0.37
Germany (W.)	0	1.0	0.37	0	0.72	0.42
Ireland	1.4					1.4
Italy	0.3	0.4	0	0	1.03	0.35
Netherlands	0.4		0.37	0	1.15	0.48
Norway	0.2		0.28			0.24
Spain	1.0					1.0
Sweden	0.5	0.6	0.28	0.73	0.70	0.56
Switzerland	1.4					1.4
United Kingdom	1.3	0.25	0	0	0.58	0.43
Japan	0	0.5	0		1.19	0.42
Australia	—	0.5	0.37		1.64	0.84
New Zealand	0					0
Canada	1.5	0.8	0		0.59	0.72
United States	0.1		0		0.43	0.18

Notes:
BLN = Bean, Layard, and Nickell 1986, Tables 3 and 5 (except the number for Spain which is taken from Dolado, Malo de Molina, and Zabalza 1986).
T = Tryväinen 1994, as reported in OECD 1994, Table 9.5 (except Sweden's number, which is from Holmlund and Kolm 1995).
AP = Alesina and Perotti 1994, Table 7, col. 4.
P-SK = Padoa-Schioppa Kostoris 1992.
Kvd W = Knoester and Van der Windt 1987.
Some of these numbers are taken directly from Leibfritz, Thornton, and Bibbee 1997, Table A1.5.
The tax wedge definitions differ somewhat between columns: 1, 2, 4 use the sum of payroll, income, and consumption tax rates; 3 and 5 omit the consumption tax rate.

tax wedge effect (col. 6) on some institutional variables[7] that relate directly to inflexibility. The results are

Tax wedge effect = Constant + 0.030 employment protection
$$(0.9)$$
$$- 0.005 \text{ labor standards}$$
$$(0.1)$$
$$- 0.16 \text{ wage bargaining coordination}$$
$$(1.7) \quad (\text{union} + \text{employer})$$
$$+ 0.004 \text{ union density}$$
$$(0.6)$$

$N = 20,\ R^2 = 0.23.$

The positive signs on employment protection and union density are consistent with the inflexibility hypothesis, but neither coefficient is significant. The only coefficient close to significance is that on coordination in wage bargaining, which suggests that if wage bargaining is more highly coordinated, tax wedge effects are smaller. It is, however, a moot point as to whether wage bargaining coordination is a sign of flexibility or inflexibility. On balance, the evidence in favor of the hypothesis that flexibility reduces tax wedge effects is not strong. Overall, however, the balance of the evidence suggests that there is probably some overall adverse tax effect on real labor costs per employee. I report the possible consequences for the impact on employment in the next section.

2.3.3   Tax Wedge Effects on Employment

An array of results in this area is presented in table 2.4. A close look at those studies that include other institutional variables as well as the tax wedge, reveals that the other institutional variables are jointly significant and reflect plausible stories as to how the labor market works (e.g., unions raise wages and reduce employment rates). Second, those studies that omit some or all the relevant institutional controls (Davis and Henrekson 2004; Prescott 2002; Daveri and Tabellini 2000; Planas, Roger, and Rossi 2003) tend to exhibit somewhat higher tax wedge effects than those that do not. On the basis of these two points, I may argue that omitting important institutional control variables is a misspecification of the model and tends to bias the tax wedge effects upward (in absolute value). If I omit those studies (noted previously) that exclude most or all of the institutional controls, I find that 10-percentage-point rise in the tax wedge reduces labor input by somewhere between 1 and 3 percent of the working-age population. Taking an average point estimate as 2 percent results in a relatively small but by no means insignificant effect. For example, the average rise in the tax wedge in the advanced OECD countries from the early 1960s to the late 1990s is around 15 percentage points, worth a reduction in labor input of around 3 percent of the working-age population.[8] Comparing the big three countries of continental Europe (France, Germany, and Italy) with the United States, the difference in the tax wedge (around 16 percentage points) would explain around 3.2 percentage points of the difference in total labor input. That is around one quarter of the overall difference in the employment rate. The remainder would be down to other factors including, in particular, the substantial differences in the social security systems, as well as other labor market institutions. In section 2.4 we pursue these issues a little further by looking more closely at the labor input rates for different groups in the working-age population.

2.4   Labor Inputs across Different Groups

The overall picture for OECD countries is presented in tables 2.5 and 2.6. We ignore inactivity rates among the young because these are strongly influenced by the extent of postschool education and whether or not postschool education takes place mainly within educational institutions, as in the United States, or in firms, as in Germany.

Focusing first on prime-age men (ages 25–54), we see that even among this group, in most countries more are inactive than are unemployed. Furthermore, the inactivity rate in this group is higher in the United States than in the European Union. Interestingly, most inactive men in this age group are classified as sick or disabled, the majority of whom are claiming some form of state benefit. Furthermore, the size of this disability group has risen substantially since the 1970s in nearly every country, and in those that have been analyzed, this increase has been driven by changes in the entry rules and the available benefits (see Bound and Burkhauser 1999 for some detailed evidence).

Among older men, unemployment rates are generally much the same as for prime-age men, but inactivity rates are enormously larger and vary dramatically from one country to another. In some European countries, more than half the older men are inactive, whereas in

Table 2.4
Recent results on the impact of taxation on employment

Reference	Impact (percentage points)	Sample	Controls
Long-run impact on employment/population rate (%) of a 10-percentage-point rise in the tax wedge			
Cross-section or random effects panel			
Scarpetta 1996 (Table 4, col. 3)	−0.3	17 OECD countries 1983–1993	Standard labor market institutions
Nickell and Layard 1999 (Table 16, col. 1)	−2.4	20 OECD countries 1983–1994	Standard labor market institutions
Fixed effects panel			
Nicoletti and Scarpetta 2001 (Table 5, col. 1)	−1.5	20 OECD countries 1982–1998	Standard labor market institutions
Nickell et al. 2003 (Table 15, col. 1)	−2.7	20 OECD countries 1961–1992	Standard labor market institutions
Davis and Henrekson 2004 (Table 4, row 8)	−2.2	17 OECD countries 1977–1994	Time dummies only
Long-run impact on average hours per week worked by the population of working age (see table 2.1, final column) of a 10-percentage-point rise in the tax wedge			
Cross-section or random effects panel			
Nickell and Layard 1999 (Table 16, col. 3)	−1.0 hours (−2.5 pps)[a]	20 OECD countries 1983–1994	Standard labor market institutions
Prescott 2002[b] (Table 3)	−3.0 hours (−7.5 pps)[a]	7 OECD countries 1993–1996	No controls
Davis and Henrekson 2004 (Table 3, row 4)	−1.8 hours (−4.5 pps)[a]	14 OECD countries 1995	No controls

Long-run impact on the unemployment rate (%) of a 10-percentage-point rise in the tax wedge

Euro area aggregate time series			
Planas, Roger, and Rossi 2003 (Tables 2, 3)	3.2	Euro area aggregate 1970–2002	No controls
Cross-section or random effects panel			
Scarpetta 1996 (Table 3, col. 3)	1.1	17 OECD countries 1983–1993	Standard labor market institutions
Elmeskov, Martin, and Scarpetta 1998 (Table 4, col. 4)	1.2	18 OECD countries 1983–1995	Standard labor market institutions; Impact at average levels of coordination
Nickell and Layard 1999 (Table 15, col. 1)	2.0	20 OECD countries 1983–1994	Standard labor market institutions
Fixed effects panel			
Daveri and Tabellini 2000 (Table 9, col. 1)	5.5	14 OECD countries 1965–1991	Restricted set of labor market institutions; Impact at average levels of coordination
Nickell et al. 2003 (Table 13, col. 1)	1.1	20 OECD countries 1961–1992	Standard labor market institutions; Impact at average levels of coordination

Notes:

[a] An impact of x hours on average weekly working hours is equivalent to 2.5x percentage points (pps) taking a full work week as forty hours.

[b] Prescott computes the tax wedge and predicted hours for seven countries. For each country we compute (*predicted hours − mean predicted hours*) ÷ (*taxwedge − mean taxwedge*) where the means are across the countries. The computed impact is the average of this ratio across the seven countries. It is also worth noting that Prescott approximates a measure of the marginal tax wedge by multiplying the income tax rate by 1.6 in all countries. In practice this makes little difference to the overall cross-country pattern of the tax wedge.

Table 2.5
Unemployment, inactivity, and employment by age and gender in 2001

	Unemployment (%)				Inactivity rate (%)				Employment rate (%)			
	Men		Women		Men		Women		Men		Women	
	25–54	55–64	25–54	55–64	25–54	55–64	25–54	55–64	25–54	55–64	25–54	55–64
Europe												
Austria	3.4	5.7	3.8	5.2	6.5	59.8	23.1	81.7	90.3	37.9	74.0	17.4
Belgium	4.8	3.9	6.1	0.9	9.1	63.4	29.3	84.2	86.5	35.1	66.4	15.6
Denmark	2.9	4.0	4.1	4.0	8.6	34.3	16.5	48.1	88.7	63.1	80.1	49.8
Finland	6.9	8.9	8.0	8.8	9.0	48.8	15.0	50.5	84.7	46.7	78.2	45.1
France	6.3	5.6	10.1	6.6	5.9	56.2	21.3	65.9	88.1	41.4	70.8	31.8
Germany	7.3	10.3	7.7	12.5	5.7	49.4	21.7	67.6	87.5	45.4	72.2	28.4
Ireland	3.4	2.6	3.0	2.7	8.2	33.6	33.9	70.8	88.7	64.6	64.1	28.4
Italy[a]	6.4	4.6	12.5	4.9	9.6	57.8	42.1	84.1	84.6	40.3	50.7	15.2
Netherlands	1.4	1.7	2.1	1.1	6.0	48.6	25.8	71.7	92.7	50.5	72.6	28.0
Norway	2.7	1.7	2.5	1.4	8.6	26.4	16.7	36.8	88.9	72.3	81.2	62.3
Portugal	2.6	3.2	4.4	3.1	7.2	36.4	21.9	58.1	90.4	61.6	74.7	40.6
Spain	6.3	5.6	13.7	8.0	8.4	38.6	38.8	76.4	85.9	57.9	52.8	21.8
Sweden	4.4	5.3	3.7	4.5	9.4	26.5	14.4	32.7	86.6	69.6	82.5	64.3
Switzerland	1.0	1.8	3.4	1.6	3.7	17.5	20.7	43.8	95.3	81.0	76.6	55.3
United Kingdom	4.1	4.4	3.6	1.8	8.7	35.6	23.6	56.0	87.6	61.6	73.6	43.2
European Union	5.5	6.3	7.9	6.6	8.2	47.8	28.4	68.1	86.8	48.9	66.0	29.8
Non-Europe												
Australia	5.5	5.6	5.0	3.3	10.1	40.0	28.6	63.1	85.0	43.3	67.8	35.7
Canada	6.3	6.0	6.0	5.6	8.9	38.8	20.9	58.2	85.4	57.6	74.3	39.4
Japan	4.2	7.0	4.7	3.7	3.1	16.6	32.7	50.8	92.8	77.5	64.1	47.3
New Zealand	4.0	4.0	4.1	2.8	8.7	25.7	25.5	48.2	87.6	71.3	71.5	50.3
United States	3.7	3.4	3.8	2.7	8.7	31.9	23.6	47.0	87.9	65.8	73.5	51.6

Source: OECD 2002, Table C.

Note: These data do not include those in prison. This makes little difference except in the United States where counting those in prison would raise the inactivity rate among prime age men by around 2 percentage points.

[a] In 2000.

Table 2.6
Youth unemployment rate (%) in 2001 (ages 15–24)

	Total	Men	Women
Europe			
Austria	6.0	6.2	5.8
Belgium	15.3	14.3	16.6
Denmark	8.3	7.3	9.3
Finland	19.9	19.6	20.2
France	18.7	16.2	21.8
Germany	8.4	9.1	7.5
Ireland	6.2	6.4	5.8
Italy	27.0	23.2	32.2
Netherlands	4.4	4.2	4.5
Norway	10.5	10.6	10.3
Portugal	9.2	7.2	11.9
Spain	20.8	16.1	27.0
Sweden	11.8	12.7	10.8
Switzerland	5.6	5.8	5.5
United Kingdom	10.5	12.0	8.7
European Union	13.9	13.1	15.0
Non-Europe			
Australia	12.7	13.3	12.0
Canada	12.8	14.5	11.0
Japan	9.7	10.7	8.7
New Zealand	11.8	12.1	11.5
United States	10.6	11.4	9.7

Source: OECD 2002, Table C.

Norway and Sweden, the inactivity rate is closer to one quarter. As Blondal and Scarpetta (1998) note, these large cross-country variations were not apparent as recently as 1971, when nearly all the countries had inactivity rates for this group below 20 percent, the major exception being Italy with a rate of 41 percent (Blondal and Scarpetta 1998, Table V.1, 72). The main factor explaining the current variations and the consequent large changes since 1971 has been the structure of the social security system. Incentives for men to stay in the labor force vary widely, with generous incentives to retire early being introduced in many countries (Blondal and Scarpetta 1998, Table 5; Disney 2004; Werding 2004). This was often done in order to reduce labor supply in the mistaken view that this would help to resolve the problem of unemployment. As a consequence, Belgium, France, Germany, and Italy, for example, all have exceptionally high inactivity rates among older men on top of their exceptionally high unemployment rates.

Inactivity rates among prime-age women (ages 25–54) also vary widely, with the Scandinavian countries having the lowest rates in the OECD, and Italy and Spain having the highest. While the majority of inactive women in this age group report themselves as looking after their family, Italy and Spain in fact have the lowest fertility rates in the OECD. What is important here is the structure of the tax system, particularly the marginal tax rate facing wives when their husbands work, the existence of barriers to part-time work, and the availability of publicly funded child care. A key tax issue that is relevant here is whether husbands and wives are taxed jointly or separately (OECD 1990, Table 6.3).

Finally, it is worth noting how unemployment in Italy, Spain, and to a lesser extent France is heavily concentrated among young people and women. This is partly due to the role of employment protection laws in generating barriers to employment for new entrants and partly due to the social mores surrounding entry into work. For example, in Italy many young people, particularly if they are well-qualified, will live at home for many years without working but effectively queuing for a particularly desirable job and contributing to measured unemployment (although perhaps not to true unemployment).

To summarize, looking at different subgroups of the working-age population, the numbers suggest that many factors other than standard tax rates are important in determining the extent of non-employment. This is consistent with the overall conclusion of section 2.3 that tax rates explain only a fraction, albeit a significant one, of the cross-country differences in employment rates (see also Bertola, Blau, and Kahn 2002, where the results have similar implications). Of course many of these "other factors" are, in fact, characteristics of the tax and benefit system taken more broadly, including the unemployment, disability, and pension benefit systems. Taken together with the standard tax rates, these would probably explain a significant proportion of the cross-country variation in market work.

2.5 Summary and Conclusions

Our basic conclusion is that tax rates are a significant factor in explaining differences in the amount of market work undertaken by the working-age population in different countries. However, the evidence

suggests that standard tax rate differentials only explain a minority of
the market work differentials, the majority being explained by other
relevant labor market institutions, many related to the tax and benefit
system more broadly. Particularly important are the differences in social security systems that provide income support to various nonworking groups including the unemployed, the sick and disabled, and the
early retired.

Notes

This chapter is based on a paper prepared for the CESifo Workshop on Tax Policy and
Labor Market Performance. The conference took place in Venice on July 21–23, 2003. I
am most grateful to conference participants, Jonas Agell, Peter Birch Sørensen, and two
anonymous referees for helpful comments on an earlier draft.

1. Who gets the better dinners is, as yet, an unresolved question.

2. The unemployed are those without jobs who are seeking work; the inactive are those
without jobs who are not seeking work.

3. The reason I do this is because, despite the huge number of microeconometric studies
of labor supply referring to weekly hours, annual hours, unemployment, employment,
and so on, there is, to my knowledge, no published work that translates these numerous
empirical results in a coherent way into explanations of cross-country variations in aggregate employment rates or overall labor inputs.

4. Of course, there are numerous other types of wage-setting models, notably efficiency
wage models and rent-sharing models. However, in my view, bargaining models better
reflect how most wages are determined outside the competitive sector.

5. The use of average coefficients and average t statistics to summarize sixteen separate
regressions is unusual. However, it is clear that an average t above 2 indicates that the
null that all sixteen coefficients on a particular variable are equal to 0 may be rejected.

6. Namely, Australia, Belgium, France, Germany, Italy, Netherlands, Spain, and the
United Kingdom (pre-1980).

7. The four variables in this regression are defined here. Employment protection is an index of the strength of employment protection legislation. (Nickell and Layard 1999, Table
6, col. 2). Labor standards is an index of the strength of legislation covering working
time, fixed-term contracts, employment protection, minimum wages, and employee rep-
resentation rights. It is increasing in inflexibility (Nickell and Layard 1999, Table 6, col.
1). Coordination refers to the extent to which wage bargaining is coordinated both across
unions and across employers (ibid., Table 7, sum of cols. 3 and 4). Union density is trade
union membership as a percentage of employees (ibid., Table 7, col. 1).

8. In fact the average employment/population ratio in these same countries has risen
over the same period, so there are obviously other forces at work aside from taxes. This
overall change is because the rise in the employment/population ratio among women
has more than offset the fall among men.

References

Alesina, A., and R. Perotti. 1994. "The Welfare State and Competitiveness." NBER Working Paper No. 4810, Cambridge, Mass.

Bean, C. R., R. Layard, and S. J. Nickell. 1986. "The Rise in Unemployment: a Multi-country Study." *Economica* 53: S1–522.

Bertola, G., F. D. Blau, and L. M. Kahn. 2002. "Labor Market Institutions and Demographic Employment Patterns." European University Institute, Fiesole, Italy, June.

Blondal, S., and S. Scarpetta. 1998. "The Retirement Decision in OECD Countries." OECD Economics Department Working Paper No. 202, OECD, Paris.

Bound, J., and R. V. Burkhauser. 1999. "Economic Analysis of Transfer Programs Targeted on People with Disabilities." In *Handbook of Labor Economics*, vol. 3, ed. O. Ashenfelter and D. Card, 3417–3528. Amsterdam: North-Holland.

Daveri, F., and G. Tabellini. 2000. "Unemployment, Growth and Taxation in Industrial Countries." *Economic Policy* (April): 49–90.

Davis, S. J., and M. Henrekson. 2004. "Tax Effects on Work Activity, Industry Mix and Shadow Economy Size: Evidence from Rich Country Comparisons." Mimeo., University of Chicago Graduate School of Business.

Disney, R. 2000. "Fiscal Policy and Employment I: A Survey of Macroeconomic Models, Methods and Findings." Mimeo., IMF, Washington, D.C., May.

Disney, R. 2004. "Are Contributions to Public Pension Programmes a Tax on Employment?" *Economic Policy* (July): 267–311.

Dolado, J. J., J. L. Malo de Molina, and A. Zabalza. 1986. "Spanish Industrial Unemployment: Some Explanatory Factors." *Economica* 53: S313–S334.

Elmeskov, J., J. P. Martin, and S. Scarpetta. 1998. "Key Lessons for Labour Market Reforms: Evidence from OECD Countries' Experiences." *Swedish Economic Policy Review* 5, no. 2: 205–252.

Freeman, R. B., and R. Schettkat. 2001. "Marketization of Production and the US-Europe Employment Gap." *Oxford Bulletin of Economics and Statistics* (Special Issue: The Labour Market Consequences of Technical and Structural Change) 63: 647–670.

Gruber, J. 1997. "The Incidence of Payroll Taxation: Evidence from Chile." *Journal of Labor Economics* 15, no. 3 (Part 2): S72–S101.

Holmlund, B., and A. Kolm. 1995. "Progressive Taxation, Wage Setting and Unemployment—Theory and Swedish Evidence." Tax Reform Evaluation Report No. 15, National Institute of Economic Research, Stockholm.

Hoon, H. T., and E. S. Phelps. 1995. "Taxes and Subsidies in a Labor-turnover Model of the Natural Rate." Columbia University, March.

Knoester, A., and N. Van der Windt. 1987. "Real Wages and Taxation in Ten OECD Countries." *Oxford Bulletin of Economics and Statistics* 49, no. 1: 151–169.

Koskela, E. 2002. "Labour Taxation and Employment in Trade Union Models: A Partial Survey." In *Towards Higher Employment: The Role of Labour Market Institutions*, ed. S.

Ilmakunnas and E. Koskela, 63–85. Helsinki: Government Institute for Economic Research, Vatt Publications.

Layard, R., S. Nickell, and R. Jackman. 1991. *Unemployment: Macroeconomic Performance and the Labour Market*. Oxford: Oxford University Press.

Liebfritz, W., J. Thornton, and A. Bibbee. 1997. "Taxation and Economic Performance." Working Paper No. 176, OECD, Paris.

Nickell, S. J., and R. Layard. 1999. "Labour Market Institutions and Economic Performance." In *Handbook of Labor Economics*, vol. 3, ed. O. Ashenfelter and D. Card, 3029–3084. Amsterdam: North-Holland.

Nickell, S. J., L. Nunziata, W. Ochel, and G. Quintini. 2003. "The Beveridge Curve, Unemployment and Wages in the OECD from the 1960s to the 1990s." In *Knowledge, Information and Expectations in Modern Macroeconomics: In Honor of Edmund S. Phelps*, ed. P. Aghion, R. Frydman, J. Stiglitz, and M. Woodford, 394–431. Princeton: Princeton University Press.

Nicoletti, G., and S. Scarpetta. 2001. "Interactions between Product and Labour Market Regulations: Do They Affect Employment? Evidence from OECD Countries." Paper presented at the Banco de Portugal Conference on Labour Market Institutions and Economic Outcomes, Cascais, June 3–4.

OECD 1990. *Employment Outlook*. Paris: OECD.

OECD 2002. *Employment Outlook*. Paris: OECD.

OECD 1994. *The OECD Jobs Survey, Evidence and Explanations*, vols. I and II. Paris: OECD.

Padoa-Schioppa Kostoris, F. 1992. "A Cross-country Analysis of the Tax Push Hypothesis." Working Paper No. 92/11, IMF, Washington, D.C.

Pissarides, C. 1998. "The Impact of Employment Tax Cuts on Unemployment and Wages; the Role of Unemployment Benefits and Tax Structure." *European Economic Review* 47: 155–183.

Planas, C., W. Roger, and A. Rossi. 2003. "How Much Has Labour Taxation Contributed to European Structural Unemployment?" European Commission, Economic Papers No. 183, May.

Prescott, E. C. 2002. "Why Do Americans Work So Much and Europeans So Little?" University of Minnesota, May.

Scarpetta, S. 1996. "Assessing the Role of Labour Market Policies and Institutional Settings on Unemployment: A Cross-country Study." *OECD Economic Studies* 26: 43–98.

Tyrväinen, T. 1994. "Real Wage Resistance and Unemployment: Multivariate Analysis of Cointegrating Relations in Ten OECD Economies." OECD Jobs Study Working Paper Series, OECD, Paris.

Werding, M. 2004. "Assessing Old-age Pension Benefits: The Rules Applied in Different Countries." *CESifo Dice Report* 2, no. 2 (Summer): 55–63.

3

Do Social Policies Harm Employment and Growth? Second-best Effects of Taxes and Benefits on Employment

Frederick van der Ploeg

3.1 Introduction

Many governments in western Europe have during the eighties and nineties pursued a neoliberal agenda of rolling back the welfare state and improving economic incentives. This involved trimming public spending in order to reduce tax rates in the hope of boosting employment and output. It often also involved overhauls of systems of income taxation by cutting marginal tax rates and scrapping various deductibles. The objective of lowering the progression of tax systems was to improve incentives to work and to boost the economy. Part of the agenda also involved downsizing the welfare state by cutting unemployment benefits or making eligibility conditions tougher. This neoliberal political agenda was condoned by many economists and adopted by a large number of conservative, Christian democratic, and "Third-Way" social-democratic political parties throughout Europe.

Many of these ideas have not been carefully analyzed. They make sense in economies with competitive, Walrasian labor markets, and perhaps also in noncompetitive labor markets with an elastic labor supply of individual workers. Real-world labor markets are far from Walrasian. They feature trade unions with sufficient power to set wages; firms that like to pay fair wages to boost morale, motivation, and productivity; and a mismatch between vacancies and unemployment.

In such a second-best world, social policies (e.g., redistributive policies) may boost employment, since one distortion (a progressive tax system) partially offsets another distortion (arising from the rents in non-Walrasian labor market). Social policy interacts with nontax distortions. These may result from labor market imperfections in economies with search frictions and commitment problems, the market power of trade unions, or efficiency wages arising from problems of moral hazard and or adverse selection. Social policy may also interact with imperfections in insurance markets and political distortions. A higher ratio of unemployment benefits to wages typically raises the unemployment rate in competitive and noncompetitive labor markets. However, benefits are neither indefinite nor unconditional. Benefits do not necessarily destroy jobs in such situations. Social policies may exacerbate nontax distortions, since they may reduce incentives to work and invest in education and skills. Social policies may thus lower productivity and encourage tax evasion, making it harder to finance a generous welfare state. In this chapter I highlight some cases where social policies alleviate nontax distortions.

Section 3.2 discusses the adverse effects of a higher burden of taxation and redistributive policies in the benchmark case of competitive, Walrasian labor markets. Section 3.3 investigates the effects of the tax burden, a more progressive tax system, and a higher ratio of unconditional benefits to wages in non-Walrasian labor markets characterized by trade unions, efficiency wages, and/or search frictions. The incidence of taxation depends crucially on the properties of the welfare state—in particular, on whether benefits are indexed to after-tax wages and on whether the unemployed enjoy untaxed income. If benefits are indexed or, more precisely, if unemployed people share fully in the tax burden, unemployment is unaffected by changes in average income or payroll taxes. A higher tax burden pushes up unemployment if the unemployed escape part of the tax burden. More progressive tax systems induce wage moderation and boost employment in these non-Walrasian settings of the labor market. Section 3.3 considers other efficiency arguments in favor of progressive taxation. Section 3.4 applies the shirking theory of unemployment to show that higher unemployment benefits may lower the unemployment rate and raise the vacancy rate if benefits are only granted to people who become involuntarily unemployed while voluntary quits and dismissed shirkers are not entitled to unemployment benefits. Conditional unemployment benefits may thus spur job growth. Section 3.5 briefly discusses why bashing trade unions may harm employment unless one goes the whole way and gets rid of them completely. It also highlights the potential merits of corporatism. Section 3.6 analyses the differential effects of various types of public spending cuts on employment and economic growth. In particular, the effects of scrapping public employment are contrasted with cutting public spending on private goods. Section 3.7 discusses the political economy of redistributive policies. If the distribution of income and assets is more equal, the median voter outcome leads to less populist policies that resort not as much to distortionary taxes on labor income and capital and the inflation tax. In such a political-economic equilibrium, a more equal distribution of income and assets induces higher labor supply, higher growth and lower inflation. Section 3.8 concludes.

3.2 The Benchmark Case: Walrasian Labor Markets

In order to assess the effects of social policies on employment and output in non-Walrasian labor markets, we first present the benchmark case of Walrasian labor markets with undifferentiated, homogenous labor and perfect competition.

Each household derives utility $U(C, V)$ from private consumption C and leisure V. We assume that the utility function is concave and homothetic. We normalize so that each household has one unit of time available, which can be used to work H hours or to enjoy leisure $V = 1 - H$. For simplicity, we assume that households only have wage income. Hence, their budget constraint is $C = W_A H$, where $W_A \equiv (1 - T_A)W$ stands for the after-tax wage, W is the pretax wage, and T_A denotes the average tax rate. Each household maximizes utility by setting the marginal rate of substitution between leisure and consumption equal to the marginal consumer wage, that is, $U_V/U_C = (1 - T_M)W$, where T_M denotes the marginal tax rate on labor income. Loglinearizing (ignoring constants and using $\log(1 - T_i) \cong -T_i$, $i = A, M$) this first-order condition and the household budget constraint yields labor supply:

$$\log(H) = \varepsilon_U \log(W) - \varepsilon_C T_M - \varepsilon_I T_A,$$

where $\varepsilon_I \equiv -V < 0$ is the income elasticity, $\varepsilon_C \equiv \sigma V > 0$ is the compensated wage elasticity, $\varepsilon_U \equiv (\sigma - 1)V = \varepsilon_C + \varepsilon_I$ is the uncompensated wage elasticity of labor supply, and $\sigma \equiv -\mathrm{d} \log(C/V)/\mathrm{d} \log(U_C/U_V) > 0$ denotes the elasticity of substitution between leisure and consumption goods.

A higher pretax wage has two effects. First, it makes leisure relatively more expensive than consumption goods and thus encourages substitution away from leisure and encourages each household to work more. Second, it makes each household richer so that it consumes less leisure and fewer consumption goods and thus work less. If the former (i.e., the substitution effect measured by ε_C) dominates the latter (the income effect measured by ε_I), that is, if $\sigma > 1$, a higher wage increases labor supply. Otherwise, that is, if $\sigma < 1$, the labor supply curve bends backward.

Only the income effect is relevant for changes in the *average* tax rate; hence, a higher average tax rate makes people poorer and thus makes them work harder. In contrast, only the substitution effect is relevant for changes in the marginal tax rate. A higher *marginal* tax rate thus encourages substitution toward leisure and reduces incentives to work. It is helpful for the discussion to define the following measure of the progression of the labor income tax:

$$S \equiv d \log(W_A)/d \log(W) = (1 - T_M)/(1 - T_A).$$

This measure S is the coefficient of residual income progression and gives the percentage increase in the after-tax wage resulting from a 1 percent increase in the pretax wage. Because most tax systems are progressive and allow for many deductibles, the marginal tax rate is typically higher than the average tax rate and thus $S < 1$. A more progressive tax system for a given average tax rate corresponds to a reduction in S, which depresses labor supply:

$$\log(H) = \varepsilon_U[\log(W) - T_A] + \varepsilon_C \log(S) = \varepsilon_U \log(W_A) + \varepsilon_C \log(S),$$

where $\log(S) \approx T_A - T_M$. For a given degree of tax progression S, a higher average tax rate only raises labor supply if the income effect dominates the substitution effect. It is the after-tax wage that matters for labor supply. There are N households, so aggregate labor supply equals NH.

Firms maximize profits under perfect competition. The optimal level of employment L follows from setting the marginal productivity of labor to the product wage, that is $F'(L) = (1 + T_L)W$ where $F(L)$ is a standard production function with diminishing returns to scale ($F' > 0, F'' < 0$) and T_L denotes the payroll tax firms have to pay. Hence, labor demand falls if the pretax wage or the payroll tax rises:

$$\log(L) = -\varepsilon_D[\log(W) + T_L],$$

where $\varepsilon_D \equiv -(1 + T)W/F''L > 0$ is the wage elasticity of labor demand.

In a competitive labor market, the wage adjusts until labor demand L equals labor supply NH. This yields the following expressions for the producer wage and the consumer wage:

$$\log((1 + T_L)W) = [\varepsilon_U(T_A + T_L) - \varepsilon_C \log(S)]/(\varepsilon_U + \varepsilon_D),$$

$$\log(W_A) = [-\varepsilon_D(T_A + T_L) - \varepsilon_C \log(S)]/(\varepsilon_U + \varepsilon_D).$$

In an economy with a competitive, Walrasian labor market, it thus does not matter for employment whether taxes are imposed on firms or workers (or indeed on consumers). A higher payroll tax on firms is partially shifted to workers by lowering the wage, particularly if labor demand is relatively elastic and labor supply inelastic. In that case, the fall in employment is relatively small. A higher average tax on workers depresses the after-tax wage, but not fully, since firms have to pay a higher wage. Clearly, the burden of this tax rise is shifted to firms, especially if labor supply is relatively elastic and labor demand inelastic. The higher labor income tax rate then causes a relatively large drop in employment. In fact, microeconometric studies of labor supply suggest that labor supply for males is very inelastic ($\varepsilon_U \approx 0$), though for females the uncompensated wage elasticity may be small and positive. This suggests that, in practice, producer wages, employment, and output hardly change if the average income tax or the payroll tax changes and that the burden of taxation falls almost entirely on households. Even though labor supplies for males may be relatively inelastic on the *intensive* margin (i.e., hours worked), recent empirical work suggests that labor supply of especially low-skilled workers and single mothers may be rather elastic on the *extensive* margin (i.e., the participation decision); see Heckman 1993, Kimmel and Kniesner 1998, Meyer 2002, and Saez 2002. Part of the burden of labor taxation is then borne by firms as well.

A more progressive tax system (lower S) pushes up wages and depresses employment. The underlying disincentives operate through the substitution effect and are particularly strong if σ is large and people are already enjoying a lot of leisure.

An unconditional benefit (say, a tax credit or basic income) makes people work fewer hours, drives up the wage, and cuts employment and output. If this benefit is paid for by distortionary taxes on labor, the fall in employment and output is even greater. Unconditional benefits give people an incentive to enjoy leisure rather than to work. With competitive, Walrasian labor markets, social policies such as a higher tax rate to pay for, say, education or public health or a more progressive tax system, on the one hand, push up pretax wages and damage employment, and, on the other hand, depress after-tax wages. However, if benefits are taxed, an increase in the tax burden may boost the supply of labor. In fact, sections 3.3 and 3.4 show that the employment effects of taxation in non-Walrasian labor markets also depends on whether benefits (and other informal incomes) are taxed or not.

3.3   Progressive Taxation and Unemployment Benefits in Non-Walrasian Labor Markets

The competitive view of the labor market is not very realistic. Many economies experience "real" unemployment, not leisure or holidays disguised as unemployment. Most people can buy consumption goods as long as they are prepared to pay the market price and are thus not rationed. This is generally not the case in the labor market. Many jobs are not available to outsiders who offer to work at the going wage. Jobs, in contrast to most consumption goods, are rationed. In fact, wages are typically set by trade unions, by firms, or in negotiations between workers and firms rather than as the outcome of clearing labor markets. Also, macroeconometric evidence suggests that wages are not very sensitive to employment and that aggregate demand shocks induce large fluctuations in employment and output and almost no fluctuations in the real wage. This evidence in favor of real wage rigidity is at invariance with microeconometric evidence that suggests very low wage elasticities of labor supply. More realistic views of the labor market thus stress non-Walrasian features such as real wage rigidity— for example, Layard, Nickell, and Jackman 1991 and Heijdra and van der Ploeg 2002. This yields equilibrium with involuntary unemployment where *effective* labor supply is below *notional* labor supply. In this section I examine the effects of changes in the tax burden and in the progression of the tax system on wages, employment, and output within the context of non-Walrasian labor markets. In particular, I analyze the incidence of taxation and the effects of the degree of tax progression on employment in settings with trade unions, efficiency wages, and search frictions. Wages are set, respectively, by unions, by firms, and jointly by firms, and workers.

If the unemployed do not escape the burden of taxation, changes in the average labor tax rate do not affect the unemployment rate or the producer wage. However, if unemployment benefits are not fully indexed to after-tax wage income or the unemployed enjoy untaxed, informal income, the unemployed escape part of the burden of taxation. In that case, a higher tax rate on labor pushes up unemployment and wages. In non-Walrasian settings there is a surplus to be divided between firms and workers. Progressive taxes then tilt the balance in favor of less purchasing power and more jobs. This explains why in many econometric estimates of wage equations, higher average tax rates give rise to upward wage pressure while higher marginal tax rates induce downward wage pressure—see, for example, Lockwood and Manning 1993, Holmlund and Kolm 1995, and Lockwood, Sløk, and Trances 2000. The analysis also builds on Bovenberg and van der Ploeg 1994 and Pissarides 1998. Although we do not consider insider-outsider explanations of unemployment—for example, Lindbeck and Snower 2002—some of the results carry over to such settings. Insiders' positions are protected by rent-related labor turnover costs (mainly firing costs), and thus insiders will be able to bargain for higher wages than is necessary to recruit, retain, or motivate them. Insiders also insist on seniority rules ("last in, first out"), severance pay, advance notices of dismissal, and other terms of employment that diminish chances of outsiders. In a sense, the insider-outsider view explains the power of trade unions, and thus a move toward more progressive taxation is likely to boost jobs in the same way.

More generally, tax incidence under imperfect competition is discussed in Fullerton and Metcalf 2002. Tax incidence in general equilibrium models with nonlabor markets are discussed in Agell and Lundberg 1992 for the case of efficiency wages and in Davidson, Marin, and Matusz 1987 and 1988 for the case of search unemployment. Here I restrict my discussion to tax incidence (and the degree of tax progression) in partial equilibrium models of labor markets.

3.3.1 Trade Unions

Substantial parts of the labor force are unionized. In some countries trade union agreements are legally extended to all workers, thus making the power of trade unions even stronger. A competitive, Walrasian labor market obviously does not make sense then. One must allow for the power of trade unions to influence wages and employment. We do not examine right-to-manage and Nash bargaining models of trade unions (see, e.g., Booth 1995), but simply consider monopoly trade unions that have sufficient monopoly power in their sector of the labor market to set the wage for its members given knowledge of the labor demand curve. Firms subsequently take the wage set by the monopoly union as given when maximizing profits.

Right-to-manage models allow the trade union to bargain with firms over the wage, but not the level of employment. This does not change

the results very much, because the outcome is still on the labor demand curve. We assume middle-sized trade unions, which are big
enough to set wages but too small to internalize the adverse effects of
higher wages on prices and thus on purchasing power of their members. The unions are also too small to engage in bargaining with the
government over taxation, benefits, child care, pensions, training, and
other matters that may concern employees. In other words, trade
unions do not internalize the government budget constraint and thus
ignore the (small) effects of a rise in the wage on, say, taxes and unemployment benefits the government might set and thus indirectly on the
welfare of trade union members; however, see section 3.5. The welfare
of trade union members is captured by a utilitarian welfare function,
or, equivalently, by an expected utility approach where L/N denotes
the probability of being employed and $U \equiv 1 - L/N$ the probability of
being unemployed.

Firms face a concave production function $Y = F(L)$, where Y denotes
output and L employment. Maximization of profits implies firms set
the marginal productivity of labor equal to the real producer wage,
that is, $F'(L) = (1 + T_L)W$, so the demand for labor is a decreasing
function of the producer wage. The monopoly trade union operates
under a Rawlsian "veil of ignorance" and maximizes expected utility
of its members. Alternatively, it chooses the wage to maximize the welfare of its members, $Lv(W_A) + (N - L)v(B)$, subject to the labor demand
curve, where $v' > 0$, $v'' < 0$, and B indicates the level of the unemployment benefit. This yields the following union wage markup:

$$[v(W_A) - v(B)]/[W_A v'(W_A)] = S/\varepsilon_D.$$

The left-hand side gives the difference in utility of an employed and an
unemployed trade union member, converted from utility units into
production units and expressed as a fraction of the after-tax wage. The
right-hand side indicates that, given the level of the unemployment
benefit, this union wage markup is particularly large and thus unemployment is high if the wage elasticity of labor demand ε_D is low. Also,
given the level of the unemployment benefit, the union wage markup
falls and employment rises if the tax system becomes more progressive
(lower S). This result contrasts with that under competitive, Walrasian
labor markets. If the coefficient of relative aversion is unity, the union
wage markup yields $W_A = \exp(S/\varepsilon_D)B$. The unemployment benefit sets
a "floor" in the after-tax wage, so that a rise in the benefit immediately
translates into a rise in the wage and a fall in employment. For a given

degree of tax progression, a higher average tax rate on labor income T_A leaves the after-tax wage unaffected and thus the pretax wage rises. The after-tax wage displays real wage rigidity in the face of this shock, hence the whole burden of the labor income tax is borne by firms. An increase in the payroll tax to be paid by firms also leaves the after-tax wage unaffected, so labor costs rise and employment falls. Firms not workers carry the burden of taxation.

So far, we assumed that an unemployed trade union member is unable to find a job elsewhere in the economy and has to rely on unemployment benefit. It is realistic, especially for middle-sized trade unions, to assume that unemployed members have probability $1 - U$ of finding a job and probability U of being on the dole, where U denotes the unemployment rate. In that case, expected outside income, namely, $W_O = (1 - U)W_A + U(B + I)$ is the relevant alternative income and not the benefit B, where I stands for (utility of leisure or) untaxed income from the informal sector. Since $W_A - W_O = U(W_A - B - I)$, the income differential of a union job increases if the differential between the after-tax wage and the benefit plus informal income is high and if the chance of falling back on the dole is high (i.e., if the unemployment rate is high). With risk-neutral preferences (linear $v(.)$) we obtain the equilibrium unemployment rate:

$$U = (S/\varepsilon_D)/[1 - (B/W_A) - (I/W_A)].$$

Equilibrium unemployment is high if the replacement ratios for benefits $\rho \equiv B/W_A$ and informal income are high, the tax system is not so progressive and labor demand is fairly inelastic.[1] If benefits are indexed to after-tax wages and informal incomes are indexed to before-tax wages, $\rho_I \equiv I/W$, the equilibrium unemployment rate $U = (S/\varepsilon_D)/[1 - \rho - (\rho_I/(1 - T_A)]$ rises when the replacement rates for benefits and informal incomes rise and when the average tax rate rises. If benefits or informal incomes are not indexed, the preceding equation gives a wage-setting equation in which the wage rises with both the level of employment and the benefit. Together with the labor demand curve, one can solve simultaneously for employment and the wage. Although cuts in payroll taxes do not affect the unemployment rate if benefits are indexed to after-tax wages and informal incomes are absent, they raise the wage, boost employment, and reduce the unemployment rate if benefits are not indexed (cf. Bovenberg and van der Ploeg 1994; Pissarides 1998). Hence, if benefits are not indexed or the unemployed enjoy untaxed, informal income, the wage-setting

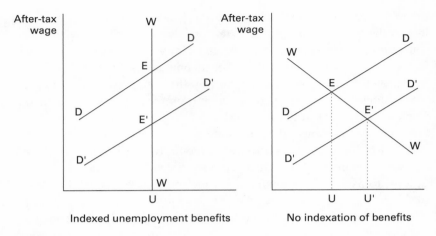

Figure 3.1
Indexation of benefits and incidence of taxes in noncompetitive labor markets

equation is flatter and payroll taxes boost employment by cutting the replacement rate and increasing the incentive to work (figure 3.1). Another way of putting it is that the effects of a higher average labor tax depend on whether unemployment benefits are taxed (rather than indexed) or, more precisely, the unemployed escape the burden of taxation. There is no increase in unemployment if the unemployed share fully in the higher tax burden, namely, if the outside option is fully taxed and the net replacement rate is not increased. Of course, it is then debatable whether this is a social policy and presumably the answer depends on time perspective and liquidity constraints. In practice, it is unlikely that the unemployed share fully in the tax burden. Unemployed people enjoy untaxed leisure and income in the informal economy, so that a higher average tax rate on labor destroys jobs.

The result that with a fixed after-tax replacement rate a more progressive tax system moderates wages and boosts employment and output also holds in a "right-to-manage" model where the wage follows from a Nash bargain between trade unions and firms and employment is subsequently set by firms. The ratio of the wage-bargaining outcome to outside income is again high if labor demand is fairly inelastic and the degree of tax progression is small. In addition, the wage is high if the "ability to pay" (as measured by the share of profits relative to that of wages) is high and the bargaining power of firms relative to that of unions is relatively weak. Also, imperfect competition in product markets lowers the wage elasticity of labor demand and bolsters the power of trade unions. Koskela and Vilmunen (1996) also show that more tax progression lowers wages and raises employment under efficient Nash bargaining between firms and unions. Aronsson, Löfgren, and Sjögren (2002) argue that tax progressivity boosts the wage and *does* harm employment within the context of a Ramsey growth sector with monopolistic households setting the wage as well as choosing consumption and saving subject to a labor demand schedule. However, their result does not allow for real unemployment and a union setting wages for its members behind a Rawlsian "veil of ignorance." Their result does not really differ from under perfect competition except that wages are set above the marginal rate of substitution between leisure and consumption. Tax progressivity simply implies that people demand more leisure and work less. This causes more underemployment, not more unemployment.

If unemployment benefits are indexed to after-tax wages and unemployed people share fully in the tax burden, changes in labor taxes do not affect unemployment and are fully borne by workers. However, Graafland and Huizinga (1999) offer evidence for the Netherlands that the tax rate adversely affects unemployment even after correcting for the effects of changes in the net replacement rate. Also, Daveri and Tabellini (2000) provide empirical evidence that suggests that changes in labor taxes are strongly correlated with changes in unemployment rates, particularly for those European countries with substantial unionization and less so for the Nordic European countries with centralized trade unions. One reason is that unemployed people enjoy both untaxed incomes from the informal sector and the utility of untaxed leisure. In that case, the *true* replacement rate is not constant and a higher tax wedge can boost unemployment even if productivity growth must be consistent with stationary unemployment (Bovenberg and van der Ploeg 1994, 1998; Sørensen 1997; and chapter 1, this volume).

These insights also hold for an open economy with international capital mobility and constant returns to scale in production. With interest rates determined on world markets, the producer wage is pinned down by the factor price frontier. A higher replacement rate or a less progressive tax system then reduces the demand for capital from abroad and the demand for labor but leaves the producer wage unaffected. The end result is the same: more unemployment.

3.3.2 Efficiency Wages

The main idea behind efficiency wages is that workers produce more output if they are paid more, so that firms can increase their profits by paying their workers more than the market-clearing wage. Typically, it is assumed that the efficiency of workers depends on the wages firms pay relative to opportunities in other firms and to income on the dole. This leads to leapfrogging, which is often observed in labor markets. With efficiency wages the wage is no longer determined by the marginal productivity of labor, namely, by the capital labor intensity and the state of technology, but by sociological considerations. The "law of one price" is repealed, so that inter-industry wage differences occur even if abilities (resulting from education, experience, etc.) are the same and jobs are equally unpleasant.

Firms want to pay relatively high wages in order to recruit, retain, and motivate workers. Typically, it is hard for firms to monitor the abilities and effort of its workers. However, by paying a bit more than elsewhere, firms can attack the problem of adverse selection by trying to improve the average quality of the workforce. This works if workers' reservation wages and abilities are positively correlated. Paying a "fair" wage makes people feel as though they are treated well, so it reduces work disruption and raises morale and work effort. Since high morale may be more important in some professions (pilots, firemen) than in others, homogenous labor earns different wages in different industries.

We thus assume that effort by workers in firm i depends on differences in indirect utility if one works and if one is without a job, so that effort depends on relative wages:

$$E_i = [v(W_{Ai}) - v(W_O)]^{\varepsilon} \quad \text{with} \quad W_O \equiv U(B+I) + (1-U)W_A$$
$$= \{1 - [1 - (B+I)/W_A]U\}W_A,$$

where $\varepsilon > 0$, W_{Ai} is the after-tax wage of a worker in firm i. The $v(.)$ represent the indirect utilities as before. Outside income of workers in firm i are with probability $(1-U)$ the after-tax wage elsewhere W_A if employed in another firm and with probability U unemployment benefit B plus informal income I. Effort thus depends on relative wages (leapfrogging). Effort also increases if the chance of becoming unemployed and experiencing a large drop in income is high, that is, if the unemployment rate U is high and the replacement rates are low.

Firm i faces a simple linear production function, $Y_i = E_i L_i$, so that output increases if the efficiency or the volume of labor increases. Firm i sets the wage it pays so as to maximize profits, $[E_i - (1 + T_L)W_i]L_i$, or equivalently to minimize the wage to ensure a given level of efficiency. This yields the wage markup set by firm i:

$$[v(W_{Ai}) - v(W_O)]/[W_{Ai}v'(W_{Ai})] = \varepsilon S,$$

where use has been made of $E_i = (1 + T_L)W_i$ in equilibrium. This leap-frogging formula shows that firm i sets relatively high wages if the efficiency wage effect ε is strong and the tax system is not very progressive. Also, more risk-averse workers imply that firms have to pay less to recruit, retain, and motivate workers. Again, in contrast to competitive, Walrasian labor markets, a more progressive tax system reduces the wage markup. Firms have in the margin less incentive to offer higher wages in order to boost morale and so forth if the government grabs a bigger slice of the wage rise. This makes it less attractive for workers to exert effort. In (symmetric) equilibrium, all firms pay the same, $W_{Ai} = W_A$, and the wage markup is $(1 - \rho)U$. Leapfrogging thus causes a higher unemployment rate. With risk-neutral preferences we obtain[2]

$$U = \varepsilon S/[1 - \rho - \rho_I/(1 - T_A)],$$

where $\rho \equiv B/W_A$ and $\rho_I \equiv I/W$. A bigger efficiency wage effect (higher ε), a higher replacement rate, a less progressive tax system (higher S) and, if there is untaxed informal income, a higher average rate all induce a higher unemployment rate. More risk aversion among workers also leads to a lower unemployment rate. A more progressive tax system boosts employment and output and reduces unemployment, since it is less attractive to pay high wages and to leapfrog other firms and for workers to do their best. Consequently, labor productivity and the pretax wage fall. This contrasts with competitive, Walrasian labor markets, where more progressive taxes destroy incentives to work more hours and lower employment and output. Indeed, if we allow for optimal choice of hours worked and efficiency wages, a more progressive tax system lowers labor supply per household (i.e., reduces hours worked per job), which generates upward wage pressure. Total demand for labor will not rise as much and may even fall. The number of jobs will rise despite the fact that each job has shorter working hours. This may be what some advocates of social policies have in mind, but the size of the national income need not necessarily rise.

To assess the effects on the unemployment rate, it is crucial to know what the characteristics of the welfare state are. If unemployment benefits are fixed automatically to after-tax wages (p fixed) and informal income is absent, a higher average income tax rate T_A or payroll tax T_L does *not* affect the unemployment rate (cf. section 3.3.1). However, if benefits or informal incomes are not indexed to after-tax wages, the unemployment rate is a decreasing function of after-tax wages and one needs the expressions for pretax and after-tax wages (ignoring constants) in order to assess the incidence of taxes and the effects on the unemployment rate:

$$\log(W) = [1/(1 - \varepsilon)][\varepsilon\{\log(S) - T_A\} - T_L] \quad \text{and}$$

$$\log(W_A) = [1/(1 - \varepsilon)][\varepsilon\log(S) - T_A - T_L].$$

If one considers an increase in taxation while keeping the degree of tax progression unchanged, the marginal and the average tax rates rise together and the pretax wage falls. After-tax wages then fall by more than 100 percent and thus workers bear more than 100 percent of the tax burden. Again, these results are very different from the standard ones for a competitive, Walrasian labor market. They also differ from the outcomes under a monopoly trade union, because there it was the firms rather than the workers who carried the burden of labor income taxation. This is not very surprising, since under monopoly unions workers set wages and under efficiency wages firms set wages. If unemployed benefits are not indexed to after-wages or the unemployed enjoy income from untaxed activities, a higher average labor income or payroll taxes depresses after-tax wages more than 100 percent, increases the replacement rate, and thus increases the unemployment rate. The effect of taxes thus depends crucially on the properties of the welfare state. The beneficial effects of a more progressive tax system— namely, wage moderation and a lower unemployment rate—are less if benefits are not indexed to after-tax wages, because then the replacement rate is pushed up by the fall in after-tax wages. Clearly, the components of the welfare state can not be seen in isolation.

3.3.3   Search and Matching Frictions

We now consider the effects of taxation and benefits in a non-Walrasian economy in which it is costly and takes time to match preferences, skill, and needs. Unemployment results, since it takes time to match vacancies and the unemployed. Jobs and workers are heterogeneous. Each job corresponds to a match between one firm and one worker. Nash bargaining between the worker and the firm divides the surplus of the match. We abstract from on-the-job search. This economy with search frictions is based on Pissarides 1990.

Let N denote the number of workers, U the unemployment rate, V the vacancy rate, and X the matching rate. The constant-returns-to-scale and concave matching function $G(.)$ gives the number of matches being made: $XN = G(UN, VN)$. The instantaneous probability of a job being filled thus equals $q \equiv XN/VN = G(U/V, 1) \equiv q(\theta)$, where $\theta \equiv V/U$ denotes the vacancy unemployment ratio ("labor-market tightness") and $q' < 0$. We assume $0 < -\theta q'/q < 1$. Equilibrium in the "bathtub" of unemployed requires that expected inflow $s(1 - U)N$, where s stands for the exogenous job separation rate, equals expected outflow of the pool of unemployed $q(\theta)VN$. Using $V = \theta U$, we obtain the Beveridge curve:

$$U = s/[s + \theta q(\theta)].$$

A low separation rate s or, alternatively, legal restrictions on firing a worker (cf. Saint-Paul 1996) and a tighter labor market (higher θ) lower the unemployment rate.

Output follows from a concave, constant-returns-to-scale production function $F(K, 1)$, where K denotes the firm's capital stock. Free entry and exit of firms drives the value of a vacant job to zero, so in equilibrium firms do not make profits. This yields the zero-profit condition:

$$[F_L(K, 1) - (1 + T_L)W_A/(1 - T_A)]/(R + s) = \gamma/q(\theta),$$

where R denotes the interest rate and the constant γ indicates search costs per unit of time. The left-hand side shows that the value of an occupied job equals the present value of the rents or surplus of a job, for as long the job is expected to last. This must in equilibrium equal the right-hand side, that is, the expected value of search costs being the search costs γ times the expected duration of a vacancy $1/q(\theta)$. The demand for capital follows from the condition that the marginal productivity of capital equals the user cost of capital, that is, $F_K(K, 1) = R + \delta$, where δ denotes the depreciation rate of the capital stock.

The wage follows from maximizing the Nash product, that is, the weighted average of the log of the surplus of the worker and that of the firm $\beta \log(V_E - V_U) + (1 - \beta) \log(V_O - V_V)$, where V_E, V_U,

$V_O = [F_L - (1 + T)W_L]/(R + s)$ and $V_V = 0$ denote, respectively, the value of an employed worker, the value of an unemployed worker, the value of an occupied job, and the value of a vacant job. The weight β denotes relative bargaining strength of the worker, and $1 - \beta$ that of the firm. The annuity value of an employed worker equals $RV_E = W_A - s(V_E - V_U)$, that is, the after-tax wage minus the expected loss in value if the job is lost. V_U is taken as given. Since $V_E - V_U = (W_A - RV_U)/(R + s)$, we obtain the optimal rent-sharing condition

$$(1 - \beta)(1 + T_L)(V_E - V_U) = \beta(1 - T_M)(V_O - V_V).$$

If we abstract from informal incomes, the value of an unemployed worker is given by

$$RV_U = B + \theta q(\theta)(V_E - V_U),$$

which says that the reservation wage of an unemployed worker (RV_U) equals the unemployment benefit plus the expected increase in value if a job match occurs. Substitution of the expressions for the various value functions into the rent-sharing condition yields the following Nash bargaining outcome for the wage:

$$W_A = [(1 - \beta)B + \beta S\{F_L(K, 1) + \theta\gamma\}(1 - T_A)/(1 + T_L)]/[1 - \beta(1 - S)].$$

The worker gets an average of the unemployment benefit and the surplus, where the surplus is the sum of the marginal productivity of labor and the expected search costs that are saved if the deal is struck (i.e., average hiring costs per unemployed worker). The worker can ask more from the firm, since he knows the firm has to incur search costs if it has to look for another job match when the deal is not struck. If the worker has most of the bargaining strength (β close to one), the worker is able to extract most of the surplus. If the firm is very strong (β close to zero), the worker must make do with a wage close to the unemployment benefit.

The solution is recursive: first solve for K from $F_K = R + \delta$, then solve simultaneously for W and θ from the zero-profit and Nash bargaining conditions, and finally compute U and V from the Beveridge curve. Some of the comparative statics results are familiar. An increase in the unemployment benefit or an increase in the relative bargaining strength of the worker induces a higher wage bargain, but does not shift the zero-profit condition or the Beveridge curve. The new wage bargain pushes up the after-tax wage, diminishes labor market tight-

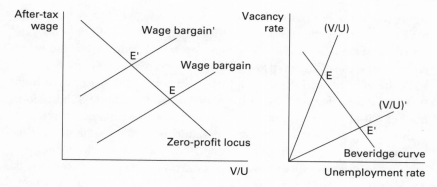

Figure 3.2
Effects of higher unemployment benefits, greater bargaining strength of workers, or less progressive taxation in labor markets with search and matching

ness, reduces the vacancy rate, and increases the unemployment rate (figure 3.2). A fall in the job destruction rate or tougher firing regulations (cf. Saint-Paul 1996) (lower s) shifts out the Beveridge curve in $V - U$ space *and* shifts out the zero-profit condition in $W_A - \theta$ space. This can be shown to raise the power of workers and push up after-tax wages, make the labor market tighter, raise the vacancy rate, and increase the unemployment rate. In this particular model the fall in the firing rate is thus outweighed by the fall in the hiring rate. The point is that, if it is more difficult to fire workers, firms react by hiring fewer workers. Conversely, more labor market flexibility lowers the unemployment rate.

Indexing unemployment benefits yields a steeper wage bargaining locus (albeit not vertical as in sections 3.3.1 and 3.3.2). Hence, the adverse effects of, say, tougher firing regulations on the equilibrium unemployment rate are weakened. A lower job destruction rate thus yields a bigger increase in after-tax wages of those lucky enough to keep their job.

A less progressive tax system (higher S for given T_A) induces a higher wage bargain, since pushing for higher wages is no longer punished so severely by progressive taxes in the margin. Consequently, the wage is pushed up and the labor market becomes less tight. This lowers the vacancy rate and raises the unemployment rate, again the opposite of what happens in competitive, Walrasian labor markets. Conversely, a more progressive tax system encourages wage moderation and results in a higher vacancy rate and a lower unemployment rate, as in figure 3.2. If unemployment benefits are not indexed to after-tax wages (or the unemployed enjoy untaxed income), a higher average tax rate on labor income T_A and a higher payroll tax T_L shift down the wage equation because higher taxes lower after-tax wages. They also shift back the zero-profit locus, since they reduce the ability to pay a high wage. The net effect is a fall in the after-tax wage and a less tight labor market with a lower vacancy rate and a higher unemployment rate.

Bovenberg and van der Ploeg (1994) and Bovenberg (chapter 1, this volume) discuss the employment effects of tax changes in economies with trade unions, efficiency wages, or search frictions when benefits are indexed to producer prices, consumer prices, and market wages. They also discuss the effects of changes in consumer taxes and productivity shocks.

There is a case for conditioning unemployment benefits on imperfectly observed search efforts (Boone et al. 2001). In particular, it is optimal to monitor search efforts and to sanction workers who do not search sufficiently. The sanction could be to reduce the income from unemployment benefit (i.e., unemployment insurance) to welfare (i.e., unemployment assistance). Risk aversion is necessary to get this result. Otherwise, if monitoring is costly, it is optimal to raise the sanction indefinitely and reduce the monitoring rate to an arbitrarily small number. Shavell and Weiss (1979) and Fredriksson and Holmlund (2001) argue that the optimal benefit should fall with the duration of the unemployment spell in order to stimulate search activities. However, Cahuc and Lehmann (2000) demonstrate that this induces wage pressure and strengthens insider power in wage negotiations and thus diminishes the case for a declining unemployment benefit. Also, Hopenhayn and Nicolini (1997) show that the wage tax upon reemployment should rise with the duration of the unemployment spell.

3.3.4   Other Efficiency Arguments for Progressive Taxation

The real world does not have Walrasian markets. Markets are distorted in many ways. Markets may fail or disappear altogether if there are legal restrictions, institutional rigidities, high transaction costs, external effects, adverse selection, and moral hazard problems arising from asymmetric information and/or imperfect competition. In the real world prices need not equal marginal costs and labor may well be paid a wage higher than its marginal product. There are rents to be shared between employers and employees. In such a second-best world, it is not clear that reducing one distortion improves welfare. In fact, it may happen that the distortion arising from a more progressive tax system offsets the distortion arising from an imperfectly functioning labor market.

Indeed, in the presence of trade union power, efficiency wage, and/or search frictions, a more progressive tax system tends to moderate wages and boost employment. The boost to the number of jobs may be enhanced, since a more progressive tax system typically reduces the number of hours worked per employee. Indeed, Sørensen (1999) shows that a union concerned with the employment of its members restricts working hours below the level that the individual employed member would prefer at the going after-tax wage. Since tax progression drives an additional wedge between the marginal disutility of work and the marginal productivity of labor, hours worked per worker falls and labor supply is further distorted. Wage moderation boosts employment, that is, the total hours of labor demanded by firms. Together with the induced shorter working week, this boosts the total number of jobs in the economy. Labor supply effects thus remain important in non-Walrasian labor markets. In fact, it is a priori not clear what happens to unemployment. We need to closely examine the evidence from microeconometric studies, since some agents may face high marginal tax rates and exhibit elastic labor supply (chapter 1, this volume). In any case, it is better to focus on the employment effects, which also seems more relevant in the analysis of problems arising from the aging of the population. Cross-country comparisons of employment are also easier for statistical reasons.

Many politicians are concerned about the unequal distribution of labor within the family. Men typically work more hours in the labor market than women, but engage in less shopping, child care, and other household chores. A more progressive tax system has, if the tax system is individualized, the added benefit that the partner who works most hours is stimulated to work less while the other partner is encouraged to work more hours on the labor market. Hence, a more progressive tax system can contribute to a more equal distribution of labor between men and women in the family.

Failing capital and insurance markets may also provide efficiency grounds for progressive taxation (van Ewijk et al. 2003). Future labor income is usually not accepted by commercial banks as a guarantee for a loan, since people cannot be forced to work and pay back in the future. Problems of adverse selection imply that good risks do not borrow, thus the bad risks remain. As a result, interest rates go up and credit is rationed (Stiglitz and Weiss 1981). People thus are unable to borrow when they are young and to smooth consumption over their lifespan. Progressive taxes redistribute incomes from when people are old and earn a lot to when people are young and do not earn a lot. In this sense, a progressive tax system acts as an implicit credit market and thus alleviates some of the distortions of rationed credit markets (cf. Hubbard and Judd 1986). Rationing of credit particularly hurts students with poor parents. This is bad for society, since the full potential of human capital remains underdeveloped. Since a progressive tax system also redistributes from rich to poor parents, it alleviates some of the adverse effects of credit rationing on schooling (Jacobs 2003).

Insurance markets fail to fully insure the risks of losing income if people become ill, disabled, or unemployed. People typically have a better knowledge of their own chances of becoming ill, disabled, or unemployed than do insurance companies. The good risks thus leave the market and the insurance companies are left with the bad risks. Insurance premiums go up while some insurance markets disappear altogether (Rothschild and Stiglitz 1976). As a result, people engage in less risky jobs and activities. Since a progressive tax system also redistributes income from people with good luck to people with bad luck, it also corrects to a certain extent for failing insurance markets (cf. Sinn 1995). A progressive tax system also encourages risk-averse people to invest in risky studies (Eaton and Rosen 1980).

Increasingly, economists have come to realize that people's happiness does not depend on money and absolute levels of consumption alone (van de Stadt, Kapteyn, and van de Geer 1985). For example, job satisfaction of British workers is only weakly correlated with absolute income, but decreases if reference wages of other comparable workers increase (Clark and Oswald 1998). People feel better if they do better than their peers. Money can buy happiness, but the well being of people depends on relative income as well and is badly affected by unemployment and divorce (Blanchflower and Oswald 2003). Abundance resulting from economic growth evidently makes some people unhappier and others more content. In fact, for neoclassical economics with its emphasis on selfishness, it is a puzzle why abundance breeds discontent.

Understanding this puzzle requires one to consider habituation and the importance of relative positions for happiness (Layard 1980, 2003). Habituation implies that people quickly adjust to higher living standards and find it difficult to adjust downward. Hence, improvements in material living standards make people happy for a while but the effect quickly fades. Extra money does not necessarily make people better off either, because people tend to compare their lot with others. If everybody works hard to get more income and spend more, they do not necessarily become happier. The extra income earned makes other people unhappy, so this adverse externality should be corrected for by a progressive tax on labor income. Moreover, to a certain extent, people tend to engage in a wasteful rat races, which leaves less room for leisure and provides additional grounds for progressive taxes (Akerlof 1976). Developed societies thus have a tendency to work too hard, engage in rat races, consume too much, and enjoy too little leisure. Efficiency can be improved with a progressive tax system (also see section 3.7).

I have given many arguments why social policies and redistributive taxation may alleviate nontax distortions in second-best economies, but I stress that social policies such as progressive taxation also exacerbate nontax distortions and may reduce output. They distort markets, reduce the incentive to work, and can exclude many people from the labor markets. If unemployment benefits are taxed or the unemployed enjoy untaxed, informal income, tax progression raises the *effective* net replacement rate and can thus induce wage pressure and destroy jobs. If labor supply is endogenous, the effect of progressive taxation on employment is ambiguous. Tax progression may harm the incentive to invest in training and human capital, so that it may lower the productivity of the economy. Tax progression may also encourage tax evasion, reduce working hours, lower productivity by lowering the employers' optimal efficiency wage relative to the level of unemployment benefit, and lower the efficiency of the job matching process by reducing workers' expected marginal return to job search. Even if employment rises with more tax progression, output may fall and finance of a generous welfare state may become more difficult. Conversely, a by-product of a less progressive tax system is that some low-wage earners may face higher average and marginal tax rates. Since low-wage earners are likely to have relatively elastic labor supplies, the OECD (1995) argues that the efficiency costs of taxation may actually increase rather than decrease.

Sørensen (1999), Røed and Strøm (2002), and Bovenberg (chapter 1, this volume) rightly point out that, in general, there is an optimal degree of tax progression. It is an empirical matter to find out whether the efficiency grounds for social policies dominate the costs of market distortions. All we can say is that the case for social policies may be greater in economies plagued by many nontax and nonbenefit distortions.

3.4   Unemployment Benefits, Shirking, and the Reserve Army of Unemployed

So far, unemployment benefits have been modeled in the way that it is normally done in the literature. Atkinson (2002), however, rightly argues the case for dealing properly with the institutional details of the welfare state. It is clearly not realistic to model unemployment benefits as indefinite and unconditional "income during unemployment." Most countries require workers to have worked a certain period in order to qualify for benefit and do not offer benefits to people who have become unemployed after voluntary quits or misconduct. Furthermore, one is only eligible for an unemployment benefit if the claimant makes a serious effort to search and is available for employment if suitable job offers are made. Typically, one can reject job offers a number of times, but eventually one must accept a job offer. The duration of unemployment benefits is often limited to a number of years. Afterward, unemployed people may get welfare assistance, which is unrelated to the wage, that one once earned as an employee. In practice, low-skilled workers benefit from welfare more or less indefinitely as eligibility conditions are seldom policed, especially not in deep recessions when the chance of finding a job is very low. If the conditions can be policed, conditional benefits and active labor market policies imply substantial administrative costs.

To understand the consequences of rolling back the welfare state, we must allow for these real-life features of unemployment benefit systems. If we merely treat benefits as indefinite and unconditional income, we are bound to overestimate the adverse effects of unemployment benefits on unemployment. To make the point that conditional unemployment benefits may boost employment, we modify the no-shirking efficiency wages theory of unemployment and moral hazard developed by Shapiro and Stiglitz (1984). We assume that workers who have been fired for misconduct (shirking) are not entitled to an unemployment benefit, while people who get laid off through no fault of their own do qualify for a benefit. For simplicity, we abstract from the effects of taxes. Unemployment arises, because the impossibility of monitoring workers precisely causes a moral hazard problem of workers having a potential incentive to shirk. Firms avoid shirking by paying more than the market-clearing wage.

Let s be the exogenous separation rate, that is, the instantaneous probability of a worker having to leave job without fault of its own, and let h be the endogenous instantaneous probability of an unemployed person finding a job. Due to asymmetric information, firms are unable to perfectly monitor whether workers are doing what is expected of them or not, so let q be the instantaneous additional probability of a worker being detected and fired if caught shirking. We focus on steady-state analysis and flow equilibrium, so ignore the dynamics of unemployment. The inflow into the pool of unemployed thus equals the outflow, so that $s(1 - U) = hU$. The unemployment rate $U = s/(s + h)$ increases in the separation rate s and decreases with the probability of finding a job h.

Since we focus on the steady state, we abstract from capital gains in the value of nonshirking and shirking workers and the transient dynamics in the number of unemployed individuals. Hence, the (expected) value of a worker who does not shirk is given by

$$V_W = [W - d + (1 - s)V_W + sV_B]/(1 + R) = (W - d + sV_B)/(R + s),$$

where R stands for the interest (discount) rate and V_B indicates the (expected) value of an unemployed person who is entitled to a conditional benefit. The value of a worker is in steady state equal to the present value of his earnings W *minus* the disutility of work d *plus* his expected value next period. During the next period he is employed with probability $1 - s$ and then has value V_W, and he is unemployed with probability s and value V_B.

On the one hand, the (expected) value of a shirker V_S is higher because he does not suffer the disutility of work. On the other hand, the value of a shirker is lower because he has an additional probability q of being caught and dismissed and is then not entitled to the conditional unemployed benefit:

$$V_S = [W + (1 - s - q)V_S + sV_B + qV_U]/(1 + R)$$
$$= (W + sV_B + qV_U)/(R + s + q),$$

where V_U denotes the (expected) value of an unemployed person who has been dismissed for misconduct and is not entitled to a conditional benefit. To make sure that employees have on average no incentive to shirk, $V_W \geq V_S$, firms pay workers just enough to prevent them from shirking:

$$W \geq RV_U + (R + s + q)d/q - s(V_B - V_U).$$

The last term on the right-hand side of this no-shirking condition does not appear in Shapiro and Stiglitz 1984. It shows that firms need to pay workers less to prevent them from shirking. Effectively, denying dismissed shirkers a conditional unemployment benefit raises the penalty of misconduct.

To complete the model, we need to know the value of the two types of unemployed. The value of a person who lost his job through no fault of his known is

$$V_B = [B + v + hV_W + (1 - h)V_B]/(1 + R) = (B + v + hV_W)/(R + h),$$

where v is the utility of leisure. The value of such a person during this period must in steady state equal the present value of utility of leisure plus the benefit plus, with probability h, the value when he finds a job, and, with probability $1 - h$, the value when he remains unemployed next period.

The value of a dismissed shirker V_U is lower than the value of other unemployed, since he is not entitled to an unemployment benefit:

$$V_U = [v + A + hV_W + (1 - h)V_U]/(1 + R)$$

$$= (v + A + hV_W)/(R + h) < V_B < V_S \leq V_W,$$

where A is the level of unconditional welfare assistance (or informal earnings in the shadow economy). We can use the expressions for V_W, V_B, and V_U to solve for these values and substitute them into the no-shirking condition. If we also substitute $h = s(1 - U)/U$ from the flow labor market equilibrium condition, we finally obtain the no-shirking condition:

$$W \geq v + A + d + (R + s/U)d/q - s(B - A)/[R + s(1 - U)/U].$$

The first three terms on the right-hand side show that the wage a firm needs to pay to prevent its workers from shirking is higher if the utility of leisure, welfare assistance (or informal earnings), and the disutility of work are high. The fourth term shows that, in addition, the firm has to pay workers more to prevent them from shirking if the job destruction rate is high, the unemployment rate is low, and the additional probability of being detected and dismissed q is small. Hence, if the

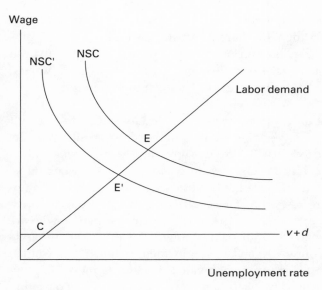

Figure 3.3
Higher conditional benefits B reduce shirking and boost employment

chance of being caught shirking is small or the probability of finding another job is large, the firm has to pay more to discipline workers given that they dislike work. This fourth term is the main reason why the no-shirking condition (NSC) in figure 3.3 slopes down. Effectively, a lower wage needs to be paid if unemployment is high.

The final term on the right-hand side of the no-shirking condition is new and is not in Shapiro and Stiglitz 1984. It shows, at first sight rather surprisingly, that a firm needs to pay less to prevent its employees from shirking if the conditional unemployment benefit is high relative to the unconditional welfare payment. The unemployment benefit is given only if the worker has lost his job through no fault of his own. A higher sanction for misconduct, namely, a bigger gap between the conditional and the unconditional benefit, raises the effective penalty of shirking, so firms can afford to pay workers less. Hence, a higher level of the conditional unemployment benefit boosts employment and output. Figure 3.3 shows that a higher conditional benefit B shifts the no-shirking condition down and thus reduces the wage, boosts employment, and lowers unemployment (move from E to E'). In contrast, a higher welfare payment shifts up the no-shirking condition and depresses employment. Note that equilibrium wages are higher than in the competitive outcome C, where wages are driven down to the unconditional welfare payment plus utility of leisure plus disutility of work. Equilibrium unemployment is thus higher than in the competitive outcome. Unemployment here is akin to the Marxist idea of the need to have a reserve army of unemployed in order to discipline workers.

The drop in the unemployment rate is even larger if there is a shift from unconditional to conditional unemployment benefits, namely, from earnings-related benefit to flat-sum welfare assistance ($dB = -dA > 0$). The penalty for shirking increases for two reasons. First, dismissed shirkers do not get the conditional benefit. Second, the unconditional welfare assistance falls and thus stimulates the incentive to work. This last incentive to work also increases for people who are unemployed through no fault of their own. These extra two effects mean that the fall in wages and unemployment is much greater than with a straight increase in unemployment benefit. If the unemployment benefit is financed by distortionary taxes, there will be offsetting adverse effects on employment and output.

In practice, unemployment benefits are conditional in other ways as well. They usually last for a limited period, and an unemployed person is only eligible if available for work and actively seeking a job. A "rough-and-ready" way to capture this is to assume that with probability $p > 0$, unemployment benefits are stopped. If there is no sanction for misconduct, the unemployed get the same benefit irrespective of whether they have been fired for industrial misconduct or not, $B = A$. In that case, the no-shirking condition becomes

$$W \geq [(R+h)/(R+h+p)]B + d + v + (R+s/U)d/q.$$

Since the unemployment benefit no longer lasts forever, the penalty for shirking and misconduct is *increased* and thus firms have to *pay less* to prevent workers shirking. Consequently, employment will be higher and the unemployment rate will be lower. On the other hand, if there is a sanction and with probability $p > 0$ the conditional benefit B is terminated and replaced by the everlasting, lump-sum welfare assistance A, the no-shirking condition becomes

$$W \geq v + d + A + (R+s/U)d/q - s(B-A)/[R+p+s(1-U)/U].$$

The main effect of limiting the duration of a conditional benefit is that the penalty for shirking and misconduct is *reduced* and that firms must *pay more* to ensure workers' discipline. As a result, the unemployment rate will be higher.

Another possible modification is to allow dismissed workers to have a smaller probability of finding a job than other unemployed. Since this raises the shirking penalty, firms have to pay less to prevent shirking. Consequently, equilibrium unemployment is lower. If lump-sum taxes are not available, a higher conditional benefit is typically paid for by a higher tax rate on labor. Obviously, this induces an offsetting adverse effect on unemployment.

In the model presented earlier nobody shirks, so all unemployed receive *conditional* unemployment benefits. With a continuum of heterogeneous workers $i \in [0, 1]$, which differ in their disutility of work d_i, firms set a wage just high enough to attract the least "lazy" workers:

$$d_i \leq \{W - A - v + s(B - A)/[R + s(1 - U)/U]\}/[1 + (R + s/U)/q]$$

$$\equiv d^*(W, v, A, B, U; Rq, s).$$

More lazy workers do not take a job. Firms set the wage to discipline just enough workers, so that $1 - U = F[d^*(W, v, A, B, U; Rq, s)]$ where $F[.]$ is the cumulative probability density function of d_i. This yields a similar no-shirking condition schedule as in figure 3.3, so that the comparative statics are qualitatively the same. However, if workers (who are not caught shirking) enjoy protection against firing, then a negative shock to labor demand after hiring has taken place induces workers with the highest disutility of work to stay on the job and shirk rather than quit. Some of them may be caught and end up on welfare rather than benefit, so the unemployment pool consists of dismissed shirkers and other unemployed who are entitled to a high benefit. The insight that a higher level of conditional benefit or a higher replacement rate reduces equilibrium unemployment does not change.

One critique that can be leveled at the analysis is that it is unclear that the government is able to monitor perfectly whether the employee has indeed been fired for misconduct or whether the employer and employee are just using it as an attractive way to stop their relationship. If the government runs the unemployment insurance scheme, there are additional problems of moral hazard and thus there are incentives to abuse the social insurance scheme. Of course, if the firm runs the unemployment insurance scheme itself, these problems would not arise.

The result that higher conditional benefits boost employment may carry over to other settings of noncompetitive labor markets (see

Atkinson 2002, chap. 4). Moreover, redundancy payments in a dynamic no-shirking model induce firms to fire less. This internalizes the externality arising from foregone rents imposed by firms on fired workers (Fella 2000).

More generally, conditional benefits seem to hurt employment less than unconditional benefits. In settings with search frictions a higher benefit harms employment, since those who search for a job are less likely to accept lower-wage jobs. In dividing the surplus of a job match, a bigger part of it goes to the worker, so wages are higher and employment lower. However, if unemployment benefits are of limited duration, the unemployed who search for a job are more likely to accept a job for fear of not finding a job and having to fall back on the lower welfare payment. Similarly, the harmful effects on employment are attenuated in a search context if the unemployed who want to be eligible for a conditional benefit face a work test and can only reject a job offer a maximum of, say, two or three times. In fact, when allowing for search in both labor and product markets in a general equilibrium context, a higher unemployment benefit induces firms to offer more high-wage jobs and may lower unemployment even if the benefit is unconditional (Axell and Lang 1990).

3.5 Corporatism

Many governments in the developed world have followed Ronald Reagan and Margaret Thatcher in reducing the power of trade unions. Trade unions are believed to interfere with the proper functioning of labor markets. The neoliberal advocates regard them as a public enemy, whose only interest is to push up wages for their members at the expense of employment and chances for outsiders to get a job. They also fear that different trade unions engage in leapfrogging, so it is important to be tough. The danger is that if one trade union succeeds in bargaining for higher wages, all the others will want higher wages as well. The question is whether this view of trade unions is a realistic one.

Some argue that trade unions, as long as they are big and powerful enough, will become more concerned with the general interest. They may try to internalize certain externalities, for example, by forsaking wage increases in favor of investment in training the workforce, child care facilities, and so forth. This may overcome free-riding problems such as a worker being trained in one firm leaving for another firm without a training program for a higher wage. In fact, Calmfors and Driffill (1988) argue that there is a hump-shaped relationship between the degree of centralization of trade union power and the unemployment rate. Countries with competitive labor markets (the United States, Canada, and the United Kingdom) have more wage competition and thus lower unemployment. Conversely, countries with a few big trade unions, whose power increases by extending coverage of the bargaining agreements to nonunionized workers as well (Austria, Sweden, and the Netherlands), show substantial wage moderation and have low unemployment. Countries with medium-sized trade unions (the rest of the European Union) suffer from upward wage pressure and have relatively high unemployment.

What are the reasons behind this hump-shaped relationship? The main one is that centralized trade unions internalize the adverse effects of higher wages on aggregate prices and thus on the purchasing power of trade union members. A small union realizes that an increase in wages for its members hardly has any effect on the aggregate price level, but a large professional union covering many industries anticipates that setting higher wages feeds into higher price levels. Consequently, large trade unions moderate wages more than medium-sized trade unions. They also engage less in leapfrogging. Big, professionally organized trade unions are more likely to internalize such adverse effects than are industrially organized trade unions.

Another reason for the hump-shaped relationship is that bigger trade unions are more likely to internalize the fiscal externalities implied by the government budget constraint. Hence, a big trade union anticipates that pushing up the wage causes unemployment and thus increases the benefit bill for the government. If benefits are indexed to wages, the price as well as the volume of benefits goes up, and thus the total cost to the government rises even more. In addition, if civil servants' salaries are indexed to market wages as well, the cost for the government goes up even more. Clearly, if the union pushes for a higher wage, the government will have to put up tax rates to balance the books (assuming that the tax base effect of a higher wage is relatively small to the three other effects just discussed). A big trade union knows that the consequences of pushing for higher wages is that taxes will have to be raised and that this will adversely effect the purchasing power of its members. Consequently, a big trade union is more likely to moderate wages, which will keep the unemployment rate low.

Alesina and Perotti (1997) suggest a related hump-shaped relationship, namely, that in relatively centralized labor markets the distortionary effects of fiscal policy are likely to be lower than in countries with intermediate degrees of labor market centralization. Larger trade unions are thus better able to internalize the fiscal externalities implied by the government budget constraint. Driffill and van der Ploeg (1993, 1995) show that globalization and more international product market integration reduce the power of trade unions. Effectively, opening up to international trade implies that domestic trade unions face more indirect competition from foreign trade unions, which drives down wages and spurs job growth. This suggests that countries in Europe may have moved more in the direction of less centralized trade unions. In general, deregulation and more competition on product markets reduces unemployment (cf. Blanchard and Giavazzi 2001).

Large unions care not only about internalizing wage-price spirals or fiscal externalities and combating free riding, but about reputation, and thus they have a longer time horizon. This way they can address commitment and holdup problems and avoid wage pressure. Unions concerned with their reputation may also wish to internalize their impact on outsiders, and thus abstain from insider pressure. Such unions may want to combat adverse selection and attempt to provide a better insurance against human capital risks such as disability. Corporatist unions may also internalize profit externalities and in this way help provide for occupational, funded pension schemes, but this may be more difficult in open economies.

3.6 Public Employment and Economic Growth

Musgrave (1959) and Atkinson (2002) stress the importance of analyzing the differential impacts on economic outcomes of the various categories of public spending. If one wants to cut back government, it matters *how* one rolls back the welfare state. Many governments have tried to do this by scrapping jobs for teachers, nurses, and policemen. Holmlund (1997), Finn (1998), Yann, Cahuc, and Zylberberg (2002), Alesina et al. (2002), and van der Ploeg (2006) give an analysis of the effects of public employment on macroeconomic outcomes. Instead of scrapping public employment, governments may cut spending on goods produced by the private sector. Both options enable a reduction in the tax rate and are meant to boost employment and output. However, the effects of cutting back public employment on private employment, consumption, investment, wages, and interest rates are very different from the macroeconomic effects of cutting back public consumption.

Alesina et al. (2002) find evidence to support the strong positive effects of cutting back public employment on private investment. A 1-percentage point cut in ratio of the public wage bill to GDP boosts the investment to GDP ratio by 0.48 percentage points on impact and by 2.56 cumulatively after five years. Rolling back the welfare state in this way reduces the demand for labor and exerts downward wage pressure. This induces firms to substitute away from capital toward labor. The lower capital intensity gives a higher return on private investment and raises the equilibrium interest rate. Both the substitution and the output effect raise private employment. If the decline in public employees permits a decline in the income tax rate, wages fall and the interest rate rises even further, thus leading to yet more private investment.

Van der Ploeg (2006) shows, within the context of a Ramsey model of economic growth with public and private employment, that it indeed matters how one rolls back the welfare state. If labor supply is inelastic, cutting public expenditures on private goods leads to immediate 100 percent crowding out of private consumption and thus leaves investment and capital accumulation, on the one hand, and wages and employment, on the other hand, unaffected. If labor supply is elastic, a temporary wage hike with a corresponding dip in the labor-capital ratio occurs. The associated dip in the capital intensity and the interest rate depresses saving and private investment. In the short run, more than 100 percent crowding out of private consumption occurs. In the long run, the lower capital stock depresses labor demand and the extra wealth of households reduces labor supply; hence, long-run employment falls. Conversely, if the government buys *more* goods from the private sector, employment and output rise.

Firing public employees leads, however, to temporary wage moderation and a lower capital intensity. The temporary hike in the interest rate boosts private saving and investment, thus raising capital in the long run. In the short run, there is less than 100 percent crowding out of private consumption. In the long run, the output effect is responsible for a boost to private-sector labor demand while the wealth effect depresses labor supply. Hence, the fall in public-sector employment is in the long run not fully offset by the rise in private sector-employment. These results may be used to comment on the situation where the government desperately tries to hire more nurses, teachers, and police personnel in a tight labor market. This pushes up wages and lowers interest rates, thus reducing the incentives to save and depressing private investment. In the end employment increases, because the fall in private-sector employment does not fully offset the gain in public-sector employment. These results for changes in public employment hold even if labor supply is inelastic. Changes in public employment thus have "first-order" welfare effects, while changes in public expenditures on private goods have "second-order" welfare effects. Cuts in public employment, in contrast to cuts in public spending on private goods, produce non-Keynesian effects in the sense that a fiscal contraction induces higher growth and more private-sector employment. Conversely, raising public employment reduces investment and harms employment and output.

If the savings in public revenue are handed back to the public in the form of a lower tax rate rather than lower tax credits, there is a further fall in the pretax wage and rise in the interest rate. This strengthens the investment boom resulting from a cut in public employment and attenuates the fall in saving and investment resulting from a cut in public spending on private goods. If a cut in public spending on private goods is associated with a cut in the tax rate, there is also an investment boom and increase in capital. The positive effects of the tax cut outweigh the negative effects of a cut in public spending on private goods.

The adverse effects of increasing public employment on investment and growth may be overturned in economies with endogenous growth (Barro and Sala-i-Martin 1999). If public employment raises the productivity of private workers, more public employment may stimulate saving and investment sufficiently to offset the adverse effects discussed earlier.

3.7 Political Economy of Redistribution

The recent literature on modern political economy, surveyed by Persson and Tabellini (2000), also details how social outcomes might affect the setting of economic policies and thus economic outcomes. It investigates the decisive role of the electorate on economic policy outcomes. Since the majority of the electorate decides in a democracy, attention is focused on median voter outcomes. A more unequal distribution of assets, incomes, and productivities leads to a poorer median voter who is more likely to vote for three kinds of "populist" policies. First, a poorer median voter will vote for more redistributive policies with higher marginal tax rates on labor, thus depressing employment and output (Romer 1975; Roberts 1977; Meltzer and Richard 1981). Second, a poorer median voter is more likely to resort to taxes on capital and thus to depress economic growth (Alesina and Rodrik 1994; Persson and Tabellini 1994). Third, a poorer median voter is more likely to resort to inflation taxes and to fuel inflation (Beetsma and van der Ploeg 1996). Each of these "populist" policies harms the economy and illustrates the merits of a more equal distribution of income and assets.

To illustrate how the political process endogenizes economic policy, consider the model of redistributive taxation put forward by Meltzer and Richard (1981) and discussed by Persson and Tabellini (2000). To keep matters simple, we assume a linear technology and normalize so that the pretax wage is equal to unity. Furthermore, we abstract from income effects in labor supply and assume quasi-linear preferences of worker i, that is $U_i = C_i + u(V_i)$, where the concave function $u(.)$ stands for utility of leisure. The budget constraint of worker i is $C_i = (1 - T_M)L_i + A$, where A is the tax credit. A more distributive policy requires a higher tax credit A financed by a higher marginal tax rate T_M. Worker i has a time constraint, $L_i + V_i = 1 + \Pi_i$, so that the time available for work and leisure equals 1 plus an individual-specific productivity Π_i. Hence, workers differ in their ability to work fast and enjoy leisure. Since the marginal utility of leisure is set to the after-tax wage, $u'(V_i) = 1 - T_M$, leisure of each worker is given by $V_i = v(T_M)$ with $v' = -1/u'' > 0$. Hence, leisure increases and labor supply falls if the marginal tax rate rises, that is, $L_i = 1 + \Pi_i - v(T_M)$. If Π denotes average productivity, average labor supply is $L = 1 + \Pi - v(T_M)$ and thus $L_i = L + \Pi_i - \Pi$. Labor supplies of different workers thus differ to the extent that their productivities differ. Effectively, more talented people work more hours, earn more, and consume more, but enjoy the same amount of leisure as less talented people.

The tax credits given to each individual A must be financed by taxes on labor $T_M L$, so that the indirect utility of worker-household i is given by

$$U_i = (1 - T_M)(\Pi_i - \Pi) + 1 + \Pi - v(T_M) + u(v(T_M)).$$

Since this utility function is single-peaked for each worker i, the median voter theorem holds. Hence, the median voter chooses the optimal tax rate (the Condorcet winner):

$$T_M = (\Pi - \Pi_{\text{median}})/v'(T_M).$$

The tax rate chosen in a democracy is higher if the adverse effect of the tax rate on labor supply (v') is small. This is the usual Ramsey tax rule, which says that relatively price-inelastic activities should be taxed more than others. Even more interesting, for a given average productivity level Π, more inequality (proxied by a lower Π_{median}) leads to a higher tax rate in a democracy. More inequality implies that the median voter is relatively poor and thus votes for a relatively large basic income and a large amount of redistribution. Hence, the marginal tax rate is relatively high and employment and output are relatively low. Conversely, a more equal distribution of productivities (and incomes) induces a political outcome with a lower tax rate and higher levels of employment and output. In general, the size of general redistributive programs reflect the preferences of the middle classes.

People care not only about absolute levels, but also about relative levels of consumption and income. Jealousy and keeping up with the Joneses are important features of human nature. People compete with each other to afford status goods and thus attempt to earn more than one another. A more realistic specification of preferences may thus be $U_i = C_i - \lambda C + u(V_i)$, with $0 < \lambda < 1$ and where C denotes the average consumption level. Hence, people feel worse off if other people consume more. Layard (2003) suggests that λ is about 0.3. Leisure is still given by $V_i = v(T_M)$, but utility of voter i is now given by $U_i = (1 - T_M)(\Pi_i - \Pi) + (1 - \lambda)[1 + \Pi - v(T_M)] + u(v(T_M))$. When jealousy and keeping up with the Joneses matter, the median voter sets the tax rate to

$$T_M = (\Pi - \Pi_{\text{median}})/v'(T_M) + \lambda.$$

The first term is the familiar selfish redistribution term discussed earlier. The second term λ in the expression indicates that the majority of the electorate judges progressive taxation to be a good thing, even if talents and pretax incomes are equally distributed. Since people compete to consume more than their neighbors do, they work too hard from a social perspective. To correct for this externality, labor is taxed progressively to make room for a society with more leisure and less consumption. The tax rate is at least 30 percent and even higher if there is inequality in talents and pretax incomes. The tax rate is thus the sum of a Pigovian term to correct for the consumption rat race and a redistributive term to correct for talent and pretax income inequality.

Investing in long-term education can lead to a narrowing of productivities among workers. In that case one obtains political outcomes with low tax rates and high levels of employment and output. In this sense, it may be more efficient to reduce inequalities ex ante through the education system than ex post through the tax system. In a dynamic setting with repeated voting over distortionary income redistribution, the future constituency for redistributive taxation depends positively on current redistribution, since this affects both private investment and the future distribution of voters (Hassler et al. 2003). The young can affect their chances of becoming successful when old by investing in human capital. In such a framework multiple equilibria are possible, ones with positive redistribution existing forever and others where voters eventuallly induce a collapse of the welfare state. The latter is more likely to occur if there is substantial skill-biased technical change (Besley and Coate 1998).

The same political economy arguments can be used in other contexts as well; for example, Boadway and Wildasin (1989) and Boldrin and Rustichini (2000) consider median voter models of social security, and Bénabou (2000) examines unequal societies and the social contract. If there is a relatively unequal distribution of financial asset holdings among the population, the median voter is relatively poor and votes for higher taxes on capital. This depresses the rate of economic growth (Bertola 1993; Alesina and Rodrik 1994; Persson and Tabellini 1994). Conversely, a more equitable distribution of asset holdings goes hand in hand with less "populist" policies and thus higher economic growth. Perotti (1996) surveys the empirical evidence for this proposition. Due to the dearth of data, the empirical evidence is ambiguous. Perotti considers marginal tax rates and spending on social security, housing, and education. He finds a positive relationship between redistribution and growth. In addition, Rodriquez (1999) finds empirically that pretax inequality negatively affects income and capital transfers. Figini (1999) even finds evidence of reverse causation; namely, redistribution is lower if there is inequality. Saint-Paul and Verdier (1994) and Aghion and Bolton (1997) demonstrate theoretically that growth can be higher in more unequal societies, since redistribution boosts opportunities to invest in human capital formation. Haile and Meijdam 2003 establish a nonmonotonic relationship between growth and inequality.

Empirical evidence exists that countries with a more equitable distribution of nominal asset holdings are more likely to end up with political outcomes that support low inflation (Beetsma and van der Ploeg

1996). With a more equal distribution, the median voter is likely to be richer and thus less likely to vote for an unanticipated inflation tax that wipes out nominal asset holdings. A more equal distribution of nominal assets reduces the time inconsistency and credibility problems of a government tempted to use the unanticipated inflation tax as a mode of government finance.

A related strand of literature examines the political economy of labor market reforms (Saint-Paul 1996, 2000). Politicians do not implement many labor market reforms recommended by economists. Why is that politicians resist reducing particular types of job protection legislation, minimum wages, extending coverage of collective wage bargaining agreements, and the extent of eligibility requirements for welfare benefits if these would boost job growth? Many of these labor market rigidities create rents for employers and employees and lead to strong lobbies of political insiders in the labor market. Typically, the lower-skilled unemployed and the employed higher-skilled workers lose out from such labor market reforms. These groups are too small and have insufficient power to create a majority for such reforms. The employed lower-skilled workers and part of the skilled workers, who dislike more redistributive conflict between skilled and unskilled workers, are a majority and block such labor market reforms. This is a waste, since having a large part of the labor force idle and excluding the poorest from the labor market are a very inefficient way to redistribute income through the tax system. The middle class of employed workers with intermediate skill levels is crucial. It blocks reforms and imposes a big burden on the unemployed. Labor market rigidities thus make the middle class more cohesive. It can be argued that the rent-creating and rent-protecting arguments reinforce each other and that the underlying complementarities give rise to a strong status quo bias. If a country has many labor market rigidities, it creates new constituencies to protect them and one is more likely to be stuck with them.

In a different context, Alesina and Angeletos (2003) and Bénabou and Tirole (2005) argue in their analysis of the welfare state in the United States and Europe that there may be multiple equilibria; see also Piketty 1995. In the United States there is little redistribution and a small welfare state, because the majority of Americans believe that education, effort, and risk taking are rewarded with higher incomes. In Europe most people believe that poor people are poor because of bad luck, so there is a lot of redistribution and a big welfare state. It is difficult to move from the high redistribution, bad equilibrium to the low redistribution, good equilibrium, because of a status quo bias and because of the difficulties in changing people's beliefs.

3.8 Concluding Remarks

From the eighties onward, many governments in Europe have tried to push back the welfare state. Governments of different political persuasions have done this by pursuing a neoliberal political agenda of reducing the size of the public sector by cutting public spending on private goods, cutting public employment, and cutting the level and the eligibility of various benefits. The ambition was to start a virtual spiral of tax cuts followed by boosts to private-sector employment and output. This agenda of cutting back the welfare state was complemented with a policy of reducing redistribution from the rich to the poor by overhauling income tax systems to make them less progressive. This objective was to improve incentives to work and to better oneself. Since most of these policies were supported by acts of faith and a certain backlash to the laissez-faire revolution that started in the eighties exists, there is need for theoretical and empirical analysis of the robustness of these claims.

The faith in the neoliberal agenda is justified for economies with competitive, Walrasian labor markets. Social policies defined as those that pump up public-sector employment, generate generous welfare benefits, and induce more income redistribution harm employment and output. Although this may be reasonable for the United States, non-Walrasian labor markets with strong trade unions, efficiency wages, problems of adverse selection and moral hazard, costly search and mismatch, and high transaction costs are prevalent in Europe. We thus need to enter the realm of second-best economics where a faith in the neoliberal agenda is much harder to justify, especially if one distortion offsets another. Social policies such as progressive taxation, high conditional unemployment benefits, or facilitating corporatism may then induce wage moderation and boost employment and output. They may also reduce working hours, thus boosting employment further. In a second-best world, the usual effects of social policies on employment can thus be overturned.

With an individualized tax system, such redistributions of income from the high-earning partner to the low-earning partner favor a more equal distribution of household duties (shopping, child care, cleaning, etc.) within the family. They make men work less and women work more hours. Failing capital and insurance markets may also provide efficiency grounds for progressive taxation. Future labor income is not accepted by commercial banks as a guarantee for a loan. People cannot borrow when they are young and smooth consumption over their lifespan. Progressive taxes redistribute incomes from when people are old and earn a lot to when people are young and do not earn a lot. In this sense, a progressive tax system acts as an implicit credit market and thus alleviates some of the distortions of rationed credit markets. Rationing of credit particularly hurts students with poor parents and hampers development of the full potential of human capital. Since a progressive tax system also redistributes from rich to poor parents, it reduces some of the adverse effects of credit rationing on schooling. Insurance markets fail to fully insure the risks of losing income if people become ill, disabled, or unemployed. As a result, people engage in fewer risk jobs and activities. Since a progressive tax system also redistributes income from people with good luck to people with bad luck, it corrects to a certain extent for failing insurance markets. A progressive tax system also encourages risk-averse people to invest in risky studies.

Increasingly, economists have come to realize that people's happiness does not depend on money and absolute levels of consumption alone but also on relative incomes. Jealousy matters and abundance can breed discontent, because people adjust quickly to higher living standards and find it difficult to adjust downward. If everybody works hard to get more income and spend more, they do not necessarily become happier. Hard work gives rise to an adverse externality, which should be corrected for by a progressive tax on labor income.

I have given a large number of arguments why social policies and redistributive taxation may alleviate nontax distortions in second-best economies. It is important to emphasize that social policies can also exacerbate nontax distortions, since they distort markets, reduce incentives to work hard, and invest in human capital and encourage tax evasion. They also reduce working hours, lower productivity by lowering the employers' optimal wage relative to the level of unemployment benefit, and lower the efficiency of the job matching process by reducing workers' expected marginal return to job search. Even though employment may rise as a result of a more progressive tax system, output may fall and it may make it more difficult to finance a generous welfare state. Sørensen (1999) rightly points out that, in general, there is an optimal degree of tax progression. It is an empirical matter to find out whether the efficiency grounds for social policies dominate the standard neoclassical critique of market distortions. All we can say is that the case for social policies may be greater in economies plagued by many nontax and nonbenefit distortions.

If unemployed benefits are indexed or unemployed people share fully in the tax burden, lowering the tax rate on labor does not lower unemployment. Only if unemployed people enjoy untaxed income from the informal sector and leisure does a lower labor tax rate reduce jobs. It may seem that the neoliberal agenda of lowering the tax burden on labor is not compatible with indexing unemployment benefits to after-tax wages and the absence of informal incomes. However, Altenburg and Straub (2002) combine efficiency wages and shirking when firms both choose employment and the minimum performance level required of their employees with right-to-manage bargaining and demonstrate that a higher tax rate on labor *does* increase unemployment even if benefits are indexed to after-tax wages and informal incomes are absent.

If dismissed shirkers and, more generally, unemployed people who were fired for misconduct receive unconditional benefits, unemployment is pushed up. Hence, eligibility conditions should be designed in such a way that benefits are temporary and conditional on work experience, search efforts, and having lost a job by bad luck only. It may also help to link unemployment benefits to individual saving schemes, especially for skilled workers. Large reductions in unemployment can be achieved by switching from unconditional to conditional benefits even if the level of the benefit is not cut. The welfare state should thus have checks and balances and only by being tough on eligibility can society afford to be generous on the level of benefits. The crucial problem is how the government can obtain *verifiable* information about, for example, whether layoffs are voluntary or not and whether misconduct has taken place or not. The employer and employee have a joint incentive to shift the cost of breaking their relationship to the government. To overcome these free-rider problems, the government must monitor and obtain information on search efforts. This may sometimes conflict with privacy considerations. Some conditions on the benefit (e.g., experience rating) do not suffer from these problems. Other options such as sanctions and limited duration of benefits may not be credible for unskilled workers, especially in large recessions. There seems to be a case for tagging benefits (cf. Akerlof 1978).

High public spending on privately provided public goods raises employment, investment, and output. In contrast, more public employment pushes wages up and private employment down. It also drives up interest rates and reduces private saving and investment. The median voter in a full political-economic equilibrium with a more equitable distribution of income and assets is better off and thus votes for less "populist" policies. Employment and economic growth are thus higher and inflation lower in countries with more equitable distribution of income and assets. A strong middle class of workers supports much rigidity in the labor market, such as minimum wage or job protection legislation. Such social policies are, in fact, detrimental to the prospects of the unemployed and are not in the interests of the higher-skilled employees either. Since they keep a large part of the labor force idle, they are wasteful from a social point of view. The median voter is thus likely to be middle class, so that there is a status quo bias and wasteful rigidities in the labor market are difficult to remove.

Coming from an international perspective, Rodrik (1997) argues more that markets and the state are complementary and questions the supremacy of the idea that social policies are bad for the economy (the "Washington consensus"). Both governments and markets have their failures, but they must interact to grapple with the problems of conflicting information and offer the right incentives since first-best outcomes in the real world rarely occur. However, Dixit (1996) does not see this as proof of the inefficiency of government. Indeed, weak incentives and the various second-best constraints and prohibitions may even occur in a game equilibrium outcome. Rodrik (1997) thus stresses that the maintenance of social safety nets is not a luxury but an essential ingredient of a market economy (cf. Sinn 1995). Markets produce many benefits, but they also make life riskier and more insecure for many people. A reliable welfare state thus contributes to a proper functioning of the market economy. Rodrik (1998) shows that countries that are more exposed to the risks of international trade have bigger governments, possibly because governments offer social insurance to cushion the effects of exposure to external risk. De Grauwe and Polan (2002) show that countries that spend most on social security rank highest, on average, in the competitiveness leagues of Lausanne's IMD or of the World Economic Forum. The causation is very unlikely to run in reverse, so that the link going from strong competitiveness to a stronger economy and more funds for the welfare state is weak. The general picture that emerges is that laissez-faire advocates have some explaining to do, since neither theory nor empirical evidence suggests that social policies must necessarily harm the economy.

This may particularly be the case if the general public does not see redistribution as unfair. The World Values Survey suggests that people's attitudes toward the rewards from effort and taking risks are quite different in the United States than in Europe. Around 30 percent of Americans believe that the poor are trapped in poverty and cannot do anything to get out of their miserable situation. Moreover, 30 percent of Americans believe that luck, rather than effort or education, determines income. In contrast, these percentages are almost double in Europe. Americans are much more likely to think that the poor are lazy and that the rich have become so by hard work and effort. Europeans are much more likely to think that luck, family ties, and other connections matter. Alesina and Angeletos (2003) and Bénabou and Tirole (2005) show, using different arguments, that two self-fulfilling equilibria are possible. There is one equilibrium in which a lot of redistribution exists and where people believe that people have become poor or rich by bad or good luck (Europe). There is another equilibrium in which little redistribution exists but where people firmly believe that effort, education, and hard work pay off (the United States). This suggests that people are much more prepared to sacrifice income by paying higher taxes if the proceeds go to people who are laid off, sick, or disabled through no fault of their own rather than to people who are lazy or have cheated the system. Obviously, this is in line with the arguments in favor of high conditional benefits developed in section 3.4. To put it another way, it is much easier to build up support for a generous welfare state if the principle of reciprocity is respected (Fong, Bowles, and Gintis 2003). Conversely, people do not mind taxing rich people as long as they got rich by luck or connections rather than by hard work.

Social interactions and the effects of neighbors on individual behavior are important for understanding unemployment (Akerlof 1980; van de Klundert 1990) and welfare stigma (Besley and Coate 1992; Lindbeck, Nyberg, and Weibull 1999). It is a mistake to think that all interactions between people are mediated through the price and wage mechanism alone. The individual's voluntary choice between living on welfare and working depends very much on social norms and interactions. Åberg, Hedström, and Kolm (2003) study the social and psychological costs of involuntary unemployment empirically and within the context of a search-theoretic model of the labor market. Examining the behavior of young people in Stockholm, they find evidence that these costs are low if people live in a neighborhood where many people are unemployed and vice versa. Consequently, ratchet effects occur in unemployment. If unemployment is high in an area, psychological costs of unemployment are low and thus people search less intensively for a new job and are more likely to become and remain unemployed themselves. Conversely, if unemployment is low, psychological costs of unemployment are low, people search harder for a new job, and unemployment is more likely to remain low. This work emphasizes the importance of communities and social norms.

In the future, I wish to further investigate whether any of these propositions hold up empirically. I know from the Dutch experience, for example, that it is possible to have a low unemployment rate and a generous welfare state, but this is not true for all countries. In empirical work it seems sensible to contrast Anglo-Saxon Europe characterized by its emphasis on Beveridge social assistance of last resort for people of working age, weak unions, and lots of wage dispersion with continental Europe. Continental Europe is characterized by its emphasis on extending the coverage of trade unions and the Bismarckian tradition of insurance-based non-employment benefits such as disability and old-age pensions. It may also be necessary to distinguish Nordic Europe with the highest levels of social protection, universal welfare provision, high tax wedges, and an active labor market policy from Mediterranean Europe. Mediterranean Europe has, in contrast, strong wage compression, strong unions supported by extended coverage, employment protection, and early retirement provisions (Bertola and Boeri 2001). It is no good to look for cross-country correlations between spending on social policies and unemployment rates, but one should see whether there exist correlations between the generosity of various welfare state provisions and wages and unemployment rates. To investigate this for the OECD countries is a challenge for the future.

Notes

Presented at the CESifo Workshop on Tax Policy and Labor Market Performance, Venice Summer Institute, San Servolo, July 21–23, 2003, the 7th Schumpeter Institute Lecture Series on Topics on Macroeconomics and Public Finance, Humboldt University, Berlin, December 17–19, 2002, and the Sienna Summer School, the 16th Workshop on Inequality and Economic Integration, CRISS, July 2–6, 2003. I thank my Venice discussant, Lans Bovenberg, Peter Birch Sørensen, and an anonymous referee for their detailed comments, and Sam Bowles, Bas Jacobs, and seminar participants in Berlin, Florence, Rome (Tor Gervata), Siena, and Venice for helpful comments.

1. With a unit coefficient of relative risk aversion,

$$U = [1 - \exp(-S/\varepsilon_D)]/[1 - (B/W_A)].$$

In general, more risk aversion tends to make unions moderate wages in order to avoid the risk of unemployment for its members. Consequently, the unemployment rate is lower if union members are risk-averse.

2. If workers have a unit coefficient of relative risk aversion, one obtains

$$U = [1 - \exp(-\varepsilon S)]/[1/(B/W_A)].$$

In general, risk-averse workers can be paid less in order to lower the chance of layoffs, and thus in equilibrium unemployment is lower than with risk-neutral workers.

References

Åberg, Y., P. Hedström, and A.-S. Kolm. 2003. "Social Interactions and Unemployment." Mimeo., Nuffield College, Oxford and Uppsala University.

Agell, J., and P. Lundborg. 1992. "Fair Wages, Involuntary Unemployment and Tax Policies in a Simple General Equilibrium Model." *Journal of Public Economics* 47: 299–320.

Aghion, P., and P. Bolton. 1997. "A Theory of Trickle-down Growth and Development." *Review of Economic Studies* 64: 151–172.

Akerlof, G. 1976. "The Economics of Caste and of the Rat Race and other Woeful Tales." *Quarterly Journal of Economics* 90, no. 4: 599–617.

Akerlof, G. 1978. "The Economics of "Tagging" as Applied to the Optimal Income Tax, Welfare Programs, and Manpower Planning." *American Economic Review* 68, no. 1: 8–19.

Akerlof, G. 1980. "A Theory of Social Custom, of which Unemployment May Be One Consequence." *Quarterly Journal of Economics* 84: 749–775.

Alesina, A., and D. Rodrik. 1994. "Distributive Politics and Economic Growth." *Quarterly Journal of Economics* 109: 465–490.

Alesina, A., and R. Perotti. 1997. "The Welfare State and Competitiveness." *American Economic Review* 87, no. 5: 921–939.

Alesina, A., S. Ardagna, R. Perotti, and F. Schiantarelli. 2002. "Fiscal Policy, Profits and Investment." *American Economic Review* 92, no. 3: 571–589.

Alesina, G., and G-M. Angeletos. 2003. "Fairness and Redistribution: U.S. versus Europe." Working Paper 9502, NBER, Cambridge, Mass.

Altenburg, L., and M. Straub. 2002. "Taxes on Labour and Unemployment in a Shirking Model with Union Bargaining." *Labour Economics* 8: 721–744.

Aronsson, T., K-G. Löfgren, and T. Sjögren. 2002. "Wage Setting and Tax Progressivity in Dynamic General Equilibrium." *Oxford Economic Papers* 54: 490–504.

Atkinson, A. B. 2002. *The Economic Consequences of Rolling Back the Welfare State*. Munich Lectures in Economics. Cambridge, Mass.: MIT Press.

Axell, B., and H. Lang. 1990. "The Effect of Unemployment Compensation in General Equilibrium with Search Unemployment." *Scandinavian Journal of Economics* 92: 531–540.

Barro, R. J., and X. Sala-i-Martin. 1999. *Economic Growth*. Cambridge, Mass.: MIT Press.

Beetsma, R. M. W. J., and F. van der Ploeg. 1996. "Does Inequality Cause Inflation? The Political Economy of Inflation, Taxation and Government Debt." *Public Choice* 87, nos. 1–2: 143–162.

Bénabou, R. 2000. "Unequal Societies: Income Distribution and the Social Contract." *American Economic Review* 90, no. 1: 96–129.

Bénabou, R., and J. Tirole. 2005. "Belief in a Just World and Redistributive Politics." CEPR Discussion Paper 4952, CEPR, London.

Bertola, G. 1993. "Factor Shares and Savings in Endogenous Growth." *American Economic Review* 83: 1184–1198.

Bertola, G., and T. Boeri. 2001. "EMU Labour Market Reforms Two Years On: Microeconomic Tensions and Institutional Evolution." In *EMU and Economic Policy in Europe: The Challenge of the Early Years*, ed. M. Buti and A. Sapir, 249–280. Aldershot: Edward Elgar.

Besley, T., and S. Coate. 1992. "Understanding Welfare Stigma: Tax Payers Resentment and Statistical Discrimination." *Journal of Public Economics* 48: 165–183.

Besley, T., and S. Coate. 1998. "Sources of Inefficiency in a Representative Democracy: A Dynamic Analysis." *American Economic Review* 88, no. 1: 139–156.

Blanchard, O. J., and F. Giavazzi. 2001. "Macroeconomic Effects of Regulation and Deregulation in Goods and Labor Markets." Mimeo., IGIER, Bocconi, Milan.

Blanchflower, D. G., and A. J. Oswald. 2004. "Well-being over Time in Britain and the USA." *Journal of Public Economics* 88: 1359–1386.

Boadway, R. W., and D. E. Wildasin. 1989. "A Median Voter Model of Social Security." *International Economic Review* 30, no. 2: 307–328.

Boldrin, M., and A. Rustichini. 2000. "Political Equilibria with Social Security." *Review of Economic Dynamics* 3, no. 1: 41–78.

Boone, J. P., P. Fredriksson, B. Holmlund, and J. C. van Ours. 2001. "Optimal Unemployment Insurance with Monitoring and Sanctions." Discussion Paper No. 401, IZA, Bonn.

Booth, A. 1995. *The Economics of the Trade Union*. Cambridge: Cambridge University Press.

Bovenberg, A. L., and F. van der Ploeg. 1994. "Effects of the Tax and Benefit System on Wage Setting and Unemployment." Mimeo., CentER, Tilburg University, the Netherlands.

Bovenberg, A. L., and F. van der Ploeg. 1998. "Tax Reform, Structural Unemployment and the Environment." *Scandinavian Journal of Economics* 100, no. 3: 593–610.

Cahuc, P., and E. Lehmann. 2000. "Should Unemployment Benefits Decrease with the Unemployment Spell?" *Journal of Public Economics* 77: 135–153.

Calmfors, L., and E. J. Driffill. 1988. "Bargaining Structure, Corporatism and Macroeconomic Performance." *Economic Policy* 6: 13–62.

Clark, A. E., and A. J. Oswald. 1998. "Comparison-concave Utility and Following Behaviour in Social and Economic Settings." *Journal of Public Economics* 70: 133–155.

Daveri, F., and G. Tabellini. 2000. "Unemployment, Growth, and Taxation in Industrial Countries." *Economic Policy* 30: 47–101.

Davidson, C., L. Marin, and S. Matusz. 1987. "Search, Unemployment, and the Production of Jobs." *Economic Journal* 97: 857–876.

Davidson, C., L. Marin, and S. Matusz. 1988. "The Structure of Simple General Equilibrium Models with Frictional Unemployment." *Journal of Political Economy* 96: 1267–1293.

de Grauwe, P., and M. Polan. 2002. "Globalisation and Social Security. A Race to the Bottom?" Mimeo., University of Leuven, Belgium.

Dixit, A. K. 1996. *The Making of Economic Policy: A Transaction-cost Politics Perspective*, Cambridge, Mass.: MIT Press.

Driffill, E. J., and F. van der Ploeg. 1993. "Monopoly Unions and the Liberalisation of International Trade." *Economic Journal* 103, no. 417: 379–385.

Driffill, E. J., and F. van der Ploeg. 1995. "Trade Liberalization with Imperfect Competition in Goods and Labour Markets." *Scandinavian Journal of Economics* 97, no. 2: 223–242.

Eaton, J., and H. S. Rosen. 1980. "Taxation, Human Capital, and Uncertainty." *American Economic Review* 70: 705–715.

Fella, G. 2000. "Efficient Wages and Efficient Redundancy Pay." *European Economic Review* 44, no. 8: 1473–1490.

Figini, P. 1999. "Inequality and Growth Revisited." Mimeo., Trinity College, Dublin.

Finn, M. G. 1998. "Cyclical Effects of Government's Employment and Goods Purchases." *International Economic Review* 39, no. 3: 635–657.

Fong, C. M., S. Bowles, and H. Gintis. 2003. "Reciprocity and the Welfare State." Mimeo., Siena University.

Fredriksson, P., and B. Holmlund. 2001. "Optimal Unemployment Insurance in Search Equilibrium." *Journal of Labor Economics* 19: 370–399.

Fullerton, D., and G. E. Metcalf. 2002. "Tax Incidence." In *Handbook of Public Economics*, vol. 4, ed. A. Auerbach and M. Feldstein, 1787–1872. Amsterdam: North-Holland.

Graafland, J. J., and F. H. Huizinga. 1999. "Taxes and Benefits in a Non-linear Equation." *The Economist* 147: 39–54.

Haile, D. T., and L. Meijdam. 2003. "The Political Economy of Inequality, Redistribution and Growth." Mimeo., CentER, Tilburg University, the Netherlands.

Hassler, J., J. V. Rodríquez, K. Storesletten, and F. Zilibotti. 2003. "The Survival of the Welfare State." *American Economic Review* 93, no. 1: 87–112.

Heckman, J. J. 1993. "What Has Been Learned about Labor Supply in the Past Twenty Years?" *American Economic Review* 83, no. 2: 116–121.

Heijdra, B. J., and F. van der Ploeg. 2002. *Foundations of Modern Macroeconomics*. Oxford: Oxford University Press.

Holmlund, B. 1997. "Macroeconomic Implications of Cash Limits in the Public Sector." *Economica* 64, no. 253: 49–62.

Holmlund, B., and A-S. Kolm. 1995. "Progressive Taxation, Wage Setting and Unemployment: Theory and Swedish Evidence." *Swedish Economic Policy Review* 2: 423–460.

Hopenhayn, H. A., and J. P. Nicolini. 1997. "Optimal Unemployment Insurance." *Journal of Political Economy* 105: 412–438.

Hubbard, R. G., and K. L. Judd. 1986. "Liquidity Constraints, Fiscal Policy, and Consumption." *Brookings Papers on Economic Activity*, no. 1: 1–50.

Jacobs, B. 2003. "Optimal Taxation of Human Capital and Credit Constraints." Discussion Paper No. 044/2, Tinbergen Institute, Amsterdam and Rotterdam, the Netherlands.

Kimmel, J., and T. J. Kniesner. 1998. "New Evidence on Labor Supply: Employment versus Hours Elasticities by Sex and Marital Status." *Journal of Monetary Economics* 42, no. 2: 289–301.

Kolm, A-S. 2000. "Labour Taxation in a Unionised Economy with Home Production." *Scandinavian Journal of Economics* 102: 689–705.

Koskela, E., and J. Vilmunen. 1996. "Tax Progression Is Good for Employment in Popular Models of Trade Union Behaviour." *Labour Economics* 3, no. 1: 65–80.

Layard, R. 1980. "Human Satisfactions and Public Policy." *Economic Journal* 90: 737–750.

Layard, R. 2003. "Lectures on Happiness." Lionel Robbins Memorial Lectures 2003, Centre for Economic Performance, London School of Economics.

Layard, R., S. Nickell, and R. Jackman. 1991. *Unemployment: Macroeconomic Performance and the Labour Market*. Oxford: Oxford University Press.

Lindbeck, A., S. Nyberg, and J. Weibull. 1999. "Social Norms and Economic Incentives in the Welfare State." *Quarterly Journal of Economics* 114, no. 1: 1–35.

Lindbeck, A., and D. Snower. 2002. "The Insider-Outsider Theory: A Survey." Discussion Paper No. 534, IZA, Bonn.

Lockwood, B., and A. Manning. 1993. "Wage Setting and the Tax System: Theory and Evidence from the United Kingdom." *Journal of Public Economics* 52: 1–29.

Lockwood, B., T. Sløk, and T. Trances. 2000. "Progressive Taxation and Wage Setting: Evidence for Denmark." *Scandinavian Journal of Economics* 102, no. 4: 707–724.

Meyer, B. 2002. "Labor Supply at the Extensive and Intensive Margins: The EITC, Welfare and Hours Worked." *American Economic Review, Papers and Proceedings* 92, no. 2: 373–379.

Meltzer, A., and S. Richard. 1981. "A Rational Theory of the Size of Government." *Journal of Political Economy* 89: 914–927.

Musgrave, R. A. 1959. *The Theory of Public Finance*. New York: McGraw-Hill.

OECD. 1995. *The OECD Jobs Study. Taxation, Employment and Unemployment*. Paris: OECD.

Perotti, R. 1996. "Growth, Income Distribution and Democracy: What the Data Say." *Journal of Economic Growth* 1: 149–188.

Persson, T., and G. Tabellini. 1994. "Is Inquality Harmful for Growth?" *American Economic Review* 84: 600–621.

Persson, T., and G. Tabellini. 2000. *Political Economics*. Cambridge, Mass.: MIT Press.

Piketty, T. 1995. "Social Mobility and Redistributive Politics." *Quarterly Journal of Economics* 110, no. 3: 551–584.

Pissarides, C. A. 1990. *Equilibrium Unemployment Theory*. Oxford: Basil Blackwell.

Pissarides, C. A. 1998. "The Impact of Employment Tax Cuts on Unemployment and Wages: The Role of Unemployment Benefits and Tax Structure." *European Economic Review* 42: 155–183.

Roberts, K. 1977. "Voting over Income Tax Schedules." *Journal of Public Economics* 8: 329–340.

Rodrik, D. 1997. "The 'Paradoxes' of the Successful State." *European Economic Review* 41, nos. 3–5: 411–442.

Rodrik, D. 1998. "Why Do Open Economies Have Bigger Governments?" *Journal of Political Economy* 106: 997–1032.

Rodriquez, F. 1999. "Does Inequality Lead to Redistribution? Evidence from the United States." *Economics and Politics* 11: 2.

Røed, K., and S. Strøm. 2002. "Progressive Taxes and the Labour Market: Is the Trade-off between Equality and Efficiency Inevitable?" *Journal of Economic Surveys* 16, no. 1: 77–110.

Romer, T. 1975. "Individual Welfare, Majority Voting and the Properties of a Linear Income Tax." *Journal of Public Economics* 7: 163–168.

Rothschild, M., and J. E. Stiglitz. 1976. "Equilibrium in Competitive Insurance Markets." *Quarterly Journal of Economics* 90: 629–649.

Saez, E. 2002. "Optimal Income Transfer Programmes: Intensive versus Extensive Labor Supply Responses." *Quarterly Journal of Economics* 117: 1039–1074.

Saint-Paul, G. 1996. "Exploring the Political Economy of Labor Market Institutions." *Economic Policy* 23: 265–315.

Saint-Paul, G. 2000. *The Political Economy of Labour Market Institutions*. Oxford: Oxford University Press.

Saint-Paul, G., and G. Verdier. 1994. "Education, Democracy and Growth." *Journal of Development Economics* 42: 399–407.

Shapiro, C., and J. E. Stiglitz. 1984. "Equilibrium Unemployment as a Worker Discipline Device." *American Economic Review* 74: 433–444.

Shavell, S., and L. Weiss. 1979. "The Optimal Payment of Unemployment Insurance Benefits over Time." *Journal of Political Economy* 87: 1347–1363.

Sinn, H-W. 1995. "A Theory of the Welfare State." *Scandinavian Journal of Economics* 97: 495–526.

Sørensen, P. B. 1997. "Public Finance Solutions to the European Unemployment Problem?" *Economic Policy* 25: 223–264.

Sørensen, P. B. 1999. "Optimal Tax Progressivity in Imperfect Labour Markets." *Labour Economics* 6: 435–452.

Stiglitz, J. E., and A. Weiss. 1986. "Credit Rationing in Markets with Imperfect Information." *American Economic Review* 71, no. 3: 393–410.

van de Klundert, T. 1990. "On Socioeconomic Causes of 'Wait Unemployment.'" *European Economic Review* 34, no. 5: 1011–1022.

van der Ploeg, F. 2006. "Rolling Back the Welfare State: Differential Effects on Employment, Investment and Growth." *Oxford Economic Papers* 58, no. 1: 103–122.

van de Stadt, H., A. Kapteyn, and S. van de Geer. 1985. "The Relativity of Utility: Evidence from Panel Data." *Review of Economics and Statistics* 67: 179–187.

van Ewijk, C., B. Jacobs, R. de Mooij, and P. Tang. 2003. "Tien Doelmatigheidsargumenten voor Progressive Belastingen." *Tijdschrift voor Openbare Financiën* 1: 30–35.

Yann, A., P. Cahuc, and A. Zylberberg. 2002. "Public Employment. Does It Increase Unemployment?" *Economic Policy* 34: 7–65.

II

Taxation, Labor Supply,
and Wage Formation

4

Welfare Effects of Tax Reform and Labor Supply at the Intensive and Extensive Margins

Nada Eissa, Henrik Jacobsen Kleven, and Claus Thustrup Kreiner

4.1 Introduction

A central finding of the modern empirical labor literature is that labor supply responses tend to be concentrated more along the extensive margin (labor force participation) than along the intensive margin (hours of work). Evidence from expansions of tax-based transfers in the United States and the United Kingdom seems to indicate substantial effects on labor force participation, but only modest effects on hours of work for those who are working (Eissa and Liebman 1996; Meyer and Rosenbaum 2001; Blundell 2001). These recent findings support direct and indirect evidence from earlier work on labor supply. Direct evidence from the Negative Income Tax (NIT) experiments in the United States shows that the average participation response from all experiments was slightly larger than the annual hours-of-work response for both single female heads and married women (Robins 1985). For married women, Mroz (1987) and Triest (1990) estimate larger wage and income elasticities when including all (working and nonworking) women than when including only working women, suggesting that the participation margin is more sensitive to taxes than hours worked by working women.

This chapter argues that the concentration of labor supply responsiveness along the extensive margin carries important implications for the welfare evaluation of tax reform. The theoretical public finance literature has largely ignored the participation margin and instead has focused on labor supply at the intensive margin. An important exception is Saez 2002, which extends the theory of optimal taxation to account for both margins of labor supply response. Saez demonstrates that if participation elasticities are relatively high at the bottom of the earnings distribution—as indeed seems to be the case—the optimal policy subsidizes low-income earners. Interestingly, this result is broadly in line with the recent tax reforms in the United States and the United Kingdom, which have incorporated large subsidies for low-income workers. The optimality approach is limited in the evaluation of actual tax reforms, however. First, this approach deals with the properties of tax systems where all taxes and transfers have been optimized. This never occurs, since actual reforms change specific elements of the tax code and leave other, potentially inefficient, elements unchanged. Second, optimal taxation depends on the magnitude of elasticities at the optimal point, which is presumably different from the current position, or anything else previously observed. The evaluation of actual tax reforms, on the other hand, depends only on behavioral responses in the current equilibrium.

To understand the implications of the participation decision for evaluating tax reform, we embed the extensive margin in a simple welfare theoretic framework. A central issue is whether to model the extensive response within a standard convex labor supply model or within a model incorporating non-convexities in budget sets or preferences. In the convex framework, labor force participation is determined by a reservation wage and is nondiscrete at the individual level. Thus, a tax reform lowering the marginal tax rate by a small amount at or around the reservation wage level induces some individuals to enter the labor market at few working hours. In the chapter we show that extensive labor supply responses of this type create only second-order welfare effects, and are therefore inconsequential for the welfare evaluation of (small) tax reforms. Moreover, the kind of participation responses predicted by the standard convex model is inconsistent with the empirical evidence. Empirical evidence shows that almost no workers choose to enter the labor market at very small hours of work.

A realistic model must account for discrete participation behavior, where people enter the labor market at some minimum hours of work, say, twenty or thirty hours per week. This type of behavior is typically explained by non-convexities created by work costs (Cogan 1981; Heim and Meyer 2003). Based on Eissa, Kleven, and Kreiner (2004), we outline a simple framework incorporating fixed costs of work, and we show that extensive labor supply responses generate first-order welfare effects within such a framework. The extensive welfare effect from tax reform depends on the size of the participation elasticity, and it depends on the pre-reform levels of tax rates and on the changes in tax rates introduced by the reform. In particular, the welfare effect from participation responses is related to the effective *average* tax rate, including the average benefit reduction rate for welfare benefits. Due to nonlinearities and discontinuities in taxes and transfers, the average tax rate may be significantly different from the marginal tax rate associated with the intensive margin of labor supply.

It is exactly because of nonlinearities in the tax transfer system and the implied difference in average and marginal tax rates that it is necessary to distinguish between the intensive and extensive margins in the welfare analysis. In the case of linear taxes and transfers, we argue that there is no loss from conflating the two margins in a total labor supply response. But nonlinearities are significant in practice, especially at the lower end of the distribution where welfare benefits and tax-based transfers play an important role. In the United States, for example, the Earned Income Tax Credit (EITC) implies a marginal tax rate equal to −36 percent in the phase-in range (in 2002), while the marginal tax rate implied by the phase-out of the credit is +21 percent. Since most individuals eligible for the EITC have income beyond the phase-in range, the credit tends to reduce incentives to supply labor along the intensive margin. At the same time, the program reduced average tax liabilities and therefore average tax rates, thereby improving the returns to work. In the welfare evaluation of an EITC reform, it is important to distinguish explicitly between intensive and extensive responses and to account for the different incentives created along the two margins. Moreover, even if one were to consider a linear tax reform (say, a proportional tax change), one needs to distinguish between the two margins of response as long as the pre-reform tax system involves nonlinearities.

Finally, we consider an empirical application to the Tax Reform Act of 1986 (TRA86) in the United States. This reform constituted the most fundamental change in the federal income tax system in nearly forty years. By design, the reform had its largest impact on high-income earners, but it also included substantial benefits at the lower end of the distribution. Our concern is with the welfare effects for single mothers, a group characterized by low earnings and long spells of non-employment. This group experienced large tax cuts from the reform due to an expansion of the EITC, and because of increases in the standard deduction, personal exemptions, and a more favorable tax rate schedule. The combination of all these elements implied substantial improvements in the incentives to supply labor along both the intensive and extensive margins. We show that the reform created substantial welfare gains for single mothers and that most of the effect was generated by positive participation responses. Hence the application serves to confirm that large errors can be made by omitting the extensive response in the welfare analysis of tax reform.

The chapter is organized in the following way. Section 4.2 discusses the theoretical analysis of tax reform. Section 4.3 describes a number of tax reforms passed in the United States over the past two decades, while section 4.4 reviews the empirical evidence on the effects of tax reform on labor supply. Section 4.5 presents microsimulation results for the welfare effects of TRA86, and section 4.6 concludes.

4.2 A Theoretical Analysis of Tax Reform

4.2.1 Labor Supply Responses

In general, tax reforms may affect labor supply along both the intensive and the extensive margins. Along the intensive margin, a tax reform that changes the marginal net wage induces employees to adjust their weekly hours of work from, say, forty to thirty-nine hours. At the same time, a tax reform may create extensive responses by affecting the incentive to participate in the labor market. This effect is likely to be particularly relevant for certain subgroups of the population such as married females, single mothers, low-educated individuals, the young, and the elderly (retired). For these individuals, higher tax burdens may make it worthwhile to leave the labor market entirely, going from, say, thirty or twenty hours per week to zero hours per week.

The bulk of the literature on taxation and labor supply is based on the standard static labor supply model, where preferences and budget sets are assumed to be convex. This model underlies Mirrlees' (1971) exploration into optimal income taxation. The framework has subsequently been used to examine the welfare cost of taxation by Ballard, Shoven, and Whalley (1985), Ballard (1988), Triest (1994), Browning (1995), and Dahlby (1998). In the convex model, optimal labor supply is given by the tangency of the budget line and the indifference curve, implying that marginal changes in prices and endowments give rise to marginal changes in individual behavior. In other words, the model is one of continuous choice.

Figure 4.1 illustrates the choice of labor supply in the standard model. In the figure, we consider two individuals facing the same budget constraint, where y_0 is nonlabor income and $(1 - t)w$ is the mar-

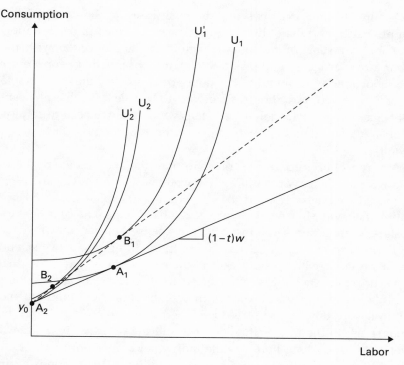

Figure 4.1
Intensive versus extensive responses in the convex model

ginal net-of-tax wage. The indifference curves of the two individuals are drawn such that individual 1 has a relatively low valuation of leisure, while individual 2 has a relatively high valuation of leisure. Consequently, it is optimal for the first individual to work many hours, while the second individual chooses to stay outside the labor market since there is no point of tangency at positive hours. Consider now a reduction in the tax rate causing an increase in the slope of the budget line. This induces individual 1 to increase his or her hours of work a little bit (an intensive response). For individual 2, on the other hand, the higher net wage gives rise to an interior solution such that he or she decides to enter the labor market (an extensive response). However, the extensive response involves a change in labor supply from zero hours to some small (infinitesimal) number of hours. Thus, the type of participation response predicted by this framework is a marginal one, just like the change in hours of work for those who are working.

As already indicated, this may be misleading in the case of labor supply behavior, where discrete jumps seem to be empirically important. In particular, discreteness is significant in connection with the labor force participation decision. We do not observe that people enter the labor market at infinitesimal hours of work, but that they do so at, say, twenty or forty hours. Therefore, to be able to realistically capture labor supply behavior at the extensive margin, we need to employ a different framework. In particular, some type of non-convexity is required.

A way to introduce a non-convexity into the analysis would be to allow for fixed costs of working. In a well-known paper, Cogan (1981) proposed a model with fixed costs of working to explain discrete labor supply behavior. In Cogan's analysis, the fixed costs may be monetary costs (say, child care and transportation expenses) or they may take the form of a loss of time (e.g., commuting time). In figure 4.2, we extend the analysis of labor supply choice along these lines. An individual who chooses to stay outside the labor market receives nonlabor income y_0. If he decides to enter the labor market, he loses Δy_f in income and Δl_f in leisure time upon entry, thereby creating a discontinuity in the budget set. In the initial situation, it is still the case that individual 1 works relatively long hours, while individual 2 does not work at all. Now, if we reduce the tax rate a little bit, individual 1 responds again with a marginal change in working hours. In contrast, individual 2 now reacts by making a discrete jump from not working at all to working nearly as many hours as individual 1. Thus, the incorporation of fixed costs of working in the budget constraint seems to provide a more realistic model of participation behavior.[1] Indeed, the studies by Cogan (1981) for the United States and by Blundell, Ham, and Meghir (1987) for the United Kingdom show that fixed costs are empirically important for the labor supply of married women.

The design of the tax transfer system may in itself be part of the explanation for the observed discontinuity in labor supply. For example, in some countries individuals face a U-shaped pattern of marginal tax rates. Effective marginal tax rates are high for low-income individuals due to the phasing out of welfare benefits, while marginal tax rates are high at the top of the earnings distribution where the progressivity of the tax system kicks in. Such a system gives rise to an S-shaped budget line as illustrated in figure 4.3. In the figure, the individual initially stays out of the labor market. But a small reduction in tax rates, creat-

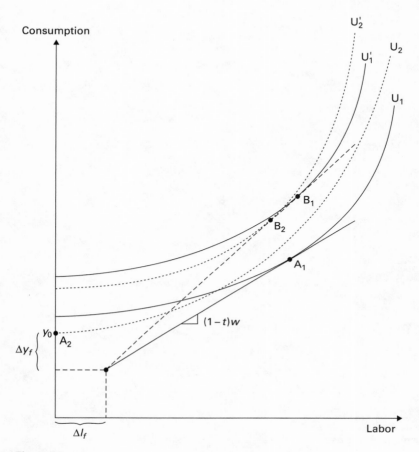

Figure 4.2
Intensive versus extensive responses with fixed costs of working

ing an upward shift in the budget line, induces the individual to jump in at l^* hours.

So far we have considered labor supply problems involving only one candidate for an interior solution, which is then compared to the corner solution with non-participation. In this situation, labor supply is discontinuous at the point of entry and exit, whereas hours of work for those who are working is a continuous choice variable. Such a model is fine as long as the non-convexity in the budget set is concentrated at the lowest earnings points as in the case of fixed work costs or welfare benefits that are (quickly) phased out upon entry. But if

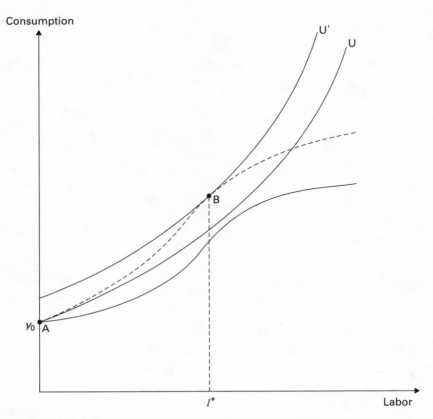

Figure 4.3
Discrete extensive response with a U-shaped pattern of marginal tax rates

there are discontinuities or other non-convexities further into the interior of the budget set, even the intensive labor supply response may become discrete. Such a situation is depicted in figure 4.4, where the budget line is discontinuous at l_1^* hours. The discontinuity could reflect that a benefit is lost completely once income exceeds a certain threshold or that some tax is imposed on the entire income above the threshold.[2] In the figure, it is initially optimal for the worker to locate at the notch l_1^* so as to avoid the discontinuous tax payment. But a tax reform creating a small upward shift in the budget line induces the worker to move discretely from l_1^* (part-time) to l_2^* (full-time).

To summarize, we note that tax reforms entail intensive as well as extensive labor supply responses, and to account for the observed

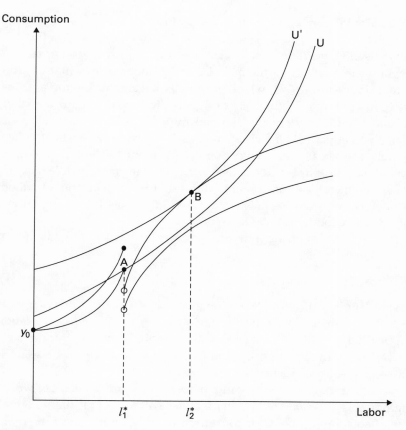

Figure 4.4
Discrete intensive response with a non-convex budget set

discreteness of responses, they have to be modeled by introducing non-convexities into the standard framework. The presence of non-convexities and discreteness is presumably more important for the extensive response, because of fixed work costs.

One may question the value of distinguishing explicitly between intensive and extensive labor supply responses for the evaluation of tax reform; that is, will we correctly estimate the welfare effects by combining the two margins into a single elasticity in the standard convex model? If so, Occam's Razor would suggest that we use this simpler method. We show in the following sections, however, that it is indeed important to distinguish between the two types of responses in welfare analysis, except under very special circumstances.

4.2.2   The Welfare Effect from Intensive Responses

In this section, we derive the welfare effect from intensive labor supply responses in a simple partial model. We consider a representative individual with earnings wl, where w is an exogenous wage rate and l is the hours of work. Without loss of generality, we disregard nonlabor income. The tax system is described by a function $T(wl, z)$, where z is an abstract parameter that we will use to derive the effects of policy reform. The tax function gives the net payment to the public sector, embodying taxes as well as transfers. The tax transfer schedule may involve nonlinearities and discontinuities, but we will restrict attention to the case of piecewise linearity where individuals face marginal tax rates that are locally constant.

The preferences of the individual are represented by a quasi-linear utility function

$$U = wl - T(wl, z) - v(l), \tag{1}$$

where disutility of work $v(l)$ is increasing and strictly convex ($v' > 0$, $v'' > 0$). The quasi-linear specification excludes income effects on labor supply that simplifies the algebra with no loss of generality for the welfare analysis. In fact, a general utility function would provide exactly the same results (cf. section 4.2.4).

Assuming that an interior solution exists, the optimal choice of working hours is characterized by the familiar condition that the marginal rate of substitution between consumption and leisure equals the marginal net-of-tax wage rate. That is,

$$(1 - m)w = v'(l), \tag{2}$$

where $m \equiv \partial T(wl, z)/\partial(wl)$ is the marginal tax rate.

The consequences of a small tax reform may be approximated by the effects of a marginal change in the parameter z. From (1) and (2), we see that a change in z affects utility directly through the tax payment and indirectly through the effect on hours of work. However, the indirect effect disappears by the envelope theorem, since working hours are initially at the optimum. Accordingly, the change in utility is given by

$$\frac{dU}{dz} = -\frac{\partial T}{\partial z}, \tag{3}$$

which is simply the mechanical change in the tax payment, namely, the tax change exclusive of feedback effects from behavioral responses to the reform.

The utility change does not in itself constitute the welfare effect of tax reform, which is instead related to the change in the deadweight loss (or excess burden) of taxation. With quasi-linear utility, the deadweight loss is given simply by $D = U_0 - U - T$, where U_0 is the (hypothetical) utility level with no taxation. The welfare loss of tax reform is then given by

$$\frac{dD}{dz} = -\frac{dU}{dz} - \frac{dT}{dz} = \frac{\partial T}{\partial z} - \frac{dT}{dz}, \tag{4}$$

where we have inserted the derivative (3). Thus, the welfare loss is equal to the difference between the mechanical change in tax revenue and the total change in revenue accounting for both mechanical effects and behavioral feedback effects of the reform. In other words, the welfare loss of tax reform is given simply by the revenue loss created by changed behavior. Notice that this insight does not rely on the preference specification adopted here; it follows from the definition of the deadweight loss and the application of the envelope theorem.

In this model, the behavioral feedback effect on revenue is given by the change in earnings multiplied by the marginal tax rate, implying that equation (4) may be written as

$$\frac{dD}{dz} = -mw\frac{dl}{dz}. \tag{5}$$

The working hours response dl/dz may be derived from (2) and substituted into (5) so as to get

$$\frac{dD/dz}{wl} = \frac{m}{1-m} \cdot \frac{\partial m}{\partial z} \cdot \varepsilon, \tag{6}$$

where $\varepsilon = v'(\cdot)/[v''(\cdot)l]$ denotes the (compensated) elasticity of hours of work with respect to the marginal net-of-tax wage. This expression is a classic Harberger-type formula for the marginal deadweight burden of taxation. It shows that the marginal deadweight loss depends on the initial level of the marginal tax rate, the increase in the marginal tax rate, and the hours-of-work elasticity.

The previous formula suggests that welfare effects may be substantial even for moderate labor supply elasticities provided that initial marginal tax rates are high. Tax reforms should therefore aim at reducing marginal tax rates where these rates are relatively high. From this perspective, one would perhaps be skeptical about the recent moves toward "in-work" benefits for low-income families with children (mostly single mothers) such as the American EITC and the British WFTC (Working Family Tax Credit). These policies have raised marginal tax rates on average, since most eligible families are located in the phase-out region of the credit. Moreover, marginal tax rates within the eligible group were initially quite high, because many were receiving other benefits subject to phase-out (cash benefits, food stamps, etc.). This problem with the EITC is reinforced if the existing estimates of a highly elastic female labor supply (Killingsworth and Heckman 1986) are taken to indicate a high intensive elasticity ε. Indeed, this seems to be the underlying interpretation in the strong criticism of the EITC by Browning (1995). It is an incorrect interpretation, however, since high labor supply elasticities for single mothers reflect mostly extensive responses (Mroz 1987; Triest 1990).

4.2.3 The Welfare Effect from Extensive Responses in the Standard Model

A realistic model of extensive labor supply responses requires some type of heterogeneity. With no heterogeneity in preferences or in productivity, either everyone participates or nobody participates. The extensive labor supply response becomes discrete at the macrolevel in that the economy moves from no employment to full employment at some threshold. The standard method of smoothing the participation response is to introduce a continuum of productivities $w \in (0, \bar{w})$ in the convex model from section 4.2.2.

Individual labor supply is described by the first-order condition (2) and a non-negativity constraint on hours. From the first-order condition, non-negative hours correspond to a requirement that the marginal net-of-tax wage is greater than or equal to $v'(0)$. Thus, we may write individual labor supply at productivity w, denoted by l_w, as

$$(1 - m_w)w = v'(l_w) \quad \text{if} \quad (1 - m_w)w \geq v'(0); \qquad \text{otherwise } l_w = 0, \quad (7)$$

where m_w is the marginal tax rate faced by an individual with wage rate w (given the labor earnings chosen by this type). We may define a threshold wage level $\tilde{w}$ for the marginal entrant, that is, $\tilde{w} \equiv v'(0)/(1 - m_{\tilde{w}})$, such that all individuals with $w \geq \tilde{w}$ choose to enter the labor market while all those with $w < \tilde{w}$ choose not to enter. If we let wages be distributed according to $F(w)$, the participation rate in the economy is given by $1 - F(\tilde{w}) = 1 - F(v'(0)/(1 - m_{\tilde{w}}))$.

It then follows that the tax system affects labor supply at the extensive margin through the marginal tax rate $m_{\tilde{w}}$ for the marginal entrant. Accordingly, a tax reform that reduces the marginal tax rate for people at or around the reservation wage level will induce additional entry. What is the welfare effect of these extensive responses? Notice first that unemployment in this model is voluntary such that the marginal entrant is indifferent between employment and non-employment. By implication, extensive labor supply responses do not create discrete utility changes. As in the previous model, the effect on excess burden is determined solely by the feedback effect on government revenue. But since individuals enter the labor market at infinitesimal working hours in this model, no additional tax revenue is created by more participation, at least not for small reforms. In other words, extensive labor supply responses are irrelevant from the point of view of economic welfare within the standard convex model. For extensive responses to matter for the evaluation of tax policy, the responses have to be discrete as in the nonconvex framework (or non-participation would have to be involuntary).

4.2.4 The Welfare Effect from Extensive Responses in a Nonconvex Model

In this section, we present a stripped-down model to capture participation responses in a realistic way. As suggested in the previous discussion, such a model should incorporate some type of non-convexity as well as heterogeneity across individuals. The non-convexity enables us to explain discrete entry-exit behavior at the individual level, while heterogeneity is needed to get a smooth participation response at the macro level.[3]

Perhaps the simplest way to introduce a non-convexity in the model is through fixed costs of working and, as mentioned in section 4.2.1, such work costs have been shown to be empirically significant. In what follows we lay out a framework where fixed work costs are captured in a single parameter q, which may reflect monetary and time costs or a "psychic" distaste for participation. A heterogeneity may then be introduced through the fixed costs by assuming that the economy consists of a continuum of individuals with $q \in (0, \bar{q})$. For simplicity, let the productivity level be identical across individuals and, to focus on the extensive margin, let us fix hours of work for those who are working at 1 unit. Thus, individuals are simply making a choice between $l = 0$ and $l = 1$, involving utility levels

$$U = \begin{cases} w - T(w,z) - q & l = 1, \\ -T(0,z) & l = 0. \end{cases} \tag{8}$$

If the individual chooses to work, he obtains wage income net of taxes and the fixed work cost $w - T(w,z) - q$. This has to be compared to the public benefits $-T(0,z)$, which will be received in case of non-participation.

For the individual to enter the labor market, the utility from participation must be greater than or equal to the utility from non-participation, giving rise to the participation constraint

$$q \leq w - [T(w,z) - T(0,z)] \equiv \tilde{q}. \tag{9}$$

This expression defines an upper bound on the fixed cost, $\tilde{q}$, the size of which reflects the income gain from entry net of taxes and transfers. Individuals with a fixed cost below the threshold value $\tilde{q}$ decide to enter the labor market, while those with a fixed cost above the threshold value stay out. If we let q be distributed according to $P(q)$ with density $p(q)$, the labor force participation rate in the economy becomes equal to $P(\tilde{q})$. The sensitivity of the participation rate P with respect to changes in the net income gain from entry $\tilde{q}$ may be measured by the extensive labor supply elasticity

$$\eta \equiv \frac{\partial P}{\partial \tilde{q}} \frac{\tilde{q}}{P} = \frac{p(\tilde{q})\tilde{q}}{P}. \tag{10}$$

The relationship between taxation and labor force participation in this nonconvex model is different from the relationship in the convex model in section 4.2.3. In the convex model, the participation decision was related to the marginal tax rate at zero labor income whereas, in the model laid out here, the decision is related to the change in total tax transfer payments $T(w,z) - T(0,z)$ following entrance into the labor market. Obviously, this difference is related to the distinction between discrete and continuous labor supply behavior. In the standard model, individuals enter the labor market at infinitesimal hours, creating a change in the total tax liability equal to $T(y,z) - T(0,z) \approx m \cdot y$ since earnings y are small.

As in the previous model, non-employment is voluntary and the marginal entrant is indifferent between participating or not. Accordingly, the effect of extensive labor supply responses on aggregate utility envelopes out, and the marginal excess burden is therefore given by the revenue implications of changed participation. Since aggregate government revenue R is given by

$$R = T(w,z)P(\tilde{q}) + T(0,z)(1 - P(\tilde{q})), \tag{11}$$

the marginal excess burden may be written as

$$\frac{dD}{dz} = \frac{\partial R}{\partial z} - \frac{dR}{dz} = -[T(w,z) - T(0,z)]\frac{dP(\tilde{q})}{dz}. \tag{12}$$

The welfare effect of a tax reform is determined by its impact on the labor force participation rate multiplied by the increase in the net tax liability created by entry into the labor market.

By using equations (9) and (10), it is straightforward to derive the participation effect as a function of the extensive labor supply elasticity and parameters of the tax transfer system and the reform. By defining a tax rate on labor force participation, $a \equiv [T(w,z) - T(0,z)]/w$, we may write the marginal deadweight burden in proportion to aggregate income in the following way:

$$\frac{dD/dz}{wP} = \frac{a}{1-a} \cdot \frac{\partial a}{\partial z} \cdot \eta. \tag{13}$$

This deadweight formula reflects the same basic form as the traditional one in equation (6), but it is related to different policy parameters and a different elasticity. In particular, the welfare cost is no longer related to the *marginal* tax rate. It is instead related to the tax rate applying at the extensive margin. This tax rate is an effective *average* tax rate, which includes the loss in benefits from labor market entry. Finally, the welfare effect depends on the sensitivity of entry-exit behavior as measured by the elasticity of labor force participation with respect to the net-of-tax income gain from entry, η.

The policy conclusions that follow from the preceding formula are quite different from those implied by the standard analysis. Again, the EITC is a case in point. As mentioned in section 2.2, the standard analysis leads to some skepticism of the EITC, because of the implied increase in effective marginal tax rates in the phase-out region of the tax credit. The standard analysis, however, misses an essential problem with the welfare system, which is that it keeps some individuals completely out of the labor force. A model with discrete participation, on the other hand, allows the introduction of tax credits to low-wage earners to improve welfare, since lower average tax rates encourage labor force participation. This conclusion is reinforced by empirical evidence indicating high participation elasticities among those targeted by in-work benefits in both the United States and the United Kingdom (Eissa and Liebman 1996; Blundell et al. 2000).

4.2.5   A General Formula for the Evaluation of Tax Reform

Tax reforms give rise to both intensive responses and (discrete) extensive responses. The effects on welfare from these two types of responses have been illustrated in sections 2.2 and 2.4. In order to focus on the central mechanisms at work, we have kept the theory as simple as possible. To quantify the welfare effects of a reform in the tax benefit system, we would need to combine intensive and extensive responses in a more realistic theoretical setting. The theory should build on a more general specification of preferences, so as to allow for income effects in labor supply, and should also account for individual heterogeneity in productivities and preferences. In Eissa, Kleven, and Kreiner 2004, we show that the more general model gives rise to the following formula for the marginal excess burden[4]

$$\frac{dD/dz}{\sum_{i=1}^{N} w_i h_i P_i} = \sum_{i=1}^{N} \left[\frac{m_i}{1 - m_i} \frac{\partial m_i}{\partial z} \cdot \varepsilon_i + \frac{a_i}{1 - a_i} \frac{\partial a_i}{\partial z} \cdot \eta_i \right] s_i, \tag{14}$$

where $i = 1, \ldots, N$ is the index parameter for individuals and $s_i \equiv w_i l_i P_i / (\sum_{i=1}^{N} w_i l_i P_i)$ is the wage share of individual i. In this analysis, each individual works with a given probability P_i. Accordingly, the participation elasticity, η_i, measures how much the probability of working increases when the income gain of entry rises.

Formula (14) shows how to calculate the impact on aggregate welfare of a tax reform. The first term in the bracket measures the welfare effect of intensive margin responses, while the second term captures the welfare effect of extensive margin responses. Notice the resemblance to the welfare effects obtained along the two margins in the simple models, namely, equations (6) and (13). The total welfare effect is obtained by adding intensive and extensive margin effects for each individual, then calculating a weighted sum of the individual welfare effects with wage shares used as weights.

When using the previous formula to evaluate actual tax reforms, it is important to distinguish between compensated and uncompensated labor supply elasticities. The simple models are silent about this because of the absence of income effects. The general theory, however, reveals that we should apply compensated elasticities. For the participation elasticity, however, it may be shown that compensated and uncompensated responses to tax reform are identical (Eissa, Kleven, and Kreiner 2004).

A priori one might have wondered whether the standard convex framework could be saved by a reinterpretation of the labor supply elasticity. Following this interpretation, one would introduce extensive responses into the framework simply by using estimates of the *total* labor supply elasticity including both margins of response.[5] The previous formula demonstrates that, in general, this approach is not correct. This is because the extensive welfare effect is related to the effective average tax wedge (including average benefit reduction), which is different from the effective marginal tax wedge (including marginal benefit reduction) associated with the intensive effect. For tax reform in practice, the two rates generally differ in terms of both pre-reform levels and the reform-induced changes. In the case of the EITC, for example, the changes in marginal and average tax rates have opposite signs for most people eligible for the credit.

There is one special case, however, where the conventional model is valid. This is the case of a *linear* Negative Income Tax, which grants a lump-sum transfer B to all individuals in the economy (participants and non-participants) and then imposes a constant marginal tax rate on labor income, $m_i = m \, \forall i$. In this case, the tax burden on labor market entry for individual i becomes $T(w_i l_i, z) - T(0, z) = (m w_i l_i - B) - (-B)$, which implies a participation tax rate $a_i = m \, \forall i$. Moreover, if the tax reform is simply a change of tax transfer parameters within the framework of the NIT, we would have $\partial a_i / \partial z = \partial m_i / \partial z \, \forall i$. Inserting these relationships in equation (14), we get a standard Harberger formula with the intensive and extensive elasticities lumped together:

$$\frac{dD/dz}{\sum_{i=1}^{N} w_i h_i P_i} = \frac{m}{1-m} \frac{\partial m}{\partial z} \sum_{i=1}^{N} (\varepsilon_i + \eta_i) s_i.$$

The practical applicability of this special case is clearly limited since it requires that the entire welfare system be a linear NIT. Public benefits tend to be non-universal, targeted to low- and middle-income classes through earnings or work tests (creating discontinuities) or through gradual phase-outs. Consider as examples low-income support, in-work benefits, housing and education subsidies, child benefits, medical aid, food stamps, and public pensions. While some benefits may be universal in some countries, they are never collectively so. A description of the actual welfare systems prevailing in a number of European countries is provided by Immervoll et al. (2004), while the U.S. tax transfer system will be discussed in section 4.5.1.

4.3   Tax Reforms in the United States and the EITC

Over the past two decades, a series of tax acts—passed in 1981, 1986, 1990, 1993, 2001, and 2003—have substantially changed the federal income tax structure and federal income tax liabilities in the United States. To outline the major features of the tax changes, table 4.1 presents federal income tax parameters from 1984 to 2002. The table highlights the dramatic changes to the federal income tax schedule over the period. In 1984, the federal (non-EITC) tax schedule consisted of fifteen brackets, with marginal rates ranging from 0 to 50 percent. It now stands at five rates, ranging from 15 percent to nearly 40 percent. The table also highlights the central role of the Earned Income Tax Credit in altering the shape of the tax schedule.

Since the EITC is important in the empirical application that we discuss later on, it is useful to start by describing the EITC program. It began in 1975 as a modest program aimed at offsetting the social security payroll tax for low-income families with children. Since its introduction the credit was little changed, increasing from $400 to $500 (nominal dollars) by 1985 at its maximum level. Following the 1986 and subsequently the 1990 and 1993 expansions, the EITC has become the largest cash transfer program for low-income families with children at the federal level. By 2000, total EITC expenditures (tax expenditures and direct outlays) amounted to about $30 billion.

An important feature of the EITC is that eligibility is conditional on the taxpayer having positive earned income. Moreover, the size of the credit to which the taxpayer is entitled depends on the amount of earned income (adjusted gross income, or AGI) and, since 1991, the number of qualifying children who meet certain age, relationship, and residency tests. In tax year 2002, taxpayers with two or more children must have earnings no higher than $33,150 to qualify for a credit. Children must be under age 19 (or 24 if a full-time student) or permanently disabled, and must reside with the taxpayer for more than half the year.

There are three regions in the credit schedule. The initial phase-in region transfers an amount equal to the subsidy rate (currently 36 percent for larger families) times earnings. In the flat region, the family receives the maximum credit ($4,204 in tax year 2002), while in the phase-out region, the credit is phased out at a fixed phase-out rate (21 percent in 2002). The credit is refundable so that a taxpayer with no federal tax liability, for example, would receive a tax refund from the government for the full amount of the credit.

The 1986 expansion of the EITC, passed as part of the Tax Reform Act of 1986 (TRA86) increased the subsidy rate for the phase-in of the credit from 11 percent to 14 percent and increased the maximum income to which the subsidy rate was applied from $5,000 to $6,080. This resulted in an increase in the maximum credit from $550 to $851 ($788 in 1986 dollars). The phase-out rate was reduced from 12.22 percent to 10 percent. The higher maximum credit and the lower phase-out rate combined to expand the phase-out region from $11,000 in 1986 to $18,576 by 1988.

The impact of the EITC expansion on the tax liability of eligible taxpayers was reinforced by other elements of TRA86. TRA86 increased the standard deduction for a taxpayer filing as head of household from $2,480 in 1986 (included in the zero bracket) to $4,400 in 1988. TRA86 further reduced the tax liability of taxpayers with children by increasing the deduction per dependent exemption from $1080 in 1986 to $1950 in 1988. Finally, the tax schedules were changed. The tax schedule changes were particularly beneficial to head-of-household filers because the increased standard deduction and exemption amounts meant that in 1988 the typical head-of-household filer did not jump from the 15 percent tax bracket to the 28 percent tax bracket until her adjusted gross income (AGI) exceeded $33,565. Together, all these elements of the 1986 reform reduced substantially the tax liabilities for single women with children.

The Omnibus Budget Reconciliation Act of 1990 (OBRA90) further expanded the EITC for all eligible families and introduced a different EITC schedule for families with two or more children. The phase-in rate of the EITC was increased from 14 percent to 18.5 for taxpayers with one child and 19.5 percent for taxpayers with more children. OBRA90 also led to a larger (nominal and real) increase in the maximum benefit, phased in over three years.

Table 4.1
Federal income tax and EITC parameters, 1984–2002

Year	Federal income tax parameters		EITC parameters (family with one child; family with two or more children)			
	[lowest, highest marginal tax rate] (number of brackets)	Personal exemption, standard deduction[a,b]	Phase-in rate	Maximum credit	Phase-out rate	Maximum earnings
1984	[0.000; 0.500] (15)	$1,000; $0	0.100	$500	0.125	$10,000
1985	[0.000; 0.500] (15)	$1,040; $0	0.110	$550	0.122	$11,000
1986	[0.000; 0.500] (15)	$1,080; $0	0.110	$550	0.122	$11,000
TRA86						
1987	[0.110; 0.390] (5)	$1,900; $2,540	0.140	$851	0.100	$15,432
1988	[0.150; 0.330] (2)	$1,950; $4,400	0.140	$874	0.100	$18,576
1989	[0.150; 0.330] (2)	$2,000; $4,550	0.140	$910	0.100	$19,340
1990	[0.150; 0.330] (2)	$2,050; $4,750	0.140	$953	0.100	$20,264
OBRA90[c]						
1991	[0.150; 0.310] (3)	$2,150; $5,000	0.167	$1,192; $1,235	0.119; 0.124	$21,250
1992	[0.150; 0.310] (3)	$2,300; $5,250	0.176	$1,324; $1,384	0.126; 0.130	$22,370
1993	[0.150; 0.396] (5)	$2,350; $5,450	0.185	$1,434; $1,511	0.132; 0.139	$23,050
OBRA93						
1994	[0.150; 0.396] (5)	$2,450; $5,600	0.263	$2,038; $2,526	0.160; 0.177	$23,755; $25,296
1995	[0.150; 0.396] (5)	$2,500; $5,750	0.340	$2,094; $3,110	0.160; 0.202	$24,396; $26,673
1996	[0.150; 0.396] (5)	$2,550; $5,900	0.340	$2,152; $3,556	0.160; 0.211	$25,078; $28,495
1997	[0.150; 0.396] (5)	$2,650; $6,050	0.340	$2,210; $3,656	0.160; 0.211	$25,750; $29,290
2000	[0.150; 0.391] (5)	$2,900; $6,650	0.340	$2,353; $3,888	0.160; 0.211	$27,450; $31,152
EGTRRA						
2001	[0.100; 0.386] (5)	$3,000; $6,900	0.263	$2,428; $4,008	0.160; 0.211	$28,250; $32,100
2002	[0.100; 0.386] (6)	$3,050; $7,000	0.340	$2,547; $4,204	0.160; 0.211	$30,200; $33,150

Source: The Green Book and authors' calculations from Internal Revenue Service (IRS) forms and publications.

[a] The standard deductions are given for head of household tax return.

[b] In 1984–1986, there were no standard deductions because of the zero bracket. The fifteen brackets include the zero bracket.

[c] Basic EITC only. Does not include supplemental young child credit or health insurance credit.

[d] Introduced a small benefit for taxpayers with no qualifying children, phased in at 0.0765 up to a maximum credit of $306.

The budget reconciliation act of 1993 (OBRA93) further increased the *additional* maximum benefit for taxpayers with two or more children to $1,400 by 1996 ($3,556 vs. $2,152 in 1996), and doubled the subsidy rate for the lowest-income recipients from 19.5 to 40 percent for larger families (18.5 to 34 percent for families with one child). These changes combined to dramatically expand eligibility for the EITC, such that by 1996 a couple with two children would still be eligible at incomes of almost $30,000. Other than the expansions to the EITC there was little in the way of changes to the federal income tax for lower-income individuals in OBRA93.

Finally, the 2001 Economic Growth and Tax Relief Reconciliation Act (EGTRRA) further reduced taxes at the lower end of the distribution, although to a much lesser extent than the previous reforms. This time the main change in tax liabilities did not come through the EITC but through a reduction in the lowest income tax bracket from 15 to 10 percent.

4.4   Intensive and Extensive Labor Supply Responses: A Review of the Empirical Literature

This chapter argues that recent empirical evidence on labor supply behavior has important implications for the evaluation of tax reforms. In particular, we are interested in the emerging consensus that labor supply responses tend to be concentrated more along the extensive margin (labor force participation) than along the intensive margin (hours of work). This consensus emerged over an extended period of time from three different sources of evidence: direct evidence from recent tax reforms and expansions to tax-based transfers in the United States and the United Kingdom, evidence from the Negative Income Tax Experiments, and indirect evidence from structural models of labor supply. We discuss the evidence in that order.

Perhaps the most compelling evidence on the responsiveness of the participation margin arises from the evaluation of the labor supply effects of recent reforms to the tax and to the transfer system in the United States. We focus on that evidence because it is most relevant for the empirical exercise in the chapter. The literature evaluating expansions to the Earned Income Tax Credit has generally employed both quasi-experimental (difference-in-differences) methods (Eissa and Liebman 1996, hereafter EL; Eissa and Hoynes 2004, hereafter EH; Hotz, Mullin, and Scholz 2002, hereafter HMS) and structural methods

(Dickert, Houser, and Scholz 1995, hereafter DHS; and Meyer and Rosenbaum 2001, hereafter MR).

The first set of results come from studies that use quasi-experimental methods to examine the labor supply effects of the Tax Reform Act of 1986 on female heads (EL), the 1993 EITC expansion on married women (EH), and the EITC expansions in the 1990s on welfare recipients in California (HMS).[6] EL compare the change in labor force participation and hours worked by single mothers to that of single women without children, and find a sizeable labor force participation response of 2.8 percentage points (out of a base of 74.2). Their data (the Current Population Survey, or CPS) also show no evidence of an hours-of-work response.

HMS extend this work by accounting for labor supply incentives due to state-level welfare to work programs. Using administrative data on welfare recipients in four California counties, HMS evaluate the labor supply response of larger welfare families to the marginal second child credit. Their findings are dramatic and show an increase in the employment rate of larger families between 6 and 8 percentage points relative to families with one child, implying an elasticity with respect to net income of up to 1.7.

Overall the evidence based on the difference-in-differences model is consistent and suggests fairly strong participation effects, especially for female household heads. One limitation of the reduced-form labor force participation methods (as applied in these papers) is the use of group-level variation in taxes and transfers. This approach assumes that all relevant wage and income changes are captured by group-level variation in family type and size (presence and number of children) and time.

DHS and MR exploit the fact that tax reforms typically have heterogenous effects within group to estimate the effect of EITC expansions on labor force participation. DHS use cross-sectional data from the 1990 Survey of Income and Program Participation (SIPP) and estimate a joint program and labor force participation model, identified by variations in the returns to part-time (or full-time) employment in different states. They estimate a labor force participation elasticity of 0.35. MR extend this work by using time variation in tax and welfare policies. The use of time variation allows MR to eliminate any bias that results from different state characteristics that are unobserved and correlated with labor supply incentives. MR use a discrete participation model based on comparisons of utility in and out of the labor force, and CPS data from 1985 to 1997. Their finding that the EITC accounts for about 60 percent of the increase in the employment of single mothers over the period implies a labor force participation elasticity of about 0.7.

The second major source of direct evidence comes from the Negative Income Tax experiments. The NIT experiments were randomized experiments conducted in various sites in the United States from 1968 to 1982 to study the responsiveness of labor supply to taxes (see review by Moffitt and Kehrer 1981). Program participants received over $60 million in direct benefits over the four sites (New Jersey; Gary, Indiana; rural Iowa and North Carolina; and Seattle/Denver). The experiments typically lasted three years, but a small proportion of the Seattle/Denver experiment lasted for five to twenty years. The NIT experiments varied across sites in several features, including sample size (809 to 4,800), income eligibility cutoff (1.5 to 3.25 times poverty), and in the tax benefit parameters. Robins (1985) presents a useful comparison of the labor supply findings in the NIT experiments. His summary concludes that participation responses are small for men but sizeable for females (single and married) as well as young individuals. In fact, the average employment effects across the four experiments are stronger than the annual hours worked response for both single and married females. One may argue that these findings are not relevant because of the dramatic changes to the labor market and the labor market participation of women over the past three decades. We are sympathetic to this view but present these results to show that recent findings regarding the participation responses to tax reforms should not be surprising.

Finally, indirect evidence comes from two studies that are largely focused on the statistical properties of labor supply models (Triest 1990; Mroz 1987). Triest examines labor supply behavior using nonlinear budget set models. These models allow for jumps as well stickiness in labor supply with nonproportional tax schedules and therefore are particularly useful for evaluating the effects of taxes. Using Panel Study of Income Dynamics (PSID) data, Triest estimates censored and truncated hours of work models and finds larger elasticities for married women when using the censored data. He concludes that the difference is likely due to stronger labor force participation than hours worked responsiveness to taxes. In his sensitivity analysis of married women's hours of work, Mroz (1987) finds similar results for married women using a standard model of labor supply that does not explicitly account for budget set nonlinearities. Both Triest and Mroz finds small hours worked responses by working women.

Overall, the evidence is convincing that the labor force participation margin is sensitive to taxes, and in fact more sensitive than are hours worked.

4.5   Welfare Effects from Tax Reform: The Tax Reform Act of 1986 as a Case Study

4.5.1   Methodology and Data

As described earlier, a succession of tax acts have changed work incentives in the United States quite substantially. In particular, the EITC expansions strongly improved returns to entry in the labor market, and they involved large changes on the intensive margin too because of the phasing in and out of the credit. Based on the empirical findings of large participation responses, we have argued that it is crucial to incorporate this margin of response in the welfare analysis. More specifically, we showed theoretically that it is necessary to make an explicit distinction between the extensive and intensive margins whenever nonlinearities are significant, either in the pre-reform taxes and transfers or in the reform itself. Since the EITC is a highly nonlinear transfer, our point seems to be very relevant for the recent tax reforms.

To understand the quantitative importance of these insights, we apply the theory outlined in section 4.2 to study the Tax Reform Act of 1986 (TRA86). We focus on the welfare effects of the reform on single women with dependent children. This population is particularly interesting for two reasons. First, it were affected more by the EITC than any other group in the labor market. After the full phase-in of the 1986 reform, 95 percent of all single mothers had income below the EITC maximum allowable income. Besides the effect of the EITC, tax liabilities and average tax rates of single mothers were reduced further due to increases in the standard deduction, personal exemptions, and a more favorable tax rate schedule. All these elements led to big improvements in the labor supply incentives on the extensive margin. Second, single mothers are interesting in our context because their labor supply responses to tax reform have been so well documented. In particular, we know that participation elasticities are large for this group.

We use a microsimulation approach to study the welfare effects of the reform. The simulations are based on the formula in (14). Notice that this approach is exact only for small policy reforms. Since the tax changes that were introduced by the 1986 tax act were quite substantial, our calculations should be seen as first-order approximations to the true welfare effects. The potential errors of the approximation will be discussed later.

The implementation of our deadweight formula requires information about labor supply elasticities as well as various tax transfer parameters and wage income shares. The labor supply elasticities will be taken from the empirical literature reviewed in section 4.3. To generate the tax transfer parameters, we first estimate effective marginal and average tax rates (m_i and a_i) for each individual. Calculations of marginal and average tax rates should account for all taxes on labor income (federal taxes, state taxes, and payroll taxes), and they should account for the phase-out of welfare benefits. Moreover, the tax rates should reflect values pertaining to the time immediately before the reform (we use 1985 as the pre-reform year).

The changes in tax rates introduced by the reform ($\partial m_i / \partial z_i$ and $\partial a_i / \partial z_i$) are computed as the difference between the pre-reform rates and imputed post-reform rates, reflecting the changes in the tax code after the reform is fully phased in (but not any behavioral responses). To isolate the impact of TRA86 (which was a federal tax reform), we include only the difference between pre-reform and post-reform federal tax rates. The post-reform federal tax rate is imputed by applying the post-reform federal tax code to pre-reform individual incomes (adjusted for inflation). To account for the phasing-in of the reform, we use 1988 as the post-reform year.

The data for the simulations come from the March Current Population Survey. The March CPS is an annual demographic file of approximately 60,000 households, with information on labor market and income outcomes. From CPS we extract information on unmarried females (widowed, divorced, and never married) who are between 16 and 55 years old and who have dependent children (children under the age of 19 or under 24 if a full-time student). We exclude older women to avoid complications related to modeling retirement decisions. We also exclude any female who was ill or disabled, was in the military, or reported herself retired during the previous year. Finally, we exclude any woman with negative earned income (due to negative

Table 4.2
Summary statistics: Single mothers

Age	32.60 (8.64)
Years of education	12.82 (2.54)
Number of children	1.92 (1.11)
Non-white	0.306 (0.461)
Labor force participation	0.702 (0.457)
Earned income	$7,998 (9.366)
Non-labor income	$2,837 (4,963)
Gross hourly wage	$6.49 (4.49)
Observations	4,732

Note: Authors' tabulations of the 1985 March Current Population Survey. Sample includes unmarried mothers ages 16–55. See text for further sample selection. Earned income includes wage and salary and self-employment income. Non-labor income is calculated as the difference between total income and earnings, and therefore includes income for various sources such as welfare assistance, capital income, social security income, and workers' compensation. The wage is defined for workers only. Standard errors are in parenthesis. All monetary amounts are in nominal dollars.

self-employment income), negative unearned income, or with positive earned income but zero hours of work. The resulting sample size is 4,730 observations. Table 4.2 presents summary statistics of the characteristics of all unmarried females with children used for the analysis. The typical unmarried mother is 33 years old with two children. She has a high school diploma and earns an hourly wage of $6.49 in 1985.

The tax parameters for the sample of female heads are calculated using the Tax Simulation Model (TAXSIM) of the National Bureau of Economic Research (NBER). Since we cannot observe the earnings of nonworkers if employed, we impute earnings for all individuals in the sample using a simple earnings regression.[7] The predicted earnings and CPS data on individual nonlabor income are used as input in TAXSIM to calculate the marginal tax rate and the tax liability of each individual in the sample. Because the CPS does not ask about itemized deductions, we assume everyone takes the standard deduction. The TAXSIM-generated tax rates include the federal, state and payroll tax components but do not include the transfer component.

In the United States, lower-income families are eligible to receive cash assistance from the Temporary Assistance to Needy Families, previously the Aid to Families with Dependent Children (AFDC) program. In addition, eligible families may receive in kind benefits in the form of food vouchers (food stamps) and health insurance (Medicaid).

To incorporate benefits, we augment tax data from TAXSIM with information on AFDC, food stamps, and Medicaid. Because transfer programs have differing eligibility and benefit structures at the federal and state levels, we treat each program separately. We assign unemployed parents the maximum AFDC benefit in their state of residence and apply a tax rate of 25 percent on earned income (Triest 1994). To assign Medicaid benefits, we used the average annual health expenditures on AFDC recipients by state in 1985. Because Medicaid benefits were not reduced on the margin with earned income, Medicaid eligibility and expenditures affect the total tax liability (and average tax rate) but not the marginal tax rate.

To get an impression of the shapes of the individual budget constraints, we display in figure 4.5 the budget set of a woman who is living in Pennsylvania and has two children. The graph shows that effective taxes can be very high at low incomes, especially before the 1986 tax reform. Prior to the reform, if the mother chooses to enter the labor market at $8000, she will lose $6,000 in net tax payments and withdrawal of AFDC and food stamps. In other words, the effective average tax rate relevant for the entry decision is 75 percent for this in-

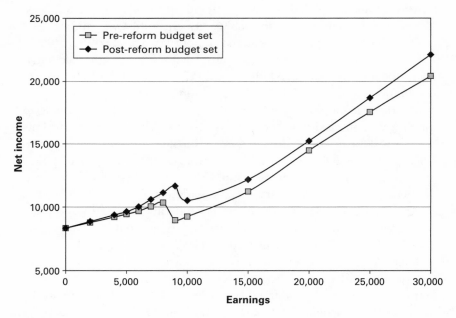

Figure 4.5
Budget set for single mother with two children (Pennsylvania)

dividual. The downward jump in net income as earnings pass $8,000 occurs because Medicaid is lost entirely at this earnings level. Immediately beyond the Medicaid threshold, there is essentially no net income gain from entry; that is, the participation tax rate is almost 100 percent. It will never be optimal for the individual to enter at this earnings level. Finally, notice that the 1986 reform provided a large increase in the incentive to work. At an earnings level of $8,000, the net income gain of working was increased from $2,000 to $3,000.

Figure 4.5 illustrates only an example of a budget set. In the sample, there is substantial variation in the budget sets across the individuals depending on state of residence, number of children, and so forth. In addition, our procedure overestimates on average the true effective tax rates because the take-up rate of benefits has been shown to be much less than 1 (see the review by Moffitt 1992). To correct this bias, we apply an empirical take-up rate, calculated from our CPS data as the share of the eligible population that reports positive benefits during the year. In the 1985 CPS, the empirical take-up rate was 56 percent. We apply this rate to the statutory benefit amount and the statutory benefit reduction rate. Therefore, both the marginal and the average tax rates are adjusted in this procedure.

Table 4.3 presents sample means and standard deviations for the tax parameters of female household heads. What the data shows is that the typical female household head loses 25.4 cents on the next dollar of earnings to federal and state income taxes, and an additional 17.7 cents to the welfare authorities through reduced cash and food benefits. In total, she pays 43 percent on the marginal dollar earned. On average, however, she loses about 52 percent of her total earnings to the tax and welfare authorities with entry into the labor market. As a consequence, the tax rate on the extensive margin is higher than the tax rate on the intensive margin. The table also reports "tax ratios" to be used in the welfare calculations, namely, $t/(1 - t)$, where t denotes the marginal or average tax rate. The average tax ratio associated with the extensive welfare effect is higher than the intensive tax ratio important for the intensive welfare effect. Finally, as shown at the bottom of the table, TRA86 had a large impact on the tax treatment of single mothers. On average, their effective marginal and average tax rates were reduced by 6 and 8 percentage points, respectively. The standard deviations indicate substantial heterogeneity, however, especially for the changes in the marginal tax rate due to the phasing in and out of the EITC.

Table 4.3
Tax-benefit parameters for single mothers for TRA86

Tax rate on the intensive margin (pre-reform)	
Marginal tax rate without benefits	0.254 (0.164)
Marginal tax rate with benefits	0.431 (0.156)
Marginal tax ratio	1.129 (3.137)
Tax rate on the extensive margin (pre-reform)	
Average tax rate without benefits	0.144 (0.106)
Average tax rate with benefits	0.518 (0.109)
Average tax ratio	1.359 (3.742)
Effect of the 1986 tax reform act	
Change in the effective marginal tax rate	−0.060 (0.095)
Change in the effective average tax rate	−0.075 (0.029)

Note: The reported parameter values are sample means while numbers in parenthesis are standard deviations. The tax parameters include federal, state, and social security payroll rates. The effective tax rates account for the withdrawal of benefits and include cash assistance (AFDC), food stamps, and Medicaid adjusted for an empirical 54 percent take-up rate. The tax ratios are derived by calculating the average over the individuals of $t/(1-t)$, where t is the relevant tax rate of the individual. The tax ratios include benefits. The pre-reform tax benefit rates are from 1985. The changes in the marginal and average tax rates reflect only changes at the federal level. The data come from the 1985 March Current Population Survey.

4.5.2   Welfare Effects

In this section, we use the tax and benefit calculations described earlier to simulate the welfare effects arising from the behavioral responses of single mothers to the 1986 tax act. Before turning to the simulation results, we attempt to gauge the effects of the tax reform simply by looking at the sample means presented in table 4.3, using a representative agent approach. In this approach, the welfare effect from the intensive margin is calculated by multiplying the means of the marginal tax ratio and the marginal tax rate change, then applying an (compensated) hours-of-work elasticity. To calculate the welfare effect from the extensive margin of response, we repeat the procedure using the average tax ratio, the average tax rate change, and the elasticity of labor force participation. Based on the tax and benefit parameters presented in table 4.3, this approach yields substantial positive welfare effects from both reforms and on both margins even for very small elasticities.

This approach is unlikely to yield precise results, however, because single mothers are quite hetergeneous as a group. More precisely, the shortcoming of the representative agent approach in this evaluation arises from the fact that tax rates, tax rate changes, and wage income

Table 4.4
Welfare effects from TRA86 on single mothers for different elasticity scenarios

Elasticity scenarios	Elasticities		The welfare gain from tax reform			Welfare gain per dollar spent
	Extensive	Intensive	Extensive	Intensive	Total	
Low	0.3	0.1	3.27	0.81	4.08	2.07
		0.2	3.27	1.62	4.89	2.62
		0.3	3.27	2.43	5.70	3.59
Middle	0.5	0.1	5.46	0.81	6.27	4.81
		0.2	5.46	1.62	7.08	9.50
		0.3	5.46	2.43	7.89	352.22
High	0.7	0.1	7.64	0.81	8.45	Laffer
		0.2	7.64	1.62	9.26	Laffer
		0.3	7.64	2.43	10.07	Laffer

Note: The welfare gain is measured in percentage of wage income and is calculated using equation (14) in the text. The total welfare gain is calculated as the sum of the intensive and extensive gains. The welfare gain per dollar spent measures the total welfare gain in proportion to the aggregate reduction in tax burden. A Laffer curve effect arises if the welfare gain is larger than the reduction in tax burden, in which case the reform creates a net tax revenue. The data come from the 1985 March Current Population Survey.

shares are highly correlated. For example, in our sample those initially in the phase-out range of the EITC experience a reduction in the effective average tax rate of 10 percentage points while the effective average tax rate of those in the phase-in interval decreases by only 6 percentage points. Since those in the phase-out range have higher productivities, their behavioral responses have more weight in the welfare calculation. Such heterogeneity is critically important for correctly simulating the welfare effects of tax reforms. As such, one should interpret with caution welfare calculations that do not account fully for the type of heterogeneity just described.

The simulations that we present here exploit all the individual heterogeneity in the sample. The results are shown in table 4.4, where we consider different elasticity scenarios. We examine three different participation elasticities (0.3, 0.5, and 0.7) that are each combined with three different values of the (compensated) hours-of-work elasticity (0.1, 0.2, and 0.3). All these scenarios seem to fall within the range of elasticities estimated in the literature on female labor supply. In particular, the scenarios reflect that the weight of empirical evidence indicates that the extensive elasticity is significantly larger than the intensive elasticity, especially for single mothers.

Columns 4–6 present the estimated welfare gains from the reform in proportion to the aggregate wage income of single mothers, decomposed into effects arising from labor supply responses along the two different margins. The last column shows the welfare gain to single mothers per dollar of revenue spent on their tax relief. This last number corresponds also to the so-called marginal cost of public funds, which is the estimate one would get when thinking about raising additional government revenue by reversing the reform.

Turning to the results in table 4.4, we find that TRA86 generated substantial welfare gains. In the middle scenario, the total gain is about 7.1 percent of wage income, and the welfare effects spanned by the different elasticity scenarios are from 4.1 to 10.1 percent. According to these estimates, the welfare gain per dollar spent is at least $2.00. In fact, for all the high elasticity scenarios—not out of the bounds of empirical estimates—we obtain Laffer curve effects. In these cases, the labor supply responses to the reform create an increase in government revenue that is sufficiently large to finance the initial reductions in the tax liabilities of single mothers. With Laffer effects, the gain per dollar spent is negative and hence difficult to interpret, which is why we do not show it. Notice also that, as we approach the maximum of the Laffer curve, the gain per dollar spent goes to infinity. This explains the very large number in one of the scenarios.

The table shows that the aggregate welfare gain is the result of positive effects along each of the two margins of labor supply. The 1986 tax reform act reduced average tax rates for almost all single mothers (99.7 percent of our sample), thereby increasing labor force participation and creating positive welfare effects along this margin. The effect on marginal tax rates, on the other hand, was not unambiguous due to the phasing in and out of the EITC. In particular, some people experienced higher marginal tax rates due to an expanded phase-out region for the EITC. Yet our tax simulations show that the marginal tax rate was reduced for 81.8 percent of the individuals in our sample, which explains the positive welfare effects created on the intensive margin. Taking a closer look at the size of the welfare effects at the two margins, we observe that for all elasticity combinations, the welfare effect along the extensive margin is greater than that along the intensive margin. In the middle elasticity scenario, almost 80 percent of the overall welfare gain is generated by movements into the labor market.

Of course, one reason for the larger welfare effects along the extensive margin is simply that participation elasticities are higher than hours-of-work elasticities. However, this difference in labor supply responsiveness cannot account entirely for the difference in welfare effects. As an example, consider the elasticity scenario where both elasticities are equal to 0.3. Even in this scenario, the adjustment in labor supply along the extensive margin creates a larger welfare effect than that occurring on the intensive margin. This result illustrates why it is important to distinguish explicitly between the two margins of labor supply response. The distinction is important due to the difference between marginal and average tax rates created by nonlinearities (and discontinuities). The effect of nonlinearity is present both in the pre-reform tax system and in the reform.

As shown in table 4.3, the 1986 reform reduced average tax rates by more than it reduced marginal rates. In isolation, this generates a larger participation response than hours-of-work response and, by implication, a larger welfare gain is generated along the extensive margin. This effect is reinforced by the fact that effective average tax rates were about 9 percentage points higher than marginal tax rates prior to the reform. This implies that tax distortions were initially higher on the participation margin than on the hours-of-work margin. Therefore, a given increase in labor supply is more beneficial for economic efficiency if it is occurring along the extensive margin.

An important feature of the EITC is its heterogeneous effects on taxpayers at different points in the income distribution. To explore the role of heterogeneity, table 4.5 shows tax-benefit parameters and welfare calculations by income groups for the middle elasticity scenario. We divide the population according to the threshold levels of the EITC prior to the implementation of the 1986 reform. The overall decline in marginal tax rates reflects substantial differences across individuals. The largest reductions were concentrated among taxpayers with incomes in the flat and phase-out ranges before the reform ($5,000–$11,000), representing 49 percent of the total population and 54 percent of wage income. The lowest income taxpayers, representing over one-third of the population of female heads and 10 percent of wage income, had their marginal rates reduced by less than the average individual. Finally, taxpayers beyond the eligibility threshold, representing 36 percent of the aggregate wage income, experienced a slight increase in their marginal tax rate. The small effect on this group is the result of offsetting effects from an expanded phase-out region for the EITC and lower non-EITC federal tax rates. Turning to the average tax rate relevant for participation, we see that it was reduced for all

Table 4.5
Tax-benefit parameters for single mothers by income groups: Participation elasticity equal to 0.5 and hours-of-work elasticity equal to 0.2

	Phase-in <5,000	Plateau 5,000– 6,500	Phase-out 6,500– 11,000	Beyond >11,000	Aggregate
Group shares					
Population	0.35	0.13	0.36	0.15	1.00
Wage income	0.10	0.09	0.45	0.36	1.00
Tax benefit parameters					
Marginal tax rate	0.45	0.40	0.45	0.37	0.43
Average tax rate	0.52	0.47	0.53	0.52	0.52
Change in marginal tax rate	−0.05	−0.11	−0.08	0.01	−0.06
Change in average tax rate	−0.06	−0.08	−0.10	−0.06	−0.08
Welfare gain					
Intensive	0.12	0.30	1.15	0.05	1.62
Extensive	0.36	0.37	3.27	1.45	5.46
Total	0.48	0.67	4.42	1.50	7.08

Note: The marginal tax rate and the average tax rate incorporate benefits. See notes to tables 4.3 and 4.4 for an explanation of calculations. The decomposition into different income groups is determined by the income thresholds in the Earned Income Tax Credit before the 1986 reform.

income groups. Again, the reduction is largest for those who were located in the plateau or phase-out regions of the EITC prior to the reform.

The last panel in table 4.5 shows that the welfare gains from TRA86 are concentrated among higher-income female household heads. Females with income in the phase-out group represent the largest source of efficiency gains. In fact, the welfare effect along the extensive margin for this group contributes with nearly half of the total welfare gain. The large welfare effect for this group occurs because its members have the highest wage share, face the highest tax rate on labor force participation prior to the reform, and experience the largest reduction in the participation tax rate following the reform. This correlation among wage shares, initial tax rates, and tax rate reductions is important for the size of the total welfare effect. Our results therefore suggest that accounting for heterogeneity in the tax effects can be critical to the proper evaluations of tax reform.

Our evaluation of tax reform includes only first-order welfare effects and is therefore exact only for small reforms. This approach implies that we do not have to apply specific functional forms. On the other hand, the tax changes introduced by the 1986 tax act were quite substantial and may have created non-negligible second-order effects. One type of second-order effect derives from the fact that the marginal excess burden is positively related to the size of the tax wedge (cf. equation 14). In the simulations, the welfare gain from the increase in labor supply is evaluated at the pre-reform tax wedge. However, as the tax wedge is reduced, so is the marginal welfare gain. By evaluating the entire labor supply response at the pre-reform tax wedge, we tend to overstate the welfare gains. Another type of second-order effect works through the labor supply elasticities. These may go up or down as we move away from the pre-reform equilibrium. The direction and magnitude of the implied welfare effects depend on third derivatives of the utility function of which we have no knowledge.

4.6   Concluding Remarks

This chapter has argued that recent empirical evidence on labor supply behavior has important implications for the evaluation of tax reforms. Our interest in particular is the emerging consensus that labor supply responses tend to be concentrated more along the extensive margin (labor force participation) than along the intensive margin (hours of work). To understand the implications of the empirical research for evaluating tax reform, we have outlined a simple welfare theoretic framework incorporating (discrete) participation responses. We show that it is necessary to distinguish explicitly between intensive and extensive responses in welfare analysis whenever nonlinearities are present either in the pre-reform tax transfer system or in the policy reform under consideration. This is because labor force participation is related to a different tax rate than hours worked. While the welfare effects from hours-of-work responses are related to the marginal tax rate, the welfare effects from participation responses are instead linked to the effective average rate of taxation (including the average phase-out for transfers). Differences between these two tax rates are driven by the degree of nonlinearity in the tax transfer schedules, particularly important at the lower end of the income distribution.

To examine the quantitative importance of the theoretical points, we presented a microsimulation exercise to evaluate the welfare effects of TRA86 on female household heads. The results suggest that substantial welfare gains were created by the reform, mostly along the extensive margin of labor supply. The application therefore confirms the quantitative importance of accounting for the extensive margin of labor supply for a particular tax reform. Eissa, Kleven, and Kreiner (2004) extend the results in this chapter to a wider range of reforms. It is shown that some of the points made here are even more important for some of the more recent reforms in the United States. In particular, we are thinking of the tax acts passed in 1990 and 1993, which introduced very large expansions of the EITC.

In general, our results indicate that policy simulations that do not account for (discrete) participation responses may make significant errors. The error will be larger at the bottom of the earnings distribution for two reasons: participation responses are large, and nonlinearities in taxes and transfers tend to be very important. This criticism seems to apply to, among others, Browning and Johnson (1984), Ballard (1988), Triest (1994), and Browning (1995).

Finally, although we have focused exclusively on tax reform in the United States, the results may carry implications for welfare reform in other countries as well. In particular, many European countries are characterized by large taxes and transfers creating very poor incentives to participate in the labor market for low-wage earners. This implies that in-work benefit reform may be a good policy to adopt in these countries. Indeed, the findings of Immervoll et al. (2004) suggest that this is the case. Interestingly, a number of European countries, including the United Kingdom, Ireland, and France, have introduced various forms of in-work benefits in recent years.

Notes

Comments by Jonas Agell, Isabelle Robert-Bobée, Peter Birch Sørensen, two anonymous referees, and participants at the CESifo Workshop on Tax Policy and Labor Market Performance are gratefully acknowledged. We also wish to thank Emmanuel Saez for helpful discussions on this topic. The activities of EPRU (Economic Policy Research Unit) are supported by a grant from The Danish National Research Foundation.

1. Alternatively, one may introduce the non-convexity directly in the preferences through fixed "psychic" costs of participation.

2. These types of discontinuities in benefits and taxes apply, for example, to Medicaid in the United States (cf. section 5.1), to the national insurance tax in the United Kingdom (see Blundell, Duncan, and Meghir 1998), and to housing benefits in some continental European countries (Immervoll et al. 2004).

3. A general framework for analyzing welfare effects with discrete choice is provided by Small and Rosen (1981).

4. Kleven and Kreiner (2002) discuss the marginal cost of public funds in a similar context.

5. Indeed, it is not uncommon that simulation studies based on the standard convex model employ total elasticities in their calibration. For example, this seems to be the case in Browning and Johnson 1984; Ballard, Shoven, and Whalley 1985; Ballard 1988; Browning 1995; and Bourguignon and Spadaro 2002a, 2002b. In all these studies, high female labor supply elasticities (around 0.5–1.0) are used in the calibration, although elasticity estimates of this magnitude tend to be based on censored specifications including observations with 0 hours of work (Mroz 1987; Triest 1990). By implication, these studies are lumping together extensive and intensive responses in the simulations.

6. More detailed information on eligibility and benefits is provided in Hotz and Scholz 2003.

7. The log of earnings (by workers) is regressed on demographic characteristics, including age, education, age-education interactions, race, and state of residence. We also control for self-selection into the labor force using a propensity score correction. The selection term is identified by the number of children.

References

Ballard, C. L. 1988. "The Marginal Efficiency Cost of Redistribution." *American Economic Review* 78: 1019–1033.

Ballard, C. L., J. B. Shoven, and J. Whalley. 1985. "General Equilibrium Computations of the Marginal Welfare Costs of Taxes in the United States." *American Economic Review* 75: 128–138.

Blundell, R. 2001. "Evaluating Labour Supply Responses to In-work Benefit Reforms for Low Income Workers." In *Taxation, Welfare and the Crisis of Unemployment in Europe*, ed. Marco Buti, Paolo Sestito, and Hans Wijkander, 157–187. London: Edward Elgar.

Blundell, R. W., A. Duncan, J. McCrae, and C. Meghir. 2000. "The Labour Market Impact of the Working Families Tax Credit." *Fiscal Studies* 21: 75–104.

Blundell, R. W., A. Duncan, and C. Meghir. 1998. "Estimating Labor Supply Responses Using Tax Reforms." *Econometrica* 66: 827–861.

Blundell, R. W., J. Ham, and C. Meghir. 1987. "Unemployment and Female Labour Supply." *Economic Journal* 97: 44–64.

Bourguignon, F., and A. Spadaro. 2002a. "Redistribution and Labour Supply Incentives: An Application of the Optimal Tax Theory." Mimeo., DELIA (Department and Laboratory of Applied and Theoretical Economics), Paris.

Bourguignon, F., and A. Spadaro. 2002b. "Tax-benefit Revealed Social Preferences: Are Tax Authorities Non-Paretian?" Mimeo., DELIA (Department and Laboratory of Applied and Theoretical Economics), Paris.

Browning, E. K. 1995. "Effects of the Earned Income Tax Credit on Income and Welfare." *National Tax Journal* 48: 23–43.

Browning, E. K., and W. R. Johnson. 1984. "The Trade-off between Equality and Efficiency." *Journal of Political Economy* 92: 175–203.

Cogan, J. F. 1981. "Fixed Costs and Labor Supply." *Econometrica* 49: 945–963.

Dahlby, Bev. 1998. "Progressive Taxation and the Social Marginal Cost of Public Funds." *Journal of Public Economics* 67: 105–122.

Dickert, S., S. Houser, and J. K. Scholz. 1995. "The Earned Income Tax Credit and Transfer Programs: A Study of Labor Market and Program Participation." In *Tax Policy and the Economy*, 9th ed., ed. J. Poterba, 1–50. Cambridge, Mass.: MIT Press.

Eissa, N., and H. Hoynes. 2004. "Taxes and the Labor Market Participation of Married Couples: The Earned Income Tax Credit." *Journal of Public Economics* 88: 1937–1958.

Eissa, N., H. J. Kleven, and C. T. Kreiner. 2004. "Evaluating Tax Reform: Labor Supply at the Intensive and Extensive Margins." Mimeo.

Eissa, N., and J. Liebman. 1996. "Labor Supply Response to the Earned Income Tax Credit." *Quarterly Journal of Economics* 61: 605–637.

Heim, B. T., and B. D. Meyer. 2004. "Work Costs and Nonconvex Preferences in the Estimation of Labor Supply Models." *Journal of Public Economics* 88: 2323–2338.

Hotz, V. J., C. H. Mullin, and J. K. Scholz. 2002. "The Earned Income Tax Credit and Labor Market Participation of Families on Welfare." Mimeo., University of California, Los Angeles, Vanderbilt, and University of Wisconsin-Madison.

Hotz, V. J., and J. K. Scholz. 2003. "The Earned Income Tax Credit." In *Means-tested Transfer Programs in the United States*, ed. R. A. Moffitt, 141–197. Chicago: University of Chicago Press.

Immervoll, H., H. J. Kleven, C. T. Kreiner, and E. Saez. 2004. "Welfare Reform in European Countries: A Micro-Simulation Analysis." CEPR Discussion Paper No. 4324, March. Forthcoming in *The Economic Journal*.

Killingsworth, M. R., and J. J. Heckman. 1986. "Female Labor Supply: A Survey." In *Handbook of Labor Economics*, vol. 1, ed. O. Ashenfelter and R. Layard, 103–204. Amsterdam: North-Holland.

Kleven, H. J., and C. T. Kreiner. 2002. "The Marginal Cost of Public Funds in OECD Countries: Hours of Work versus Labor Force Participation." CESifo Working Paper No. 935, München.

Meyer, B., and D. Rosenbaum. 2001. "Welfare, the Earned Income Tax Credit, and the Labor Supply of Single Mothers." *Quarterly Journal of Economics* 66: 1063–1114.

Mirrlees, J. A. 1971. "An Exploration in the Theory of Optimal Income Taxation." *Review of Economic Studies* 38: 175–208.

Moffitt, R. 1992. "Incentive Effects of the U.S. Welfare System." *Journal of Economic Literature* 30: 1–61.

Moffitt, R., and K. C. Kehrer. 1981. "The Effects of Tax and Transfer Programs on Labor Supply." In *Research in Labor Economics*, ed. R. Ehrenberg, 103–150. Amsterdam: Elsevier.

Mroz, T. A. 1987. "The Sensitivity of an Empirical Model of Married Women's Hours of Work to Economic and Statistical Assumptions." *Econometrica* 55: 765–799.

Robins, P. K. 1985. "A Comparison of the Labor Supply Findings from the Four Negative Income Tax Experiments." *Journal of Human Resources* 20: 567–582.

Saez, E. 2002. "Optimal Income Transfer Programs: Intensive versus Extensive Labor Supply Responses." *Quarterly Journal of Economics* 117: 1039–1073.

Small, K., and H. Rosen. 1981. "Applied Welfare Economics with Discrete Choice Models." *Econometrica* 49: 105–130.

Triest, R. K. 1990. "The Effect of Income Taxation on Labor Supply in the United States." *Journal of Human Resources* 25: 491–516.

Triest, R. K. 1994. "The Efficiency Cost of Increased Progressivity." In *Tax Progressivity and Income Inequality*, ed. J. Slemrod, 137–176. Cambridge: Cambridge University Press.

5

The Hours of Work Response of Married Couples: Taxes and the Earned Income Tax Credit

Nada Eissa and Hilary Hoynes

5.1 Introduction

Low-income transfer policy in the United States has undergone a radical transformation in the past fifteen years. Assistance to the needy (traditional welfare) is no longer an entitlement without conditions, but is instead temporary assistance with work requirements. More generally, the changes can be characterized as a shift from out-of-work benefits to in-work benefits. This shift to "making-work-pay" is not limited to the United States, however. A number of countries have adopted policies to enable work by lower-income families, including the United Kingdom, Canada, Finland, and New Zealand (Blundell and Hoynes 2004; Duncan 2003). A number of other countries yet are considering making-work-pay policies (Denmark, Australia).

In the United States, in-work benefits for low-income families are provided largely through the Earned Income Tax Credit (EITC). In a relatively short period of time, the EITC has been transformed from a very small program to become the largest cash transfer program for lower-income families with children. About twenty million families are projected to have benefited from the EITC in 2003, at a total cost to the federal government of nearly $34 billion (Internal Revenue Service, 2003).[1] By contrast, only seven million families received the EITC in 1986, at a total cost of $2 billion.

The design of the EITC is unusual and includes three regions: phase-in, flat, and phase-out. The credit is a pure earnings subsidy in the phase-in region. Workers continue to receive the maximum credit over some range of earnings, after which the credit is gradually phased out. In 2005, a family with two children would have received a 40 percent subsidy rate per dollar earned, and a 21 percent phase-out rate on income up to about $35,000. Families with one child had a less generous credit schedule. Although the credit may be received as part of a worker's regular paycheck, only a very small share of taxpayers avails itself of that option, choosing instead to receive the transfer in the form of a lump-sum payment when annual taxes are filed.[2]

Advocates of the credit argue that redistribution occurs with much less distortion to labor supply than that caused by other elements of the welfare system. In particular, the credit is said to encourage labor force participation. Critics, however, point to the marginal tax rates in the phase-out of the credit to argue that the credit (when combined with federal, state, and payroll taxes) can impose very high marginal tax rates that may substantially reduce hours worked.

In this chapter, we examine the impact of the EITC on the labor supply of married couples. This group is particularly interesting for several reasons. First, the popular view that the credit "encourages work effort" is unlikely to hold among married couples. Primary earners (typically men) may slightly increase labor force participation, but most secondary earners in recipient families are expected to reduce their labor supply. In fact, the EITC causes the budget constraint faced by many secondary earners to look strikingly similar to that faced by welfare (Aid to Families with Dependent Children, or AFDC, and Temporary Assistance to Needy Families, or TANF) recipients. In addition, empirical research suggests that the reduction in labor supply may be substantial for affected groups. That work finds that labor supply of secondary earners, typically married women, is particularly sensitive to taxes (Triest 1992). Finally, these incentives affect a significant portion of the EITC population: in 1994 one-third of all recipients and about 40 percent of the phase-out population are married couples (U.S. General Accounting Office 1996).

In earlier work, we found that EITC expansions over the past decade increased the likelihood of married men's labor participation only slightly but *reduced* the likelihood of married women's labor force participation by over a full percentage point (Eissa and Hoynes 2004). In this chapter, we extend that work and examine the impact of the EITC on the hours worked of married couples. We use Current Population Survey (CPS) data from 1984–1996, which allows us to examine the expansions in the EITC in 1986, 1990, and 1993. Whereas our primary interest is in the response to changes in the budget set induced by the EITC, our estimation strategy takes account of budget set changes caused by federal tax policy and of cross-sectional variation in income and family size.

The problems of estimating the impact of taxes on labor supply are well known in the literature, and they include the joint determination of hours worked and tax rates. We estimate instrumental variables models to address the endogeneity of the net-of-tax wage to labor supply. Our instruments trace the budget set and take advantage of both time (tax reform) variation and cross-sectional (nonlabor income and family size) variation in the tax schedule. As a preliminary analysis, we evaluate the impact of the EITC expansion using quasi-experimental methods where we compare changes in labor supply among EITC eligible and ineligible groups.

This chapter makes two important contributions. First, while a number of papers have evaluated the EITC's effect on the labor supply of single women, few have examined the labor supply decisions of married couples using tax reform variation (see the review in Hotz and Scholz 2003). Second, the chapter also contributes to the empirical labor supply literature by using a new instrument based on tax reforms that capture (changes to) the individual's entire budget.

Our main estimates are based on a sample of married couples with less than twelve years of schooling, chosen because they are most likely to be affected by the EITC. In 1996, almost 60 percent of less-educated married couples with children were eligible for the EITC. By comparison, only 20 (10) percent of couples with twelve (more than 12) years of schooling were eligible for the EITC. Our findings are consistent with existing evidence showing that married men's labor supply is not responsive to taxes whereas their spouses' labor supply is moderately responsive to taxes. For married women, the estimated elasticity of hours worked with respect to the net-of-tax wage is between 0.1 and 0.4.

Our simulations show that EITC expansions between 1984 and 1996 led to modest reductions in hours worked by married men and married women. Overall, married women in the labor force are estimated to decrease work by between 1 and 4 percent. Women in the phase-out range of the credit experience the greatest reductions, between 3 and 17 percent. Overall, the evidence suggests that family labor supply and pretax earnings fell.

The remainder of the chapter is as follows. Section 5.2 describes relevant features of the EITC, reviews the existing literature, and discusses the expected effects of the credit on family labor supply. Section 5.3 outlines our empirical methodology. Our data are summarized in section 5.4. Results are presented in sections 5.5 and 5.6. We conclude in section 5.7.

5.2   Background

5.2.1   The EITC and the Federal Income Tax

The EITC provides transfers primarily to working families with children. Eligibility and the amount of the credit received depend on total family earnings and, since 1990, the number of children in the family.[3] The design of the EITC includes three regions: phase-in, flat, and phase-out. The credit is a pure earnings subsidy in the phase-in region. Workers continue to receive the maximum credit over some range of earnings, after which the credit is gradually phased out. In 2005, a family with one (two) children would have received a 34 (40) percent subsidy rate per dollar earned up to a maximum credit of $2,662 ($4,400), and a 16 (21) percent phase-out rate on income up to $31,030 ($35,263).

The credit is refundable so that a taxpayer with no federal tax liability, for example, would receive a tax refund from the government for the full amount of the credit. Taxpayers may also receive the credit throughout the year with their paychecks; but in 1989, less than one-half of 1 percent of all EITC recipients availed themselves of this early payment option (U.S. General Accounting Office 1992). Consequently, most recipients receive the credit as a single lump-sum payment when annual taxes are filed.

The EITC began in 1975 as a modest program aimed at offsetting the social security payroll tax for low-income families with children. Since its introduction the credit was changed very little, increasing from $400 to $500 (nominal dollars) by 1985 at its maximum level. Following the 1986 and subsequently the 1993 expansion, the EITC has become the largest cash transfer program for low-income families with children at the federal level. By 2000, total EITC expenditures (tax expenditures and direct outlays) amounted to about $30 billion.

Our data cover the period 1984–1996, and our estimation strategy exploits changes to the budget sets of lower-income families with children due to the 1986, 1990, and 1993 tax acts. To outline the major features of the tax changes, table 5.1 presents the parameters of the EITC and other federal income tax parameters from 1984 to 1997. The table highlights the dramatic changes to the federal income tax schedule over the period. In 1984, the federal (non-EITC) tax schedule consisted

Table 5.1
Federal income tax and EITC parameters, 1984–1997

Year	Federal income tax parameters		EITC parameters (family with one child; family with two or more children)			
	Lowest, highest marginal tax rate	Personal exemption, Standard deduction[a,b]	Phase-in rate	Maximum credit	Phase-out rate	Maximum earnings
1984	[0.000; 0.500]	$1,000; $0	0.100	$500	0.125	$10,000
1985	[0.000; 0.500]	$1,040; $0	0.110	$550	0.122	$11,000
1986	[0.000; 0.500]	$1,080; $0	0.110	$550	0.122	$11,000
TRA86						
1987	[0.110; 0.390]	$1,900; $2,540	0.140	$851	0.100	$15,432
1988	[0.150; 0.330]	$1,950; $4,400	0.140	$874	0.100	$18,576
1989	[0.150; 0.330]	$2,000; $4,550	0.140	$910	0.100	$19,340
1990	[0.150; 0.330]	$2,050; $4,750	0.140	$953	0.100	$20,264
OBRA90[c]						
1991	[0.150; 0.310]	$2,150; $5,000	0.167; 0.173	$1,192; $1,235	0.119; 0.124	$21,250
1992	[0.150; 0.310]	$2,300; $5,250	0.176; 0.184	$1,324; $1,384	0.126; 0.130	$22,370
1993	[0.150; 0.396]	$2,350; $5,450	0.185; 0.195	$1,434; $1,511	0.132; 0.139	$23,050
OBRA93[d]						
1994	[0.150; 0.396]	$2,450; $5,600	0.263; 0.300	$2,038; $2,526	0.160; 0.177	$23,755; $25,296
1995	[0.150; 0.396]	$2,500; $5,750	0.340; 0.360	$2,094; $3,110	0.160; 0.202	$24,396; $26,673
1996	[0.150; 0.396]	$2,550; $5,900	0.340; 0.400	$2,152; $3,556	0.160; 0.202	$25,078; $28,495
1997	[0.150; 0.396]	$2,650; $6,050	0.340; 0.400	$2,210; $3,656	0.160; 0.211	$25,750; $29,290

Source: U.S. House of Representatives 1996 and 2000 and authors' calculations from OBRA93.

[a] The standard deductions are given for head of household tax return.

[b] In 1984–1986, there were no standard deductions because of the zero bracket. The fifteen brackets include the zero bracket.

[c] Basic EITC only. Does not include supplemental young child credit or health insurance credit.

[d] Introduced a small benefit for taxpayers with no qualifying children, phased in at 0.0765 up to a maximum credit of $306.

of fifteen brackets, with marginal rates ranging from 0 to 50 percent. It now stands at five rates, ranging from 15 percent to nearly 40 percent. The table also highlights the central role of the EITC in altering the shape of the tax schedule.

The real value of the EITC increased only modestly in the early years and was mostly due to inflation.[4] The 1987 expansion of the EITC, passed as part of the Tax Reform Act of 1986 (TRA86), represents the first major expansion of the EITC. TRA86 increased the subsidy rate for the phase-in of the credit from 11 percent to 14 percent and increased the maximum income to which the subsidy rate was applied from $5,000 to $6,080. This resulted in an increase in the maximum credit from $550 to $851 ($788 in 1986 dollars). The phase-out rate was reduced from 12.22 percent to 10 percent. The higher maximum credit and the lower phase-out rate combined to expand the phase-out region from $11,000 in 1986 to $18,576 by 1988.

The positive impact of the EITC expansion on the tax liability of eligible taxpayers was reinforced by other elements of TRA86. TRA86 increased the standard deduction for taxpayers filing jointly from $3,670 in 1986 (included in the zero bracket) to $5,000 in 1988. TRA86 further reduced the tax liability of taxpayers with children by increasing the deduction per dependent exemption from $1,080 in 1986 to $1,950 in 1988. Finally, the tax schedules were changed, which led to increases in marginal tax rates for some married couples and reductions for others.

The Omnibus Budget Reconciliation Act of 1990 (OBRA90) further expanded the EITC for all eligible families and introduced a different EITC schedule for families with two or more children. The phase-in rate of the EITC was increased from 14 percent to 18.5 for taxpayers with one child and to 19.5 percent for taxpayers with more children. OBRA90 also generated a larger (nominal and real) increase in the maximum benefit, phased in over three years.

The largest single expansion over this period was contained in the Omnibus Reconciliation Act of 1993 (OBRA93) legislation. The 1993 expansion of the EITC, phased in between 1994 and 1996, led to an increase in the subsidy rate from 19.5 percent to 40 percent (18.5 to 34 percent) and an increase in the maximum credit from $1,511 to $3,556 ($1,434 to $2,152) for taxpayers with two or more children (taxpayers with one child). This expansion was substantially larger for those with two or more children. The phase-out rate was also raised, from 14 percent to 21 percent (13 to 16 percent) for taxpayers with two or more children (taxpayers with one child). Overall, the range of the phase-out was expanded dramatically, such that by 1996 a couple with two children would still be eligible with income levels of almost $30,000.

Figure 5.1 illustrates the shape of the EITC budget constraint and the effect of these three expansions, by plotting the value of the EITC (in 1996 dollars) against real family earnings for eligible taxpayers with one child (panel A) and two or more children (panel B). These figures show that the expansion in 1996 (TRA86) increased the eligible range substantially, while the 1993 expansion (OBRA93) primarily expanded the maximum credit, through an increase in the subsidy rate. This 1993 expansion was particularly large for families with two or more children (panel B). Overall, the subsidy rate increased from 10 percent in 1984 to 34 percent (40 percent) in 1996 for families with one (two or more) children and the real value of the maximum credit increased 185 percent (370 percent) for families with one child (two or more children).

Figure 5.2 plots the 1996 EITC against annual earnings for three different hourly wage levels. Again, panel A presents the schedule for families with one child and panel B presents the schedule for families with two or more children. The vertical line indicates full-time full-year hours of work (2,080 hours). Families earnings minimum wage ($4.75 per hour in 1996) could remain eligible for the credit even with both parents working full-time. At an hourly wage of $10, a family with one earner would be in the phase-out range. The secondary worker, therefore, would experience first-hour marginal tax rates that include this phase-out rate. At an hourly wage of $20, the primary earner in a family with one (two or more) children is eligible until 1,200 (1,400) hours per year. This result illustrates the often cited feature of the EITC—it is transferring income to *low-earnings* families that are not necessarily *low-wage* families.

5.2.2 Family Labor Supply and the EITC

To evaluate the impact of the EITC on married couples' labor supply, we begin with the impact of the EITC on an unmarried taxpayer. Because the EITC is available only to taxpayers with earned income, standard labor supply theory predicts that the EITC will encourage labor force participation among single parents. Figure 5.3 shows how the introduction of an EITC shifts the budget constraint of an otherwise untaxed individual from ADE to ABCDE. The well-being of a taxpayer

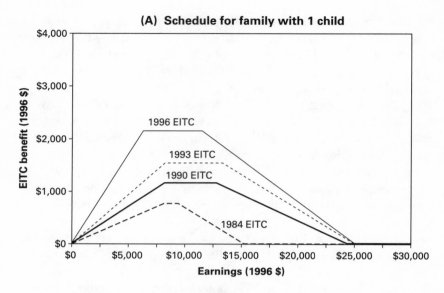

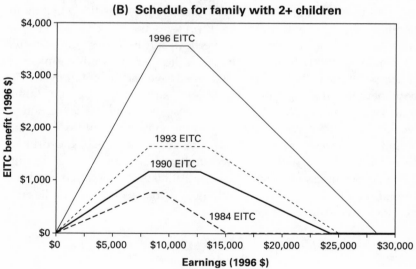

Figure 5.1
EITC benefit for selected tax years, by real earnings (1996 dollars). *Source:* Authors' tabulations of tax parameters in table 5.1.

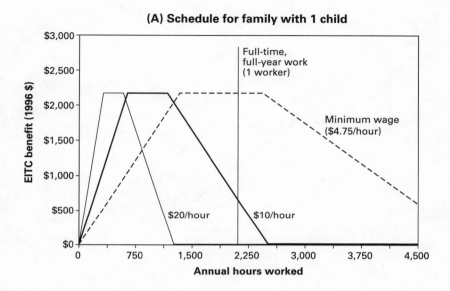

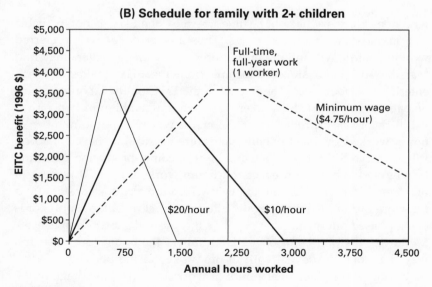

Figure 5.2
EITC benefit for selected hourly wage levels, by annual hours worked (1996 tax year).
Source: Authors' tabulations of tax parameters in table 5.1. Figure shows the value of the EITC by wage level + annual hours worked, assuming there is one worker in the family and no other sources of income.

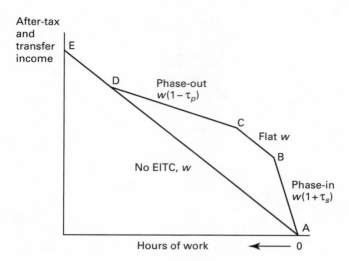

Figure 5.3
Stylized EITC budget constraint

who does not work has not changed because the EITC is not available to a taxpayer with zero earnings. Thus any taxpayer who preferred working before will still prefer working, and some taxpayers may find that the additional after-tax income from the EITC makes it worth entering the labor force. The impact of the EITC on the labor force participation of unmarried taxpayers is therefore unambiguously positive.

But theory also predicts that the credit will reduce the number of hours worked by most eligible taxpayers already in the labor force. While the credit initially increases with income, producing offsetting income and substitution effects on hours worked, over 70 percent of recipients have incomes in regions in which the credit is constant (and therefore produces only a negative income effect on labor supply) or is being phased out (producing negative income and substitution effects). Moreover, the phase-out of the credit alters the budget set in such a way that some taxpayers with incomes beyond the phase-out region may choose to reduce their hours of work and take advantage of the credit. Therefore, the EITC's only unambiguous positive effect on labor supply occurs on the participation margin.

Among married couples, the effects of the EITC on labor supply are more complicated because even the labor force participation effect is ambiguous.[5] This also occurs because the credit is based on *family* earnings and income. The simplest way to show how this effect operates is to consider sequential family labor supply decisions, with the husband as the primary mover and the wife as the secondary mover. In this model, the effect of the credit on the labor supply of primary earners is the same as that of single taxpayers. Labor force participation increases unambiguously. The impact on hours worked is again ambiguous but, for the reasons argued earlier, will most likely decline.

Secondary earners, however, receive the EITC even if they remain out of the labor force because of the husband's earnings. Suppose, for example, that the husband earns $12,700 (in 2000), thus placing the family at the beginning of the phase-out region of the credit. If the wife remains out of the labor force, her family receives the maximum credit of $3,888 if the couple has two children ($2,352 if one child). For each dollar of income she earns, however, the family's credit is reduced by 21 cents (about 18 cents if one child). Additionally, she pays the social security payroll and, possibly, state tax. With marginal tax rates approaching 50 percent, the incentive not to participate in the labor force can be quite strong. For these women, the EITC creates a budget set similar to that faced by traditional welfare programs (with a guarantee and high benefit reduction rate), which have been criticized for generating adverse work incentives. Of course, it is also possible for the wife's work effort to increase the family's credit if the husband's earnings are in the subsidy region ($6,800–$9,500 depending on family income), but very few married couples can be found with such low incomes.

To summarize, secondary earners whose spouses have incomes in the flat to phase-out regions should be less likely to work and should work fewer hours, while those whose spouses have income in the phase-in region should be more likely to work with ambiguous effects on hours worked. The net effect on the hours worked of married mothers is expected to be negative, and the magnitude will depend on the distribution of family income. Table 5.2 presents the distribution of families in different regions of the EITC, based on Internal Revenue Service (IRS) data (top panel), and CPS data (bottom panel). IRS data show that 73 percent of married EITC recipients have income in the phase-out range of the credit (compared to 53 percent of single recipients), where they face the highest marginal tax rates. CPS data show in addition that a substantial share of *less-educated* couples are eligible for the EITC (almost 60 percent), and affected by the high marginal tax rates (74 percent of eligible and 43 percent of all married couples have incomes in the phase-out range of the credit).

Table 5.2
Distribution of families by EITC credit range

	Married couples		Single parents
Percent distribution of EITC recipients with children by marital status (tax year 1994)			
Phase-in or flat	27%		47%
Phase-out	73%		53%
Total	100%		100%
	Including women's earnings	Excluding women's earnings	
Percent distribution of married couples with children (tax year 1996)			
Less than twelve years of schooling			
Phase-in	7%	10%	—
Flat	6%	8%	—
Phase-out	43%	52%	—
Above phase-out	42%	26%	—
Zero countable income	2%	4%	—
Total	100%	100%	—
Twelve years of schooling			
Phase-in	1%	4%	—
Flat	2%	3%	—
Phase-out	16%	31%	—
Above phase-out	81%	61%	—
Zero countable income	0%	1%	—
Total	100%	100%	—

Notes: Top panel from U.S. General Accounting Office 1996. Bottom panel is authors' calculations of March 1997 Current Population Survey.

Overall, this analysis suggests it is unlikely that the EITC will have *any* positive effect on the labor supply of secondary earners. In fact, it is unlikely that the EITC will have any positive effect on the labor supply of married couples because, in addition to the impact on secondary earners, evidence suggests that married men's participation and hours worked are not affected by taxes (Heckman 1992; Triest 1992).

5.2.3 Previous EITC Work

Several literatures are relevant to this study. A substantial amount of work has examined the effects of federal income taxes and transfer programs on labor market outcomes. Relevant to our work is the empirical literature on tax and labor supply, as well as the negative income tax (NIT) experiments of the 1970s; see the surveys by Moffitt (1992) and Moffitt and Kehrer (1981).

Because the EITC changes the budget set in a straightforward manner, its impact on labor supply can be imputed using static labor supply elasticities from the literature. Several studies have taken that approach and used standard elasticity estimates from the literature (Browning 1995) and the NIT experiments (U.S. General Accounting Office 1993; Hoffman and Seidman 1990; Holtzblatt, McCubbin, and Gilette 1994) to predict the impact of the credit. Browning estimates that about half of the taxpayers in the phase-out region of the credit will reduce hours of work by enough for their total disposable income to decline.

These simulations may be biased if labor supply responsiveness to taxes varies by income or over time. While no direct evidence supporting this hypothesis exist,[6] the large increase in participation by married women over the past three decades likely renders the early NIT estimates less applicable to the EITC population. Also, because of the short duration and limited sites in which the NIT experiments were implemented, extrapolating the NIT results to the more widely implemented EITC is difficult (see Moffitt and Kehrer 1981).

The most directly relevant work for this study comes from prior studies that have examined the impact of the EITC. In practice, there is little empirical evidence on the magnitude of the EITC effects for married couples with children. Several recent studies have examined the labor supply effects of the EITC on single parents (Dickert, Hauser, and Scholz 1995; Eissa and Liebman 1996; Meyer and Rosenbaum 2000, 2001; Keane and Moffitt 1998; Ellwood 2000; Hotz, Mullin, and Scholz 2002; Grogger 2003). As summarized in the recent review by Hotz and Scholz (2003), these papers consistently find that the EITC increased the labor force participation of single mothers. Dickert, Hauser, and Scholz (1995), Eissa and Hoynes (2004), and Ellwood (2000) examine the impact on the labor force participation of married couples with children, and all find that the EITC reduces the labor force participation of married women with children. None of these studies examines the impact of the EITC on the hours worked of married couples.

The literature evaluating expansions to the EITC has generally employed quasi-experimental (difference-in-difference, or DD) methods. Typically, the approach compares the outcomes of an affected group (female household heads) to the outcomes of a comparison group that is unaffected by the program (childless females/males). The comparison group generates the counterfactual necessary to evaluate the effects of policy reform by removing any nonprogram shocks affecting the outcomes of interest. The validity of the experiment rests on the quality of the comparison group, which requires the possibly restrictive assumptions that it mimics the behavior of the affected group.

This method was applied to examine the labor force participation effects of the TRA86 on the labor supply of female heads (Eissa and Liebman 1996), of the 1993 EITC expansion on the labor force participation rates of married women (Eissa and Hoynes 2004), and of the EITC expansions in the 1990s on welfare recipients in California (Hotz, Mullin, and Scholz 2002). In addition, Meyer and Rosenbaum (2000) use this approach to examine the impacts of many EITC expansions on female heads.

Eissa and Liebman (1996) use CPS data to estimate the impact of TRA86. They compare the change in labor force participation and hours worked by single mothers to that of single women without children, and they find a sizeable labor force participation response of 2.8 percentage points (out of a base of 74.2) but no discernible hours of work response. In addition, Eissa and Liebman report larger responses for women more likely to be eligible for the EITC (i.e., with less than a high school degree). Eissa and Hoynes (2004) use a similar method to examine the impact of the EITC on married women. Unlike the incentives for single parents to enter the labor market, the EITC is expected to reduce the labor force participation of married women because of the additional income it provides to the primary earner (typically the husband). Their evidence suggests that the EITC does in fact reduce the participation rate of married women. While the overall effect is modest, substantial heterogeneity exists in the effect—with the largest reduction observed among women whose tax rates are highest. Both the Eissa and Liebman and Eissa and Hoynes use policy changes enacted at the federal level.

Hotz and Scholz (2003) note that a concern arises in isolating the effects of the EITC from other reforms that occurred at the state level. Beginning in the late 1980s, states began implementing increasing numbers of demonstration projects that altered the work incentive of welfare eligible families. Hotz, Mullin, and Scholz (2002) exploit this source of variation by examining welfare recipients in four counties participating in a welfare demonstration project in California. In contrast to other work based on survey data, they use administrative data from welfare, unemployment insurance, and tax authorities. Hotz, Mullin, and Scholz also identify the EITC effect somewhat differently. They exploit the very large increase in credit for families with at least two children relative to families with one child, and they compare labor force participation of parents with at least two children to that of parents with one child. Their findings are dramatic and show an increase in the employment rate of larger families between 6 and 8 percentage points relative to families with one child. These findings imply a labor force participation elasticity with respect to net income as high as 1.7.

Overall the evidence based on the difference-in-differences model is consistent and suggests fairly strong participation effects, especially for female household heads. One limitation of the reduced-form labor force participation methods (as applied in these papers) is the use of group-level variation in taxes and transfers. This approach assumes that all relevant wage and income changes are captured by group-level variation in family type and size (presence and number of children) and time. The EITC effect is the relative (to childless) participation response of couples with children after the EITC expansion.

Tax reforms typically have heterogenous effects within groups, however. Dickert, Houser, and Scholz (1995) and Meyer and Rosenbaum (2001) exploit individual-level variation in after-tax wages and incomes to estimate the effect of EITC expansions on labor force participation. Dickert, Houser, and Scholz use cross-sectional data from the 1990 Survey of Income and Program Participation (SIPP) and estimate a joint program and labor force participation model, identified by variation in the returns to part-time (or full-time) employment in different states. They estimate a labor force participation elasticity of 0.35. The major limitation in their study is the use of cross-sectional data and the potential biases that arise from correlations between unobserved state characteristics and labor supply incentives or behavior. Meyer and Rosenbaum overcome this problem by using time variation in both federal and state tax and welfare policies. They estimate an econometric model of participation based on comparisons of utility in and out of the labor market. Meyer and Rosenbaum carefully model the set of welfare and tax systems at the federal and state level, and they incorporate the information into their utility model. Using CPS data from 1985 to 1997, they estimate that the EITC accounts for about 60 percent of the increase in the employment of single mothers over the period. Their implied labor force participation elasticities are more moderate than those of Hotz, Mullin, and Scholz 2002 and the lowest educated group in Eissa and Liebman 1996 but still large (about 0.7).

5.3 Methods

5.3.1 "Traditional" Model of Family Labor Supply

In this section, we outline the model of family labor supply used to generate our estimating equations. We adopt the more common approach to analyzing household labor supply that is based on the unitary model. It is a simple extension of the standard consumption leisure choice, and it considers the work decisions of two (or more) household members who maximize joint utility over consumption and individual leisure times.

Our empirical work is based on a simpler version of this framework. We assume a sequential, two-earner model in which the primary earner (generally, the husband) makes his work decision independent of the secondary earner. The second mover then makes her labor supply decision by maximizing utility, taking account of the primary earner's earnings and other household income. This model introduces asymmetry and drops the interdependence of the spouses' utilities: the wife's labor supply has no effect on the husband's decision while the husband's work affects the wife's decision, but only through family income. These restrictions lead to the following pair of labor supply equations:

$$H^1 = h^1(w^1, Y, X) \quad \text{and} \quad H^2 = h^2(w^2, Y + w^1 H^1, X), \tag{1}$$

where H^1 and H^2 represent hours worked by the husband and wife at wages w^1 and w^2, respectively; Y is family nonlabor income and X family characteristics. This model, which has been widely used in the empirical literature, implies that the husband does not share in the wife's earnings (although they share her unearned income).

The framework allows for consideration of non-participation (in the labor force) and as well as taxes. It is especially useful in empirical tax analysis because the assumption that the husband's work decision is independent of the wife's decision identifies exogenous variation in tax rates for secondary earners (wives).[7] We discuss the methods used to estimate the labor supply equations (1) in the next two sections.

5.3.2   Empirical Framework

Estimating labor supply models presents several difficulties. In the context of taxation, these include the joint determination of labor supply and taxes with non-proportional income tax schedules, unobserved tastes for work that affect the observed wage, and measurement error in both the marginal tax rate and the wage. Labor supply estimates based on Ordinary Least Squares (OLS) can therefore be severely biased.

Several methods have been used to address these problems. The most complete method to estimating labor supply responses is driven by the presence of several features of labor supply and taxes. The nonlinear budget set approach addresses several challenges noted extensively in the literature, including the presence of kink points and unobserved heterogeneity in work preferences. We should point out that while constraints imposed to make nonlinear budget set models tractable appear to be binding and to heavily influence the results (Heckman 1982; MaCurdy, Green, and Paarsch 1990), the expansions of the EITC and other tax policy reforms may actually allow us to relax some of the binding restrictions.

Because identification is tenuous, we do not estimate a nonlinear budget set model. Instead, in this chapter we estimate reduced form hours equations that depend on net-of-tax wages and virtual income. We estimate instrumental variables models to correct for the joint determination of hours worked and tax rates. Our instruments trace out the budget set and take advantage of tax reforms as well as variation in the tax schedule that families face given their nonlabor income and number of children. As a preliminary analysis, we evaluate the impact of the EITC expansion using quasi-experimental methods where we compare changes in labor supply among EITC eligible and ineligible groups.

5.3.2.1   Tax Reforms as Quasi Experiments

To describe the overall changes, we begin by examining the impact of the 1993 EITC expansion using a difference-in-differences method. We compare an affected group (low-income couples with children) to the outcomes of a comparison group (low-income couples without children) that is unaffected by the program. The comparison group is assumed to purge any nonprogram shocks affecting the outcomes of interest. This approach represents a natural starting point for married couples since it has been widely used to evaluate the effect of the EITC on single women. It can be summarized by the following formulation:

$$y_{it} = \gamma \delta_{gt} + \eta_g + \eta_t + X'_{it}\theta + \varepsilon_{it}, \tag{2}$$

where y refers to some measure of labor supply (participation or annual hours worked); η_g is a fixed (group) effect; η_t is a common time effect; δ_{gt} is the interaction between fixed group and time effect; X represents observable characteristics; and ε represents an error term. The program effect is measured by γ, the coefficient on the interaction term δ_{gt}. An unbiased estimate of γ requires that η_t be common across groups (ensuring that the comparison group mimics the underlying behavior of the affected group) and that η_g be fixed over time. In this setup, the impact of the policy reform is estimated as the relative change in outcomes of the affected group (EITC eligible parents).

In practice, we compare the change in labor supply of married couples with children to the labor supply of childless married couples following the OBRA93 expansion of the EITC. The identifying assumptions require that the labor supply of married couples without children be trending similarly to married couples with children and that the composition of the two groups remain the same. The composition of the two groups could change in a number of ways, such as through marriage and childbearing. While EITC expansions altered the incentives to marry and to have children, empirical evidence suggests relatively small responses on these margins (Dickert and Houser 1998, 2002; Eissa and Hoynes 2000a; Ellwood 2000).

The difference between the change in labor supply of eligible husbands (wives) with children and husbands (wives) with no children is the estimate of the EITC effect on participation. In addition, by widening the gap between the first and second child credit, the 1993 expansion created different incentives for families of different sizes thus allowing an additional degree of variation to identify the EITC effect. Clearly, the validity of the experiment rests on the quality of the comparison group, which requires the possibly restrictive assumption that its behavior exactly mimics the non-EITC behavior of couples with children.

5.3.3 Parameterizing EITC and Other Tax Changes

Once in the labor force, we assume the hours worked decision is continuous and therefore depends on the log of net-of-*marginal*-tax wage

(w_{it}^n) and virtual income (y_{it}^v).[8] In particular, our annual hours of work equation is

$$H_{it} = \alpha + X_{it}\beta + \gamma_1 \ln(w_{it}^n) + \gamma_2 y_{it}^v + \varepsilon_{it}. \tag{3}$$

We maintain the secondary earner assumption throughout this analysis. Therefore, the net-of-tax wages and virtual income for the married women are calculated taking into account the actual earnings of the husband. The X vector includes demographic variables, state labor market variables, and state and time fixed effects.

We use instrumental variables (IV) methods to address the endogeneity of the net wage and income to hours worked. Instrument sets used previously in the literature include the gross wage and taxable unearned income (Triest 1987), demographic characteristics such as education, age, home ownership and region (Flood and MaCurdy 1992), and tax parameters and demographics (Blundell, Duncan, and Meghir 1998). Some of these instruments are not convincing. It is difficult to argue, for example, that transformations of observable characteristics (education or age) are not correlated with the error in the hours worked equation. In addition, demographic variables have been rejected as valid instruments for wages and virtual income because the R^2s on the first stage are low (Blomquist 1995).

We propose a new instrument for the net-of-tax wage and income based on the individual's entire budget set. Essentially our instrument traces out the income tax schedule that a person faces—given their family size and nonlabor income. In particular, we calculate the marginal tax rate at $5,000 earnings intervals up to $100,000. The marginal tax rates are calculated using current year tax law and observed nonlabor income and family size. Again, we maintain the secondary earner assumption, and consequently the nonlabor income of the married women includes the husband's earnings. These methods essentially trace out the different seqments of the nonlinear budget set.

In addition, we use a second IV based on statutory income tax parameters, including the EITC tax parameters, the first federal income tax bracket, and EITC tax parameters interacted with cohort dummies. This instrument set is motivated by the Blundell, Duncan, and Meghir (1998) approach used to evaluate tax reforms in the United Kingdom. To be valid, these instruments must be correlated with the endogenous variables (net wage and virtual income), but uncorrelated with the error in the hours worked equation. The instruments vary by year, family size (number of children), and the amount of nonlabor income.

In addition, they are exogenous under the maintained assumptions in the chapter. Nonetheless, to assess their validity, we construct all relevant test statistics in the chapter.

IV methods can lead to biased estimates of the wage and income effects if individuals bunch at or near kink points along the convex budget set. In their evaluation of the effect of tax reforms in the United Kingdom, Blundell et al. (2000) address this potential bias by dropping workers near kink points. Empirical evidence from the United States finds weak evidence of bunching by taxpayers along the tax schedule (Liebman 1998; Saez 2000). More relevant to our study is the finding that "the large jumps in marginal tax rates created by the Earned Income Tax Credit generate no bunching by wage-earner recipients" (Saez 2002).[9] One potential explanation is that the U.S. tax schedule is relatively more complicated, making it difficult for taxpayers to locate such points. Consequently, we do not drop any observations from our sample.

5.4   Data

The data we use come from the March CPS from 1985 to 1997. The March CPS is an annual demographic file of between 50,000 and 62,000 households. It includes labor market and income information for the previous year, so the data we have are for tax years 1984 to 1996, a time period covering the three EITC expansions outlined in table 5.1. We choose to begin our analysis just before the TRA86 expansion because it represents the first major expansion since the EITC was introduced in 1975.

The relevant unit of analysis for this study is the tax-filing unit. The CPS has information on households, families, and individuals, however. We use CPS families to construct tax-filing units; therefore, subfamilies (both related and unrelated) are allocated to separate tax-filing units from the primary family. We consider any member of the tax-filing unit who is under the age of 19 (or under 24 and a full-time student) to be a dependent child for tax purposes. We do not impose the support test for dependents because we do not have enough information to impose the EITC six-month residency test.

The sample includes married couples residing in the same household, who are between 25 and 54 years old. We exclude those couples where one spouse was ill or disabled, in the military, or in school full-time during the previous year. We also exclude any couple with negative earned income (due to negative self-employment income), negative unearned income, or positive earned income but zero hours of work.[10] The resulting sample size, after pooling all twelve years and including all education groups, is 182,958 observations.

The main estimates in the chapter are based on a sample of couples with less than a high school education, where the selection is based on the wife's education. We use this criteria to better select couples that are most likely to receive the EITC.[11] As shown in table 5.2, over 60 percent of married couples with less than a high school education are eligible for the EITC compared to only 20 percent of those with exactly a high school degree. Restricting the sample to less-educated couples reduces the sample size to 22,671 observations.

Table 5.3 presents summary statistics of the low educated sample of married couples separately by gender and by family size. The demographic variables used in the analysis are fairly standard and include age, race, education, number and ages of children, and the state unemployment rate. Summary statistics show that married men with children are younger, less educated, and more likely to be white, and earn lower wages and have less nonlabor income than childless married men without children.

To generate net-of-tax wages and virtual income, and to construct the instrumental variables, we construct a tax calculator that simulates federal income and social security payroll taxes. The tax calculator is discussed more comprehensively in section 5.6 and in the appendix.

5.5 Comparison Group Results

To begin, we describe the changes over this period using a quasi-experimental approach. In particular, we examine the expansion in 1993 (OBRA93) and compare the hours of work of married couples with children to married couples without children. The CPS sample for this preliminary analysis includes tax years 1989 to 1996, with 1989–1993 as the pre-OBRA93 period and 1994–1996 as the post-OBRA93 period. Because the majority of married couples are beyond the phase-in range, we expect that hours should fall for *working* women with children relative to those with no children, and that hours should fall more for taxpayers with more than one child. The net effect on total hours worked depends on the relative size of the responses of participation and hours worked by workers.

In the case of the EITC, the difference-in-difference approach is unsuitable for the analysis of hours for several reasons. First, the EITC

Table 5.3
Summary statistics for married couples with and without children

	Married couples			
	All	No children	One child	Two or more children
State unemp. rate	6.6 (1.7)	6.5 (1.7)	6.5 (1.7)	6.7 (1.7)
# children	1.81 (1.51)	0	1	2.9 (1.1)
# preschool children	0.44 (0.74)	0	0.20 (0.40)	0.72 (0.87)
Husband				
Age	40.4 (7.8)	45.4 (7.4)	41.6 (7.7)	37.8 (6.7)
Non-white	0.13	0.14	0.11	0.13
Education	9.7 (3.2)	10.2 (2.9)	10.1 (3.1)	9.4 (3.4)
Annual hours	1922 (718)	1937 (739)	1976 (674)	1897 (725)
Labor force participation	0.959	0.955	0.969	0.958
Unearned income	$1,669 (3,767)	$2,046 (4,452)	$1,658 (3,897)	$1,513 (3,364)
Net nonlabor income	—	—	$1,535 (3,600)	$1,518 (3,335)
Gross hourly wage	—	—	$12.7 (7.3)	$11.39 (6.72)
ln(net wage)	—	—	2.11 (0.50)	2.05 (0.48)
Wife				
Non-white	0.13	0.15	0.12	0.13
Age	38.0 (7.6)	43.8 (7.2)	39.1 (7.5)	35.1 (6.1)
Education	8.5 (2.5)	8.9 (2.2)	8.8 (2.2)	8.2 (2.6)
Annual hours	873 (932)	1040 (968)	987 (938)	753 (896)
Labor force participation	0.577	0.644	0.632	0.524
Unearned income	$24,928 (16,310)	$27,312 (17,925)	$26,726 (17028)	$23,206 (15047)
Net non-labor income	—	—	$23,233 (12236)	$21,279 (11,091)
Gross hourly wage	—	—	$7.63 (4.9)	$7.36 (5.2)
ln(net wage)	—	—	1.58 (0.46)	1.57 (0.48)
Observations	22,671	5,493	4,890	12,288

Notes: Authors' tabulations of the 1985–1997 March Current Population Surveys. Sample includes married couples where the wife has less than a high school education. See the text for further sample selection. Standard errors are in parentheses. All dollar amounts are in 1995 dollars. Wages are defined for workers only.

schedule generates very different incentives for hours worked depending on family income. Married women in the phase-in are predicted to work more hours, while married women beyond the phase-in are predicted to work fewer hours. Aggregating these populations therefore conflates the hours effect across different groups. Moreover, without panel data, we would not be able to distinguish whether responses are shifts across budget segments or responses within segments. For these reasons, we only summarize the results of the quasi-experimental estimation. The results are available on request.[12]

Controlling for demographics, business cycles, and state fixed effects, when we examine unconditional hours (including workers and non-workers), we find that women with one child worked twenty-five *additional* hours, while women with at least two children worked fifty-four *fewer* hours per year after the 1993 EITC expansion. Overall, family labor supply (hours worked by husband and wife) rose by about sixty annual hours.

Although the EITC can raise total family labor supply if its effect on the participation decision is stronger than that on hours worked by workers, the family labor supply results are surprising for a number of reasons. First, they suggest stronger labor supply responses by men than by women. Second, in Eissa and Hoynes (2004), we find that only men increased their participation rates and not by enough to dominate the lower participation rates by women.

The results for the sample of working individuals are even more implausible: they suggest that men worked up to one hundred more hours, while women worked sixty-seven more hours after the EITC expansion. Our explanation for these results is that childless married couples represent a poor comparison group for couples with children in this exercise. Figure 5.4 shows the age distributions of the two groups and highlights one reason why childless women (and men) may be poor comparison groups when evaluating the labor supply of married couples.

5.6 Using Variation in Taxes, Wages, and Income

5.6.1 Annual Hours Worked: Instrumental Variables

In this section, we report IV estimates of the relationship between hours worked and their after-tax wages and income. We limit the sample to workers and estimate equation (3). Because of concerns about the validity of childless married couples as a control group, this IV analysis

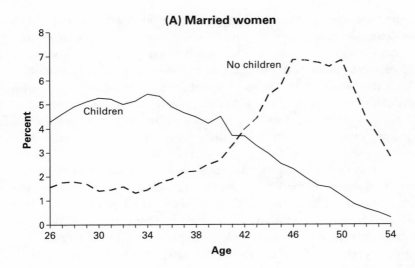

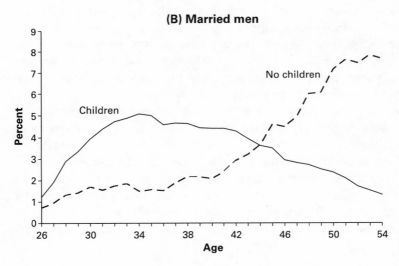

Figure 5.4
Age distributions for married couples by presence of children. *Source:* Authors' calculations of the 1985–1997 March Current Population Surveys.

is limited to married couples with children. The net-of-marginal-tax wage (w^n) and virtual income (y^v) are evaluated at observed hours of work.[13]

Figure 5.5 (panels A and B) show marginal tax rates in 1984, 1990, and 1996 for the sample of working women and men, respectively, and illustrate the extensive variation in tax rates. In each figure, we present minimum, mean, and maximum tax rates by (own) gross annual earnings. At a particular earnings point for any given year, marginal tax rates vary by family size and nonlabor income. For married women, nonlabor includes husband's earnings. We note two interesting observations in our data. First, tax schedules broadly mimic the combined federal income and payroll tax schedules in any given year and therefore reflect the changes over time in tax law. By 1996, we observe substantial changes in marginal tax rates at the bottom of the income distribution. It is this variation that identifies our labor supply responses. Second, married women's tax schedules are relatively flat, and their marginal tax rates are everywhere higher and more dispersed than those of their spouses (see Eissa and Hoynes 2000b). This occurs because we assume that couples file married joint tax returns and that the wife is the secondary earner in the household. As a result, married women's earnings are taxed further up the schedule.

Our main results are presented in tables 5.4a and 5.4b. Table 5.4a (5.4b) presents OLS and IV results for the annual hours worked equation for women (men). We present results for two sets of instruments (IV1 and IV2). IV-1 includes a vector of marginal tax rates evaluated at $5,000 earnings increments from $0 to $100,000 (column 2). IV-2 includes EITC parameters and interactions of those tax parameters with birth cohort, and a variable for the location of the first non-EITC kink in the budget constraint (column 3). All specifications control for the number of children and preschool children, race, birth cohort (defined over 10 years), state unemployment rate, and time and state dummies.[14] All demographics show the expected signs so we do not refer to them here.[15]

Consistent with existing empirical labor supply work, our estimated wage and income effects for married women are greater and more sensitive to specification than those of men. For women, the uncompensated wage elasticity is between 0.07 (IV-1) and 0.44 (IV-2). The estimated income elasticity is between −0.04 (IV1) and −0.36 (IV2). This range of estimates is relatively tight given the wide range of estimated elasticities for married women present in the literature. For men, the range of estimates is quite tight and consistent with the

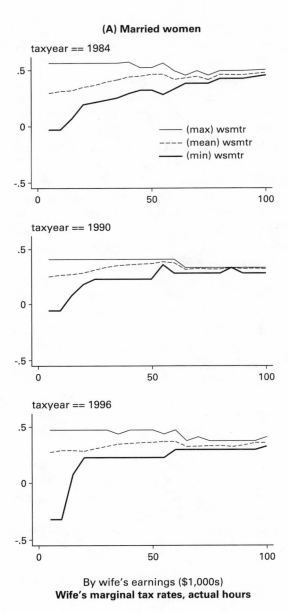

By wife's earnings ($1,000s)
Wife's marginal tax rates, actual hours

Figure 5.5
Marginal tax rates for married couples with children by own actual earnings (earnings
in 1,000s of 1996 dollars). *Source:* Authors' tabulations of the March Current Population
Surveys. Figures show maximum, mean, and minimum marginal tax rates.

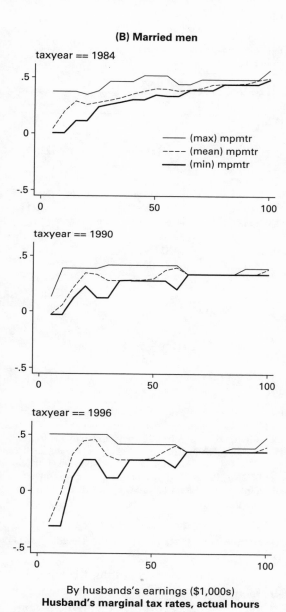

By husbands's earnings ($1,000s)
Husband's marginal tax rates, actual hours

Figure 5.5
(continued)

Table 5.4a
Parameter estimates for annual hours of work equation: married couples with children,
1984–1996 (sample: wife's education < 12)

Variable	Estimates for working married women		
	OLS	IV-1	IV-2
constant	1942.89 (192.2)	1836.38 (240.7)	1454.6 (629.9)
# of children	−50.91 (7.07)	−50.32 (7.10)	−55.75 (10.33)
# preschool children	−89.55 (12.61)	−91.06 (12.94)	−132.39 (25.27)
Black	82.22 (29.81)	81.40 (29.98)	4.88 (55.52)
Other race	192.07 (31.82)	192.49 (31.86)	149.36 (45.83)
Cohort 2	109.85 (44.94)	108.92 (45.00)	120.75 (52.04)
Cohort 3	57.90 (45.63)	58.32 (45.68)	61.18 (51.41)
Cohort 4	56.90 (44.56)	60.89 (44.91)	66.87 (55.76)
State unemp. rate	−22.89 (7.44)	−22.94 (7.46)	−28.53 (9.01)
Mills ratio	−309.54 (190.0)	−308.22 (190.25)	−214.20 (220.43)
Net wage (ln)	31.4 (15.8)	99.1 (100.3)	662.5 (360)
Virtual income	−3.2 (0.7)	−3.0 (0.74)	−25.3 (14.8)
Test statistics			
First-stage F stat, $\ln(w)$	—	12.3 ($p = 0$)	1.2 ($p = .2$)
First-stage F stat, y	—	300 ($p = 0$)	1.2 ($p = .2$)
Mean of dep. var.	1,477	1,477	1,477
Observations	9,532	9,532	9,532
Behavioral elasticities			
Wage	0.02	0.07	0.44
Income	−0.05	−0.04	−0.36

Notes: Authors' tabulations of the 1985–1997 March Current Population Surveys. Sample
includes married couples with children. See the text for details. Instrument set 1 (IV-1)
includes the marginal tax rate the individual faces at 5,000 earnings increments from 0
up to $100,000 (0, 5000, 10,000, . . . , 95,000, 100,000). The tax calculations account for the
EITC, other federal taxes, and payroll taxes and condition on the person's level of unearned income. Instrument set 2 (IV-2) includes EITC tax parameters (phase-in rate,
phase-out rate, kink points), kink point where federal taxes begin, and tax parameters
interacted with education and birth cohort dummies.

existing literature. The net-of-tax wage elasticity from the IV estimates
is in the range of 0.05 to 0.09.

Tables 5.4a and 5.4b also present the F statistic testing the joint significance of the set of instruments from the first stage regression. For
women's hours worked, IV-1 is more highly correlated with the endogenous variables. This result is not surprising since IV-1 and IV-2 differ
in two important ways. First, IV-2 uses statutory EITC and tax parameters up to the maximum EITC earnings limit ($30,000 in 1996 dollars),
while IV-1 uses marginal tax rates evaluated up through earnings of
$100,000. Second, IV-2 uses tax parameters and varies only by family

Table 5.4b

Parameter estimates for annual hours of work equation: married couples with children, 1984–1996 (sample: wife's education < 12)

Variable	Estimates for married men		
	OLS	IV-1	IV-2
constant	2557.56 (73.94)	2119.08 (287.9)	1899.2 (393.4)
# of children	−22.85 (4.18)	−19.23 (4.57)	−19.01 (4.87)
# preschool children	−24.78 (7.23)	−21.27 (7.91)	−17.87 (8.62)
Black	−117.62 (20.26)	−107.00 (23.08)	−92.49 (26.89)
Other race	−66.25 (21.75)	−51.83 (24.20)	−43.02 (26.19)
Cohort 2	−10.20 (17.08)	−13.62 (17.47)	−7.25 (18.68)
Cohort 3	−5.98 (17.49)	2.46 (19.25)	11.86 (23.36)
Cohort 4	−41.71 (22.22)	−45.77 (27.42)	−27.21 (32.92)
State unemp rate	−24.93 (4.69)	−23.74 (4.80)	−24.51 (4.92)
Net wage (ln)	−136.7 (10.1)	100.8 (130.9)	174.5 (176.2)
Income (virtual)	+4.0 (1.39)	−16.8 (3.40)	−10 (19.4)
Test statistics			
First-stage F stat, $\ln(w)$	—	8.6 ($p = 0$)	2.8 ($p = 0$)
First-stage F stat, y	—	350 ($p = 0$)	4.6 ($p = 0$)
Mean of dep. var.	1,477	1,477	1,477
Observations	9,532	9,532	9,532
Behavioral elasticities			
Wage	−0.07	0.05	0.09
Income	+0.01	−0.04	−0.02

Notes: Authors' tabulations of the 1985–1997 March Current Population Surveys. Sample includes married couples with children. See the text for details. Instrument set 1 (IV-1) includes the marginal tax rate the individual faces at 5,000 earnings increments from zero up to $100,000 (0, 5000, 10,000, . . . , 95,000, 100,000). The tax calculations account for the EITC, other federal taxes, and payroll taxes and condition on the person's level of unearned income. Instrument set 2 (IV-2) includes EITC tax parameters (phase-in rate, phase-out rate, kink points), kink point where federal taxes begin, and tax parameters interacted with education and birth cohort dummies.

size and year, while IV-1 includes husband earnings in the wife's nonlabor income.

To reconcile the somewhat different magnitudes for the estimates in IV-1 and IV-2 for married women, we consider each of these differences in turn. To see the first point, consider that the instruments used affect workers at different points in the distribution. So if labor supply elasticities of working women vary across the earnings distribution, we would expect different wage and income estimates.

To explore this, we re-estimate the hours equation by limiting the instrument to lower points in the earnings distribution (e.g., $60,000, $40,000, $25,000). The results are presented in table 5.5 (top). These

Table 5.5
Parameter estimates for annual hours of work equation for married women using alternative instrument sets (LATE)

		Wage and income estimates	
		Net wage (ln)	Virtual income
Results for IV-2 (marginal tax rates at $5,000 intervals), including husband earnings			
Basic results (0–100K)		99.1 (100)	−3.0 (0.7)
		[0.08]	[−0.04]
LATE	(0–60K)	124.6 (101)	−3.4 (0.8)
		[0.08]	[−0.05]
	(0–40K)	143.8 (103)	−3.4 (0.8)
		[0.10]	[−0.05]
	(0–25K)	163.2 (106)	−3.3 (0.8)
		[0.11]	[−0.05]
Results for IV-2 (marginal tax rates at $5,000 intervals), excluding husband earnings			
Basic results (0–100K)		226.4 (34.3)	−9.8 (3.6)
		[0.15]	[−0.14]
LATE	(0–60K)	647.5 (418)	−12.8 (4.1)
		[0.44]	[−0.19]
	(0–40K)	949.9 (52.7)	−13.1 (4.5)
		[0.64]	[−0.19]
	(0–25K)	1111.9 (593.9)	−13.5 (4.8)
		[0.75]	[−0.20]
Results for IV-1 (EITC parameters)			
Basic results		662.5 (360)	−25.3 (14.8)
		[0.44]	[−0.36]

Notes: Each row corresponds to estimates from an annual hours worked equation for married women. In each case, the estimates are from instrumental variables estimation. The rows differ in the specification of the instrument sets. The estimated equations are identical to those reported in table 5.4a and include net wages, virtual income, demographics, mills ratio, and state and time dummies. The table reports parameter estimates, standard errors in ( ), and elasticities in [ ].

results show that the estimated wage effect progressively increases as we limit IV-1 to lower-earning workers. We refer to these estimates as local average treatment effects (LATE) (Imbens and Angrist 1994). The wage elasticity (in brackets) rises to 0.11 while the income effect remains fairly constant at −0.05. Note also that the estimated standard errors do not change very much across specifications. One explanation for this modest change is that the marginal tax schedule is fairly proportional at the upper end of the income distribution. We observe a similar pattern for men's hours worked: limiting the instruments to the lower end of the earnings distribution increases the estimated elasticities (see table 5.6).

Table 5.6
Parameter estimates for annual hours of work equation for married men using alternative instrument sets (LATE)

	Wage and income estimates	
	ln(net wage)	Virtual income/100
Results for IV-1 (marginal tax rates at $5,000 intervals)		
Basic Results (0–100K)	100.8 (130.9)	−16.8 (3.4)
	[0.07]	[−0.03]
LATE (0–60K)	236.5 (135.8)	−14.1 (3.5)
	[0.12]	[−0.03]
(0–40K)	451.2 (182.6)	−17.0 (3.9)
	[0.23]	[−0.04]
(0–25K)	396.9 (200.8)	−13.9 (4.1)
	[0.20]	[−0.03]

Notes: Each row of the table corresponds to estimates from an annual hours of work equation for married men. In each case, the estimates are from instrumental variables estimation. The rows differ only in the specification of the instrument sets. The specification of the equations are identical to those reported in table 5.4b and include net wages, virtual income, demographics, state dummies and time dummies. The table reports the parameter estimate, standard errors in ( ), and elasticities in [ ].

Limiting the marginal tax rates to $25,000 in earnings begins to marginally close the gap between the estimates using IV-1 and IV-2 in the women's hours worked equations, but a substantial difference remains. Next, we exclude husband's earnings when calculating IV-2. These results are shown in table 5.5 (bottom). The results show that excluding husband earnings explains much of the divergence between the two instrument sets. The estimated wage and income responses become much larger and statistically not different than IV-2 estimates. While the evidence presented explains the divergence between the estimated hours worked responses under IV-1 and IV-2, we do not conclude from it that one instrument set dominates another. Each set has its advantages and drawbacks, and we choose to present these results as bounds on the responsiveness of married women's hours of work.

5.6.2   Simulations

To evaluate the effect of the EITC on hours worked, we perform simulations of our estimated equations. Our simulations are based on the 1996 sample of less-educated married couples. We compare predicted hours worked using the 1996 tax law to hours worked under different EITC schedules. In particular, we consider two alternative simulations.

We examine how labor supply would change if the household faces (1) the 1984 EITC schedule and (2) the 1993 EITC schedule. In each case, we assume that all other parameters remain fixed, including gross wages, nonlabor income, family structure, spouse's earnings (for the wife), and income taxes. The simulations are discussed more completely in appendix B.

Using the tax calculator, we generate after-tax wages and incomes under 1996 law and then under each alternative scenario. These values are used to predict hours worked, presented in table 5.7 for the full

Table 5.7
Simulated change in annual hours, EITC expansion 1984–1996

| | Married men | | | | Married women | | | |
| | IV-1 (MTR 0–100K) | | IV-2 (EITC, tax) | | IV-1 (MTR 0–100K) | | IV-2 (EITC, tax) | |
	Level	Percent (%)	Level	Percent (%)	Level	Percent (%)	Level	Percent (%)
Overall	−54	−2.6%	−15	−0.7%	−11	−0.7%	−81	−3.9%
Grouping by husband's actual wage								
Decile 1	−2	−0.10%	27	1.29%	−19	−1.15%	−141	−8.57%
Decile 2	−41	−1.84%	0	0.00%	−28	−1.77%	−197	−12.45%
Decile 3	−61	−3.15%	−12	−0.62%	−19	−1.12%	−132	−7.77%
Decile 4	−92	−4.23%	−31	−1.43%	−19	−1.24%	−134	−8.74%
Decile 5	−100	−4.60%	−39	−1.80%	−11	−0.66%	−74	−4.43%
Decile 6	−101	−4.71%	−41	−1.91%	−11	−0.67%	−80	−4.90%
Decile 7	−89	−4.40%	−37	−1.83%	−6	−0.43%	−39	−2.79%
Decile 8	−40	−1.87%	−16	−0.75%	−3	−0.19%	−19	−1.23%
Decile 9	−12	−0.55%	−4	−0.18%	−1	−0.07%	−9	−0.60%
Decile 10	−8	−0.41%	−2	−0.10%	−3	−0.19%	−19	−1.22%
Husband not working	—	—	—	—	−10	−0.59%	−80	−4.69%
Grouping by location in 1996 EITC schedule								
Phase-in	29	6.55%	46	10.38%	26	5.99%	172	39.63%
Flat	−9	−0.86%	22	2.11%	5	0.45%	24	2.15%
Phase-out	−87	−4.67%	−28	−1.50%	−34	−2.45%	−241	−17.41%
Above phase-out	−40	−1.81%	−16	−0.72%	0	0.00%	0	0.00%

Notes: The simulations are based on estimates of the annual hours of work equations reported in tables 5.4a and 5.4b. The equations control for the log of net wages, virtual income, demographics, state dummies, and time dummies. The simulations are based on predictions of the hours worked using 1993 EITC tax parameters compared to 1996 EITC tax parameters. All other taxes and regression variables are held constant in the simulations. The percent change in hours is calculated using the cell-specific average hours.

sample, and for two different groupings of married couples: by deciles of the husband's gross hourly wage distribution and regions of the 1996 EITC schedule (phase-in, flat, phase-out, above phase-out). The regions of the EITC are assigned using the 1996 EITC schedule and are based on actual family earnings and adjusted gross income.

Table 5.7 (7) presents the simulated hours worked response to the 1984–1996 (1993–1996) EITC expansion, based on the wage and income responses from IV-1 and IV-2. Because the sample includes working men and working women, the husband and wife samples are different.

Table 5.7 shows that the 1993 expansion in the EITC led to declines in hours worked for married men and women. Men decreased work by between 10 and 32 hours (0.5–1.5 percent), and women decreased work by between 7 and 49 hours (0.4–2 percent). Taking into account the three EITC expansions over the period 1984–1996, table 5.8 shows that married men decreased hours by between 1 and 3 percent (15–54 hours) and women decreased hours by between 1 and 4 percent (11–81 hours).

These rather modest overall effects mask some more substantial responses in subsets of the population. Tables 5.7 and 5.8 also present the simulated change in hours worked by deciles of the husband's wage distribution and by location in the 1996 EITC schedule. Table 5.8 shows that men in the phase-in region worked *more* hours, while men in the phase-out range worked 87 fewer hours (4.7 percent). Men in the middle of the wage distribution face the strongest disincentive effects (from the phase-out). Women married to low-wage men reduced their work hours substantially more than women married to high-wage men. Further, women in the phase-in range worked more hours, while those in the phase-out worked 34–241 fewer hours (3–17 percent) per year.

5.7   Conclusions

This chapter examines the hours worked response of married couples to the expansions of the earned income tax credit using Current Population Survey data from 1984–1996, using both a quasi-experimental approach and instrumental variables estimates of reduced form labor supply methods.

Our main estimates are based on a sample of married couples with less than twelve years of schooling, chosen because they are most

Table 5.8
Simulated change in annual hours, EITC expansion 1993–1996

	Married men				Married women			
	IV-1 (MTR 0–100K)		IV-2 (EITC, tax)		IV-1 (MTR 0–100K)		IV-2 (EITC, tax)	
	Level	Percent (%)	Level	Percent (%)	Level	Percent (%)	Level	Percent (%)
Overall	−32	−1.52%	−10	−0.5%	−7	−0.4%	−49	−2.4%
Grouping by husband's actual wage								
Decile 1	−10	0.48%	10	0.48%	−12	−0.73%	−86	−5.22%
Decile 2	−44	−1.98%	−15	−0.67%	−14	−0.88%	−13	−0.82%
Decile 3	−44	−2.28%	−15	−0.78%	−13	−0.77%	−93	−5.48%
Decile 4	−42	−1.93%	−14	−0.64%	−9	−0.59%	−67	−4.37%
Decile 5	−42	−1.93%	−15	−0.69%	−8	−0.48%	−55	−3.29%
Decile 6	−42	−1.96%	−16	−0.75%	−7	−0.43%	−49	−3.00%
Decile 7	−49	−2.42%	−19	−0.94%	−3	−0.21%	−23	−1.64%
Decile 8	−30	−1.40%	−12	−0.56%	−2	−0.13%	−16	−1.03%
Decile 9	−9	−0.41%	−3	−0.14%	−1	−0.07%	−5	−0.33%
Decile 10	−6	−0.31%	−2	−0.10%	−1	−0.06%	−9	−0.58%
Husband not working	—	—	—	—	−8	−0.47%	−63	−3.69%
Grouping by location in 1996 EITC schedule								
Phase-in	20	4.51%	31	7.00%	16	3.69%	98	22.58%
Flat	−24	−2.30%	0	0.00%	−6	−0.54%	−46	4.11%
Phase-out	−52	−2.79%	−19	−1.02%	−20	−1.45%	−142	−10.26%
Above phase-out	−20	−0.90%	−8	−0.36%	0	0.00%	0	0.00%

Notes: The simulations are based on estimates of the annual hours of work equations reported in tables 5.4a and 5.4b. The equations control for the log of net wages, virtual income, demographics, state dummies, and time dummies. The simulations are based on predictions of the hours worked using 1993 EITC tax parameters compared to 1996 EITC tax parameters. All other taxes and regression variables are held constant in the simulations. The percent change in hours is calculated using the cell-specific average hours.

likely to be affected by the EITC. Our results suggest that hours worked by both married men and women are moderately affected by taxes. The elasticity of hours worked with respect to the net-of-tax wage is between 0.1 and 0.44 for married women and less than 0.1 for married men. We present evidence that shows the hours worked elasticities for men and women are larger for lower-earnings individuals.

A large literature has pointed out the strong labor supply disincentives faced by low-income women from traditional welfare, and recent work has shown that the EITC offsets these distortions. This chapter points out that traditional welfare-type disincentives exist for EITC eligible married women. In the aggregate, these distortions are modest. In previous work (Eissa and Hoynes 2004), we estimated that the EITC expansions between 1984 and 1996 reduced the likelihood of married women's labor force participation by more than a full percentage point. Here, the results show that EITC expansions between 1984 and 1996 led to modest reductions in hours worked by married men and married women. Overall, married women in the labor force are estimated to decrease work by 11–81 hours (1–4 percent), while married men in the labor force are estimated to work 15–54 fewer hours (1–3 percent). These modest overall effects, however, mask substantial heterogeneity across the population of married EITC eligible families. Women in the phase-out range of the credit experience the greatest reductions, between 3 and 17 percent. Overall, the evidence suggests that family labor supply and pretax earnings fell.

Our results imply that the EITC is effectively subsidizing married mothers to stay at home, and therefore has implications for the design of the program. We make no value judgment about this feature of the credit. In fact, empirical evidence in the United States has generated little consensus on the effects of maternal employment on child outcomes (such as health and education). We note, however, that the EITC incentives for single mothers are exactly the opposite—namely, to encourage work.

Advocates in the United States and other countries point to the positive labor supply incentives of work-subsidy programs. This chapter, along with other work in the United States and in the United Kingdom, shows that the employment effects of work subsidies are in fact more complicated and "uneven across demographic groups" (Duncan 2003).

In the United States, differing labor supply incentives can be traced to the joint (as opposed to individual) income basis of the EITC and the federal income tax system. If the main objective of the EITC is to encourage work, however, an EITC based on individual earnings is preferred to one based on family earnings. A system of individual-based transfers, however, raises two serious concerns. The first concern is about its distributional implications of such a system, as benefits reach higher into the income distribution. The second concern is cost. An individual-based EITC is estimated to cost at least $11 billion more per year, according to the Congressional Budget Office. These additional dollars allocated to the EITC will themselves have efficiency costs and/or distributional implications. Policymakers therefore face a trade-off between implementing positive labor supply incentives for two-earner households and targeting the credit to lower-income families.

A second option to address secondary-earner labor supply distortions is to make the credit a wage (as opposed to earnings) subsidy, possibly implemented as an earnings subsidy with minimum hours requirement. Implementation of such a wage subsidy for married couples would be complicated by the need to take into account the spouse's hours and earnings. It is worth noting that the U.K. Working Families Tax Credit (more recently disentangled into the Working Tax Credit and Child Tax Credit) includes a minimum-hours requirement imposed on the *family*. Not surprisingly, similar secondary-earner labor supply effects have been documented for married women in the United Kingdom (Blundell et al. 2000).

Evaluating these and other alternatives to the current setup of making work-pay policies should be of high priority for economists interested in tax transfer program design.

Appendix A: Tax Calculator

Our tax model calculates federal taxes and payroll taxes and covers tax years 1984–1996. We assume that all married couples file jointly and take the standard deduction. Our tax calculator does not include state income taxes. Therefore we do not model the presence of the state supplements to the EITC, now available in many states. These are growing in importance but were small relative to the federal credit during most of our sample. While in principle these simplifications could lead to measurement problems, in practice our estimated tax rates are very highly correlated with those produced by NBER's TAXSIM model (which includes state taxes and models itemizers).

Two tax variables are used in the estimation of the reduced form hours equation: net-of-tax wages and virtual income. The net wage is the slope of the budget set at the observed level of hours of work and is equal to the gross wage times one minus the marginal tax rate (MTR). Virtual income is the vertical intercept (e.g., after-tax income) at 0 hours of work if the budget set is linearized through the person's observed budget segment.

All of the tax calculations assume a secondary-earner model. Accordingly, the primary earner's (husband's) taxes are computed without taking account of the spouse's labor supply choice. For example, the husband's net nonlabor income is the family's after tax nonlabor income. All of the wife's calculations, on the other hand, use actual husband's earnings. Her MTR will therefore depend on in which EITC region her husband's earnings place the family.

Appendix B: EITC Simulations

The goal of our simulations is to obtain estimates of the effect of the EITC on the labor supply of married couples. The simulations are based on our sample of low education married couples in 1996. We compare predicted labor supply based on tax laws in 1996 to what their labor supply would be if they faced a different EITC schedule. In particular, we consider two alternative simulations. We consider how labor supply would change if the household faces (1) the 1984 schedule for the EITC or (2) the 1993 schedule for the EITC. In each case, we assume that all other values remain fixed. In particular, there is no change in gross wages, nonlabor income, family structure, and spouse's earnings (for the wife) and no other changes in taxes. That is, we do not apply all tax laws in 1984, but just the EITC schedule for 1984.

We use our tax calculator to generate values for the after-tax wage and income variables under 1996 law and the alternative simulation. Labor supply is predicted in each case, and the simulation tables present the change in labor supply. We show the results of the simulations for the full sample, and for two different groupings of married couples: by deciles of the husband's gross hourly wage distribution and regions of the 1996 EITC schedule (phase-in, flat, phase-out, above phase-out). The regions of the EITC are assigned using the 1996 EITC schedule, and they are based on actual family earnings and adjusted gross income.

Notes

We are grateful to Alan Auerbach, Ken Chay, David Card, Steve Davis, Stacy Dickert-Conlin, Andrew Hildreth, Tom MaCurdy, Bruce Meyer, Steve Rivkin; to participants at various seminars, conferences, and the CESifo Summer Institute; and to an anonymous referee for comments and suggestions. Darren Lubotsky and Doug Schwalm provided excellent research assistance. Hoynes received financial support from National Institute for Child Health and Human Development and from the Department of Health and Human Services. Eissa received financial support from the Institute for Industrial Relations at U.C. Berkeley. Computing support was provided by the Econometrics Laboratory at U.C. Berkeley.

1. Federal spending on Temporary Assistance to Needy Families (TANF), which block grants Aid to Families with Dependent Children (AFDC), is fixed at about $16 billion per year through 2001 (U.S. House of Representatives 1996).

2. This feature of the transfer has implications for the interpretation of the labor supply responses. We discuss this later in the chapter.

3. Children must be under age 19—or 24 if a full-time student—or permanently disabled and must reside with the taxpayer for more than half the year.

4. The EITC was first indexed to inflation in 1987.

5. The hours of work effects are exactly the same as those for single parents.

6. One exception is Hoynes (1996), who estimates the effect of AFDC benefits on the labor supply of married couples. This work suggests that low-income couples may have higher wage and income elasticities than the overall population of married couples.

7. CPS data show that less-educated women are predominantly secondary earners when measured by the share of family earnings they contribute. Overall, about 90 percent earn less than their husbands, while among working couples, that figure is 85 percent.

8. Virtual income is the vertical intercept (e.g., after-tax income) from the worker's current budget segment at 0 hours of work.

9. Saez also finds that the EITC generates substantial bunching for self-employed recipients, but these are excluded from our sample.

10. We also exclude families with taxable unearned income in excess of $30,000 (in 1995 dollars). This group would not be eligible for the EITC in any year during this period. We drop couples where either the husband or wife has hourly earnings of less than $2 or over $100 per hour (in 1995 dollars) or who derives more than half of their earned income from self-employment.

11. A married woman's education is highly correlated with her spouse's education (0.67 in our sample). We experimented with classifying groups based on the husband's education and the qualitative results were unchanged.

12. In addition, we note that the response of working couples requires correcting for any self-selection bias, which in this context, is likely to be exacerbated by the EITC's effect on the labor force participation decision. Because the differencing approach is not valid for hours worked, we do not correct for self-selection.

13. We correct for self-selection into the labor force by standard methods (Mills ratio) but find that the correction does not have substantive effects on the estimated wage and income elasticities. The selection equation is estimated using full interactions among education, tax year, and birth cohort. As an alternative, we used estimates of the reduced form labor force participation model in Eissa and Hoynes (2004) to generate the Mills ratio. In theory, that model is attractive because it models the EITC's effect on participation. In practice, identification is tenuous at best since there are no valid exclusion restrictions.

14. The ten-year birth cohorts are defined as 1930–1939, 1940–1949, 1950–1959, and 1960–1969. Because of the controls for time and cohort, we do not include any controls for age. The results are not sensitive to alternative specifications of age, time, and cohort.

15. We also estimated models with instruments used in the literature. We found demographic variables (education, education*age) to be substantially weaker in the first stage relative to IV-1. The estimates of the wage and income effects were quite unstable in these specifications, reflecting the weak first stage. We also used gross wages and nonlabor income as instruments. These were very strong in the first stage and were relatively stable and similar to those based on IV-1.

References

Blomquist, Soren. 1995. "Estimation Methods For Male Labor Supply Functions: How to Take Account of Non-linear Taxes." *Journal of Econometrics* 70: 383–405.

Blundell, Richard, Alan Duncan, Julian McCrae, and Costas Meghir. 2000. "The Labour Market Impact of the Working Families Tax Credit." *Fiscal Studies* 21: 75–104.

Blundell, Richard, Alan Duncan, and Costas Meghir. 1998. "Estimating Labor Supply Responses Using Tax Reforms." *Econometrica* 66: 827–861.

Blundell, Richard, and Hilary Hoynes. 2004. "Has 'In-work' Benefit Reform Helped the Labour Market?" In *Seeking a Premier League Economy*, ed. Richard Blundell, David Card and Richard Freeman, 411–459. Chicago: University of Chicago Press.

Browning, Edgar. 1995. "Effects of the Earned Income Tax Credit on Income and Welfare." *National Tax Journal* 48: 23–43.

Dickert, Stacy, and Scott Houser. 1998. "Taxes and Transfers: A New Look at the Marriage Penalty." *National Tax Journal* 51, no. 2: 175–218.

Dickert, Stacy, and Scott Houser. 2002. "EITC and Marriage." *National Tax Journal* 55, no. 1: 25–40.

Dickert, Stacy, Scott Houser, and John Karl Scholz. 1995. "The Earned Income Tax Credit and Transfer Programs: A Study of Labor Market and Program Participation." In *Tax Policy and the Economy*, ed. James Poterba, 1–50. Cambridge, Mass.: MIT Press.

Duncan, Alan. 2003. "Making Work Pay Policies and Employment Incentives." Invited Lecture, CESifo Summer Institute, July.

Eissa, Nada, and Hilary Hoynes. 2000a. "Good News for Low Income Parents: Tax-Transfer Schemes and Marriage." Mimeo., University of California, Berkeley.

Eissa, Nada, and Hilary Hoynes. 2000b. "Explaining the Fall and Rise in the Tax Cost of Marriage: The Effect of Tax Laws and Demographic Trends, 1984–1997." *National Tax Journal* 53, no. 3, pt. 2: 683–711.

Eissa, Nada, and Hilary Hoynes. 2004. "Taxes and the Labor Market Participation of Married Couples: The Earned Income Tax Credit." *Journal of Public Economics* 88: 1931–1958.

Eissa, Nada, and Jeffrey Liebman. 1996. "Labor Supply Response to the Earned Income Tax Credit." *Quarterly Journal of Economics* III: 605–637.

Ellwood, David. 2000. "The Impact of the Earned Income Tax Credit and Social Policy Reforms on Work, Marriage and Living Arrangements." *National Tax Journal* 53, no. 4, pt. 2 (December): 1063–1106.

Flood, Lennart, and Thomas MaCurdy 1992. "Work Disincentive Effects of Taxes: An Empirical Analysis of Swedish Men." *Carnegie-Rochester Conference Series on Public Policy* 37: 239–277.

Grogger, Jeffrey. 2003. "The Effects of Time Limits and Other Policy Changes on Welfare Use, Work, and Income among Female-headed Families." *Review of Economics and Statistics* 85, no. 2: 394–408.

Heckman, James. 1992. "Comment." In *Behavioral Simulations in Tax Policy Analysis*, ed. Martin Feldstein, 70–82. Chicago: University of Chicago Press.

Hoffman, Saul, and Laurence Seidman 1990. *The Earned Income Tax Credit: Antipoverty Effectiveness and Labor Market Effects*. Kalamazoo, Mich.: Upjohn Institute for Employment Research.

Holtzblatt, Janet, Janet McCubbin, and Robert Gilette. 1994. "Promoting Work through the EITC." Mimeo., U.S. Department of the Treasury, June 4.

Hotz, V. Joseph, Charles Mullin, and John Karl Scholz. 2002. "The Earned Income Tax Credit and the Labor Market Participation of Families on Welfare." Mimeo., University of California, Los Angeles.

Hotz, V. Joseph, and John Karl Scholz. 2003. "The Earned Income Tax Credit." In *Means-Tested Transfer Programs in the United States*, ed. Robert Moffitt, 141–197. Chicago: University of Chicago Press.

Hoynes, Hilary Williamson. 1996. "Welfare Transfers in Two-parent Families: Labor Supply and Welfare Participation under the AFDC-UP Program." *Econometrica* 64, no. 2: 295–332.

Imbens Guido, and Joshua Angrist. 1994. "Identification and Estimation of Local Average Treatment Effects." *Econometrica* 62, no. 2: 467–475.

Internal Revenue Service. 2003. "Individual Income Tax Returns." Statistics of Income Division, IRS.

Keane, Michael, and Robert Moffitt. 1998. "A Structural Model of Multiple Welfare Program Participation and Labor Supply." *International Economic Review* 39, no. 3: 553–589.

Liebman, Jeffrey. 1998. "The Impact of the EITC on Incentives and Income Distribution." In *Tax Policy and the Economy*, vol. 12, ed. James Poterba, 83–119. Cambridge, Mass.: MIT Press.

MaCurdy, Thomas, David Green, and Harry Paarsch. 1990. "Accessing Empirical Approaches for Analyzing Taxes and Labor Supply." *Journal of Human Resources* 25, no. 3: 415–490.

Meyer, Bruce, and Daniel Rosenbaum. 2000. "Making Single Mothers Work: Recent Tax and Welfare Policy and Its Effects." *National Tax Journal* 53, no. 4, pt. 2 (December): 1027–1062.

Meyer, Bruce, and Daniel Rosenbaum. 2001. "Welfare, the Earned Income Tax Credit, and the Labor Supply of Single Mothers." *Quarterly Journal of Economics* 116, no. 3 (August): 1063–1113.

Moffitt, Robert. 1992. "Incentive Effects of the U.S. Welfare System: A Review." *Journal of Economic Literature* 30: 1–61.

Moffitt, Robert, and Kenneth Kehrer. 1981. "The Effect of Tax and Transfer Programs on Labor Supply: The Evidence from the Income Maintenance Experiments." In *Research in Labor Economics*, vol. 4, ed. R. G. Ehrenberg, 103–150. Greenwich, CT: JAI Press.

Saez, Emmanuel. 2002. "Do Taxpayers Bunch at Kink Points?" NBER Working Paper No. 7366, Cambridge, Mass.

Triest, Robert K. 1987. "A Monte Carlo Test of the Robustness of Alternative Estimators if Labor Supply Functions." Working Paper 198, Department of Economics, Johns Hopkins University.

Triest, Robert K. 1992. "The Effect of Income Taxation on Labor Supply in the United States." *The Journal of Human Resources* 25: 491–516.

U.S. General Accounting Office. 1992. *Earned Income Tax Credit: Design and Administration Could Be Improved*. Washington, D.C.: GAO.

U.S. General Accounting Office. 1993. *Earned Income Tax Credit: Design and Administration Could Be Improved*. Washington, D.C.: GAO.

U.S. General Accounting Office. 1996. *Earned Income Tax Credit: Profile of Tax Year 1994 Credit Recipients*. Washington, D.C.: GAO.

U.S. House of Representatives. 1996. *Background Materials and Data on Programs within the Jurisdiction of the Committee on Ways and Means*. Washington, D.C.: Government Printing Office.

U.S. House of Representatives. 2000. *Background Materials and Data on Programs within the Jurisdiction of the Committee on Ways and Means*. Washington, D.C.: Government Printing Office.

6 Progressive Taxation and Wages: Microevidence

Torben Tranæs, Søren Arnberg, and Anders Holm

6.1 Introduction

This chapter studies the relationship between income tax progression and wages in unionized and nonunionized sectors using microdata from the highly unionized Danish labor market. Tax progressivity is the ratio between marginal and average income retained after tax. Assuming perfect competition, economic theory has traditionally proposed that progressive taxation forces wages up. This received wisdom has lately been challenged by a new hypothesis that predicts that tax progression will moderate wages if the labor market is imperfectly competitive. A number of interesting empirical questions are raised by this. Do imperfectly competitive labor markets in fact react as predicted? Is any given labor market either perfectly or imperfectly competitive? Rather than trying to characterize the type of wage setting that takes place in the Danish labor market, in this chapter we test directly whether income tax progression increases wages.

This question is of course very important for welfare state policy. The traditional view is that there is a clear trade-off between equity and efficiency: a progressive tax system can create greater equality of consumption opportunities, but only at the price of reduced efficiency, because wages will increase and employment decrease. Under sufficiently strong assumptions, this is indeed still the hypothesis if the labor market is without imperfections. On the other hand, if there are imperfections—be they agents with market power or informational asymmetries—then the new theories predict that income tax distortions will play a different role. In general terms, this is not a surprise. What is surprising is that not only will these imperfections neutralize the traditional distortionary effect of progressive taxation, they will reverse the sign so that progressive taxation can reduce inequality and increase efficiency at the same time.

This proposition should be considered in a context where the stylized facts across countries are hard to reconcile with the traditional
view that tax progression reduces economic activity. Countries like
Denmark and Sweden used to have some of the most steeply progressive income tax systems in the world, and yet they also had some of
the highest employment rates. Is this in accordance with the new
theories? Are the labor markets in Scandinavian countries sufficiently
characterized by imperfect competition that their progressive tax systems work in the opposite way to that which traditional economic
theory would predict?

The empirical investigations made into these important questions
have not yet arrived at any final conclusion, and more work needs to
be done. Many of the first studies did in fact support the new theories,
but some more recent studies have not been able to confirm the earlier
findings. Our study also raises some doubts about the overall predic-
tive power of the new theories, but at the same time we partially vindi-
cate them since we do find *relative* wage moderation in unionized
sectors; in response to higher tax progressivity, the wages increase *by*
less in the unionized than in the nonunionized sectors, except at the
top of the job hierarchy, where there is no union effect.

6.1.1 The Theoretical Background

In an imperfectly competitive labor market, an increase in average
taxes while progressivity is held constant is expected to increase pretax
wages, because it drives a wedge between the wage enjoyed by
workers and the wage bill faced by firms. An increase in the marginal
tax rate while average tax is held constant is expected to have the opposite effect, because it increases tax progressivity: a proportional tax
scheme is a tax on the wage level, whereas a progressive tax is a tax
on wage *increases*, and therefore greater progressivity is expected to reduce wage increases in a market where the wage is not a parameter for
economic agents.

A number of recent studies have investigated theoretically the impact of income tax progressivity on wage determination in unionized
labor markets, in markets where firms set efficiency wages and in
frictional labor markets where firms seek to get vacancies filled and
workers seek to find jobs. In markets where workers are represented
by unions with preferences for both wages and employment, wage
increases are traded for higher employment levels. If the marginal tax

rate goes up (while the average rate is held constant) the price of higher take-home wages goes up in terms of forgone employment, so the demand for higher wages goes down (Hersoug 1984; Malcolmson and Sator 1987; Lockwood and Manning 1993; Koskela and Vilmunen 1996). In cases where firms set wages in order to elicit effort, the effect is similar. Higher marginal rates increase the price of greater effort (i.e., the wage costs), so the incentives to use wages to increase effort diminish (Pisauro 1991). This effect also exists in labor markets with search externalities (e.g., Hansen 1999).

Of course, all this stands in sharp contrast to the predictions of the competitive model, which admits only a labor supply effect from tax progression. The labor supply effect of an increase in the marginal tax rate when the average tax rate is held constant shifts the labor supply schedule to the left, and thus tends to increase wages (a pure substitution effect); the opposite is the case if the average tax rate is increased while the marginal rate is held constant (a pure income effect).

6.1.2 Previous Empirical Studies

Until recently, the empirical findings were supportive of a wage-moderating effect of tax progression (see Sørensen 1997 for a survey of these results). Most of the studies used aggregate time-series data, and, as we discuss in section 6.2, there are reasons why these results are more likely to be found if macrodata are used. However, wage moderation is also found in studies using more disaggregated data. In general, the earlier studies have found a significant wage-moderating effect independent of the country being studied. In the case of Sweden, the same effect was found at all earnings levels (Holmlund and Kolm 1995), which was not the case for Denmark (Lockwood, Sløk, and Tranæs 2000).

The study at hand produces very different results, as does the independent study by Brunello, Parisi, and Sonnedda (2002) who, like us, base their study on derived individual tax rates, average as well as marginal. We use administrative microdata for the full fiscal system to obtain these rates, whereas Brunello, Parisi, and Sonnedda use household survey data.

The two studies differ, however, on some important counts. When studying responses to tax progression, the difficult part is to get good measures of the marginal tax rates affecting individuals; the average tax rates are usually obtained relatively directly. There are basically two ways to proceed. One can put together all relevant fiscal rules and laws to draw up the complete tax and fiscal schedules for the relevant socioeconomic types of workers, and then simply compute the individual marginal tax rates. This is the approach used in Brunello, Parisi, and Sonnedda 2002. Alternatively, one can estimate tax functions for the relevant types of workers and then derive the marginal rates from these functions, which is the approach taken in this chapter.

6.1.3 This Study

We have chosen to estimate tax functions for two reasons. First, some subsidies are given on the basis of discretion rather than on rules. Furthermore, the take-up rates for subsidies are far from 100 percent; for example, only 85 percent of those eligible for housing subsidies claim these in Denmark (Hansen and Hultin 1997). By estimating tax functions, we obtain the realized tax schedules. Second, tax rates are endogenous to the wage rate because tax rates are functions of income, and income is of course influenced by the wage rate. This is a problem, in particular, because it is very difficult to find instruments for the marginal rates. For this reason we estimate tax functions; we do this on the basis of predicted income, since there are many good instruments for income.

From the estimated tax functions, we then derive both the effective marginal and average tax rates for each individual. These variables, along with the standard human capital variables, are then used to explain the variations in wages.[1]

The estimations are performed for the municipality of Copenhagen.[2] We believe that wage-setting institutions differ by occupational levels, and therefore we divide the employed labor force into the following occupational groups: unskilled workers, skilled blue- and white-collar workers, and professionals. At each of these three levels, we use a proxy for union membership to identify a "union effect," which we expect to be noncompetitive and thus point toward a negative association between the degree of tax progressivity and the wage level.[3] It should be mentioned that one might also expect to find noncompetitive effects in nonunionized sectors to the extent that wages are not parameters but strategic variables to workers and firms, whether in a search or efficiency wage environment.

The estimation approach used here is different to that of earlier studies on this topic. We look at first-difference estimators to factor out unobserved individual effects, and we do this at different points of the business cycle, boom and bust, in order to test its influence. Because of endogeneity problems involving tax rates and wages, we also use the variations generated by a tax reform, the 1986 reform (see section 6.2). Here we also use a difference-in-difference estimator in order to control for trend breaks.

The estimations across the tax reform yield a significant competitive effect at the upper end of the occupational hierarchy, and no significant effects at the lower end. The 1986 tax reform was implemented over a period, from 1987 to 1989, where the business cycle changed from boom to bust, and we cannot fully control for this with our data. We can control for a trend break that could be due to either the tax reform or the changed economic climate, but if the wage response to progressivity itself depends on whether unemployment is high or low, we cannot do anything about this. Therefore we attach weight to the estimations at the points in time where unemployment is low and high, and the estimations across the turnaround: the first two are free from business-cycle changes but have no variations from the tax reform, whereas the second ones have variations both from the reform and from the business cycle.

The overall conclusion is the same, nevertheless: significant competitive effects are to be found at the top of the job ladder, and no effect at the bottom. But looking at different points of the business cycle reveals something else. A priori we would expect to find union effects in the unionized sectors for skilled and unskilled workers, where the union traditions are the strongest, and we would expect to find it when unemployment is high, as it is concern about employment that drives the union effect. We do indeed find union effects when unemployment is high, in the years 1990–1991, and we find it only for unskilled and skilled union workers. Here both a significant competitive effect and a significant noncompetitive effect (wage moderation) are identified. The net effect is the competitive effect, nevertheless, since this is the strongest. But the result suggests that at least in a recession, where the unemployment risk is high, the unions do moderate wages relative to wages outside the unionized sector in response to steeper tax progression. There is no such effect for the professionals during periods of boom or bust.

Our results are compatible with those of Brunello, Parisi, and Sonnedda (2002) who study Italian data, although they do not compare unionized and nonunionized sectors. This is particularly striking because Scandinavia, of all places, with its high level of union coverage (above 80 percent), is where one would expect to find wage responses compatible with an imperfectly competitive labor market; yet we do not find such effects. If workers care about relative wages, this could help explain why the wage-moderating effect of unions is small or even nonexistent (see Brunello and Sonnedda 2002).

Tax progressivity aside, we also identify other effects of unions. Unions reduce significantly the influence of average income taxation on pretax wages. Wages are simply less flexible in the unionized sectors. As expected, wage levels also seem to be affected by unions. For unskilled workers the wage effect of unionization is positive and strong; for skilled workers it is also significantly positive but less strong; and for professionals there is no significant wage-level effect of unions when taxation is held constant. The results are only suggestive, since important controls for studying union wage effects, for example, industrial sector, have not been included.

6.2   Endogenous Tax, Problems, and Cures

As discussed in section 6.1, the time-series (macro)studies of the relationship between income tax progression and wages arrive at a conclusion very different from ours. With few exceptions, they confirm the hypothesis that tax progression moderates wages. But why should there be a systematic difference between micro- and macrostudies based on this question? In fact, there are problems of endogeneity when using aggregate time-series data that pull in this direction. These are problems that do also exist when using micropanels, but here there are more tools available for dealing with the problem.

Consider first the macrostudies, and suppose that we study a period during which the tax structure remained fixed. In this case a macrostudy is likely to contain very little variation in the marginal tax rates, but some increase in the average tax rate due to background increases in productivity. Thus, we simply get pairs of observations monotonically moving along a linear segment of the tax schedule; or in the most extreme case, we could get a series of points distributed around a kink. In both cases the average tax rate increases with the income, while the marginal rate is constant or changes only once. This implies that the progressivity variable V will be positively correlated with income (almost everywhere), just as the hypothesis based on imperfectly competitive labor markets predicts. However, this is simply by definition and not due to a behavioral response. In other words V is endogenous and, in general, it is hard to find good instruments for V; it is particularly hard to find good macroinstruments.

This is not a problem if the tax system is fully indexed, in which case V remains constant in the situation described. Most countries do not have a fully indexed system but rather an underindexed system (resulting in the so-called fiscal drag problem). For these countries there is a bias; changes in the real wages due to productivity growth will themselves generate the result that decreasing tax progression increases wages, without this being a behavioral response. Denmark is an exception in that the system has been more or less fully indexed for long periods, and in Denmark it is in fact hard to obtain the noncompetitive result using time-series macrodata. Looking at groups at different earning levels, one either obtains confirmation of the noncompetitive hypothesis (for low and medium earners) or the classical hypothesis is confirmed (for high earners).[4] However, this could simply reflect imperfect indexation at the disaggregated level; indexation of the tax system is of course according to the average wage increases. If different groups have experienced different rates of increase, some will be underindexed and other will be overindexed.

Turning to the microdata, this tendency is also here a potential problem, because two persons who differ only with respect to income (as far as observables are concerned) will represent a negative correlation between income tax progression and income, given an affine tax system. Here the challenge is again to instrument out these relationships, which the micropanel allows for better than the macro time series. With microdata the average income differences between groups can to a large extent be explained by observable characteristics, and it is possible to simply factor out variations due to unobservable characteristics. We can, furthermore, look at subgroups in order to utilize the variation in progressivity that comes from people having arranged their lives differently with respect to their assets portfolios and families. Thus, the phenomenon that hidden productivity differences lie behind the income differences (growth), and that it is these differences that determine the variation in the tax rates rather than vice versa, is less of a problem when using a rich micropanel.

This does not mean that there is no problem with endogeneity when using microdata. The variation in progressivity mentioned earlier comes from variations in asset portfolio and family structure, and none of these can safely be assumed to be exogenous to the wage rate. In this chapter we use this variation both as it is and in relation to a general tax reform. By comparing wage setting before and after the reform, we introduce some exogenous variations into our tax variables. However, this is a general reform and we do not have a control group, since everybody is affected. We do get some exogenous variation from the reform in our data, which we could in principle also obtain using macrodata. But in both cases we cannot get rid of the endogenous variation that we might have had to begin with, and it is much harder to do anything about this if one has only macrodata.

The limitation of this study lies here. In order to take the final step of ensuring that there are no endogenous variations between tax rates and wages, either we would need to study a reform with clearly defined target and control groups, or we would have to concentrate on a small area around the kinks of the tax schedule. Whether with or without a reform (though better with), such a technique could also provide treatment and control groups that were reasonably similar.

6.3 Theory

Wage equations for a parameterized tax system are now standard and have been derived for many different market institutions, as discussed in section 6.1. In this section we will sketch the derivation for a competitive labor market using the model in Bovenberg and van der Ploeg 1994. This model is sufficiently general with respect to the way the tax parameters appear for the resulting wage equation to also encompass unionized labor markets, markets in which firms set wages on the basis of efficiency considerations and markets with search frictions.

Consider an individual worker i with ability Q_i and convex and homothetic preferences. The worker's preferences are represented by the strictly concave function $U_i(C, S)$ over consumption, C, and leisure, S. The worker's labor supply is given by $L^s = 1 - S$. The worker has made a number of long-term decisions in the past that have shaped his or her asset portfolio and family status. These decisions are assumed to be irrevocable in the short run, and this has two important implications. First, the decisions of the past influence the initial point of the utility function upon which a worker bases his or her employment decision. This we capture by an individual-specific U_i. Second, the decisions of the past regarding wealth and family structure will influence a worker's tax liability and thus the wage-setting process.

Worker i faces the budget constraint $P^c C_i = (L_i^s W_i + R_i)(1 - T_i^a)$, where P^c is the consumer price, W_i is the wage rate, and $T_i^a \equiv T(L_i^s W_i; R_i, \phi_i)/(L_i^s W_i + R_i)$, where $T(L_i^s W_i; R_i, \phi_i)$ is the tax paid on income $L_i^s W_i$ given capital income R_i and family type ϕ_i. A key variable is $V_i \equiv (1 - T_i^m)/(1 - T_i^a)$, the *coefficient of residual income progression* as defined by Musgrave and Musgrave (1976), where T_i^m is the marginal tax rate for individual i given $L_i^s W_i$, R_i, and ϕ_i. The variable V_i will be our central explanatory variable in the empirical wage equation.

We assume that there are different types of workers characterized by their gender, ability, and trade or industry. Workers of the same type supply labor and are demanded according to the same schedules. Within a type, supply and demand decisions vary with individual characteristics. We assume that workers are employed in firms that use only labor in production. Let $Q_i f(L)$ be the output produced from L units of labor, where $f' > 0$, $f'' < 0$, and where Q_i is the individual productivity (including ability) parameter. The firms take wages and prices as given, and they hire workers until the marginal product equals the firm's producer wage. Since the firms do not pay taxes, we have that $Q_i f'(L) = W_i$. Finally, $P^c = 1 + T^c$, where T^c is the consumer tax rate. Hence, $t^c \equiv dT^c/(1 + T^c) = p^c$.

For nontax variables we let small italics indicate loglinear changes from an initial equilibrium, for example, $l \equiv dL/L \equiv d \log L$. The assumption that workers maximize utility yields the following relative change in labor supply for a worker of a particular type:

$$l_i^s = \varepsilon^{ul}(w_i - p^c - t_i^a) + \varepsilon^{cl} v_i,$$

where $t_i^k \equiv dT_i^k/(1 - T_i^k)$, $k = a, t$, and $T_i^m \equiv T'(L_i^s W_i; R_i, \phi_i)$, and $v_i = t_i^a - t_i^m$. The terms ε^{cl} and ε^{ul} are the compensated and uncompensated wage elasticity of labor supply: $\varepsilon^{cl} \equiv S(\sigma - 1)$ and $\varepsilon^{ul} \equiv S\sigma > 0$, where σ is the elasticity of substitutions between leisure and consumption.

Solving the firms problem yields the following relative change in labor demand for a worker of type i:

$$l_i = \varepsilon^d(q_i - w_i),$$

where ε^d is the wage elasticity of labor demand and $\varepsilon^d \equiv -W/Lf''(L) > 0$. Assuming labor market clearing then yields the wage equation

$$w_i - p^c - t_i^a = \frac{\varepsilon^d}{\varepsilon^{ul} + \varepsilon^d}(q_i - t^c - t_i^a) - \frac{\varepsilon^{cl}}{\varepsilon^{ul} + \varepsilon^d}v_i. \tag{1}$$

Both p^c and t^c are constant across individuals, and we will ignore them. Thus, our basic wage equation for a group of workers of a particular type is

$$w_i = \frac{\varepsilon^d}{\varepsilon^{ul} + \varepsilon^d}q_i + \left(\frac{\varepsilon^{ul}}{\varepsilon^{ul} + \varepsilon^d}\right)t_i^a - \frac{\varepsilon^{cl}}{\varepsilon^{ul} + \varepsilon^d}v_i.$$

We will mainly be interested in estimations in log changes (but we will also do log levels). The point of departure here will be the following wage equation:

$$\log W_i = \beta_0 + \beta_1 \log Q_i + \beta_2 \log(1 - t_i^a) + \beta_3 \log V_i, \tag{2}$$

where we follow the tradition and use average retained income $(1 - T_i^a)$ rather than average taxation. Equation (2) is the relationship that we will be estimating.

Due to great variation in R_i and ϕ_i, capital income and family type, we will get a whole distribution of marginal rates, T_i^m, for workers with the same characteristics in terms of productivity/ability, occupation, and union status.

Although the predictions of the various theories of imperfect labor markets are different, assuming equilibrium rather than market clearing, these theories produce a reduced-form wage equation with the same variables as equation (2) plus a measure of net unemployment benefits, level, or replacement rate, whichever is exogenous. There is variation in opinion as to whether some measure of long-term unemployment should enter into the wage equation as well. We estimate (2) on a local labor market, a region further divided by occupation. Hence, by not including unemployment in (2) we assume that there is one labor market for a given occupation in a given municipality, and thus any influence from the unemployment in that market is picked up by the constant term in the empirical equations, changes in unemployment by the constant term in first-difference equations, and so forth.[5]

Theory in general predicts that $\beta_1 > 0$; the theories assuming imperfectly competitive labor markets predict that $\beta_3 > 0$, while the competitive theory predicts that $\beta_3 < 0$, assuming that $\varepsilon^{ul} > -\varepsilon^d$ so that $\varepsilon^{cl}/(\varepsilon^{ul} + \varepsilon^d)$ is positive. Precise predictions regarding β_2 require some extra assumptions on the elasticity of substitution between leisure and consumption, σ.

6.4   The Data

We have estimated the wage equations using administrative data from Statistics Denmark. From these registers a longitudinal database has been created consisting of 10 percent of the Danish adult population. This is approximately 500,000 individuals for each year. The sample covers the period 1985–1991. From this database we selected workers between the ages of 18 and 66 who live in the Copenhagen municipality (approximately 40,000 individuals). The tax rates vary considerably between municipalities, and the tax schedules for identical individuals are different if they live in different municipalities. So in order to get the individual tax functions as correct as possible, we need to estimate them separately for each municipality. In this chapter we use only data from Copenhagen, the biggest municipality in Denmark. It is obvious that we could estimate tax functions for other municipalities as well in order to have the tax variations across municipalities in our analysis. This we will do in future studies.

From the data, we construct one sample for the estimation of the yearly wage earnings and another sample for the estimation of the hourly wage equations. For the first sample, only full-time workers with no unemployment are selected; the sample contains 9,079 individuals for 1985 and 9,230 for 1991. For the second sample, only workers with a low measurement error in the hourly wage are selected. This sample contains 14,800 individuals for 1985 and 13,577 for 1991. A brief summary of the data is presented in table 6.1.

Information on the total income of each individual, wage and non-wage income, is collected by the tax authorities, who use it to calculate the income tax of the individual. Information on subsidies are reported by the social authorities. All this information, plus additional information on demographics, education, and occupation, is contained in our panel. As a proxy for union membership, we use information on whether the individual is insured against unemployment, which is recorded in the registers as well. There is a close connection between union membership and unemployment insurance (UI) take-up, which is voluntary in Denmark. Between 85 and 100 percent of the insured are union members, and typically more than 90 percent are union members. The net average and net marginal tax rates (including subsidies) are calculated from the coefficients of the estimated tax equations. This is the subject of section 6.5.

Table 6.1
Means and standard deviations

Variable			1985	1986	1990	1991
Taxable income*			148.69	155.88		
			(61.68)	(62.85)		
Personal income**					204.97	212.35
					(76.77)	(80.95)
Capital income**					−13.18	−13.22
					(25.64)	(25.70)
Taxable capital			72.25	91.43	70.50	65.63
			(376.27)	(372.42)	(256.61)	(282.40)
Taxable income × Capital income*			−1394.68	−1734.50		
			(7014.98)	(7014.99)		
Personal income × Capital income**					−3384.21	−3592.64
					(9238.15)	(12196.68)
Age			36.37	36.20	36.01	36.16
			(12.34)	(12.16)	(11.48)	(11.42)
Education			1.99	2.02	2.10	2.14
			(1.06)	(1.07)	(1.11)	(1.12)
Sex (1 = male, 2 = female)			1.46	1.47	1.48	1.49
			(0.50)	(0.50)	(0.50)	(0.50)
Single	Tenant	No children	0.39	0.40	0.40	0.40
			(0.49)	(0.49)	(0.50)	(0.49)
		1 child	0.03	0.03	0.03	0.03
			(0.18)	(0.18)	(0.17)	(0.17)
		2 or more children	0.01	0.01	0.01	0.01
			(0.09)	(0.09)	(0.09)	(0.09)
Single	Homeowner	No children	0.03	0.03	0.02	0.02
			(0.16)	(0.17)	(0.15)	(0.15)
		1 child	0.00	0.00	0.00	0.00
			(0.05)	(0.05)	(0.05)	(0.05)
Couple	Tenant	No children	0.28	0.28	0.28	0.28
			(0.45)	(0.45)	(0.45)	(0.45)
		1 child	0.09	0.09	0.09	0.10
			(0.28)	(0.28)	(0.29)	(0.29)
		2 or more children	0.06	0.06	0.06	0.06
			(0.24)	(0.24)	(0.24)	(0.23)
Couple	Homeowner	No children	0.04	0.04	0.04	0.04
			(0.20)	(0.20)	(0.20)	(0.20)
		1 child	0.03	0.03	0.03	0.03
			(0.17)	(0.17)	(0.17)	(0.17)
		2 or more children	0.03	0.03	0.03	0.03
			(0.17)	(0.17)	(0.17)	(0.17)
$\mathrm{Log}(1 - T_a)$			−0.53	−0.54	−0.53	−0.56
			(0.28)	(0.29)	(0.24)	(0.25)
$\mathrm{Log}(1 - T_m)$			−0.80	−.85	−0.90	−0.94
			(0.11)	(0.12)	(0.15)	(0.16)
$\mathrm{Log}(V)$			−0.28	−0.31	−0.38	−0.38
			(0.30)	(0.30)	(0.26)	(0.28)
Wage per hour			94.85	98.22	131.59	138.36
			(30.93)	(32.61)	(43.43)	(47.58)

Notes: Standard deviations in parentheses. Tax, income, and capital variables are in DKK thousands. The data set only contains individuals for which the variation in their estimated hourly wage is less than 50 percent. *indicates data observed before the tax reform of 1987–1989, and **indicates data observed after the reform.

Table 6.2
Means and standard deviations for the occupation groups

Variable	Unskilled workers		Skilled or salaried workers		Professionals	
	1985	1991	1985	1991	1985	1991
Taxable income*	131.02		140.05		180.97	
	(48.90)		(42.94)		(84.63)	
Personal income**		178.98		195.43		258.74
		(65.84)		(54.34)		(99.70)
Capital income**		−8.37		−11.464		−18.97
		(17.23)		(20.72)		(34.38)
Taxable income	36.03	31.78	57.22	54.40	134.65	105.16
	(223.81)	(101.52)	(163.71)	(304.33)	(637.67)	(311.56)
Age	36.67	36.55	35.69	35.43	37.80	37.76
	(12.75)	(12.15)	(12.45)	(11.63)	(11.34)	(10.26)
Education	1.34	1.40	1.78	1.84	2.96	3.05
	(0.71)	(0.74)	(0.70)	(0.79)	(1.17)	(1.16)
$\text{Log}(1 - T_a)$	−0.53	−0.53	−0.51	−0.55	−0.55	−0.59
	(0.31)	(0.25)	(0.24)	(0.25)	(0.29)	(0.25)
$\text{Log}(1 - T_m)$	−0.79	−0.88	−0.80	−0.92	−0.82	−1.01
	(0.11)	(0.15)	(0.10)	(0.13)	(0.13)	(0.17)
$\text{Log}(V)$	−0.26	−0.35	−0.29	−0.37	−0.27	−0.42
	(0.33)	(0.27)	(0.26)	(0.27)	(0.31)	(0.29)
Wage per hour	88.86	124.39	89.96	128.26	109.22	162.26
	(29.50)	(41.73)	(25.02)	(24.69)	(36.60)	(57.54)

Notes: Standard deviations in parentheses. Income and capital variables are in DKK thousands. The data set only contains individuals for which the variation in their estimated hourly wage is less than 50 percent. *indicates data observed before the tax reform of 1987, and **indicates data observed after the reform.

Statistics Denmark provide an estimate of the hourly wage, based on information on the yearly wage income and the yearly payments to a compulsory pension fund. The latter depends step-wise on the yearly amount of work hours and can be used to calculate the minimum, maximum, and average hourly wage rates. In the hourly wage equation, we only use wage rates where possible variation is less than 50 percent.

6.5 Evidence

In this section we discuss the main evidence, namely, the results of the estimations of wage equation (2). But first we estimate the tax functions, since these will produce the predicted average and marginal tax rates to be used in the wage equations.

6.5.1   The Tax Equation

In order to analyze the effect from taxes on wage formation, we need to have both average and marginal tax rates at an individual level. Average tax rates are in principle easily obtained from the register data, whereas the marginal rates must be obtained indirectly, since they are not observable. As mentioned earlier in this chapter both the average and the marginal tax rates are estimated, and thus the marginal rates are not calculated according to tax regulations. The reason for this will become clear in the following.

The effective tax rate is determined by the regulations not only on the income liable to taxation, but also on the relationship between personal income and potential social benefits. Thus, in determining total loss in net income due to effective taxes, one should control not only for the influence from the tax levied on personal income, but also for how benefits are conditioned on the level of income. This can be done not only by regressing income on tax payments, but by including other information in the regression as well. Recovering the tax rates in this way can create marginal rates of well over 80 percent even for low-income groups, due to loss of benefits resulting from increases in earned income.

Therefore, by estimating taxes on the individual level rather than calculating them, it is possible to study how the effective tax rates affect economic behavior. For the calculations, we split the sample into subgroups with similar socioeconomic environments. These groups are determined by marital status, number of children, and whether the individuals own or rent their homes. Individual tax payment is determined empirically from the following tax equation:

$$T(L_{ti}^s W_{ti}; R_{ti}; \phi) = \alpha_{0\phi} + P_{1t\phi}(\widehat{I_{ti\phi}}) + \boldsymbol{a}_{1t\phi}\boldsymbol{\varpi}_{ti\phi} + P_{2t\phi}(\widehat{R_{ti\phi}}) + e_{ti\phi},$$

$$i = 1, \ldots, n_t; \quad t = 1985, \ldots, 1991; \quad \phi = 1, \ldots, J,$$

using

$$\log I_{ti} = \theta_t' \mathbf{z}_{ti} + u_{ti} \tag{3}$$

and

$$\log R_{ti} = \theta_t' \mathbf{z}_{ti} + v_{ti} \tag{4}$$

as auxiliary regressions, where ϕ indicate family and socioeconomic type; $P_{1t\phi}(\widehat{I_{ti\phi}})$ and $P_{2t\phi}(\widehat{R_{ti\phi}})$ are polynomials in income using equations

(3) and (4) to obtain predicted income with z_{ti} as explanatory variables;[6] and finally the variables in $\varpi_{ti\phi}$ are other type-specific covariates. The reason for using predicted rather than observed income is to avoid tautological relationships between taxes and the wages in the wage equations in section 6.5.2. The index ϕ splits the sample in $J(=12)$ socioeconomic subgroups that are assumed to be homogenous with respect to the tax scheme applicable to them (same tax function); the index for the individuals in group ϕ in year t runs from 1 to n_{tj}.

This is an indirect way of instrumenting the endogenous tax variables in the wage equation here. Alternatively, we could have estimated the tax function using actual observed income and then instrumenting the resulting tax progressivity and average taxation variables before using them in the wage equation. This traditional procedure gives very imprecise predictions of progressivity with the instruments at hand. The instruments, however, predict income well, which is why we do the instrumenting in this indirect way.[7] We have not been able to derive tests for the validity of the instruments using this indirect approach.

6.5.1.1 The Tax Reform

A central feature of the period covered by this study is the 1986 tax reform, implemented during the years 1987–1989.[8] Income taxation in Denmark consists of a flat rate municipality tax, on average 27 percent in 1986, and a progressive state tax. In 1986, the state tax brackets were (DKK 0–85,000), (DKK 85,000–144,000), and (>DKK 144,000), and the respective state tax rates were 16, 32, and 44 percent.[9] The combined municipality and state tax on earned income could not exceed 72 percent. Finally, significant tax relieves and deductions such as mortgage interest were allowed at the margin.

The reform only concerned the state tax, for which a number of things were changed: (1) Earned income and pensions (personal income) continue to be taxed progressively, but now the brackets were to be (DKK 0–130,000), (DKK 130,000–200,000), and (>DKK 200,000), and the respective state tax rates 22, 28, and 40 percent. (2) Capital income was to be taxed proportionally at 50 percent. (3) The combined municipality and state personal tax was not to exceed 68 percent. (4) Almost all relieves and deductions could thenceforth only reduce the municipality and the 22 percent tax; most important, this applied to mortgage interest relief, which on average now would have a tax value of 50 percent rather than 72 percent as before the reform.

Table 6.3
Average T^a, T^m, and V

	Unskilled workers		Skilled workers		Professionals	
	1985	1991	1985	1991	1985	1991
T^a	0.41	0.41	0.40	0.42	0.42	0.45
T^m	0.55	0.59	0.55	0.60	0.56	0.64
V	0.76	0.69	0.75	0.69	0.76	0.65

Thus, the different elements of the reform worked in opposite directions, both reducing and increasing the marginal rates for the same individuals. The net effect depended on an individual's earned income level, capital income, home ownership, and so forth. It is impossible to see from the reform whether it increased or decreased progressivity in general. From the changes in the rates and tax brackets, one would expect that the reform decreased progressivity at the top and increased it at the bottom. The tax reform was implemented over the three-year period from 1987 to 1989. In fact, it increased earned income tax progression at all levels, unskilled, skilled, and professional (see table 6.3, computed from our data), mainly due to the increase in the marginal rates. For the unskilled, only the marginal rate increased; they had less mortgage interest to deduct, and the average was affected by some having to pay 22 percent rather than 16 percent in state tax (the average municipality tax was 29 percent in 1991). For the skilled workers and professionals, an increase in the average tax rates moderated the increase in progressivity coming from the increase in the marginal rates. The feature that interest reliefs could not be deducted at the margin any more obviously had a very big effect on the professionals. In 1985 it was possible to pay 72 percent at the margin, yet the average marginal rate was only 56 percent; while in 1991 where it was not possible to pay more than 68 percent at the margin, the average marginal rate was nevertheless as high as 64 percent.

Thus, before the tax reform all income was taxed progressively, whereas this was only the case for personal income after the reform; nonwage income was thenceforth taxed proportionally. For most employees, nonwage income is interest, and this is usually negative, reflecting net interest payments as a result of having debts (e.g., a mortgage). In effect, the tax reform meant a substantial decrease in tax-deductible interest payments, especially for individuals with relatively high incomes.

6.5.1.2 The Empirical Tax Functions

The differences in how income liable to taxation is calculated before and after the tax reform have to be accounted for in the estimations. Therefore, income before 1987 enters wage equation (2) as a polynomial in taxable income. Nonwage income after 1987 is taxed differently from wage income. Therefore, two polynomials are estimated: one for nonwage income and one for wage income. In table 6.4 we show tax regression results for a particular socioeconomic group. Other results are available from the authors on request.

From table 6.4 we see that for all the years shown there is a very good fit of the model, with R^2 ranging from 0.91 to 0.99. This is also the variation in the fit for the remaining regressions not shown in the table.[10] The results for 1990 and 1991 could also indicate that nonwage income is taxed proportionally and not progressively. Altogether we note that the estimation of the tax equations for the different socioeconomic groups has a good fit that will enable their use in the wage regressions as the foundation for individual marginal tax rates.

From the tax regressions we obtain estimates of individual average and marginal tax rates, which constitute the main variables in the analysis to follow.

6.5.2 The Wage Equation

In this section we estimate a wage equation that measures the effects of the tax structure on wage formation. We use the model introduced in section 6.2 and the tax variables predicted by the tax functions estimated in the previous section.

Specifically, we estimate equation (2) with the key variable being $\log V_i$, where $V_i = (1 - T_i^m)/(1 - T_i^a)$ is our measure of tax progressivity and $\log(1 - T_i^a)$ is the measure of average taxation. We measure productivity by age and education, as discussed previously.

The wage equation is (2) augmented by a time index t:

$$\log W_{til} = \beta_{0l} + \beta_{1l} \log(1 - \widehat{t_{til}^a}) + \beta_{2l} \log \widehat{V}_{til} + \beta_{3l}' \mathbf{x}_{til} + \alpha_{il} + \tau_{tl} + e_{til},$$

$$i = 1, \ldots, n_{tl}; \ t = 1985, \ldots, 1991; \ l = 1, \ldots, 3, \tag{5}$$

where $\mathbf{x}_{til}$ is a vector of explanatory variables in addition to the tax variables; α_{il} is an error term comprising the unobserved elements of individual productivity ($\beta_{1l} \log Q_{il}$ in (2)) and are assumed to be constant

Table 6.4
Tax functions for an employed person, living with a spouse, with two or more children and living in an owner-occupied dwelling

Variable	OLS regression coefficients by year			
	1985	1986	1990	1991
Constant	−101.743	−14.081	22.994	−66.741
	(−3.785)	(−0.522)	(1.624)	(−1.542)
Predicted income	1.640	0.322	−0.092	1.308
	(5.349)	(0.824)	(−1.068)	(2.094)
$(Income)^2$	−0.009	0.0035	0.0038	−0.0056
	(−3.553)	(1.1101)	(6.1216)	(−1.4139)
$(Income)^3$	3.136e-05	−1.957e-05	−9.684e-06	1.9903e-05
	(3.548)	(−1.748)	(−4.730)	(1.6994)
$(Income)^4$	−4.954e-08	4.562e-08	1.200e-08	−3.0991e-08
	(−3.542)	(2.573)	(3.982)	(−1.9335)
$(Income)^5$	2.829e-11	−3.564e-11	−5.743e-12	1.7351e-11
	(3.560)	(−3.515)	(−3.573)	(2.114)
Predicted nonwage income	N/A	N/A	0.544	0.551
			(8.534)	(4.890)
$(Non\text{-}wage\ income)^2$	N/A	N/A	0.0004	−0.0007
			(0.4494)	(−0.3836)
$(Non\text{-}wage\ income)^3$	N/A	N/A	1.382e-06	2.648e-06
			(0.165)	(0.120)
$(Non\text{-}wage\ income)^4$	N/A	N/A	1.212e-08	2.587e-08
			(0.175)	(0.199)
$(Non\text{-}wage\ income)^5$	N/A	N/A	2.639e-11	5.804e-11
			(0.169)	(0.255)
Wealth	1.339e-05	1.104e-05	−9.684e-07	4.490e-07
	(4.172)	(4.174)	(−0.545)	(0.100)
Interf	−0.0019	−0.0011	−0.0002	5.711e-05
	(−13.3791)	(−8.385)	(−0.8607)	(0.127)
$(Interf)^2$	−5.041e-08	−2.068e-08	2.126e-09	−5.922e-09
	(−6.836)	(−5.351)	(0.454)	−0.751
$(Interf)^3$	−2.696e-13	−4.384e-14	−2.703e-06	5.527e-06
	(−2.125)	(−0.767)	(−0.614)	(0.671)
Biund1	−0.476	−1.119	−0.695	−1.638
	−(2.887)	(−7.049)	(−6.845)	(−8.312)
Biund2	N/A	N/A	−0.013	−0.010
			(−1.090)	(−0.377)
Education	−1.221	−2.854	0.079	3.980
	(−0.360)	(−0.855)	(0.044)	(1.152)
$(Education)^2$	0.172772	0.464	−0.035	−0.778
	(0.266)	(0.730)	(−0.105)	(−1.179)
Age	0.208	−1.573	−0.377	0.286
	(0.162)	(−1.534)	(−0.503)	(0.212)
$(Age)^2$	−0.00064	0.024	0.006	−0.0019
	(−0.03587)	(1.750)	(0.625)	(−0.1036)

Table 6.4
(continued)

Variable	OLS regression coefficients by year			
	1985	1986	1990	1991
Sex	13.393	10.857	−5.809	−6.163
	(8.293)	(6.752)	(−7.057)	(−3.873)
R^2	0.937	0.912	0.991	0.964
N	424	442	411	415

Note: For years before 1987, income in the table covers all income liable to tax; for years after 1986, it covers only wage income. T-values are in parentheses.

across time; τ_{tl} is a time effect constant across individuals; and finally e_{til} is an idiosyncratic error term assumed to be independent of everything else in the model. Note that $\widehat{t_{til}^a}$ and $\widehat{V_{til}}$ are functions of instrumented income. If the instruments in equations (3) and (4) are correlated with α_{il} (which is unobserved) OLS on (5) will yield biased estimates. First-difference estimations, however, will yield unbiased estimates of β_{1l} and β_{2l} $l = 1, \ldots, 3$ since both $\widehat{t_{til}^a}$ and $\widehat{V_{til}}$ are time varying.

The index l separates the sample into three different submarkets: unskilled workers, skilled workers (both blue- and white-collar), and professionals (including academics in the public sector). We estimate the wage equation for these three groups separately because we believe that wage-setting institutions differ by occupational levels. We suppress the index l in what follows.

The noncompetitive theories in general suggest that we might want to control for unemployment benefits and for unemployment in some way. One might think of the latter as a measure of important characteristics of the market(s) at which the individual competes with others for jobs. As we conduct the estimations for a particular local market (Copenhagen) and furthermore divide this local market by occupational level, we believe that any relevant unemployment feature is picked up by the constant term (and the changes in unemployment are picked up by the constant term in first-difference equations, and so forth). So by construction we do control for aggregate unemployment at relevant markets. Rather than aggregate measures, one could alternatively try to obtain individual unemployment risk measures (by estimation). This measure would be strongly endogenous to the individual wage, which is why we have not followed this avenue.

With respect to unemployment benefits, the situation is the same for skilled workers and professionals, because they are all entitled to the same benefit level; (almost) all qualify for maximum UI benefits. For unskilled workers, for whom this is not the case, the UI benefits are a linear function of the dependent variable (the benefits to individual i are $0.9 * W_i$) and the replacement rate is a constant across individuals, 0.9, to be picked up by the constant term of the regression equation. Thus, with our individual wage equations either the UI benefit level is constant across individuals and the replacement rate is a linear function of the dependent variable, or the replacement rate is constant across individuals and the UI benefit level is a linear function of the dependent variable. This is why we do not include UI benefits. If we were to include "out-of-work" income for unemployed workers as an independent variable in our individual wage equations, we would need a very rich computation including, for instance, individual transportation costs, in-work benefits, child care costs, and so forth. These costs and benefits do vary across individuals and some are also exogenous, at least in the short run. However, we do not in any case have this information in our data set.

We focus on four years, 1985, 1986, 1990, and 1991, and look at pooled OLS estimators, pair-wise first-difference estimators for 1985–1986 and 1990–1991, and finally, difference-in-difference estimators between these two pairs of years.

6.5.2.1   Identification

The tax functions are estimated using capital income, socioeconomic status, and predicted income (the last in order to account for the endogeneity of tax rates and income).

The identifying variation in the tax variables then comes from two sources, variations in R, and ϕ and the tax reform. The variations in capital income, R, and socioeconomic status, ϕ, involve variations in both subsidies and deductions. During the period we look at, different tax deductions could and should be deducted from different parts of the income. This implies that a group of individuals with the same wage could have the same marginal tax rate but different average taxation rates (the tax functions are shifted and generate parallel functions as R and ϕ vary). But two individuals with the same wage could also have the same average tax rate and different marginal rates (i.e., their individual tax functions cross, which was only possible because different tax deductions were related to different elements of the individual's income, bottom, middle, and top income, each with their associated tax rate). Thus, the average and the marginal tax rates can vary independently in our data, which makes for identification of effects of both average taxation and progressivity.

In the long run R and ϕ are endogenous to the wage, however, and even though job changes and, for instance, changes in marital status take time, endogeneity could be a problem even when looking at first differences. This is why we also want to use the variations generated by the tax reform implemented in 1987–1989. Performing estimations across this period will introduce exogenous variations. It will not remove any endogenous variations between tax rates and wages that might have been in the data to begin with. Furthermore, the estimation across the tax reform may also introduce variations in the parameters, due to the changing mode of the business cycle; 1986–1987 were peak years of an economic boom, and 1990–1991 were years with high and increasing unemployment. Therefore, we emphasize both the separate estimations at the boom years (1986–1987) and bust years (1990–1991) and the estimations across the implementing period of the tax reform.

Apart from endogenous regressors there is also another problem, namely, that of unobserved heterogeneity. More able individuals might have an advantage in using any tax legislation to reduce their own tax, which could give a downward bias in the marginal rates for any given wage at the high end of the job hierarchy. Similarly, tastes for work might affect the way taxes influence labor supply. To deal with these concerns, we estimate the equation in first differences to factor out unobserved individual characteristics, α_i:

$$\Delta_{t,t+1} \log W_i = \beta' \Delta_{t,t+1} \mathbf{z}_i + \Delta_{t,t+1} \tau + \Delta_{t,t+1} e_i,$$

where $\Delta_{t,t+1} x_i = x_{i,t+1} - x_{i,t}$, and where $\mathbf{z}_i$ now denotes all the left hand side explanatory variables in (5). Allowing for $\tau_t \neq \tau_{t+1}$ implies that $\Delta_{t,t+1} \tau$ becomes a (the) constant term of the regression to capture general wage increases due to productivity trends, changes in the level of general unemployment, and so forth. Wage growth might be different before and after the tax reform, just as it might influence wage setting whether the unemployment rate was decreasing or increasing. To control for this, when we estimate across the implementation of the tax reform, we estimate the equation in difference-in-differences as well:

$$\Delta_{t',t'+1} \Delta_{t,t+1} \log W_i = \beta' \Delta_{t',t'+1} \Delta_{t,t+1} \mathbf{z}_i + \Delta_{t',t'+1} \Delta_{t,t+1} \tau + \varepsilon_i,$$

where $\Delta_{t',t'+1} \Delta_{t,t+1} x_i = (x_{i,t'+1} - x_{i,t'}) - (x_{i,t+1} - x_{i,t})$ and $\varepsilon_i = \Delta_{t',t'+1} \Delta_{t,t+1} e_i$. When we include a constant term here, we allow a trend break in wages to be explained by a general trend break—for instance, in productivity (which could be an effect of the tax reform) and/or by moving from one point to another in the business cycle (from decreasing unemployment to increasing unemployment); that is, we test whether $\Delta_{t',t'+1}\Delta_{t,t+1}\tau = 0$.

By the difference-in-difference approach, we also introduce exogenous variations in the tax variables as mentioned earlier. As long as the β's are stationary over time, the difference-in-difference version is preferred. If the β's are not stationary over time—that is, the way in which wages respond to changes in the tax structure depends, for instance, on whether unemployment is high or low—then the first-difference approach is the best we can do.

The way we identify a union effect is by interacting the two tax variables with union membership, having nonmembers as the base (model A), and similarly by interacting nonmembers with the two tax variables, having union members as the base (model B). In this way we get results separately for the unionized and the nonunionized sectors and test whether the coefficients are significantly different between these two sectors.

6.5.2.2 Results
Tables 6A.1–6A.3 contain the full set of results. The effect of education is the one that varies the most across the three different models, mainly reflecting the difference between including the variations from the entire stock of observations (as in the pooled OLS) and only from the individuals who are newly educated (as in the difference approach). The age variables, on the other hand, behave very similarly across the models and years, which suggests that the polynomial form is well specified.

With respect to the tax variables, with and without interaction terms, the pooled OLS, the first difference, and the difference-in-difference estimators all point in the same direction almost everywhere, between the year pairs and between the three occupational levels. In general, the coefficients for 1990–1991 and for the pooled OLS are numerically bigger and more significant than the coefficients for 1985–1986 and in the first-difference estimations, which are in turn more significant than the coefficients produced by the difference-in-difference estimator— probably due to loss of efficiency.

The coefficients for the tax variables are summarized in table 6.5, in order to give an overview. With regard to progressivity, the coefficients of the nonunionized groups have a negative sign, suggesting a

Table 6.5
Resumé of wage responses to tax variables (dependent variable: log hourly wage)

		Unskilled workers		Skilled workers		Professionals	
		Coefficient	T-value	Coefficient	T-value	Coefficient	T-value
1986–1985, first difference							
Non-union	$\text{Log}(1 - T_a)$	−0.1618	−2.70	−0.1728	−4.14	−0.1174	−2.13
	$\text{Log}(V)$	−0.0909	−1.77	−0.0534	−1.76	−0.0915	−2.27
Union	$\text{Log}(1 - T_a)$	0.0095	0.28	−0.0457	−1.77	0.0124	0.40
	$\text{Log}(V)$	−0.0232	−0.72	−0.0390	−1.62	−0.0510	−1.84
Union compared to non-union	$\text{Log}(1 - T_a)$	0.1713	2.65	0.1272	2.73	0.1298	2.13
	$\text{Log}(V)$	0.0677	1.18	0.0143	0.39	0.0405	0.86
	Union = 1	0.2366	4.74	0.1500	4.28	0.1891	4.19
1991–1990, first difference							
Non-union	$\text{Log}(1 - T_a)$	−0.5843	−8.16	−0.6839	−15.93	−0.1282	−4.52
	$\text{Log}(V)$	−0.3607	−5.52	−0.5964	−17.17	−0.0951	−3.97
Union	$\text{Log}(1 - T_a)$	−0.2851	−8.40	−0.3909	−15.05	0.1744	−7.38
	$\text{Log}(V)$	−0.2149	−6.79	−0.2951	−12.77	−0.0754	−3.96
Union compared to non-union	$\text{Log}(1 - T_a)$	0.2992	4.26	0.2930	6.94	−0.0462	−1.38
	$\text{Log}(V)$	0.1458	2.28	0.3013	8.69	−0.0197	−0.68
	Union = 1	0.2153	3.88	0.3027	9.55	0.0180	0.60
(1991–1990)–(1986–1985), difference-in-difference							
Non-union	$\text{Log}(1 - T_a)$	−0.3367	−5.00	−0.2944	−6.55	−0.1013	−2.73
	$\text{Log}(V)$	−0.0762	−1.19	−0.0620	−1.68	−0.0625	−2.28
Union	$\text{Log}(1 - T_a)$	0.0197	0.57	−0.1311	−4.87	0.0094	0.36
	$\text{Log}(V)$	−0.0078	−0.26	−0.0916	−3.79	−0.0474	−2.21
Union compared to non-union	$\text{Log}(1 - T_a)$	0.3541	5.15	0.1542	3.14	0.1040	2.54
	$\text{Log}(V)$	0.0645	0.99	−0.0401	−1.01	0.0060	0.18
	Union = 1	0.2554	4.59	0.0818	2.08	0.0565	1.60

Source: Tables 6A.1–6A.3. The variables "Union compared to non-union" are the interaction terms from model A. The coefficients for the variable "Union," which are the results given separately for the unionized sectors, are not shown in the appendix but only here.

competitive, wage-increasing effect of tax progressivity. The effect is less significant the lower the occupational group, and in the difference-in-difference model it is only for professionals that the effect is significant at the 5 percent level. The unionized sectors have significantly negative signs on the progressivity variable for both skilled workers and professionals. The unionized and nonunionized sectors do not behave significantly different at any of the occupational levels when we look at the difference-in-difference estimators of the progressivity variable.

However, the first-difference estimator does suggest a significant difference between union and nonunion workers for both the skilled and the unskilled. There is a significant countervailing effect of belonging to the unionized sector when unemployment is high and increasing; the wages increase less with higher progressivity in the unionized sector compared to the nonunionized sector in 1990–1991. Still, the net effect is negative, indicating that the competitive effect is the strongest.

An unbiased difference-in-difference estimator relies on some strong assumptions being fulfilled. Of particular relevance to us is a constant time effect—in particular, parameter stability. This is of some concern, given the very different business-cycle situations in 1986–1987 and 1990–1991. Aggregate unemployment in Denmark decreased between 1985 and 1986, and 1987 was the last year of an economic boom, whereas unemployment increased between 1990 and 1991, when the economy was in the middle of a recession. Comparing model A and model A2 in the appendix tables suggests that a constant term should be included in the difference-in-difference equations as well, although it only changes the estimated values marginally. Thus, the difference between the first-difference and the difference-in-difference estimators cannot be accounted for by a constant term in the latter version. This is in line with the first-difference estimators suggesting that the coefficients for the tax variables are not constant over the business cycle.

For this reason, we (also) put weight on the estimations at specific points of the business cycle—the first-difference estimators. It is, moreover, plausible that the theories for imperfectly competitive markets are more relevant empirically when unemployment is high than when it is low. The theories are typically structural models with no business cycle generated or modeled. This is also what we find, because the results for the low unemployment years 1986–1987 are the competitive ones everywhere, even though the effect is insignificant for one or two of the groups.

Giving more or less credit to the first-difference estimator does not change the overall conclusion: the effect of tax progressivity on wages we find is not the noncompetitive wage-moderating effect. On the contrary, for the main part of the Danish labor market, the competitive prediction is vindicated. An exception is the unskilled sector, where the negative coefficient for tax progressivity is insignificant.

From table 6.5 we see that the level of taxation—the average tax rate—increases pretax wages for all nonunion groups, an effect that is robust across time and models with relatively little variation. But this effect is significantly smaller (numerically) in the unionized sector compared to the nonunionized sector at all levels.

Finally, table 6.5 suggests that as expected, unions also affect the wage level if taxes are held constant. The positive influence of unions on wages is strongest for unskilled workers, and still significant but less strong for skilled workers; for professionals, the effect is not significant.

So unions seem to have a significant influence on wages, directly as well as indirectly. Unions mean higher wages and wages that are less responsive with respect to changes in the tax level. With respect to tax progressivity, the labor market as a whole seems to function like a competitive market, though with wages rising with progressivity. There are signs, however, that in the traditional trade union sectors of skilled and unskilled workers, income tax progressivity does moderate wages relative to wages in the nonunionized sector in times of high and increasing unemployment.

6.6 Conclusion

This chapter has analyzed the influence of income tax progression on wage formation, using microdata from the Copenhagen municipality. Our main conclusion is that there is a relative wage-moderating effect from the strong Danish unions, as our results for the recession years, 1990–1991, suggest. When unemployment is high and increasing, the wage response to changing tax progression does seem to reflect employment considerations; in the unionized skilled and unskilled sectors, the wages increase less than in the nonunionized sectors in response to steeper tax progression. However, the overall effects even in the unionized sectors and even during periods with high and increasing unemployment are the competitive, wage-increasing effects.

Another effect of unions is that they significantly reduce the influence of average income taxation on wages at all occupational levels. The traditional unions also seem to uphold their promises, as the wages are higher in unionized sectors for unskilled and skilled workers. But we will need to control for additional characteristics to reach a final conclusion on this issue.

Going back to the questions discussed in section 6.1, we have to conclude that this study does not lend support to the view that there is no

Table 6A.1
Results for unskilled workers (dependent variable: log hourly wage)

		Method											
		Pooled OLS				First difference				Difference-in-difference			
		Model A		Model B		Model A		Model B		Model A		Model A2	
Years	Variable	Coefficient	T-value	Coefficient	T-value	Coefficient	T-value	Coefficient	T-value	Coefficient	T-value	Coefficient	T-value
1985 and 1986[1]	Constant	3.1965	25.89	3.3520	29.24	0.2453	7.25	0.2453	7.25				
	$\log(1 - T_a)$	-0.9875	-13.67	-0.7297	-17.28	-0.1618	-2.70	0.0095	0.28				
	$\log(V)$	-0.6152	-8.71	-0.7001	-17.23	-0.0909	-1.77	-0.0232	-0.72				
	Education	0.0117	2.39	0.0117	2.39	-0.0415	-1.94	-0.0415	-1.94				
	Age	0.0587	6.27	0.0587	6.27	Const.	Const.	Const.	Const.				
	$(\text{Age})^2$	-0.0013	-5.53	-0.0013	-5.53	-0.0046	-5.08	-0.0046	-5.08				
	$(\text{Age})^3$	0.0000	4.90	0.0000	4.90	0.0000	4.31	0.0000	4.31				
	Sex = female	-0.1907	-27.78	-0.1907	-27.78	N/A	N/A	N/A	N/A				
	U-status	0.1555	2.42	-0.1555	-2.42	0.2366	4.74	-0.2366	-4.74				
	U-status × $\log(1 - T_a)$	0.2578	3.13	-0.2578	-3.13	0.1713	2.65	-0.1713	-2.65				
	U-status × $\log(V)$	-0.0849	-1.06	0.0849	1.06	0.0677	1.18	-0.0677	-1.18				
	R^2	0.277		0.277		0.049		0.049					
1990 and 1991[1]	Constant	3.2429	29.05	3.9518	34.89	0.1755	4.97	0.1755	4.97	0.0045	1.50	N/A	N/A
	$\log(1 - T_a)$	-1.8224	-36.92	-0.9847	-32.85	-0.5843	-8.16	-0.2851	-8.40	-0.3367	-5.00	-0.3322	-4.93
	$\log(V)$	-1.5202	-32.58	-0.8598	-30.91	-0.3607	-5.52	-0.2149	-6.79	-0.0762	-1.19	-0.0699	-1.09
	Education	-0.0051	-1.23	-0.0051	-1.23	0.0278	1.52	0.0278	1.52	0.0601	1.39	0.0629	1.46
	Age	0.0084	0.94	0.0084	0.94	Const.	Const.	Const.	Const.	N/A	N/A	N/A	N/A

(Age)²	−0.0001	−0.55	−0.0001	−0.55	−0.0032	−3.44	−0.0032	−3.44	−0.0037	−3.67	−0.0034	−3.47
(Age)³	0.0000	0.35	0.0000	0.35	0.0000	3.19	0.0000	3.19	0.0000	3.12	0.0000	2.93
Sex = female	−0.1029	−16.24	−0.1029	−16.24	N/A	N/A	N/A	N/A	N/A	N/A	N/A	N/A
U-status	0.7090	16.15	−0.7090	−16.15	0.2153	3.88	−0.2153	−3.88	0.2554	4.59	0.2515	4.52
U-status × Log(1 − T_a)	0.8377	14.89	−0.8377	−14.89	0.2992	4.26	−0.2992	−4.26	0.3541	5.15	0.3519	5.11
U-status × Log(V)	0.6604	12.53	−0.6604	−12.53	0.1458	2.28	−0.1458	−2.28	0.0645	0.99	0.0621	0.95
R^2	0.482		0.482		0.07		0.07		0.047		0.046	

Note: In model A, U-status indicates a unionized sector. In model B, U-status indicates a nonunionized sector.

[1] For the difference models, the results are shown for the differences between these two years. The difference-in-difference model shows the results for the differences between the differences, namely, 1991–1990 and 1986–1985.

Table 6A.2
Results for skilled workers (blue- and white-collar) (dependent variable: log hourly wage)

		Method											
		Pooled OLS				First difference				Difference-in-difference			
		Model A*		Model B		Model A		Model B		Model A		Model A2	
Years	Variable	Coefficient	T-value	Coefficient	T-value	Coefficient	T-value	Coefficient	T-value	Coefficient	T-value	Coefficient	T-value
1985 and 1986[1]	Constant	2.3328	29.91	2.4751	33.81	0.2681	10.44	0.2681	10.44				
	Log(1 − T_a)	−0.7304	−15.73	−0.5180	−20.54	−0.1728	−4.14	−0.0457	−1.77				
	Log(V)	−0.3399	−7.80	−0.4382	−18.31	−0.0534	−1.76	−0.0390	−1.62				
	Education	0.0199	6.46	0.0199	6.46	−0.0016	−0.10	−0.0016	−0.10				
	Age	0.1339	22.11	0.1339	22.11	Const.	Const.	Const.	Const.				
	$(Age)^2$	−0.0030	−19.22	−0.0030	−19.22	−0.0052	−7.58	−0.0052	−7.58				
	$(Age)^3$	0.0000	16.77	0.0000	16.77	0.0000	6.54	0.0000	6.54				
	Sex = female	−0.1603	−37.85	−0.1603	−37.85	N/A	N/A	N/A	N/A				
	U-Status	0.1423	3.50	−0.1423	−3.50	0.1500	4.28	−0.1500	−4.28				
	U-Status × Log(1 − T_a)	0.2124	4.06	−0.2124	−4.06	0.1272	2.73	−0.1272	−2.73				
	U-Status × Log(V)	−0.0983	−2.00	0.0983	2.00	0.0143	0.39	−0.0143	−0.39				
	R^2	0.293		0.293		0.034		0.034					
1990 and 1991[1]	Constant	2.5172	35.05	2.8707	39.90	0.2212	9.86	0.2212	9.86	0.0069	3.34	N/A	N/A
	Log(1 − T_a)	−1.6117	−40.25	−1.2850	−62.53	−0.6839	−15.93	−0.3909	−15.05	−0.2944	−6.55	−0.2887	−6.42
	Log(V)	−1.4517	−44.14	−1.1354	−60.59	−0.5964	−17.17	−0.2951	−12.77	−0.0620	−1.68	−0.0557	−1.51
	Education	0.0184	7.55	0.0184	7.55	0.0045	0.62	0.0045	0.62	0.0400	1.70	0.0440	1.87
	Age	0.0612	10.35	0.0612	10.35	Const.	Const.	Const.	Const.	N/A	N/A	N/A	N/A

$(Age)^2$	−0.0013	−8.66	−0.0013	−8.66	−0.0043	−7.03	−0.0043	−7.03	−0.0051	−6.96	−0.0047	−6.52
$(Age)^3$	0.0000	7.40	0.0000	7.40	0.0000	6.20	0.0000	6.20	0.0000	6.27	0.0000	5.86
Sex = female	−0.0581	−15.45	−0.0581	−15.45	N/A	N/A	N/A	N/A	N/A	N/A	N/A	N/A
U-status	0.3535	10.68	−0.3535	−10.68	0.3027	9.55	−0.3027	−9.55	0.0818	2.08	0.0813	2.07
U-status × Log$(1 − T_a)$	0.3268	7.41	−0.3268	−7.41	0.2930	6.94	−0.2930	−6.94	0.1542	3.14	0.1576	3.21
U-status × Log(V)	0.3163	8.63	−0.3163	−8.63	0.3013	8.69	−0.3013	−8.69	−0.0401	−1.01	−0.0360	−0.90
R^2	0.517		0.517		0.116		0.116		0.033		0.031	

Note: In model A, U-status indicates a unionized sector. In model B, U-status indicates a nonunionized sector.
[1] For the difference models, the results are shown for the difference between these two years. The difference-in-difference model shows the results for the differences between the differences, namely, 1991–1990 and 1986–1985.

Table 6A.3
Results for professionals (dependent variable: log hourly wage)

		Method											
		Pooled OLS				First difference				Difference-in-difference			
		Model A		Model B		Model A		Model B		Model A		Model A2	
Years	Variable	Coefficient	T-value	Coefficient	T-value	Coefficient	T-value	Coefficient	T-value	Coefficient	T-value	Coefficient	T-value
1985 and 1986[1]	Constant	2.8481	19.05	2.9127	19.38	0.2679	7.81	0.2679	7.81				
	$\log(1 - T_a)$	-0.4754	-10.29	-0.2895	-8.04	-0.1174	-2.13	0.0124	0.40				
	$\log(V)$	-0.1377	-3.55	-0.2303	-6.84	-0.0915	-2.27	-0.0510	-1.84				
	Education	0.0379	13.22	0.0379	13.22	-0.0572	-2.45	-0.0572	-2.45				
	Age	0.1114	9.67	0.1114	9.67	Const.	Const.	Const.	Const.				
	$(Age)^2$	-0.0022	-7.91	-0.0022	-7.91	-0.0053	-5.80	-0.0053	-5.80				
	$(Age)^3$	0.0000	6.57	0.0000	6.57	0.0000	5.04	0.0000	5.04				
	Sex = female	-0.2325	-35.54	-0.2325	-35.54	N/A	N/A	N/A	N/A				
	U-status	0.0646	1.39	-0.0646	-1.39	0.1891	4.19	-0.1891	-4.19				
	U-status × $\log(1 - T_a)$	0.1859	3.20	-0.1859	-3.20	0.1298	2.13	-0.1298	-2.13				
	U-Status × $\log(V)$	-0.0926	-1.81	0.0926	1.81	0.0405	0.86	-0.0405	-0.86				
	R^2	0.285		0.285		0.045		0.045					
1990 and 1991[1]	Constant	3.4821	23.16	2.8344	18.81	0.2526	7.35	0.2526	7.35	0.0125	4.86	N/A	N/A
	$\log(1 - T_a)$	-0.5949	-16.52	-1.2011	-41.56	-0.1282	-4.52	-0.1744	-7.38	-0.1013	-2.73	-0.1021	-2.75
	$\log(V)$	-0.2175	-7.77	-0.8429	-32.00	-0.0951	-3.97	-0.0754	-3.96	-0.0625	-2.28	-0.0618	-2.25
	Education	0.0154	6.12	0.0154	6.12	-0.0078	-1.43	-0.0078	-1.43	-0.0083	-0.55	-0.0030	-0.20
	Age	0.0850	7.39	0.0850	7.39	Const.	Const.	Const.	Const.	N/A	N/A	N/A	N/A

$(Age)^2$	−0.0017	−6.10	−0.0017	−6.10	−0.0042	−4.88	−0.0042	−4.88	−0.0022	−2.48	−0.0014	−1.59
$(Age)^3$	0.0000	5.00	0.0000	5.00	0.0000	4.17	0.0000	4.17	0.0000	1.63	0.0000	0.82
Sex = female	−0.1611	−26.59	−0.1611	−26.59	N/A	N/A	N/A	N/A	N/A	N/A	N/A	N/A
U-status	−0.6477	−16.43	0.6477	16.43	−0.0180	−0.60	0.0180	0.60	0.0565	1.60	0.0583	1.65
U-status × Log$(1 − T_a)$	−0.6062	−13.39	0.6062	13.39	−0.0462	−1.38	0.0462	1.38	0.1040	2.54	0.1115	2.72
U-status × Log(V)	−0.6254	−16.62	0.6254	16.62	0.0197	0.68	−0.0197	−0.68	0.0060	0.18	0.0144	0.43
R^2	0.406		0.406		0.035		0.035		0.019		0.013	

Note: In model A, U-status indicates a unionized sector. In model B, U-status indicates a nonunionized sector. For the difference models, the results are shown for the differences between these two years. The difference-in-difference model shows the results for the differences between the differences, namely, 1991–1990 and 1986–1985.

trade-off between equity and efficiency when deciding on an income tax policy if the labor market is imperfectly competitive. As discussed previously, our study is not conclusive and there is a need for further empirical work on this question, in particular, work that addresses the endogeneity problems involved in having tax rates as regressors in wage equations.

Appendix

The results discussed in section 6.5.2.2 are presented here in a version that includes all the control variables. Table 6A.1 contains the results for unskilled workers, table 6A.2 the results for skilled workers, and table 6A.3 the results for professionals.

Notes

We wish to thank Claus Thustrup Kreiner and Nada O. Eissa for their comments and helpful suggestions, and Nis Vilhelm Benn for his excellent research assistance.

1. Earlier studies either use no information on tax deduction and subsidies (Holmlund and Kolm 1996, for Sweden) or use this information only to compute average tax rates, not marginal rates (Pedersen, Smith, and Stephensen 1999, for Denmark). This creates large measurement errors, and these might have biased the results.

2. Subsidies and deductions are based mainly on a person's civil status, number of children, and whether he or she owns a house. Therefore, we have estimated tax functions for eight different socioeconomic groups (homeowners and tenants; single and married persons; and people with and without children). We estimate these functions for a specific municipality since, for a given socioeconomic group, tax functions vary a lot across municipalities; not only are the conduct and take-up rates different, the tax rates also differ across municipalities, because the largest slice of an individual's tax payment goes to the municipality where he or she lives, and the percentage is decided locally. Eventually we would like to make analyses of all municipalities, both in order to utilize the cross-municipality variations in taxes and in order to address mobility between the municipalities. This will have to await future studies.

3. As a proxy for union membership, we use membership of an unemployment insurance fund, which is voluntary in Denmark, and about which we have information. Most insured workers are also union members.

4. See Lockwood, Sløk, and Tranæs 2000.

5. We consider the following occupations: unskilled, skilled, and professionals. One could argue that these groups consist of subgroups operating at different submarkets with different unemployment characteristics and/or that the relevant markets do not coincide with municipalities. We are not sure how narrowly one can meaningfully define a market segment. If one wishes to include a measure for unemployment in the individual wage equations, a better approach would probably be to estimate individual unemployment risks.

6. The instruments used to predict income are sex, age, education, number of children, house owner or tenant, and marital status.

7. We owe thanks to Nada O. Eissa for suggesting this procedure.

8. The remainder of this section is based on Statistics Denmark 1987, 1991, and 1992.

9. The high state tax rate was 44 percent until 1985 but was 40 percent in 1986.

10. There are twelve socioeconomic groups, but we have too few observations and are forced to consider only eleven subgroups. With eight separate years, this yields eighty-eight regressions.

References

Bovenberg, A. L., and F. van der Ploeg. 1994. "Effects of the Tax and Benefit System on Wage Formation and Unemployment." Manuscript CentER, Tilburg University and the University of Amsterdam.

Brunello, G., M. L. Parisi, and D. Sonnedda. 2002. "Labor Taxes and Wages: Evidence form Italy." CESifo Working Paper No. 715(4), Munich.

Brunello, G., and D. Sonnedda. 2002. "Labor Tax Progressivity, Wage Determination and the Relative Wage Effect." CESifo Working Paper No. 721(4), Munich.

Hansen, C. T. 1999. "Lower Tax Progression, Longer Hours, and Higher Wages." Scandinavian Journal of Economics 1001, no. 1: 49–65.

Hansen, H., and M. L. Hultin. 1997. Actual and Potential Recipients of Welfare Benefits with a Focus on Housing Benefits, 1987–1992. Study No. 4. Copenhagen: The Rockwool Foundation Research Unit.

Hersoug, T. 1984. "Union Wage Responses to Tax Changes." Oxford Economic Papers 36: 37–51.

Holmlund, B., and A.-S. Kolm. 1995. "Progressive Taxation, Wage Setting, and Unemployment: Theory and Swedish Evidence." Swedish Economic Policy Review 2: 423–460.

Koskela, E., and J. Vilmunen. 1996. "Tax Progression is Good for Employment in Popular Models of Trade Union Behaviour." Labour Economics 3, no. 1: 65–80.

Lockwood, L., and A. Manning. 1993. "Wage Setting and the Tax System: Theory and Evidence for the United Kingdom." Journal of Public Economics 52: 1–29.

Lockwood, L., T. Sløk, and T. Tranæs. 2000. "Progressive Taxation and Wage Setting: Some Evidence for Denmark." Scandinavian Journal of Economics 102, no. 4: 707–723.

Malcolmson, J., and N. Sator. 1987. "Tax Push Inflation in a Unionized Labour Market." European Economic Review 31: 1581–1596.

Musgrave, R., and P. B. Musgrave. 1976. Public Finance in Theory and Practice, 2nd. ed. New York: McGraw-Hill.

Pedersen, L. H., N. Smith, and P. Stephensen. 1999. "Minimum Wage Contracts and Individual Wage Formation: Theory and Evidence from Danish Panel Data." In Macroeconomic Perspectives on the Danish Economy, ed. Torben M. Andersen, Svend E. H. Jensen, and Ole Risager. London: Macmillan Press.

Pisauro, G. 1991. "The Effect of Taxes on Labour in Efficiency Wage Models." *Journal of Public Economics* 45: 329–345.

Sørensen, P. B. 1997. "Public Finance Solutions to the European Unemployment Problem?" *Economic Policy* 25: 223–264.

Statistics Denmark. 1987, 1991, 1992. *Statistical Yearbook*. Copenhagen: Statistics Denmark.

III

Taxation and the Underground Economy

7   Insiders, Outsiders, and the Underground Economy

Dan Anderberg

7.1 Introduction

In the popular debate, labor taxes are often blamed for two things: destroying employment opportunities and encouraging tax dodging. Both questions have been examined empirically. The empirical literature linking employment to taxes have produced rather mixed results, with some contributions finding a negative relation and others finding no such relation.[1] The same literature, however, generally places more emphasis on other labor market institutions, not least the unemployment benefit regime and labor market rigidities.[2]

Looking at the relationship between taxation and the shadow economy, Schneider (2000) reports a positive correlation between a calculated measure of overall tax and social security contributions and underground economic activity as percent of GDP for eighteen OECD countries.[3] However, some authors have stressed that other institutional factors such as corruption, bureaucracy, weak legal systems and regulation tend to drive entrepreneurs underground. For example, Friedman et al. (2000), investigating sixty-nine countries, including transition countries and developing countries, find no significant effect of taxes but a significant effect of various measures of the business environment reflecting corruption and the legal environment.[4] Thus institutional factors other than taxes appear to play an important role in determining the size of the underground economy.

In order to understand what these factors may be, it is useful to consider the identities of those individuals who supply labor to the underground economy. In a particularly illuminating study using a specialized data set from Quebec, Lemieux, Fortin, and Frechette (1994) find, among other things, that the supply of labor to the underground economy comes from to a large extent individuals with

Table 7.1
Partial correlation between underground economic activity in 1995 for sixteen OECD countries with OECD index of employment protection and with overall tax wedge

Shadow economy / GDP	Partial correlation	Significance
Employment protection	0.486	0.078
Overall tax wedge	0.136	0.642

Note: For data and sources, see table 7.4.

relatively weak attachment to the regular labor market, such as the unemployed, students, and low-skilled workers.

This pattern raises the question of whether there may be a link between labor market institutions and the level of underground economic activity. Suppose, for example, that various forms of labor market rigidities reinforce the dichotomy between "insiders" and "outsiders"; by worsening the job prospects for outsiders, such rigidities may then affect their incentives to seek alternative sources of income on the fringe of the economy.

The question is thus if there is any indication that rigid labor markets are associated with widespread underground economic activities. Consider table 7.1, which shows, for fifteen OECD countries, the partial correlation between underground economic activity with a commonly used index of employment protection on the one hand and overall tax wedge on the other hand. The table highlights a surprisingly strong relationship between underground economic activity and OECD's measure of employment protection (OECD, 1999). Indeed, underground economic activity is even more strongly related to employment protection than to taxes.

More exactly, why might underground economic activity be related to labor market rigidities in general and employment protection in particular? One simple intuition is that labor market rigidities tend to worsen the employment prospects for current "outsiders" by slowing down the flows in the labor market, making it more difficult to make it into a regular job. In order to explore this intuition, this chapter builds a small model of underground trade, regular employment, taxation, and employment protection. The model focuses on the supply of labor to the underground economy by the unemployed, and shows how employment protection and taxes may increase underground economic activity.[5]

The main effect of employment protection is to reduce the rate of transition in and out of regular employment. This means that the number of jobs that are created (per unit of time) is reduced. Insofar as this also reduces equilibrium employment, it directly increases underground activities. However, more important, the slower rate of job creation also reduces the average job-finding rate among current outsiders and thus increases their incentives to participate in irregular activities at the expense of regular job search. Taxation interacts with this process: it directly encourages trading in the (untaxed) underground economy. This increased relative attractiveness of trading in the underground economy, in turn, affects job creation through the wage setting process.

The model thus also provides a theoretical foundation for an endogenous negative relation between taxes and employment. This is interesting since most standard models predict that, conditional on unemployment benefits being a fixed proportion of net earnings, labor taxes are neutral with respect to unemployment. The result (which holds both in standard matching models and efficiency wage models) is intuitive: given the structure of unemployment benefit, taxation doesn't affect the relative attractiveness of being in and out of work. This property does not hold in the current model, however, since workers who are unemployed can engage in underground economic activities, which becomes relatively more attractive at high levels of taxation.[6]

A number of recent contributions have considered the role of imperfect labor markets for underground economic activity. Boeri and Garibaldi (2002) consider a model in which jobs are randomly hit by adverse technology shocks. In equilibrium, when a bad shock occurs, the employment is continued in the underground economy. The authors focus on the role of auditing and fines and find that higher fines can actually increase underground activities. This result is partly driven by the assumption that all underground activities start out as formal jobs. The model of Boeri and Garibaldi also differs from that presented here in that a worker is, at any point in time, in one of three states: unemployed, in an underground job, or in a formal job.

Kolm and Larsen (2003b) also consider a three-state model with unemployment, formal jobs, and informal jobs. However, in their model informal jobs are directly created (rather than being made informal in response to a technology shock). Since formal and informal jobs are in direct competition for labor, they find that tougher penalties shift the allocation of labor in favor of formal employment. In the model of Fugazza and Jacques (2003), workers are heterogenous with respect to the moral considerations of working in the underground sector.[7] Labor market search by unemployed workers is directed; hence workers with low moral objections to tax evasion will always choose to work in the underground sector. In addition to standard policy instruments, Fugazza and Jacques also consider the impact of a minimum wage policy. Finally Cavalcanti (2002) presents a two-sector/three-state model (similar to Kolm and Larsen) where formal and informal jobs are assumed to differ in creation costs and without directed search. Cavalcanti shows that employment protection (in the form of a dismissal cost) increases both equilibrium unemployment and informal activities.[8]

The current model thus differs from those in the previously mentioned papers along several dimensions. First, in the current model, workers are only in one of two states. Informal activities are modeled as being performed by unemployed workers who are simultaneously searching for regular jobs. Second, we focus on employment protection; in particular, we focus on the idea that employment protection slows down the creation and destruction of formal jobs, which alters the incentives of those who are currently unemployed. Third, we do not rely on a matching model; instead, we make use of an efficiency wage model where vacancies are immediately filled. This allows us to elaborate on the idea that the unemployed workers will shift their attention away from job search when job creation slows down.

The chapter is organized as follows. Section 7.2 sets up the model. Section 7.3 characterizes the equilibrium and derives the main analytical results. Section 7.4 presents some simple simulations of the model that illustrate the interaction between taxes and employment protection. Section 7.5 concludes.

7.2 The Model

Consider an economy with a continuum (of unit size) of identical workers. Time is continuous and each worker can be either employed or unemployed. There is a single numeraire consumption good. Employed workers work full-time in regular employment. Unemployed workers divide their time into two activities: the search for a regular job and underground economic activity.[9] There is a single numeraire good and the workers maximize expected discounted lifetime income. The government taxes regular incomes at the rate θ and pays out unemployment benefits b to unemployed workers. The benefit is a fixed fraction of the average net wage during a typical employ-ment relation, $b = \beta(1 - \theta)\bar{w}$, where $\beta \in [0, 1)$ is the replacement ratio.

7.2.1 Underground Activities

A simple way of thinking about the underground economy is as a "backyard" activity; every worker is assumed to have available a sim-ple constant-returns-to-scale technology: one hour devoted to pro-duction generates one unit of output. We model diversity of goods implicitly by assuming that no worker consumes his own output. In-stead, unemployed workers swap goods with each other at S exoge-nously given "trading spots."[10] In order to trade at one of these trading spots, a worker must bring his output; however, he can only bring one unit at a time. Hence, in order to trade ξ_i units, agent i must make ξ_i visits.[11] The time it takes to travel to a trading spot is $m > 0$. (Trading on the other hand is instantaneous.) Thus, an unemployed agent who wishes to swap ξ_i units of goods must devote $(1 + m)\xi_i$ to the underground activity, ξ_i hours to production, and $m\xi_i$ hours to traveling.

The parameter m can be viewed as capturing tax enforcement; sup-pose that the tax authorities randomly inspect a fraction of the S trad-ing places. A worker who arrives at a place that is currently being inspected cannot trade there but must travel elsewhere. Thus, the more frequent are inspections, the larger is the average traveling cost per unit traded. As a result, attempts to crack down on the under-ground economy can be represented in the model with a larger value of m.

The alternative use of time is in search for regular employment. Let this search effort be denoted σ_i, and let total hours per period be nor-malized to 1. The time constraint per period facing agent i when un-employed is therefore $\sigma_i + (1 + m)\xi_i = 1$.

7.2.2 Search for Regular Employment

The unemployed workers search for the regular jobs that are being cre-ated (see section 7.2.4). We model this competition among the un-employed as a simple version of the game of "musical chairs." By searching more (less) than the other unemployed workers, an agent obtains a higher- (lower-)than-average hiring probability. Let α denote the baseline job-finding hazard, the job finding rate of a worker who searches as hard as the average unemployed worker. (The determination of α is outlined in section 7.3.) Then let f be a continuously differentiable "contest-function" f with the following properties: $f(0) = 0$, $f(1) = 1$, $f'(\cdot) > 0$, and $f''(\cdot) < 0$. Let $\bar{\sigma}$ denote the average search intensity among the unemployed. We will then assume that the job-finding rate of agent i is $\alpha f(\sigma_i / \bar{\sigma})$, which is clearly increasing and concave in σ_i. Since we will focus on symmetric equilibria, $f'(1)$ will be of particular interest; given the preceding assumptions, $f'(1)$, henceforth denoted by γ, is a real number in the interval $(0, 1)$.

7.2.3 The Behavior of Unemployed Workers

Consider the behavior of a typical unemployed worker. Let U denote the value, namely, the expected discounted future consumption, to an unemployed worker, and let $V(0)$ be the value of being newly employed (where the 0 indicates that the duration of the employment is zero). Since the worker behaves optimally, taking $\bar{\sigma}$ as given, U must satisfy the asset equation

$$rU = \max_{\xi_i, \sigma_i} \left\{ \xi_i + b + \alpha f\left(\frac{\sigma_i}{\bar{\sigma}}\right)(V(0) - U) \mid 1 = \sigma_i + (1 + m)\xi_i \right\}, \tag{1}$$

where r is the interest rate. The first-order conditions for an interior solution imply that

$$\frac{1}{(1 + m)} = \alpha f'\left(\frac{\sigma_i}{\bar{\sigma}}\right)\frac{(V(0) - U)}{\bar{\sigma}}. \tag{2}$$

We will be looking for a symmetric steady-state equilibrium, $\sigma_i = \bar{\sigma}$ for all i. Equation (2) then yields the following equilibrium condition (dropping the subscript i):

$$\xi + \alpha\gamma(V(0) - U) = \frac{1}{(1 + m)}, \tag{3}$$

where we used that $\sigma = 1 - (1 + m)\xi$ and $f'(1) = \gamma$.

7.2.4 The Regular Sector

The model captures two important aspects of employment protection. On the one hand, it generates job security to the currently employed workers. On the other hand, it also reduces the employers' flexibility;

this is captured by the fact the employment protection does not allow the firm to fire a worker even though the productivity of the match is deteriorating (see section 7.3). This latter effect makes it less attractive for entrepreneurs to create regular jobs.

While underground trade is the outcome of short-run connections, regular jobs have longer duration. The quality of a job match between a worker and an employer deteriorates deterministically over time. However, employment protection prohibits an employer from firing a worker until after a certain duration T.[12] An early closure will be penalized with a fine that we assume is so large that early closure is never optimal for an employer. Jobs are created at the highest possible productivity of one unit of output per hour.[13]

The output of a match $y(t)$ deteriorates exponentially with the duration of the employment, $y(t) = e^{-\delta t}$, where $\delta > 0$. Let $J(t)$ denote the discounted future profits of an employment with current duration t,

$$J(t) = \int_t^T (y(\tau) - w(\tau))e^{-r(\tau - t)} \, d\tau. \tag{4}$$

Free entry implies a zero-profit condition: discounted profits at entry are zero, $J(0) = 0$. Once in an employment relationship, there is a surplus to be shared by the worker and the employer: the wage given to the worker to reflect output and the worker's outside option. Let $S(t)$ denote the discounted future output of an employment with current duration t. Following Saint-Paul (2002), we assume that wage bargaining generates a gain to the worker that is a fraction of the net of tax discounted output[14]

$$V(t) - U = \phi(1 - \theta)S(t), \tag{5}$$

where $\phi \in (0, 1)$ represents the bargaining strength of the worker and where $V(t)$ is the discounted future consumption for a worker who is in a job with current duration t. The value $V(t)$ satisfies the asset equation

$$rV(t) = (1 - \theta)w(t) + V'(t), \tag{6}$$

with boundary condition $V(T) = U$.

7.2.5   Wage Determination

The wage paid to the worker declines during an employment spell.[15] To derive the equilibrium wage, we can eliminate the values from the asset equations; first we eliminate V from (6) using (5), and using the fact that $S'(t) - rS(t) = -y(t)$. The value U can then be eliminated from the resulting equation by using (1) evaluated at the equilibrium. Doing so yields the equilibrium wage equation

$$w(t) = \phi y(t) + \beta \bar{w} + (1 - \theta)^{-1}\xi + \alpha\phi S(0), \tag{7}$$

where $\bar{w}$ is the average wage (in the population, or equivalently, over an employment spell). Note that the wage decreases more slowly than output. Hence flow profits are positive at the beginning of the employment spell and negative toward the end. Integrating (7) over t yields the following expression for the average wage:

$$\beta\bar{w} = \frac{\beta}{(1-\beta)}\left(\frac{\phi}{T}\int_0^T y(t)\,dt + (1-\theta)^{-1}\xi + \alpha\phi S(0)\right). \tag{8}$$

7.3 Equilibrium

There are two endogenous variables, the job-finding rate α and the time allocation ξ, determined by free entry and optimal search/underground activity. Thus consider the free-entry condition $J(0) = 0$. Using (7) to replace $w(t)$ in (4), evaluating at $t = 0$, and using (8) to eliminate $\beta\bar{w}$, this condition can be written as

$$(1-\theta)^{-1}\xi + \alpha\phi S_0(T) = \Lambda(T,\beta), \tag{FE}$$

where

$$\Lambda(T,\beta) \equiv (1-\beta)\left(\frac{1-e^{-rT}}{r}\right)^{-1}(1-\phi)S_0(T) - \beta\frac{\phi}{T}\left(\frac{1-e^{-\delta T}}{\delta}\right), \tag{9}$$

and where the notation $S_0(T) \equiv S(0)$ is used to emphasize the dependence of the discounted output of an employment on T. The second equilibrium condition is the optimal time allocation (3), which, using (5), can be written as

$$\xi + \alpha\gamma(1-\theta)\phi S_0(T) = \frac{1}{(1+m)}. \tag{TA}$$

When depicted in (α,ξ)-space, the free entry condition (FE) is linear with slope

$$\left.\frac{d\xi}{d\alpha}\right|_{FE} = -\phi S_0(T)(1-\theta) < 0.$$

The negative slope indicates that more underground activity induces less job creation. Similarly, when depicted in (α, ξ)-space, the time allocation condition (TA) is linear with slope

$$\left.\frac{d\xi}{d\alpha}\right|_{TA} = -\gamma\phi S_0(T)(1-\theta) < 0.$$

This says that the lower the average job-finding rate α, the more the unemployed workers will engage in underground activities. Note that the slope of (TA) is γ times the slope of (FE); hence (TA) is less steep than (FE). The fact that α and ξ are negatively related in both conditions suggests that there could potentially be multiple equilibria; this is, however, ruled out by the fact that both equilibrium conditions are linear. Even though there will not be any multiple equilibria, the strategic complementarity between α and ξ is likely to give rise to large comparative static effects (snowball effects): a change in a policy parameter that, for example, strengthens the incentives for underground activity indirectly reduces the incentives for the creation of regular jobs, which further strengthens the incentives for underground activity and so forth.

PROPOSITION 1   If a symmetric steady-state equilibrium exists, it is unique and satisfies (FE) and (TA).

7.3.1 Comparative Statics

The parameters of interest to perform comparative statics on are the tax rate θ, the replacement ratio β, and employment protection T. We will restrict our attention to the limiting case where $r \to 0$; doing so simplifies the expression for $\Lambda(T, \beta)$ considerably. In the limit

$$\Lambda(T,\beta) = \frac{S_0(T)}{T}(1 - \phi - \beta), \tag{10}$$

with $S_0(T) \equiv (1 - e^{-\delta T})/T$.[16]

Consider then the impact of the replacement ratio β. β only affects the free-entry condition; in terms of figure 7.1 an increase in β simply shifts (FE) downward, thus reducing job creation for any given ξ. The equilibrium effect is thus to increase ξ and decrease α; indeed, it is easy to see that the effect on ξ is particularly strong when γ is large (close to unity). Since β decreases α (with T being constant), it also increases the equilibrium unemployment rate: note that the steady-state unemployment rate is simply equal to $1/(1 + \alpha T)$.

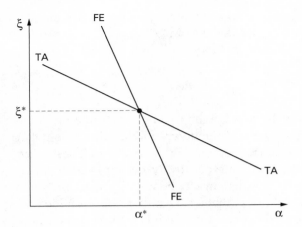

Figure 7.1
The symmetric steady-state equilibrium

Turning to the tax rate θ, we should recall that unemployment is neutral with respect to taxation in most equilibrium models of unemployment (and indeed would be so in the current model if there was no option of underground economic activity).[17] In contrast to β, θ affects both the free-entry and the time allocation condition. Simple comparative statics on (FE) and (TA) show that α (and thus equilibrium employment) decreases in θ while ξ increases in θ. Intuitively, since underground trading is untaxed, taxation increases the attractiveness of this activity relative to search for regular employment. The direct effect of θ on incentives for underground trading is then compounded by a negative effect on job creation. Since increased taxation increases both the number of unemployed and also the amount of underground trading for each unemployed individual, it obviously also increases the shadow economy's share of GDP.

Turning to the effect of T on ξ, it is important to recognize that there are likely to be effects going in opposite directions. One the one hand, an increase in T makes regular jobs more attractive by making them last longer. This effect boosts search incentives. On the other hand, an increase in T constrains employers' choices further and will hence reduce the incentives for job creation. Thus while the value of each "prize" in the job-searching contest increases, the number of prizes to be won decreases. The question is which effect will dominate. From (TA) we can see that T's effect on ξ and on $\alpha S_0(T)$ will have opposite signs; this makes sense since α is the baseline job-finding rate and

$S_0(T)$ is proportional to the gain in value from finding a job. Eliminating ξ between (FE) and (TA) reveals that the effect of T on $\alpha S_0(T)$ has the same sign as $\partial \Lambda / \partial T$. Hence we can differentiate (10), which yields

$$\frac{\partial \Lambda}{\partial T} = \frac{[(1 + \delta T)e^{-\delta T} - 1]}{\delta T^2}(1 - \phi - \beta) < 0,$$

where the sign follows from the fact that $(1 + z)e^{-z} \in (0, 1)$ for all $z > 0$. Thus we can conclude that an increase in T, just like an increase in taxation or the replacement ratio, increases ξ and decreases α. Hence while increasing T makes regular jobs more attractive by making them last longer, it decreases the number of jobs created even faster, leading to the overall conclusion that an increase in T erodes the incentives for job search and, conversely, increases the incentives for trading in the underground economy.[18]

PROPOSITION 2   Comparative statics on the symmetric steady-state equilibrium. An increase in either (i) the replacement ratio β, (ii) the labor income tax rate θ, or (iii) employment protection T increases amount of underground trading ξ and reduces the equilibrium job-finding rate α.

By solving the equilibrium equations we can also easily show that $\partial^2 \xi / \partial \theta \partial T > 0$; intuitively, smaller flows in the labor market makes the underground activities more responsive to taxation.

7.4   A Numerical Example

The purpose of this short section is to numerically illustrate the model in order to highlight how two very different policy regimes can generate similar behavior. The parameters in the model are set as follows. The time period is taken to be the month. The replacement ratio β is set to 0.35, which is reasonable in an OECD context, taking into account benefit expiration and the noneligibility. The technology deterioration rate δ is varied between 0.002 and 0.004.[19] The workers are assumed to capture three percent of the value of output, $\phi = 0.03$. Finally, the curvature γ and the cost of trading in the shadow economy m are set so as to obtain reasonable values for the monthly exit rate from unemployment at high taxes/low employment protection and vice versa; this leads us to choose $\gamma = 0.35$ and $m = 5$.[20]

Since the main mechanism stressed in the model is that of small flows on the incentives to participate in underground economic

Table 7.2

Country	ShadowEc	EmpProt	Tax Wedge	Exit Rate	ACJT
Austria	7.3	2.3	0.60	NA	NA
Belgium	21.6	2.5	0.50	0.05	17.5
Canada	15.0	1.1	0.52	0.28	2.8
Denmark	18.1	1.5	0.60	0.12	8.2
France	14.8	2.8	0.68	0.05	16.7
Germany	13.9	2.6	0.54	0.08	17.8
Ireland	15.6	1.1	0.42	NA	NA
Italy	26.2	3.4	0.71	0.04	NA
Netherlands	14.1	2.2	0.45	0.06	14.4
Norway	18.5	2.6	0.60	0.29	7.5
Spain	22.6	3.1	0.46	0.02	23.8
Sweden	18.9	2.6	0.74	0.29	8.9
Switzerland	6.9	1.5	0.37	NA	NA
Portugal	NA	3.7	0.39	0.04	30.7
United Kingdom	12.6	0.9	0.47	0.19	4.3
United States	9.0	0.7	0.46	0.4	2.8

Notes: **ShadowEc**: The size of the shadow economy in 1995 (as percent of GDP); the data are taken from Schneider 2000, Table 1. **EmpProt**: OECD employment protection index. From OECD 1999, Table 2.2 (overall employment protection legislation strictness, version 2, late 1990s). **Tax Wedge**: The sum of the employment tax rate, the direct tax rate, and the indirect tax rate in 1995. Obtained from Nickell et al. 2002. Data together with detailed documentation is available at http://cep.lse.ac.uk/. **Exit Rate**: Average monthly exit rate from unemployment. Derived from data on monthly inflow rates to unemployment and unemployment rates, 1980–1995, obtained from Nickell et al. 2002. **ACJT**: Average completed job tenure (years). Derived from data on monthly inflow rates to unemployment, 1980–1995, obtained from Nickell et al. 2002.

activity, we choose values of T that correspond to observed average completed job tenures. Average completed job tenure varies substantially across the OECD countries. Looking at table 7.2, we can spot some patterns. Shortest average tenure is in the United States and the United Kingdom; next come the Nordic countries, followed by countries in continental Europe, with the South European countries exhibiting the longest average completed tenures. Based on these observed completed tenures, we choose to vary T from four years to sixteen years; thus we let T be 48, 120, and 192 months. Similarly, we vary the labor income tax rate between 40 and 60 percent, setting θ equal to 0.4, 0.5, and 0.6. (See table 7.2.)

Table 7.3 shows the simulated values of average monthly exit rate from unemployment and the unemployment rate (given the intermediate value $\delta = 0.003$). Comparing it with table 7.2, if we attempt

Table 7.3
Simulated average monthly exit rate from unemployment and unemployment rate

T \ θ	Exit rate			Unemployment rate		
	0.4	0.5	0.6	0.4	0.5	0.6
48	34.4	28.0	18.4	5.7	6.9	10.1
120	12.4	9.5	5.3	6.3	8.0	13.6
192	6.8	4.8	1.9	7.1	9.7	21.3

Table 7.4
Simulated fraction of time devoted to underground economic activities by unemployed workers

T \ θ	$\delta = 0.002$			$\delta = 0.004$		
	0.4	0.5	0.6	0.4	0.5	0.6
48	39.2	58.4	77.4	44.5	62.7	80.9
120	47.0	64.8	82.6	58.4	74.3	90.2
192	54.1	70.7	87.3	70.0	83.9	97.9

to map countries to cells in table 7.3, we would say that the South European countries correspond to the lower-left corner of the table, the Nordic countries to the upper-right corner, the United States and the United Kingdom to the upper-left corner, and other continental European countries, such as France and Germany, to the middle of the table.

Table 7.4 gives the simulated fraction of time, $(1 + m)\xi$, devoted to underground economic activities, for two different values of δ. What is striking is how similar underground economic activities are along the opposite diagonal (in particular, at high levels of δ). This suggests that one reason why, for example, the Nordic countries can have surprisingly low levels of underground economic activities given their comparatively high levels of taxation is that they also have relatively fluid labor markets (e.g., compared to the South European countries). Thus, while high taxes do indeed induce underground economic activity, the fact that the average exit rate of transition into regular employment is comparatively large strongly works in the opposite direction.

Table 7.4 also illustrates the role of the productivity depreciation rate δ. The larger is δ, the more inefficient are long tenures; hence when δ is large, increasing T has a larger effect of choking job creation and thus reducing the average exit rate from unemployment. Hence underground activities are also more responsive to T when δ is large.

Finally, table 7.4 illustrates the impact of taxation in the current model. Note in particular how taxes have a much larger impact on underground economic activity when there is also substantial employment protection; this reflects the aforementioned complementarity between taxes and slow-moving labor markets in generating incentives for underground trade.

7.5 Conclusions

In the literature on underground economic activities, attempts to explain such activities have focused primarily on taxes, bureaucracy, and corruption. In this chapter I question whether labor market institutions may also play an important role. A finding that labor supply to the underground economy comes disproportionately from workers with a weak status in the regular labor market, for instance, the unemployed, the young, and so forth, clearly suggests that the functioning and the fluency of the labor market may be a key factor; we also report that (for 15 OECD countries) a standard index of employment protection is considerably more correlated with the size of the shadow economy than are taxes.

Employment protection has been very much in focus in the literature on unemployment. Attempts to measure employment protection have revealed significant cross-country differences. The jury is still out regarding the empirical question of whether or not employment protection increases unemployment. However, there seems to be consensus that a key effect of employment protection is to slow down the flows in the labor market. In this short chapter I have set out to link employment protection to underground economic activity, stressing exactly the slowing down of labor market flows.

The model focused on participation in underground activities by those currently unemployed and showed that slower flows have, in general, two effects on incentives that go in the opposite direction. On the one hand, when jobs last longer they are more attractive, hence increasing the incentives for job search (and, conversely, reducing the incentives for participation in the underground economy). On the other hand, employment protection also reduces the attractiveness for employers to create regular jobs; hence the average reentry rates into employment are reduced, which reduces the incentives for job search. I showed that the second effect dominates, whereby we concluded that institutions that prolong job tenure also tend to increase the incentives for current outsiders to seek alternative sources of income on the fringe of the economy.

Higher labor taxation also encourages underground economic activities for standard reasons. We argued that differences in labor market institutions and the functioning of labor markets may help explain the pattern of underground economic activities across OECD countries. Focusing only on taxes as a determinant of the shadow economies, we find it somewhat puzzling that, for example, the Nordic countries do not have larger shadow economies. We argue that a partial explanation for this may be that the labor markets are relatively fluid in these countries (compared to, e.g., the South European countries) with substantially higher reentry rates into regular employment.

Notes

I would like to thank two anonymous referees and the participants at the CESifo Workshop on Tax Policy and Labor Market Performance for helpful and insightful comments. Errors, however, are my own.

1. See, e.g., Gruber 1997; Nickell 1998; Layard, Jackman, and Nickell 1999; Madsen 1998; and Daveri and Tabellini 2000.

2. See, e.g., Nickell 1997.

3. See Andreoni, Erard, and Feinstein 1998 for a survey of theory and empirical evidence and Schneider and Enste 2000 for estimates of the shadow economy in large set countries, and for a discussion of various causes, including taxation, regulation, and corruption.

4. See also Johnson, Kaufman, and Zoido-Lobaton 1998.

5. Anderberg, Balestrino, and Galmarini (2003) examine a model (without unemployment) with heterogeneity in terms of earnings capacity. They show that workers with relatively low earnings capacity are more likely to be engaged in underground activities; they also endogenize tax policy and enforcement policy by modeling a political process and show that more high taxes need not be associated with more underground economic activities since they are likely to be combined with more tax enforcement.

6. A similar argument has recently been made by Holmlund (2001) who, rather than looking at underground economic activity, assumes that unemployed workers can engage in household production. Holmlund, however, does not consider employment protection.

7. See also Kolm and Larsen 2003a for a study of possible equilibrium multiplicity with endogenous social norms.

8. See also Bouev 2002 for a similar model and a discussion of its relevance to transition economies.

9. By underground activity, we mean productive activities that are unknown by the public administration; thus we adopt the view that underground activity is the result of tax

evasion, noncompliance with social security contributions, and so forth, but is otherwise legal.

10. An equivalent alternative to characterizing the underground economy as a "backyard activity" is to assume that an officially unemployed worker can take a number of unofficial short-run part-time jobs (each part-time job lasting exactly one period). In that case, ξ_i can be the time the worker spends searching for unofficial jobs and m is the number of odd jobs located. In each case we assume that the worker obtains the entire surplus from the underground activity; this simplifying assumption allows us to ignore the identity of underground buyers (alternate employers).

11. Note that trade need not be bilateral; hence it is no problem even if an odd number of workers arrives at the same time; as long as at least two persons arrive at the same time, everyone can trade instantaneously.

12. Our modeling of employment protection is deliberately kept to a minimum. For more detailed theoretical analysis of employment protection, see Pissarides 2001, Saint-Paul 2002, and Blanchard 2003.

13. The assumption that the underground technology is "state-of-the-art" is made simply to save notation.

14. See Saint-Paul 2002 for a microfoundation for this formulation.

15. A more realistic model would assume exogenous technological growth, in which case the wage paid could be constant or even increasing with tenure.

16. We assume that $\phi + \beta < 1$ in order to ensure some job creation.

17. To see this let $\xi = 0$; the only endogenous variable is then α which must satisfy the free entry condition $\alpha \phi S_0(T) = \Lambda(T, \beta)$. Thus while employment protection T and generous benefits β are still detrimental to employment, θ has no effect on employment.

18. Employment protection typically has an ambiguous effect on employment; however, in the current model it can easily be shown that employment protection also reduces equilibrium employment. The steps are similar to those showing the impact on $\alpha S_0(T)$.

19. The years until the productivity is halved is $\ln(2)/(12\delta)$; thus, for example, $\delta = 0.002$ implies that productivity is down to half after about twenty-nine years, while with $\delta = 0.004$ the corresponding time is only about fourteen years.

20. This value of m may seem high. However, this partially reflects the assumption that underground activity uses state-of-the-art technology (and is obviously untaxed). Indeed, the important term is $1/(1 + m)$ in (3), which, in order to generate interior time allocations, must be sufficiently below the net of tax wage. Hence, given our simplifying assumption regarding technology, the value of m needs to be set quite high in order to generate realistic endogenous values.

References

Anderberg, D., A. Balestrino, and U. Galmarini. 2003. "Search and Taxation in a Model of Underground Economic Activities." *Economic Inquiry* 41: 647–659.

Andreoni, J., B. Erard, and J. Feinstein. 1998. "Tax Compliance." *Journal of Economic Literature* 36: 818–960.

Blanchard, O. 2003. "The Economics of Unemployment: Shocks, Institutions, and Interactions." Lionel Robbins Lectures.

Boeri, T., and P. Garibaldi. 2002. "Shadow Activity and Unemployment in a Depressed Labor Market." CEPR Discussion Paper 3433, London.

Bouev, M. 2002. "Official Regulations and the Shadow Economy." Mimeo., St. Anthony's College, Oxford.

Cavalcanti, T. 2002. "Labor Market Policies and Informal Markets." Working paper, Universidade Nova de Lisboa.

Daveri, F., and G. Tabellini. 2000. "Unemployment, Growth and Taxation in Industrial Countries." *Economic Policy: A European Forum* 30: 47–88.

Friedman, E., S. Johnson, D. Kaufmann, and P. Zoido-Lobaton. 2000. "Dodging the Grabbing Hand: The Determinants of Unofficial Activity in 69 Countries." *Journal of Public Economics* 76: 459–493.

Fugazza, M., and J.-F. Jacques. 2003. "Labor Market Institutions, Taxation and the Underground Economy." *Journal of Public Economics* 88: 395–418.

Gruber, J. 1997. "The Incidence of Payroll Taxation: Evidence from Chile." *Journal of Labor Economics* 15: S72–101.

Holmlund, B. 2001. "Labor Taxation in Search Equilibrium with Home Production." CESifo Working Paper No. 462, Munich.

Johnson, S., D. Kaufmann, and P. Zoido-Lobaton. 1998. "Regulatory Discretion and the Unofficial Economy." *American Economic Review: Papers and Proceedings* 88: 387–392.

Kolm, A.-S., and B. Larsen. 2003a. "Social Norms, the Informal Sector and Unemployment." *FinanzArchiv* 59: 407–424.

Kolm, A.-S., and B. Larsen. 2003b. "Wages, Unemployment, and the Underground Economy." CESifo Working Paper No. 1086, Munich.

Layard, R., R. Jackman, and S. Nickell. 1999. "Combating Unemployment: Is Flexibility Enough?" In *Tackling Unemployment*, ed. R. Layard, 257–288. London: Macmillan Press.

Lemieux, T., B. Fortin, and P. Frechette. 1994. "The Effect of Taxes on Labor Supply in the Underground Economy." *American Economic Review* 84: 231–254.

Madsen, J. B. 1998. "General Equilibrium Macroeconomic Models of Unemployment: Can They Explain the Unemployment Path in the OECD?" *Economic Journal* 108: 850–867.

Nickell, S. 1997. "Unemployment and Labour Market Rigidities: Europe versus North America." *Journal of Economic Perspectives* 11: 55–74.

Nickell, S. 1998. "Unemployment: Questions and Some Answers." *Economic Journal* 108: 802–816.

Nickell, S., L. Nunziata, W. Ochel, and G. Quintini. 2002. "The Beveridge Curve, Unemployment and Wages in the OECD from the 1960s to the 1990s." Mimeo., Centre for Economic Performance, London School of Economics and Political Science.

OECD. 1999. *Employment Outlook.* Paris: OECD.

Pissarides, C. A. 2001. "Employment Protection." *Labour Economics* 8: 131–159.

Saint-Paul, G. 2002. "The Political Economy of Employment Protection." *Journal of Political Economy* 110: 672–704.

Schneider, F. 2000. "The Increase in the Size of the Shadow Economy of 18 OECD Countries: Some Preliminary Explanations." Paper presented at the annual meeting of the European Public Choice Society.

Schneider, F., and D. H. Enste. 2000. "Shadow Economies: Size, Causes, and Consequences." *Journal of Economic Literature* 38: 77–114.

8

Wages, Unemployment, and the Underground Economy

Ann-Sofie Kolm and Birthe Larsen

8.1 Introduction

Underground activities are unequally distributed across sectors within an economy. While analyzing comprehensive survey data for Denmark, Pedersen and Smith (1998) find that around 70 percent of the total hours performed in the informal sector is carried out within the service sector or construction sector. Hence, on a large scale, different goods are produced in the informal and in the formal sector. Although there may be different explanations for why this is the case, one reason may simply be that some types of activities and goods are easier to hide than others, and hence these goods are more likely to be produced in the informal sector. Examples include cleaning jobs in private homes, gardening services, hairdressing, home repair activities, and other types of service jobs.

The purpose of this chapter is to examine the macroeconomic effects of tax and punishment policies when different goods are being produced in the formal and the informal sector. In particular, we focus on how a revenue-neutral change in the government controls of the informal sector affects labor market performance. Hence, if the government were to control the underground economy more severely, either through higher punishment fees or through a more frequent auditing of informal sector workers and/or firms, what would then happen to unemployment, sector allocation, and wages? For example, would higher punishment fees or a higher audit rate lead to a smaller informal sector?

In order to answer these questions, we develop a two-sector general equilibrium model featuring matching frictions and worker-firm wage bargains. The two sectors correspond to the formal sector and the informal sector. Different goods are produced in the two sectors, and workers face job opportunities in both the formal sector and the informal sector. Section 4 analyzes the case when an identical good is produced in the two sectors.

We find that increased government control of the informal sector in terms of higher punishment fees (1) increases the size of the formal sector and reduce the size of the informal sector, (2) reduces real producer wages in both sectors, and (3) reduces unemployment. Considering the impact of a higher audit rate is less clear-cut. A higher audit rate has an ambiguous impact on unemployment and real producer wages, and may actually increase the size of the underground economy.

The principal contribution of the analysis in this chapter is that we incorporate an imperfectly competitive labor market. This facilitates an analysis of how tax and punishment policies affect wage setting and unemployment. Previous research has mainly been conducted within the public finance tradition.[1] In this literature wages are either assumed to be fixed or determined by market clearing, and by definition, such a framework is unable to examine how involuntary unemployment is affected by tax and punishment policies.

8.1.1 A Review of the Literature

There have been some recent studies of underground activity in models of involuntary unemployment; see Kolm and Larsen 2001, 2003a, 2003b, Cavalcanti 2002, Boeri and Garibaldi 2002, and Fugazza and Jacques 2004. The focus and modeling strategies are, however, different in these papers.

The studies by Kolm and Larsen (2001) and Fugazza and Jacques (2004) explore the consequences for unemployment when workers have moral considerations when deciding on informal sector work. With workers being heterogenous with respect to morals, only workers with low morals are willing to work in the informal sector.

Kolm and Larsen (2003a) have a different focus as they examine the potential for multiple equilibria when there are moral considerations and a social norm against tax evasion. This social norm implies that there is a psychic cost associated with tax evasion. The social norm becomes stronger the fewer people there are evading taxes, which potentially leads to the existence of multiple equilibria. There may exist one equilibria with little tax evasion and a strong norm against tax evasion, and another equilibrium including considerable more tax evasion associated with a weak norm against tax evasion.

Cavalcanti (2002) also has a different focus because he explores how labor market policies affect unemployment in a model with informal labor market opportunities. Firms in the informal sector differ from firms in the formal sector as they are assumed to face smaller job creation costs.

Boeri and Garibaldi (2002) consider control policies in a model of informal employment and involuntary unemployment. The modeling of the underground activity is very different from the modeling in this chapter. In their model, all jobs are started as legal jobs. Informal jobs come about as legal firms are hit by a bad productivity shock and face the option of becoming illegal.

Kolm and Larsen (2003b) study the impact of tax evasion on educational choice. They consider how informal sector job oppurtunities mainly available for low-skilled workers reduce the incentive to acquire skills. The tax and punishment system through the informal sector creates a distortion in the educational choice decision that has implications for welfare.

This chapter is organized as follows. Section 8.2 describes the model and the equilibrium variables are derived. In section 8.3, we examine how the equilibrium variables (tightness, relative prices, real producer wages, sector allocation, and unemployment) are affected by a fully financed change in the punishment fees and the audit rate. Section 8.4 sets out a simple model where an identical good is produced in the formal and the informal sector. Finally, section 8.5 concludes.

8.2 The Model

In this model, the economy consists of two sectors, a formal sector and an informal sector.[2] Different goods are produced in the two sectors. This captures the notion that certain types of goods and services are more likely to be produced in the informal sector than other types. For example, cleaning jobs in private homes, gardening services, hairdressing, and other types of service jobs are more likely to be produced in the informal sector, whereas cars, televisions, radios, and so forth are less likely to be produced in the informal sector.[3]

Clearly one can argue that the formal sector and the informal sector differ in a number of ways that are not modeled in this chapter. For example, as we discussed in the introduction, workers may differ in terms of morals, inducing that only low moral workers will take on jobs in the informal sector. See Kolm and Larsen 2003a. Such a

segmented market implies that workers who bargain over their wage
in the formal (informal) sector consider their fallback position to be to
search for another job in the formal (informal) sector. Changes in the
attractiveness of one sector then have little influence on the wage bargains in the other sector. This seems to be a realistic modeling strategy
for some situations, but not for all. Here instead we consider workers
who have no moral considerations and who keep their eyes open for
job offers from both the formal and the informal sector. While getting
a job in the formal (informal) sector, workers also take future employment prospects in the informal (formal) sector into account when bargaining over wages, since it affects the fallback position.

Other potential differences in between the formal and informal sector are that matching may be easier in one sector than in another, or
that productivity or wage formation, and so forth, may differ in the
two sectors.

However, in order to highlight the mechanism of how tax and punishment policies affect economic performance in an economy where
different goods are produced in the two sectors, this chapter focuses
on mainly one difference between the two sectors—namely, that the
formal sector can be taxed whereas the informal sector cannot. Rather
than taxing the informal sector, the government audits the economy.
With probability p a worker-firm pair in the underground economy is
detected and then has to pay a punishment fee, and the match will be
dissolved.[4]

8.2.1 Matching

Workers search for jobs in both the formal sector and the informal sector. We assume that only unemployed workers search for jobs. This is a
simplification; in other words, we do not acknowledge that the connection to the labor market given by working in the formal sector brings
about job opportunities not available while unemployed. Workers accept job offers as long as the expected payoff exceeds their reservation
wage.[5] We assume an undirected search as in, for example, Albrecht
and Vroman 2002. The matching function is given by

$$X = v^{1-\eta} u^{\eta},$$

where u is unemployment and v is the total number of vacancies supplied by firms. The labor force is normalized to unity, whereby we in-

terpret u as the unemployment rate and v as the vacancy rate. The number of vacancies supplied by the formal sector and the informal sector are v^j, $j = F, I$, and hence $v = v^F + v^I$. The worker's transition rates into the two sectors can be expressed as $\lambda^F = \beta(X/u) = \beta\theta^{1-\eta} = \beta\pi(\theta)$, and $\lambda^I = (1-\beta)(X/u) = (1-\beta)\theta^{1-\eta} = (1-\beta)\pi(\theta)$, where $\beta = v^F/v$ is the fraction of vacancies supplied in the formal sector and $\theta = v/u$ is overall labor market tightness. The term $\pi(\theta)$ can be interpreted as the probability of a worker getting any job offer, namely, $\lambda^F + \lambda^I = \pi(\theta)$. This implies that the transition rates facing firms is equal across firms and given by $q = X/v = \theta^{-\eta}$.[6] Furthermore, we define labor market tightness for the formal sector as $\theta^F = v^F/u$ and labor market tightness for the informal sector as $\theta^I = v^I/u$ where hence $\theta^F + \theta^I = \theta$.

8.2.2 Workers

Unemployed workers have the opportunity to apply for jobs in both the formal sector and the informal sector. We perform a steady-state analysis. Let λ^F and λ^I be interpreted as the probabilities per time unit of finding a job in the formal sector and in the informal sector, respectively. The present discounted value of unemployment, U, employment in the formal sector, E^F, and employment in the informal sector, E^I, are given in the following flow value equations:

$$rU = \frac{T}{P} + \lambda^F(E^F - U) + \lambda^I(E^I - U), \tag{1}$$

$$rE^F = \frac{T + w^F(1-t)}{P} + s(U - E^F), \tag{2}$$

$$rE^I = \frac{T + w^I(1 - p\delta)}{P} + (s + p)(U - E^I), \tag{3}$$

where r is the exogenous discount rate, t gives the income tax rate, δ captures the proportion of the evaded wage a worker has to pay as a punishment fee if he or she is detected withholding the government taxes,[7] and p is the audit rate. s is the exogenous separation rate and T is a lump-sum transfer received from the government.

The match is dissolved when detected, which implies that the separation rate in the informal sector exceeds the formal sector separation rate.

The immediate income received in each state is expressed in real terms by division with the general price level, P. P is the cost-of-living index, which is linear homogenous in the two goods prices, P^F and P^I, and derived from consumer preferences. This expression for real income could equivalently be interpreted as the instantaneous indirect utility function under certain conditions. In section 2.7 we discuss preferences in more detail.

The goods prices, and hence the general price level, is in equilibrium determined by market clearing and is taken as given by the individual firms and workers. It is hence of no importance for the results whether the flow value equations given in this section, and in the next section, are given in terms of real income or in nominal income.

8.2.3   Firms

The marginal productivity of a worker is y.[8] Hiring costs are denoted k^j, $j = F, I$, and q is the firm's probability per time unit of finding a worker. Since the value functions for workers are expressed in real terms, we express the value functions for firms also in real terms.

Firms in the formal sector are characterized by the arbitrage equations

$$rJ^F = \frac{P^F}{P} y - \frac{w^F(1+z)}{P} + s(V^F - J^F), \tag{4}$$

$$rV^F = q(J^F - V^F) - \frac{k^F}{P}, \tag{5}$$

where J^F is the value of having a filled job in the formal sector, V^F is the value of an unfilled job in this sector, and the parameter z is the payroll tax rate.

Similarly, firms in the informal sector have J^I and V^I determined by

$$rJ^I = \frac{P^I}{P} y - \frac{w^I(1+p\alpha)}{P} + (s+p)(V^I - J^I), \tag{6}$$

$$rV^I = q(J^I - V^I) - \frac{k^I}{P}, \tag{7}$$

where α is the proportion of the evaded wage the firm has to pay as a punishment fee for cheating the government on payroll taxes when supplying informal sector jobs.

8.2.4 Wages

In the wage bargains, the firm and the worker take the market clearing prices as given. Wages, w^j, $j = F, I$ solve first-order conditions from the Nash bargaining solutions with the worker's bargaining power being equal to γ:

$$\frac{\gamma}{1-\gamma}\frac{1}{\phi^j}(J^j - V^j) = E^j - U, \quad j = F, I, \tag{8}$$

where $\phi^F = (1 + z)/(1 - t)$ and $\phi^I = (1 + p\alpha)/(1 - p\delta)$ are the tax and punishment wedges.

By using equations (1)–(7) in equation (8), and assuming free entry, we have $V^j = 0$ and $j = F, I$, and with symmetric conditions facing firms and workers within each sector, the relevant real producer wages are

$$\omega^F = \frac{w^F(1+z)}{P^F} = \gamma y\left(1 + \rho\left(\theta^F + \frac{\theta^I}{\Delta}\right)\right), \tag{9}$$

$$\omega^I = \frac{w^I(1 + p\alpha)}{P^I} = \gamma y\left(1 + \rho\Delta\left(\theta^F + \frac{\theta^I}{\Delta}\right)\right), \tag{10}$$

where

$$\Delta = \psi\frac{P^F}{P^I}, \tag{11}$$

and

$$\psi = \frac{\phi^I}{\phi^F} = \frac{1 + p\alpha}{1 - p\delta}\bigg/\frac{1 + z}{1 - t}, \tag{12}$$

where we have used $k^j = \rho P^j y$, $j = F, I$. One interpretation of this specification of the vacancy cost is that the firm allocates its workforce optimally between production and recruitment activities. The cost of hiring is proportional to its alternative cost, that is, proportional to the value of the marginal product of labor. ψ is the punishment/tax wedge between the informal sector and the formal sector. We will simply refer to ψ as the wedge. It seems reasonable to focus on the case when $\psi < 1$, that is, when the government does not audit or punish the informal sector to the same extent as the formal sector is taxed. This is, however, of no importance for the results.

The wage rules in (9) and (10) capture the wage demands, namely, the bargained wages for a given relative price and for given tightness.

The relative price and sector tightness are clearly endogenous variables and will be determined in equilibrium. However, before proceeding to the determination of equilibrium, we can explore the consequences of a change in the tax and punishment rates, α, δ, z, and t, and the audit rate, p, on wage demands. For given equilibrium variables, an increase in the punishment rates or the audit rate for given tax rates will reduce the formal sector wage demands, and increase the wage demands in the informal sector. The reason is that the value of employment has fallen in the informal sector relative to in the formal sector. Workers employed in the informal sector hence face a reduced value of employment relative to unemployment and will push for higher wages. The opposite holds for workers employed in the formal sector, which causes formal sector workers to moderate their wage demands. Analogous interpretation can be given for changes in the tax rates for a given punishment policy.

It also follows from (9) and (10) that proportional changes in the tax and punishment system, leaving the wedge unaffected, will have no impact on wage demands since these changes have no effect on the value of employment relative to the value of unemployment in each respective sector.

8.2.5   Labor Market Tightness

Labor market tightness for the formal sector and the informal sector is determined by equations (4), (5), (6), and (7) using the free-entry condition and the wage equations (9) and (10):

$$(r+s)\theta^\eta = \frac{(1-\gamma)}{\rho} - \gamma\left(\theta^F + \frac{\theta^I}{\Delta}\right), \tag{13}$$

$$(r+s+p)\theta^\eta = \frac{(1-\gamma)}{\rho} - \gamma(\Delta\theta^F + \theta^I). \tag{14}$$

Note, however, that equations (13) and (14) determine labor market tightness in the formal sector and the informal sector conditioned on the relative price, namely, $\Delta = \psi(P^F/P^I)$. Thus we have two equations in the three unknowns, labor market tightness in the two sectors and the relative price, θ^F, θ^I, and P^F/P^I.

To close the system, we need to incorporate the product market. Before doing that it turns out to be useful to derive the employment rates.

8.2.6 Employment

Steady-state employment and unemployment rates are derived by considering the flows into and out of employment and the labor force identity, $n^F + n^I + u = 1$. The flow equations are given by $\lambda^F u = s n^F$ (formal sector) and $\lambda^I u = (s + p) n^I$ (informal sector).

Solving for the employment rates and the unemployment rate, we obtain

$$n^I = \frac{\frac{\theta^I \theta^{-\eta}}{s+p}}{1 + \frac{\theta^F \theta^{-\eta}}{s} + \frac{\theta^I \theta^{-\eta}}{s+p}}, \tag{15}$$

$$n^F = \frac{\frac{\theta^F \theta^{-\eta}}{s}}{1 + \frac{\theta^F \theta^{-\eta}}{s} + \frac{\theta^I \theta^{-\eta}}{s+p}}, \tag{16}$$

$$u = \frac{1}{1 + \frac{\theta^F \theta^{-\eta}}{s} + \frac{\theta^I \theta^{-\eta}}{s+p}}, \tag{17}$$

$$u^o = u + n^I = \frac{1 + \frac{\theta^I \theta^{-\eta}}{s+p}}{1 + \frac{\theta^F \theta^{-\eta}}{s} + \frac{\theta^I \theta^{-\eta}}{s+p}}, \tag{18}$$

where u^o denotes official unemployment, that is, unemployment registered by the government. The relative sector size of employment is given by

$$\frac{n^F}{n^I} = \frac{\theta^F}{\theta^I} \frac{s+p}{s}. \tag{19}$$

8.2.7 Product Market Equilibrium

Product markets clear in each period. We assume that individual preferences over the two goods are represented by a linear homogenous instantaneous utility function $v(C_i^F, C_i^I)$, where C^F is produced in the formal sector and C^I is produced in the informal sector.[9] Individuals choose the optimal mix of the two goods in each period by maximizing utility given their budget constraint. With a linear homogenous utility function, individual demand for each good is linear in the available income. Moreover, the indirect utility function is linear in income; namely, $v(I_i, P^F, P^I)^* = I_i / P(P^F, P^I)$, where I_i is the individual's available income from the budget constraint, and $P(P^F, P^I)$ is the cost-of-living index. Note that the instantaneous real income measure used in the flow value equations (1)–(3) can also be interpreted as the instanta-neous utility given workers are risk-neutral and consume their full in-come in each period.

Let us now consider market clearing. Aggregating over individual demand in order to derive aggregate demand for the two goods is sim-ply a matter of aggregating over individual income, since preferences are homothetic. Hence, we have that the aggregate demand for the two goods is given from the first-order condition for the individual con-sumer's optimal mix of commodities, that is, $v_F(C^F, C^I)/v_I(C^F, C^I) = P^F/P^I$, in conjunction with the aggregate (economy-wide) budget con-straint. The relative price is obtained by equating demand and supply of commodities. The aggregate supplies of the two goods are given by production deducted vacancy costs. In the formal sector, we have $Y^F = yn^F - v^F py = n^F y(1 - \rho\theta^\eta s)$. Similarly, in the informal sector, ag-gregate supply is $Y^I = yn^I - v^I py = n^I y(1 - \rho\theta^\eta(s + p))$.

Equalizing aggregate demand and aggregate supply leads to the fol-lowing equation:

$$\frac{v_F(Y^F/Y^I, 1)}{v_I(Y^F/Y^I, 1)} = \frac{P^F}{P^I}. \tag{20}$$

For simplicity, we assume a Cobb-Douglas utility function $U = (C^F)^\sigma(C^I)^{1-\sigma}$. Using the Cobb-Douglas assumption together with equa-tion (19), we can rewrite equation (20) as

$$\frac{\sigma}{1-\sigma}\frac{\theta^I}{\theta^F}\frac{\left(\frac{1}{s+p} - \rho\theta^\eta\right)}{\left(\frac{1}{s} - \rho\theta^\eta\right)} = \frac{P^F}{P^I}, \tag{21}$$

which is an equation in the three unknowns θ^F, θ^I, and P^F/P^I.

8.2.8 Equilibrium

Now we can characterize the equilibrium in the labor and goods mar-kets with the equations (13), (14), and (21). We have

$$(r+s)(\theta^F + \theta^I)^\eta = \frac{(1-\gamma)}{\rho} - \gamma\left(\theta^F + \frac{\theta^I}{\Delta}\right), \tag{22}$$

$$(r+s+p)(\theta^F + \theta^I)^\eta = \frac{(1-\gamma)}{\rho} - \gamma\Delta\left(\theta^F + \frac{\theta^I}{\Delta}\right), \tag{23}$$

$$\psi\frac{\sigma}{1-\sigma}\frac{\theta^I}{\theta^F}\frac{\frac{1}{s+p} - \rho\theta^\eta}{\frac{1}{s} - \rho\theta^\eta} = \Delta, \tag{24}$$

where we recall that $\Delta = \psi(P^F/P^I)$. Firms will enter into the two sectors as long as the expected vacancy costs are equal to the discounted profit. This is captured by equations (22) and (23). Equation (24) gives the relative price as a function of the relative supply derived from consumer preferences.

On the one hand, because the separation rate for informal sector jobs is higher than the separation rate for formal sector jobs, it is more attractive for a firm to enter the formal sector since jobs on the average last a longer time in the formal sector. On the other hand, if $\psi < 1$, firms in the informal sector are expected to be punished less than firms in the formal sector are taxed, which makes it more attractive to enter the informal sector. However, whether it is more attractive to enter one or the other sector also depends on the prices consumers pay for the different goods produced. Or put differently, entry into one sector rather than the other sector because of the relative attractiveness of the tax/punishment system or the difference in the separation rates will be counteracted by adjustments in the relative price. Entry into the formal sector will increase the supply of formal goods and hence reduce the relative price P^F/P^I, which in turn reduces the relative attractiveness of entering the formal sector.

We only consider fully financed reforms. Hence, the government budget restriction is always satisfied and is given by

$$n^F \omega^F \left(1 - \frac{1}{\phi^F}\right) + n^I \omega^I \frac{\psi}{\Delta} \left(1 - \frac{1}{\phi^I}\right) - c(p, n^I, n^F) = \frac{T}{P^F}, \tag{25}$$

where $c(p, n^F, n^I)$ is a function that captures that there is a cost associated with auditing.[10] The budget restriction is a function of the tax and punishment wedges, ϕ^F and ϕ^I, and the audit rate, p. Recall that the producer wages, employment rates, and Δ are functions of the wedge, $\psi = \phi^I/\phi^F$, and the audit rate p, where we note that p appears in both the wedge ψ and the informal sector separation rate, $s + p$. The tax rates, t and z, and the punishment rates, δ and α, will not appear in the government budget restriction directly when all substitutions are done. This reflects that t and z are equivalent instruments, and so are δ and α. Hence it does not matter if we tax (punish) the firm side or the worker side. A change in δ and α is captured by a change in ϕ^I, and a change in z and t is captured by a change in ϕ^F.

From (25) it is clear that an increase in ϕ^F and ϕ^I that leaves ψ and p unaffected will increase the government revenue. Hence for a given wedge, the government can choose t, z, δ, and α so as to reap any level

of revenue. This is very convenient and implies that we can investigate
the impact of various reforms on the equilibrium variables, without
explicitly incorporating the government budget restriction.

8.3 Comparative Statics

This section considers the impact of two reforms on tightness, relative
prices, real producer wages, sector allocation, and unemployment. The
first reform involves a change in the punishment rates, α and/or δ,
whereas the second reform involves a change in the audit rate p. Both
reforms are fully financed and will be discussed in turn.

Before considering the reforms we will engage in some substitution
in order to reduce the equation system in (22)–(24) and to trace down
some intuition. First, we eliminate $(\theta^F + \theta^I/\Delta)$ from (22) and (23). This
yields

$$\Delta = \frac{\frac{(1-\gamma)}{p} - (r+s+p)\theta^\eta \; > 0}{\frac{(1-\gamma)}{p} - (r+s)\theta^\eta \quad < 1}, \tag{26}$$

where $\Delta = \psi(P^F/P^I)$. Hence, the free-entry conditions determine the
relative price, P^F/P^I, conditional on total tightness θ. Changes in ψ
will induce proportional adjustments in the relative price so that Δ is
unaffected.

Equation (26) reflects the discussion in connection with equations
(22)–(24), and verifies that it is ψ and the difference in the separation
rates that are important for the entry and exit into the two sectors, and
hence for the relative price. This is easily seen by considering the following two imaginary polar cases. If $\psi < 1$ and $p = 0$, we have $\Delta = 1$
and hence $P^F/P^I = 1/\psi > 1$. That is, the informal sector is more attractive in the sense that informal firms are expected to be punished less
than formal firms are taxed. Hence, firms keep entering the informal
sector until the formal sector relative price has increased to such an extent that formal firms are fully compensated for the fact that $\psi < 1$. If
on the other hand $\psi = 1$, and $p > 0$, we have that $P^F/P^I = \Delta < 1$. That
is, the formal sector is more attractive in the sense that jobs on average
last a longer time, and the entry of firms into the formal sector will reduce the relative price on formal goods below unity. However, with
$\psi < 1$ and $p > 0$, we have $P^F/P^I = \Delta/\psi$, which can be either smaller or
larger than unity, reflecting the two counteracting incentives determining the relative attractiveness of the two sectors.

Moreover, we have

$$\frac{\partial \Delta}{\partial \theta} = -\frac{\eta \theta^{\eta-1}(1-\gamma)p}{p\left(\frac{(1-\gamma)}{p} - (r+s)(\theta^F + \theta^I)^\eta\right)^2} < 0. \tag{27}$$

That is, the relative price P^F/P^I falls with an increase in total tightness for a given ψ and for given separation rates. We know that $p > 0$ implies that the informal sector is relatively less attractive, since jobs last on average a shorter time in the informal sector. However, when θ is low, it is quite easy to fill a vacancy. The fact that jobs separate more easily in the informal sector is hence not as important since, in case of separation, the open vacancy can quickly be filled again. A large θ will, for the same reasons, increase the importance of a long job duration. An increase in total tightness will reduce the attractiveness of the informal sector for given separation rates and ψ, which induces a real-location of workers toward the formal sector with a reduction in the formal sector relative price, P^F/P^I, as a consequence.

By substituting the expression for Δ given by equation (26) into (22), we get

$$(r+s)\theta^\eta = \frac{(1-\gamma)}{p} - \gamma\left(\theta^F + \theta^I\left(\frac{\frac{(1-\gamma)}{p} - (r+s+p)\theta^\eta}{\frac{(1-\gamma)}{p} - (r+s)\theta^\eta}\right)^{-1}\right), \tag{28}$$

where $\theta = \theta^F + \theta^I$, which is one equation in the two unknowns θ^F and θ^I. We hence have a relationship between sector tightness, and most convenient this relationship is independent of the relative punishment rate, ψ. The relative price will adjust so as to make this relationship independent of ψ. It will, however, depend on p. Differentiating (28) with respect to sector tightness, we have

$$\frac{\partial \theta^F}{\partial \theta^I} = -\frac{(r+s)\eta\theta^{\eta-1} + \frac{\gamma}{\Delta}\left(1 - \frac{\theta^I}{\Delta}\frac{\partial \Delta}{\partial \theta}\right)}{(r+s)\eta\theta^{\eta-1} + \frac{\gamma}{\Delta}\left(\Delta - \frac{\theta^I}{\Delta}\frac{\partial \Delta}{\partial \theta}\right)} < -1, \tag{29}$$

where $\Delta < 1$. From (29), we have that informal tightness crowds out formal tightness, and vice versa. Moreover, a one-unit increase in informal tightness will reduce formal tightness by more than one unit. This is a consequence of Δ being smaller than unity. Recall from (26) that $\Delta < 1$ follows because $p > 0$ prevents firms from entering the informal sector to some extent, and hence induces the relative price, P^F/P^I, to be lower than elsewise would have been the case. This price premium in the informal sector makes this sector relatively more attractive in the sense that informal firms face lower real producer wages, and workers in the informal sector face higher real consumer wages.[11]

To illustrate the intuition behind this sectorial trade-off, consider the following example: an exogenous reduction in informal sector tightness. This will induce wage moderation in the whole economy as the value attached to unemployment falls; the fall in informal tightness is dampened whereas formal tightness increases. This explains the negative sign in (29). The increase in formal sector tightness will, however, induce a wage push in the economy. The wage push following the increase in formal sector tightness will never dominate the wage moderation following the reduction in informal tightness. The reason is that the employment probability increases in the sector where the payoff is the lowest (the formal sector) and falls in the sector where the payoff is the highest (informal sector). That is, as workers, in the event of unemployment, now face an increased probability of finding themselves employed in the lower-paying sector, the wage-moderating effect will dominate. This implies that tightness in the formal sector increases by more than informal tightness falls.[12]

A shorter way of expressing why the wage response following a change in informal tightness is stronger than the wage response following an equally sized change in formal tightness is to say that the informal sector is given a larger weight in the wage bargains than is the formal sector. Because the payoff in the informal sector is higher, it follows that changes in job opportunities in this sector are also relatively more important for the wage bargains.

8.3.1   Changes in the Punishment Fee

This section is concerned with the impact on tightness, relative prices, real producer wages, sector allocation, and unemployment of a fully financed change in the punishment fee given by a change in α and/or δ. Tax rates z and/or t are adjusting so as to keep the government budget in (25) balanced at all times. The audit rate p is taken as given throughout this reform. As is clear from (22)–(24), (15)–(17), (9), and (10), the equilibrium variables will only be affected by changes in α, δ, z, and t through the wedge, ψ. Hence, we can conduct comparative statics with respect to ψ without explicitly having to account for the government budget restriction since any government revenue can be reaped by appropriate changes in α, δ, z, and t at any given wedge.

8.3.1.1 Labor Market Tightness and Real Producer Wages

The effects on tightness, real producer wages, and the relative price are summarized in the following proposition:

PROPOSITION 1 A fully financed increase in the punishment fee, δ or α, will increase tightness in the formal sector, θ^F, and reduce tightness in the informal sector, θ^I. Total tightness, θ, increases, and real producer wages in the two sectors, ω^F and ω^I, fall. The relative price, P^F/P^I, falls.

All propositions in the chapter can be derived from the equilibrium equations.[13] See the appendix for details.

An increase in ψ will make it relatively worse to be in the underground economy. Hence the value of employment in the informal sector falls relative to unemployment, which increases informal sector wage demands. In the formal sector, on the other hand, wage demands fall because the value of formal employment has increased relative to the value of unemployment.

From the firms' perspective, these happenings tend to increase the producer costs in the informal sector whereas producer costs in the formal sector tend to fall. Consequently, exit from the informal sector and entry into the formal sector are initiated. That is, labor market tightness in the formal sector, θ^F, increases, and labor market tightness in the informal sector, θ^I, falls.[14]

The relative price is now affected. The reallocation of jobs toward the formal sector increases the production of formal sector goods relative to informal sector goods, which reduces the relative price, P^F/P^I. The relative price adjustments will eventually restore the equilibrium since the increase in the relative price eventually makes it profitable to produce informal goods and eliminates the profitability of producing formal goods.

Although the direct effect on real producer wages of an increase in ψ is that informal wages increase and formal wages fall, relative price adjustments fully counteracts these effects in equilibrium. The equilibrium effects on real producer wages is, in fact, entirely explained by changes in the reallocation of firms across sectors. Because $\Delta < 1$, the informal sector is given a larger weight in the wage bargains than is the formal sector. Hence the wage moderation following a reduction in θ^I is going to be larger than the wage push following an equally sized increase in θ^F. If, for the sake of the argument, total tightness where unaffected by this reallocation, also the time unit probability of finding any job would be the same, i.e., $\lambda^F + \lambda^I = \theta^{1-\eta}$. However, with total tightness being unaffected, the expected payoff from finding any job must have fallen for an unemployed worker as the probability of finding a better-paying job has fallen and the probability of finding a lesser good-paying job has increased. Hence the value of unemployment would in this case be lower, which calls for wage moderation. This wage moderation following the reallocation of jobs toward the formal sector is the driving force behind the reduction in the equilibrium real producer wages. Moreover, this wage moderation explains why total tightness must increase.[15]

8.3.1.2 Employment

We summarize the results on employment and unemployment in the following proposition:

PROPOSITION 2   A fully financed increase in the punishment fee, δ or α, will increase the employment rate in the formal sector, n^F, and reduce the employment rate in the informal sector, n^I. Both actual unemployment, u, and official unemployment, u^o, falls with the reform.

It comes as no surprise that increased punishment fees relative to tax rates induce a reallocation of workers from the informal sector toward the formal sector. An increased wedge increases the transition rate into formal sector employment, whereas the opposite movements occur in the informal sector. Actual unemployment falls both because the overall transition rate into employment, $\lambda^F + \lambda^I = \theta^{1-\eta}$, increases and because the transition rate out of employment is lower in the formal sector. Official unemployment falls as both actual unemployment and informal sector employment fall.

8.3.2 Changes in the Audit Rate

This section is concerned with the impact on tightness, the relative price, real producer wages, sector allocation, and unemployment of a fully financed change in the audit rate p. The tax rates z and/or t and the punishment fees α and/or δ are adjusting so as to keep the government budget in (25) balanced at all times. As is clear from (22)–(24), (15)–(17), (9), and (10), the equilibrium variables will be affected by changes in p both through the wedge ψ and through the informal sector separation rate, $s + p$. However, from the government budget restriction in (25), we know that there is always an appropriate adjustment in z and/or t and the punishment rates α and/or δ that will produce any level of government revenues for a given ψ. Hence to clarify how changes in p affect the equilibrium variables via the informal sector separation rate, $s + p$, this reform considers changes in p for a given ψ.

From the previous analysis, we could conclude how changes in ψ affected the equilibrium variables, and it is straightforward to extend the analysis that follows to incorporate the fact that ψ is increased by an increase in p. The discussion in sections 8.1 and 8.5 summarizes the full effects of an increase in p.

8.3.2.1 Labor Market Tightness and Real Producer Wages
The effect on tightness is summarized in the following proposition:

PROPOSITION 3   A fully financed increase in the audit rate, p (for a given ψ), will decrease total tightness, $\partial\theta/\partial p < 0$.

We first note that we cannot exclude that informal sector tightness actually increases with an increased audit rate. An increase in p reduces the profitability for firms entering the informal sector by reducing the average length of a match, which works in the expected direction of reducing informal sector tightness, θ^I tends to fall. In addition, however, the relative price, P^F/P^I, is directly reduced by an increase in p since the outflow of informal sector workers increases for given tightness, and hence the production of informal goods falls. This relative price effect will increase the attractiveness for firms to enter the informal sector, tending to increase θ^I.

Since we cannot conclude whether θ^I falls or increases with p, we cannot conclude whether θ^F increases or falls with p. The direct negative effect on the relative price tends to reduce formal sector tightness by making the formal sector less attractive for firms to enter. However, if informal sector tightness falls, formal sector tightness tends to increase since the value of unemployment is reduced and hence wages are moderated in the formal sector. The overall impact on θ^F is ambiguous.

Total labor market tightness falls with an increase in the audit rate. This follows because the direct negative effect on the relative price reduces formal sector tightness. For example, if θ^I increases with the reform, we know from (29) that θ^F falls by more. Hence total tightness falls. The fact that P^F/P^I falls as a direct effect of a higher p will further reduce θ^F and total tightness. If, on the other hand, θ^I falls with the reform, formal sector tightness increases by more, and total tightness tends to increase. However, the fact that the relative price falls as a direct effect of an increase in p will reduce formal sector tightness, and hence the fall in θ^I is larger than the increase in θ^F; total tightness falls.[16]

In general, it cannot be determined whether the relative price increases or decreases with an increase in p. Considering, for example, equation (24), we can see that the direct effect of an increase in p makes the relative price fall. There is, however, a counteracting effect working through total tightness. As total tightness falls with an increase in p, the relative supply of informal goods falls due to the fact that vacancy costs increase by more in the informal sector. In addition to that, relative tightness can move in either direction. However, if informal sector tightness falls, the relative price will fall. Hence, the effect working through vacancy costs cannot dominate the effects working through p directly and through relative tightness.

The effects on real producer wages is given by the following proposition:

PROPOSITION 4   A fully financed increase in the audit rate, p (for a given ψ), will increase the real producer wage in the formal sector, $\partial \omega^F / \partial p > 0$. The impact on the informal sector real producer wage is ambiguous.

Firms enter into the two sectors until the expected vacancy costs are equal to the discounted profits. This implies that the expected time it takes to fill a vacancy is equal to the discounted profits relative to the per period vacancy cost. For reasons given previously, we know that total tightness falls with an increase in p, although we cannot determine how sector tightness and the relative prices are affected in general. If total tightness falls with the reform, and hence a vacancy is expected to be filled at a faster rate, discounted profits in the two sectors relative to per period vacancy costs have to fall as well. The reallocation of firms across the two sectors will assure that. In the formal sector this can only be achieved by an increase in the real producer wage. In the informal sector, however, an increase in p will reduce the expected profits since a match is expected to last a shorter number of periods. It is hence not necessarily the case that the real producer wage in the informal sector increases as a consequence of a higher p.

8.3.2.2 Employment

As we cannot exclude that relative tightness, θ^F/θ^I, actually falls following an increase in p, we cannot exclude that relative employment, n^F/n^I, falls with the reform. However, if relative tightness decreases with the reform, relative employment will fall as well. This follows both because the relative transition rate into formal employment falls, and because outflow of workers from the informal sector increases.

The impact on unemployment is, however, ambiguous. It is not possible to exclude the case that the unemployment rate falls with an increase in the audit rate. This is so although we know that total tightness falls, and hence the total transition rate into employment falls, and that the exit rate from the informal sector increases.[17] The reason is the reallocation effect. Consider, for example, that this reforms brings about increased inflow into formal sector employment. This may reduce the unemployment rate although the transition rate into the informal sector falls by more than the transition rate into formal sector increases. This follows because the formal sector separation rate is lower than the informal sector separation rate and hence for a given increase in the sector transition rate into employment, formal sector employment has to increase by more than informal sector employment in order to balance inflows with outflow in steady state. That is, employment in the formal sector is more sensitive to changes in its transition rate than are informal sector employment.

8.4 Identical Goods Produced in the Formal and the Informal Sector

Throughout the chapter we have assumed that different goods are produced in the formal and the informal sector. Having different goods being produced in the two sectors captured that certain types of goods and services are more likely to be produced in the informal sector than other types. For example, cleaning jobs in private homes, gardening services, and so forth are more likely to be produced in the informal sector, whereas cars, televisions, and so forth are less likely to be produced in the informal sector. From section 8.3 it was clear that the relative price adjusted so as to guarantee a new equilibrium with the coexistence of the formal and the informal sector. Although the relative price adjustment played a central role as an equilibrating mechanism, it played no role in explaining the results. The results were solely explained by the reallocation process. This becomes clear by looking at the following stylized model where an identical good is produced in the formal sector and in the informal sector.

Assume that workers allocate their search time equally into the formal sector and the informal sector. The assumption of having workers splitting their search time exogenously between the two sectors may at first sight not seem very plausible. However, as will be explained, it delivers the same message and results as a framework where workers allocate their search time optimally between the two sectors. The matching functions for the two sectors are then given by

$$X^j = (v^j)^{1-\eta}(u/2)^\eta, \quad j = F, I.$$

The transition rates now takes the following form: $\lambda^F = \frac{1}{2}(\theta^F)^{1-\eta}$, $\lambda^I = \frac{1}{2}(\theta^I)^{1-\eta}$, $q^F = (\theta^F)^{-\eta}$ and $q^I = (\theta^I)^{-\eta}$, where tightness in each sector is defined in effective search units, $\theta^F = 2v^F/u$ and $\theta^I = 2v^I/u$. The value equations for the workers are the same as given in equations (1)–(3) apart from the fact that we normalize the price of the only good to unity, namely, $P^F = P^I = P = 1$, and consider the new arrival rates. The value equations for the firms, (4)–(7), are modified using the price normalization and noting that the firm's transition rate is q^F if located in the formal sector, and q^I if located in the informal sector. Producer wages are given by equations (9) and (10); apart from that we replace ρ with $\rho/2$ and Δ with ψ. Labor market tightness for the two sectors are determined by

$$(r+s)(\theta^F)^\eta = \frac{(1-\gamma)}{\rho} - \frac{\gamma}{2}(\theta^F + \theta^I/\psi), \tag{30}$$

$$(r+s+p)(\theta^I)^\eta = \frac{(1-\gamma)}{\rho} - \frac{\gamma\psi}{2}(\theta^F + \theta^I/\psi). \tag{31}$$

Note that the labor market equations are similar to equations (22) and (23) when $\Delta = (P^F/P^I)\psi = \psi$, except for the fact that formal and informal firms do not cause congestion for each other in this directed search framework. Hence $q^F \neq q^I$ is a possible outcome. We focus on the case when the wedge, ψ, is lower than unity as it corresponds to the case of $\Delta < 1$. Assuming ψ smaller than unity implies that the informal sector is more attractive, because the sector is not punished as severely as the formal sector is taxed. Recall that Δ smaller than unity raised the attractiveness of the informal sector to compensate for the shorter expected job duration.

As is clear, (30) and (31) define the two unknowns, θ^F and θ^I. Comparative statics with respect to δ or α yields the same results as is found in propositions 1 and 2.[18] Producer wages in the informal sector increase, whereas producer wages in the formal sector fall. Moreover, the basic intuition explaining the results goes through as well. When the punishment fees increase, it will become relatively worse to be in the underground economy. This increases wage demands in the informal sector and reduces wage demands in the formal sector, which initiates firms to reallocate toward the formal sector. Consequently, labor market tightness in the formal sector, θ^F, increases and labor market tightness in the informal sector, θ^I, falls.

In the differentiated goods case, formal sector relative prices fell, which eventually made it inoptimal for firms to further reallocate toward the formal sector. Now, identical goods are being produced, and hence there is no relative price adjustment to stop the reallocation of firms. However, with directed search, firms in the formal sector will create congestions for each other, and hence, as it becomes more crowded in the formal sector, it will eventually be inoptimal to further reallocate toward the formal sector.

Again it is the reallocation process that is the key answer as to why total tightness increases and unemployment falls. As in the differentiated goods case, this is explained by the fact that firms exiting from the informal sector is valued more in the wage bargains than firms entering into the formal sector. The wage moderation following a firm exiting the informal sector will be larger than the wage push following a firm entering the formal sector. Informal sector tightness falls by less than formal sector tightness increases; total tightness increases.

The results following an increase in the audit rate will be unclear also in the case where identical goods are being produced in the two sectors, although for partly different reasons. The effects of an increase in p working through ψ obviously works through the same mechanisms as in the differentiated goods case. However, as was clear from the analyses in section 8.3.2, there were also direct effects following a change in p on the relative price. The direct effects on the relative price affected the relative attractiveness of the two sectors. With identical goods being produced in the two sectors, these incentive effects will obviously be absent when considering identical goods. In the absence of these relative price effects, an increase in p will always reduce tightness in the informal sector and increase tightness in the formal sector.

However, in the directed search framework, we cannot know whether informal sector tightness falls by more or less than formal sector tightness increases. Hence, we cannot determine whether total tightness increases or falls with an increase in p, and hence we cannot determine whether unemployment falls or increases with p.

As previously said, the assumption of having workers splitting their search time exogenously between the two sectors may not be fully satisfactory. However, if we allow for search effort between the two sectors to be optimally determined in this framework, the same results would materialize. This becomes clear if one uses the framework set out in Kolm and Larsen 2003b, where the importance of tax evasion for educational choice is highlighted.

8.5 Conclusion

This chapter developed a two-sector general equilibrium matching model with different goods produced in the formal sector and in the informal sector. This enabled an analysis of how increased government control of the underground economy affects wage formation, sector allocation, and unemployment. This is something that to a large extent has been ignored in the previous literature where wages have been taken as either given or determined by market clearing.

Based on this framework, we have shown that increased government control of the underground economy in terms of higher punishment fees reduces the size of the underground economy, reduces real producer wages in the two sectors, and reduces actual and official unemployment.

The intuition behind these results is as follows. Increased punishment fees induce wage demands to increase in the informal sector and fall in the formal sector. As a consequence, firms find it profitable to exit the informal sector and enter the formal sector. In turn, this reallocation of production will reduce the formal sector's relative price. The relative price adjustments will fully counteract the direct effects on real producer wages in equilibrium. Both real producer wages and unemployment instead fall due to the rather strong wage moderation that follows this reallocation process. We also noted that the fall in unemployment was further reinforced because workers and firms where reallocated toward the formal sector where the separation rate was lower.

This strong wage moderation was essential and is here summarized. The reallocation of firms from the informal sector toward the formal sector will induce both increased and reduced wage demands. When firms enter the formal sector, wage demands increase since employment perspectives in the formal sector increase. Analogously, wage demands fall when firms exit the informal sector as employment perspectives in this sector fall. The wage moderation following a firm exiting the informal sector is, however, larger than the wage push following a firm entering the formal sector. The reason wages are more responsive to changes in informal tightness is that the payoff in the informal sector exceeds that of the formal sector. Hence, changes in job opportunities in the informal sector are relatively more important for the wage bargains as the payoff in this sector is higher. This rather strong wage moderation explains why real producer wages and unemployment fall.

Considering the full effects on labor market performance of an increase in the audit rate produced less clear results. In addition to the effects previously described, there was a direct positive effect on the probability of a worker-firm match being separated. The outflow from informal sector employment into the unemployment pool hence increased. Furthermore, we found that the overall transition rate into employment fell, caused by an increase in the informal sector separation rate. These effects tended to increase unemployment. Consequently, the overall impact of increased auditing on unemployment is ambiguous.

Appendix A: Proof of Propositions

8A.1   Proof of Proposition 1

Differentiate equation (24) with respect to θ^I and ψ, taking into account that Δ is a function of θ^F and θ^I as given by (26) and that θ^F is a function of θ^I through equation (28). This yields

$$\frac{d\theta^I}{d\psi} = \frac{\theta^F}{\theta^I}\frac{\Delta}{\psi}\left(\Delta\frac{\partial\frac{\theta^F}{\theta^I}}{\partial\theta^I} + \left(\frac{\theta^F}{\theta^I}\frac{\partial\Delta}{\partial\theta} + \psi\frac{\sigma}{1-\sigma}\frac{\frac{1}{s}-\frac{1}{s+p}}{\left(\frac{1}{s}-\rho\theta^\eta\right)^2}\rho\eta\theta^{\eta-1}\right)\left(\frac{\partial\theta^F}{\partial\theta^I}+1\right)\right)^{-1},$$

where $\partial(\theta^F/\theta^I)/\partial\theta^I = ((\partial\theta^F/\partial\theta^I)\theta^I - \theta^F)/(\theta^I)^2 < 0$, and $\partial\theta^F/\partial\theta^I + 1 < 0$ from (29). A sufficient condition for a negative sign is then

$$\Delta \frac{\partial \frac{\theta^F}{\theta^I}}{\partial \theta^I} + \frac{\theta^F}{\theta^I} \frac{\partial \Delta}{\partial \theta} \left(\frac{\partial \theta^F}{\partial \theta^I} + 1 \right) < 0.$$

Substituting for $(\partial \theta^F / \partial \theta^I + 1)$ and $\partial(\theta^F / \theta^I)/\partial \theta^I$ and simplifying we obtain

$$-\Delta \frac{\theta^F}{\theta^I} ((r+s)\eta\theta^{\eta-1} + \gamma) - (r+s)\eta\theta^{\eta-1} - \frac{\gamma}{\Delta} + \left(\frac{\gamma}{\Delta} \theta^I + \theta^F \gamma \right) \frac{\partial \Delta}{\partial \theta} < 0.$$

Thus, $\partial \theta^I / \partial \psi < 0$. Thereby $(\partial \theta^F / \partial \theta^I)(\partial \theta^I / \partial \psi) > 0$ and $\partial \theta / \partial \psi = (\partial \theta^F / \partial \theta^I + 1)(\partial \theta^I / \partial \psi) > 0$. Regarding the relative price we have $P^F / P^I = \Delta/\psi$ where

$$\frac{\partial \left(\frac{P^F}{P^I} \right)}{\partial \psi} = \left(\frac{\partial \Delta}{\partial \psi} \psi - \Delta \right) \Big/ \psi^2 < 0 \quad \text{since} \quad \frac{\partial \Delta}{\partial \psi} = \frac{\partial \Delta}{\partial \theta} \frac{\partial \theta}{\partial \psi} < 0.$$

Differentiating equations (9) and (10) with respect to ψ yields

$$\frac{\partial \omega^F}{\partial \psi} = \gamma p y \left(\frac{\partial \theta^F}{\partial \psi} + \frac{\partial \theta^I}{\partial \psi} \frac{1}{\Delta} - \frac{\theta^I}{\Delta^2} \frac{\partial \Delta}{\partial \theta} \frac{\partial \theta}{\partial \psi} \right), \tag{32}$$

$$\frac{\partial \omega^I}{\partial \psi} = \gamma p y \left(\frac{\partial \theta^F}{\partial \psi} \Delta + \theta^F \frac{\partial \Delta}{\partial \theta} \frac{\partial \theta}{\partial \psi} + \frac{\partial \theta^I}{\partial \psi} \right). \tag{33}$$

From (13) and (14), we have

$$\theta^\eta = \frac{(1-\gamma)}{(r+s)\rho} - \gamma \frac{\left(\theta^F + \frac{\theta^I}{\Delta} \right)}{(r+s)}, \tag{34}$$

$$\theta^\eta = \frac{(1-\gamma)}{(r+s+p)\rho} - \gamma \frac{\Delta \left(\theta^F + \frac{\theta^I}{\Delta} \right)}{(r+s+p)}. \tag{35}$$

Differentiation brings out the following expressions:

$$\eta\theta^{\eta-1} \frac{\partial \theta}{\partial \psi} = -\frac{\gamma}{(r+s)} \left(\frac{\partial \theta^F}{\partial \psi} + \frac{\partial \theta^I}{\partial \psi} \frac{1}{\Delta} - \frac{\theta^I}{\Delta^2} \frac{\partial \Delta}{\partial \theta} \frac{\partial \theta}{\partial \psi} \right), \tag{36}$$

$$\eta\theta^{\eta-1} \frac{\partial \theta}{\partial \psi} = -\frac{\gamma}{(r+s+p)} \left(\frac{\partial \theta^F}{\partial \psi} \Delta + \theta^F \frac{\partial \Delta}{\partial \theta} \frac{\partial \theta}{\partial \psi} + \frac{\partial \theta^I}{\partial \psi} \right), \tag{37}$$

where we know from the proof of proposition 1 that $\partial \theta / \partial \psi > 0$. This implies that $\partial \theta^F / \partial \psi + (\partial \theta^I / \partial \psi)(1/\Delta) - (\theta^I / \Delta^2)(\partial \Delta / \partial \theta)(\partial \theta / \partial \psi) < 0$ and $(\partial \theta^F / \partial \psi)\Delta + \theta^F (\partial \Delta / \partial \theta)(\partial \theta / \partial \psi) + \partial \theta^I / \partial \psi < 0$ have to hold. Hence we have that the equilibrium real producer wages have to fall in both sectors.

8A.2   Proof of Proposition 2

Differentiating equations (15) and (16) with respect to ψ gives

$$\frac{\partial n^I}{\partial \psi} = \frac{\frac{\partial(\theta^I(\theta)^{-\eta})}{\partial \psi}\left(1 + \frac{\theta^F(\theta)^{-\eta}}{s}\right) - \frac{\theta^I(\theta)^{-\eta}}{s}\frac{\partial(\theta^F(\theta)^{-\eta})}{\partial \psi}}{(s+p)\left(1 + \frac{\theta^F(\theta)^{-\eta}}{s} + \frac{\theta^I(\theta)^{-\eta}}{s+p}\right)^2} < 0,$$

$$\frac{\partial n^F}{\partial \psi} = \frac{\frac{\partial(\theta^F(\theta)^{-\eta})}{\partial \psi}\left(1 + \frac{\theta^I(\theta)^{-\eta}}{s+p}\right) - \frac{\theta^F(\theta)^{-\eta}}{s}\frac{\partial(\theta^I(\theta)^{-\eta})}{\partial \psi}}{s\left(1 + \frac{\theta^F(\theta)^{-\eta}}{s} + \frac{\theta^I(\theta)^{-\eta}}{s+p}\right)^2} > 0,$$

where we use the fact that

$$\frac{\partial(\theta^I(\theta)^{-\eta})}{\partial \psi} = \theta^{-\eta}\left(1 - \eta\frac{\theta^I}{\theta}\left(\frac{\partial \theta^F}{\partial \theta^I} + 1\right)\right)\frac{\partial \theta^I}{\partial \psi} < 0,$$

$$\frac{\partial(\theta^F(\theta)^{-\eta})}{\partial \psi} = \theta^{-\eta}\left(\frac{\partial \theta^F}{\partial \theta^I}\left(1 - \eta\frac{\theta^F}{\theta}\right) - \eta\frac{\theta^F}{\theta}\right)\frac{\partial \theta^I}{\partial \psi} > 0.$$

Furthermore, the unemployment rate is affected in the following way:

$$\frac{\partial u}{\partial \psi} = -\frac{\frac{s+p}{s}\frac{\partial(\theta^F(\theta)^{-\eta})}{\partial \psi} + \frac{\partial(\theta^I(\theta)^{-\eta})}{\partial \psi}}{\left(1 + \frac{\theta^F(\theta)^{-\eta}}{s} + \frac{\theta^I(\theta)^{-\eta}}{s+p}\right)^2}\frac{1}{s+p}.$$

Because $(s+p)/s > 1$ and $\partial \theta^I/\partial \psi < 0$, a sufficient condition for $\partial u/\partial \psi < 0$ is that

$$\frac{\partial \theta^F}{\partial \theta^I}\left(1 - \eta\frac{\theta^F}{\theta}\right) - \eta\frac{\theta^F}{\theta} + 1 - \eta\left(1 - \frac{\theta^F}{\theta}\right)\left(\frac{\partial \theta^F}{\partial \theta^I} + 1\right) < 0$$

$$\Leftrightarrow (1 - \eta)\left(\frac{\partial \theta^F}{\partial \theta^I} + 1\right) < 0,$$

which is satisfied. Considering u^o, we have $\partial u^o/\partial \psi = \partial u/\partial \psi + \partial n^I/\partial \psi < 0$ from this proof.

8A.3   Proof of Proposition 3

Differentiating the equilibrium system, equations (22)–(24) give

$$\frac{d\theta^F}{dp} = \frac{-\frac{\Phi\Delta + \gamma\frac{1}{\pi}H\theta^I}{\Delta}\theta^\eta + \gamma\psi\left(\theta^F\left(\Phi + \frac{\gamma}{\Delta}\right) + \frac{\Sigma+\gamma}{\Delta}\frac{\theta^I}{\Delta}\right)\frac{\sigma}{1-\sigma}\frac{\theta^I}{\theta^F}\frac{\frac{1}{(s+p)^2}}{\frac{1-\rho\theta^\eta}{s}}}{D},$$

$$\frac{d\theta^I}{dp} = \frac{\frac{\Delta(\Phi+\gamma)+\gamma\frac{\theta^I}{\theta^F}+\gamma\frac{1}{\pi}H\theta^I}{\Delta}\theta^\eta - \gamma\psi\left(\theta^F(\Phi+\gamma) + \left(\frac{\Sigma}{\Delta}+\gamma\right)\frac{\theta^I}{\Delta}\right)\frac{\sigma}{1-\sigma}\frac{\theta^I}{\theta^F}\frac{\frac{1}{(s+p)^2}}{\frac{1}{s}-\rho\theta^\eta}}{D},$$

$$\frac{d\pi}{dp} = \frac{\left(\frac{\Phi\pi+\gamma\pi}{\theta^I} + \frac{1}{\theta^F}\Phi\pi + \frac{1}{\theta^F}\gamma\frac{1}{\psi} + \frac{\gamma H}{\Delta}\left(\frac{1}{\Delta}-1\right)\right)\theta^\eta - \gamma(1-\Delta)\frac{\Sigma-\Phi\Delta}{\Delta}\frac{\sigma}{1-\sigma}\frac{\theta^I}{\theta^F}\frac{\frac{1}{(s+p)^2}}{\frac{1}{s}-\rho\theta^\eta}}{D},$$

where

$$D = -\gamma\left((\Phi+\gamma)\left(1+\frac{\theta^F}{\theta^I}\Delta\right) + \left(1+\frac{\theta^F}{\theta^I}\frac{1}{\Delta}\right)(\Sigma+\gamma) + \frac{\gamma}{\Delta}\psi H\theta\left(\frac{1}{\Delta}-1\right)\right)$$

$$< 0,$$

and

$$\Phi = (r+s)\eta\theta^{\eta-1}, \quad \Sigma = (r+s+p)\eta\theta^{\eta-1},$$

$$H = \frac{\sigma}{1-\sigma}\frac{\theta^I}{\theta^F}\frac{\frac{1}{s}-\frac{1}{s+p}}{\left(\frac{1}{s}-\rho\theta^\eta\right)^2}\rho\eta\theta^{\eta-1}.$$

Adding the derivatives for labor market tightness we obtain

$$\frac{d\theta}{dp} = \frac{1}{\Delta}\frac{\left(\Delta\gamma + \gamma\frac{\theta^I}{\theta^F}\right)\theta^\eta + \gamma\psi\left(\theta^F\gamma(1-\Delta) + \theta^I\gamma\left(\frac{1}{\Delta}-1\right)\right)\frac{\sigma}{1-\sigma}\frac{\theta^I}{\theta^F}\frac{\frac{1}{(s+p)^2}}{\frac{1}{s}-\rho\theta^\eta}}{D} < 0.$$

8A.4 Proof of Proposition 4

Differentiating equations (9) and (10) with respect to p yields

$$\frac{\partial\omega^F}{\partial p} = \gamma py\left(\frac{\partial\theta^F}{\partial p} + \frac{\partial\theta^I}{\partial p}\frac{1}{\Delta} - \frac{\theta^I}{\Delta^2}\frac{\partial\Delta}{\partial p}\right), \tag{38}$$

$$\frac{\partial\omega^I}{\partial p} = \gamma py\left(\frac{\partial\theta^F}{\partial p}\Delta + \frac{\partial\theta^I}{\partial p} + \theta^F\frac{\partial\Delta}{\partial p}\right).$$

From (13) and (14), we have

$$\theta^\eta = \frac{(1-\gamma)}{(r+s)\rho} - \gamma\frac{\theta^F + \frac{\theta^I}{\Delta}}{(r+s)},$$

$$\theta^\eta = \frac{1}{(r+s+p)}\left(\frac{(1-\gamma)}{\rho} - \gamma\Delta\left(\theta^F + \frac{\theta^I}{\Delta}\right)\right).$$

Differentiation brings out the following expression:

$$\eta\theta^{\eta-1}\frac{\partial\theta}{\partial p} = -\frac{\gamma}{(r+s)}\left(\frac{\partial\theta^F}{\partial p} + \frac{\partial\theta^I}{\partial p}\frac{1}{\Delta} - \frac{\theta^I}{\Delta^2}\frac{\partial\Delta}{\partial p}\right),$$

$$\eta\theta^{\eta-1}\frac{\partial\theta}{\partial p} = -\frac{\gamma\Delta}{(r+s+p)}\left(\frac{\partial\theta^F}{\partial p} + \frac{\partial\theta^I}{\partial p}\frac{1}{\Delta} + \frac{\theta^F}{\Delta}\frac{\partial\Delta}{\partial p}\right) - \frac{\theta^\eta}{r+s+p},$$

where we know from the proof of proposition (3) that $\partial\theta/\partial p < 0$. This implies that $\partial\theta^F/\partial p + (\partial\theta^I/\partial p)(1/\Delta) - (\theta^I/\Delta^2)(\partial\Delta/\partial p) > 0$.

Appendix B: Value Functions of Employment

This appendix gives a brief "derivation" of the flow value functions for employment in the formal and informal sectors. This serves to provide one possible interpretation for the expressions giving the flow value equations of employment in (2) and (3).

Let Δ be an arbitrary length of a time interval. We consider only steady state whereby we suppress the time index. At any date, E^F and E^I satisfy

$$E^F = \frac{1}{1+r\Delta}(w^F(1-t)\Delta + T\Delta + s\Delta U + (1-s\Delta)E^F + o(\Delta))$$

$$E^I = \frac{1}{1+r\Delta}(w^I\Delta + T\Delta + (1-s\Delta)(p\Delta(U - w^I\delta)$$

$$+ (1 - p\Delta)E^I) + s\Delta U + o(\Delta)),$$

where $o(\Delta)/\Delta \to 0$ when $\Delta \to 0$. With probability $s\Delta$, there is an exogenous separation of the match. In case the match is not separated exogenously, $1 - s\Delta$, it is detected with probability $p\Delta$ or it is not detected with probability $1 - p\Delta$.[19] The government audits the economy, and p captures the audit probability for a given time unit interval. If a worker is detected, the match is dissolved and the worker pays a punishment fee equal to a constant times the underground wage earned during this time unit interval, that is, δw^I.[20]

This yields the following flow value equations:

$$r\Delta E^F = w^F(1-t)\Delta + T\Delta + s\Delta(U - E^F) + o(\Delta),$$

$$r\Delta E^I = w^I\Delta(1 - p\delta) + T\Delta + (p\Delta + s\Delta)(U - E^I) - s\Delta p\Delta(U - w^I\delta)$$

$$+ s\Delta p\Delta E^I + o(\Delta).$$

Divide by Δ and let $\Delta \to 0$:

$$rE^F = w^F(1 - t) + T + s(U - E^F),$$

$$rE^I = w^I(1 - p\delta) + T + (s + p)(U_t - E^I).$$

Notes

We want to thank Nils Gottfries, Bertil Holmlund, Tomas Lindström, Dale Mortensen, Søren Bo Nielsen, Åsa Rosen, Fabrizio Zilibotti, two anonymous referees, and seminar participants at Aarhus Business School, the Zeuthen Workshop at the University of Copenhagen, Copenhagen Business School, the National Institute for Economic Research in Stockholm, the Trade Union Institute for Economic Research in Stockholm, Umeå University, and Uppsala University. The chapter was written while the first author was visiting the University of Michigan 2000. Their hospitality is greatfully acknowledged.

1. See Slemrod and Yitzhaki 2000 and Schneider and Eneste 2000 for two recent surveys of tax avoidance and tax evasion.

2. This model is along the lines of Pissarides 2000, extended to a two-sector version.

3. If different goods are being produced, one could ask why the workers and consumers are able to locate the informal firms whereas the tax authorities are not fully able to do so. One answer is that the tax authorities cannot officially search in the same way as workers, and they would need to use searching methods corresponding to each individual consumer. This is a time-consuming and expensive process, whereby only a fraction p of all informal firms and workers is detected. The tax authorities know what kind of firms to search for, but they do not know where to find them and their employees. The firms are not registered, they do not exist in any statistics, and officially their employees are unemployed.

4. One can view the assumption of the match being dissolved in several ways. For example, once detected there may be a court process. This court process potentially takes a long time. In case the legal system punishes one of the parties—say, the employer—the employees may simply search for a new job. Alternatively, the match may be dissolved as the detected parties fear that the tax authority will return to the firm and workers with probability one if the match is continued.

5. We focus on the nontrivial case where it is inoptimal to reject job offers from one sector and wait for a job offer from the other sector in order to ensure the existence of both a formal and an informal sector. Moreover, we disregard from moral considerations; see Kolm and Larsen 2001 for a model where workers are heterogenous in terms of moral.

6. As both formal and informal sector firms which post vacancies compete over the unemployed workers, firms in both sectors cause congestions for each other, leading to the same probability of finding a worker across all firms irrespective of sector.

7. The arbitrage equation for informal sector employment (3) includes the expression $w^I(1 - p\delta)$. This term can be interpreted as the expected consumer wage. See appendix B for the interpretation of the punishment fee as an upfront payment upon detection.
    Moreover, we note that it is not important for the results whether the punishment fee is imposed on evaded income or evaded taxes. This is not always the case in the previous

literature of tax evasion, where the choice to base the fines of evasion on evaded income or evaded taxes may be of significant importance for the results. See Yitzhaki (1974), who pointed out the importance of this critical assumption.

8. There is no apriori reason to assume that one of the productivities should be greater than the other.

9. $U_F, U_I > 0$, and $U_{FF}, U_{II} < 0$.

10. In the literature on tax evasion, it is commonly assumed that auditing is costly whereas punishment fees are costless. The auditing costs may depend on p and the number of producing firms in each sector. As will become clear in what follows, any specification of the auditing costs that includes any of the real variables in the model or the auditing rate, p, or the wedge, ψ, will yield the same results.

11. From (9) and (10), we have $\omega^F > \omega^I$, and $\omega^F(1 - t) > w^I(1 - p\delta)$.

12. One may argue, however, that the informal sector is less attractive because the sectoral separation rate is higher in itself. However, the fact that the separation rate is higher in the informal sector has no impact on the wage bargains as it affects the worker and the firm equally. In addition, the direct effect of having, for example, $\psi < 1$, has no effect on the wage bargains since this is counteracted by the relative price.

13. For an intuitive interpretation, the propositions are expressed as if an increase in ϕ^I financed by adjustments in ϕ^F implies that $\psi = \phi^I/\phi^F$ increases. Other, although perhaps less plausible cases, are of course also incorporated. The propositions simply capture fully financed changes in the tax and punishment systems that affect the relative tax and punishment rates between the formal and informal economy.

14. In fact, there is an additional effect reinforcing the reallocation process toward the formal sector. As a given reduction in θ^I induces θ^F to increase by more, total tightness increases. Thereby vacancy costs increase, which tends to reduce the supply of goods in both sectors. However, as the separation rate is higher in the informal sector, the fraction of total sector production that accounts for vacancy costs increases by more in the informal sector. This tends to further reinforce the reallocation process toward the formal sector.

15. When total tightness increases, it becomes relatively less attractive to enter the informal sector since the separation rate is higher in the informal sector than in the formal sector, which further reinforces the reallocation of firms toward the formal sector. This further reduces the relative price (i.e., further reduces the relative price than was induced in order to fully counteract the direct effects on wage demands of a change in ψ). This tends to increase real producer wages in the formal sector and reduce the informal sector real producer wages. However, this effect can never dominate the effects induced by the fact that the reallocation brings about stronger wage moderation than wage push; real producer wages fall in both sectors.

16. Due to that, the relative price, P^F/P^I, falls as a direct effect of a higher p may even make θ^F fall. But again total tightness falls.

17. Recall that the total transition rate into employment is $\lambda^F + \lambda^I = \theta^{1-\eta}$.

18. Proposition 2 can be verified by differentiating the equations for unemployment and sector employment, which again are given by $u = (1 + \lambda^F/s + \lambda^I/(s + p))^{-1}$, and $n^j = [\lambda^j/(s + p)] \cdot u$, $j = F, I$, where the arrival rates for directed search need to be used.

19. Here we have defined the discounted value as if the exogenous separations takes place before the auditing procedure. However, note that it does not matter if we assume that the match is hit by an audition prior to exogenous separation instead.

20. The discrete time unit interval could, for example, be a year, a month, or a day. In case the time unit interval is taken to be a year, the punishment fee is a constant times the yearly wage earned in the underground economy. Analogous interpretation holds for the case when the time unit interval is taken to be the month, and so forth.

References

Albrecht, J., and S. Vroman. 2002. "A Matching Model with Endogenous Skill Requirements." *International Economic Review* 43: 283–305.

Boeri, T., and P. Garibaldi. 2002. "Shadow Activity and Unemployment in a Depressed Labor Market." CEPR Discussion Paper DP3433, London.

Cavalcanti, T. 2002. "Labor Market Policies and Informal Markets." Working paper, Universidade Nova de Lisboa.

Fugazza, M., and J.-F. Jacques. 2004. "Labour Market Institutions, Taxation and the Underground Economy." *Journal of Public Economics* 88, nos. 1–2: 395–418.

Kolm, A.-S., and B. Larsen. 2001. "Moral Costs, the Informal Sector, and Unemployment." Working Paper 01-2001, Department of Economics, Copenhagen Business School.

Kolm, A.-S., and B. Larsen. 2003a. "Social Norm, the Informal Sector and Unemployment." *FinanzArchiv* 59: 407–424.

Kolm, A.-S., and B. Larsen. 2003b. "Does Tax Evasion Affect Unemployment and Educational Choice?" Working Paper 12-2003, Department of Economics, Copenhagen Business School.

Pedersen, S., and N. Smith. 1998. "'Black' Labour Supply and 'Black' Wages." (In Danish.) *Nationaløkonomisk Tidsskrift* 136: 289–314.

Pissarides, C. 2000. *Equilibrium Search Theory*. Cambridge: MIT Press.

Schneider, F., and D. Eneste. 2000. "Shadow Economices: Size, Causes, and Consequences." *Journal of Economic Literature* 38: 77–114.

Slemrod, J., and S. Yitzhaki. 2002. "Tax Avoidance, Evasion, and Administration." In *Handbook of Public Economics*, vol. 3, ed. A. J. Auerbach and F. Feldstein, 1423–1470. Amsterdam: Elsevier.

Yitzhaki, S. 1974. "A Note on 'Income Tax Evasion: A Theoretical Analysis.'" *Journal of Public Economics* 3, no. 2: 475–480.

Contributors

Jonas Agell, Stockholm University

Dan Anderberg, Royal Holloway University of London

Søren Arnberg, Institute of Local Government Studies, Copenhagen

Peter Birch Sørensen, University of Copenhagen

Lans Bovenberg, Tilburg University

Nada Eissa, Georgetown University

Anders Holm, University of Copenhagen

Hilary Hoynes, University of California, Davis

Henrik Jacobsen Kleven, University of Copenhagen

Ann-Sofie Kolm, Stockholm University

Birthe Larsen, Copenhagen Business School

Stephen Nickell, Bank of England Monetary Policy Committee

Frederick van der Ploeg, European University Institute, Florence

Claus Thustrup Kreiner, University of Copenhagen

Torben Tranæs, Rockwool Foundation Research Unit, Copenhagen

Index